DATE DUE

Doing Time in
the Depression

Guess Who's Coming to Dinner Now?
Multicultural Conservatism in America
Angela D. Dillard

One Nation Underground:
A History of the Fallout Shelter
Kenneth D. Rose

The Body Electric:
How Strange Machines Built
the Modern American
Carolyn Thomas de la Peña

Black and Brown:
African Americans and the
Mexican Revolution, 1910–1920
Gerald Horne

Impossible to Hold:
Women and Culture in the 1960s
Edited by Avital H. Bloch and Lauri
Umansky

Provincetown:
From Pilgrim Landing to Gay Resort
Karen Christel Krahulik

A Feeling of Belonging:
Asian American Women's
Public Culture, 1930–1960
Shirley Jennifer Lim

Newark:
A History of Race, Rights,
and Riots in America
Kevin Mumford

Children's Nature:
The Rise of the American Summer Camp
Leslie Paris

Raising Freedom's Child:
Black Children and Visions of
the Future after Slavery
Mary Niall Mitchell

America's Forgotten Holiday:
May Day and Nationalism, 1867–1960
Donna T. Haverty-Stacke

On the Make:
Clerks and the Quest for Capital in
Nineteenth-Century America
Brian P. Luskey

Hedda Hopper's Hollywood:
Celebrity Gossip and American
Conservatism
Jennifer Frost

Doing Time in the Depression:
Everyday Life in Texas and
California Prisons
Ethan Blue

Doing Time in the Depression

Everyday Life in Texas and California Prisons

Ethan Blue

NEW YORK UNIVERSITY PRESS
New York and London

NYU Press gratefully acknowledges
the generous support of The Australian Academy of the Humanities
in making the publication of the book possible.

NEW YORK UNIVERSITY PRESS
New York and London
www.nyupress.org

References to Internet Websites (URLs) were accurate at the time of writing.
Neither the author nor New York University Press is responsible for URLs
that may have expired or changed since the manuscript was prepared.

Library of Congress Cataloging-in-Publication Data

Blue, Ethan.
Doing time in the depression : everyday life in
Texas and California prisons / Ethan Blue.
p. cm.
Includes bibliographical references and index.
ISBN 978-0-8147-0940-5 (cloth : alk. paper)
ISBN 978-0-8147-0941-2 (ebook)
ISBN 978-0-8147-2316-6 (ebook)
1. Prisoners—California—History. 2. Prisons—California—
Social conditions. 3. Prison administration—California—History.
4. Prisoners—Texas—History. 5. Prisons—Texas—Social conditions.
6. Prison administration—Texas—History. I. Title.
HV9475.C2B58   2012
365'.976409043—dc23   2011033399

New York University Press books are printed on acid-free paper,
and their binding materials are chosen for strength and durability.
We strive to use environmentally responsible suppliers and materials
to the greatest extent possible in publishing our books.

Manufactured in the United States of America
10 9 8 7 6 5 4 3 2 1

Contents

Acknowledgments

From Austin to Sacramento and Charlottesville to Perth, I've accumulated many debts over the course of writing this book. Advisors, colleagues, friends, students, and family all gave generously of their time and advice, and even if I haven't been shrewd enough to accept it all, I am grateful. I am more grateful still for the community the discussions helped make: advisors became friends; students taught me much; family became advisors; colleagues became family. Many thanks to you all.

The University of Texas provided a warm—sweltering, even—place for graduate study. Many of the conversations I had there, in seminars and libraries, coffee shops and bars, developed the ideas that come through in the pages that follow. Neil Foley, Gunther Peck, and Robert Olwell proved a formidable trio of supervisors, whose comments expanded my thought while tightening my analysis. David Montejano, Carolyn Eastman, Kevin Kenny, Willy Forbath, David Oshinsky, James Sidbury, Harry Cleaver, Luis Alvarez, Manuel Callahan, Patrick Timmons, Alan Eladio Gómez, Ryan Carey, Steven Galpern, John Troutman, Rebecca Montes, Stephen Berrey, Norwood Andrews, and Kenneth Aslakson deserve warm thanks. The Advanced Seminar for Borderlands Research provided a model of collaborative learning and engaged research that I've carried with me ever since.

Reginald Butler, Tico Braun, Edward Ayers, and George Mentore inspired me as an undergraduate, but this inspiration paled in comparison to the scholarly challenges they would later provide. A predoctoral research fellowship at the University of Virginia's Carter G. Woodson Institute for African and African American Studies gave intellectual companionship and vital financial support: deep thanks to Reginald Butler, Scot French, Corey Walker, Deborah McDowell, Scott Saul, Wende Marshall, Hanan Sabea, Davarian Baldwin, Cheryl Hicks, Grace Hale, Eric Lott, Sandy Alexandre, Mieka Brand, and most especially to Tyrone Simpson, Jesse Shipley, and Candice Lowe.

Colleagues at the University of Western Australia have also been generous in their support for this disoriented and sunburned new arrival. Charlie Fox, Mark Edele, Rob Stuart, Susie Protschky, Richard Bosworth, Giuseppe Finaldi, Andrea Gaynor, David Barrie, Sue Broomhall, Jenny Gregory, Esta Ungar, Philippa Maddern, Norman Etherington, Jeremy Martens, Blaze Kwaymullina, David Savat, Alistair Paterson, Michael Levine, Philip Mead, Gareth Griffiths, Shalmalee Palekar, Brenda Walker, Bill Taylor, and Clarissa Ball enriched the book in many ways. Others further afield in Perth, the antipodes, and elsewhere, helped immeasurably. Many thanks to Andrew Webster, Theodore Hamm, Carolyn Strange, Frances Clarke, Clare Corbould, Janaka Biyanwila, Karen Soldatic, Mary Bosworth, Arnoldo de León, and Paul Tallion. Rhys Isaac's pointed and wry feedback was the kind that only he could provide. Special thanks to Shane White and Richard Bosworth, whose detailed comments on the full manuscript sharpened the analysis. Brooke Lamperd and George Robertson provided wonderful research assistance. So did Kevin Shupe.

I'm also grateful to the fellow travelers I've met at conferences and elsewhere. Thanks to Ruthie Gilmore, Rose Braz, Christian Parenti, Eileen Boris, Volker Janssen, Samuel Roberts, and to Stephen R. Mahoney for an early push in the right direction. Laura Saegert and John Anderson were tremendous guides to the Texas State Archives. Lucy Barber and Jeff Crawford were of special help at the California State Archives, and Marin County Free Librarians Laurie Thompson and Carol Uhrmacher continue to earn my gratitude. A University of Western Australia Research Grant, and an American Historical Association Littleton–Griswold Research Grant enabled time in those archives. Eric Zinner, Ciara McLaughlin, and the readers at NYU Press also offered sage advice that helped make the book a reality, and an Australian Academy of the Humanities publication subsidy made the book better. Alex Lichtenstein gave incisive comments on one of the first conference papers I ever gave, and his detailed notes on this manuscript were equally astute.

Since my arrival in Australia, the West Australian Deaths in Custody Watch Committee has been a source of motivation and inspiration. It has been a privilege to join in their struggle. Untold billions of dollars come into Western Australia from the mining boom, while Aboriginal Australians, from whose lands the minerals come, die in state custody in shocking numbers. The Deaths in Custody Committee's work has enriched my own, and serves as a reminder that William Faulkner's insight into America's past also holds true for Australia's: the past isn't over; it isn't even past.

assure citizens and themselves that the streets were under control, even if the economy was not.

Despite Prohibition's repeal in 1933, prison populations stayed high. As pantries emptied and belts tightened, prison ledger books grew fat. In Texas and California, the file cabinets bulged with new records, recording biometric and case histories for inmates in two of the largest systems in the nation. Each consistently had among the highest numbers of new prisoners received each year, and among the highest total numbers of prisoners in the nation.[5] The 1930s saw a considerable increase in prison populations across the land. Even before the Depression struck, health investigator Frank L. Rector worried that "with few exceptions, American prisons are greatly overcrowded."[6] Rector was concerned with the spread of disease, but officials were similarly worried about the volatility that large numbers of closely packed bodies would create. A member of California's parole board reported that prisoners were "jammed into every attic, basement, and cell."[7] It was not just riots that concerned them, but criminality could spread in these hothouse conditions too. California's San Quentin was one of the largest penal institutions in the nation, and it was also the most overcrowded; in 1933, when Edwin Owen wrote, its 6,062 inmates nearly doubled the institution's capacity. Numerically speaking (to say nothing of actual treatment), Texas was consistently among America's most punitive states, receiving more prisoners into its system each year than almost any other across the 1930s. By 1937, San Quentin had become the largest prison in the land, and Texas received the largest number of new inmates in the country (see table I.1).[8]

Crime and punishment remained at the forefront of national consciousness, inchoate as it was, in the 1930s. Gangster stories peppered newspapers and cinemas like so much buckshot, providing the public with uncertain morality tales and tough, manly antiheroes. When celebrity pilot Charles Lindbergh's infant son was kidnapped, the national hysteria the event provoked fueled the massive expansion of America's federal policing apparatus. The Bonnie Parker–Clyde Barrow and Dillinger gangs, among others, drew fascination, admiration, and scorn, robbing the banks that many regular folks felt had robbed them. Some of these famous outlaws stood trial; others were summarily shot down. In Scottsboro, Alabama, nine young black men were accused of raping two poor white women. In previous years, they would either have been lynched or given a speedy trial followed by certain execution. Yet a massive international response by the Communist Party's International Labor Defense and the NAACP saved their lives. Moreover, Tom Mooney received a belated pardon from San Quentin in 1938, after

TABLE I.1
Texas and California Prison Populations, 1926–1946

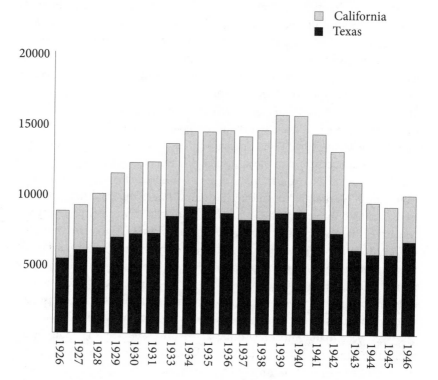

twenty-two years behind bars. Each of these cases was remarkable for the way it captured public fear and fascination, becoming both performance and battleground for the public sense of right and wrong and the role of the state in executing justice.[9] Yet in this book, I am less concerned with famous cases than with those that were mundane and unknown. Much work remains to be done on these spectacular moments in the creation of law and meaning, on how and why they came to national or international prominence—for other cases were no less remarkable or shocking. But here, I concentrate on the lives of prisoners who did not make the newspapers; mostly men, but also some women, known only by their families and the institutions that held them. These were everyday criminals and working people; they had little celebrity or notoriety. Not even their deaths would make the papers.

Prisons demand our understanding. Even if they are not analyzed as some sort of sign to be read of broader society—as microcosm, metaphor, allegory, extreme location of social relations (and they can be seen as all of these)—American prisons have housed untold millions of people, and certainly thousands upon thousands in the Depression. Yet the historiography of incarceration has by and large focused on prison officials and reformers and their shifting techniques, mentalities, or new penologies. Often even the finest of these studies focus on these broad abstractions, and leave out the prisoners themselves.[10] Many had done terrible things, and many surely suffered ordeals themselves.[11] Each person who passed through prison walls left behind families, friends, loved ones, and coworkers. They deserve to have their experiences understood, or, as E. P. Thompson once put it, "saved from the enormous condescension of posterity."[12] Doing so will also shed light on the contradictions and social conflicts all Americans faced. Bringing close attention to prisoners' worlds, as Thompson understood, is a political and analytical insistence: prisoners' lives reveal the suffering these state institutions heightened, the micropolitics of oppression and opposition in everyday forms of state formation, and the way Texas and California, these differently modern carceral states, set pressures and limits on the possibilities of prisoners' lives. Moreover, a close reading of prisoners' experience reveals new processes through which the modern state came into existence. For prisons, too, were crucial sites in Depression-era state making, and an expansion of the state's capacities. Death row was as important to the state as the governor's mansion.

Texas and California prisons were filled with people from across the country and around the world, men and women who had left worse prospects in other places to make a better life. Their movement resulted from the international geography of capital and labor, in which those displaced from America's semicolonial spheres and peripheral economic regions traveled to these border states. People from more than sixty-seven countries found themselves behind bars in Texas and California, their names and places of birth duly tracked in ledgers and annual reports. Each state shared a border with Mexico; each state had long though distinct histories of racial conflict and white supremacy; each state saw multiple populations mixing and confronting one another, and each state's multiple races and ethnicities (black, white, and Mexican in Texas; and black, white, Mexican, Chinese, Japanese, Native American, and Filipino, among others, in California)—eclipsed the dominant black-white racial categories of the United States. Los Angeles would proudly claim to be a "World City" later in the century, but San Quentin, "The Walled City," had been a world city for decades.

When newly convicted felons arrived behind the prison walls, they entered a world that only partially resembled the one they had left. This world was much smaller, and much crueler; it was both more violent and more boring, so boring that it could be deadly. Life was controlled and constricted, yet small cells grew tighter still and bunks in dormitories packed even closer as ever greater numbers of prisoners streamed in. Not even increased parole rates would keep pace with the ascending prison populations. In these alienating conditions, degrading work alternated with tedium, and the ever-present threat of violence came as much from other prisoners as from guards. Dirty looks meant even more here than they did on the outside. Yet the contrasts of prison life held bitter ironies. If many in the Depression traveled in search of work, they could find it in abundance on Texas prison farms. If they sought a thriving economy, a booming black market awaited at California's Folsom and San Quentin. While prisoners in Texas were overworked, in California, massively overcrowded institutions led to a prison-labor surplus, and inmates were as likely to be numbed from inactivity as they were to be broken from labor.

The penal worlds they entered were segregated. Despite forcibly gathering the members of the multiracial and multinational working classes in closed spaces, prisons, in many respects, were even more segregated than the outside. Prison inmates' bodies and identities were complex, multifaceted, and contextual, yet officials assiduously divided inmates into men and women, homosexuals and heterosexuals, whites and Negroes and Mexicans and Chinese and Japanese and Filipinos, the young and the old, the violent and the nonviolent, the obedient and the recalcitrant. And even though the vast majority of these people were poor, the wealthy and the educated were distinguished from the uneducated and the impoverished. Prisoners were classified and separated by sex, by race, by labor assignment, and by what officials believed to be their rehabilitative potential. They were segregated in order to save them, or so they were told. Then as now, race and its pernicious effects were a matter of a thousand indignities and slights, or, conversely, boosts and benefits—so small as to be almost unrecognizable or so bald-faced as to seem nearly uncontestable. Racial difference and power grew from the media, from the state, from policing, and from opportunities for jobs and housing and education. Racial differences became unthought differences, so fully hegemonic as to appear natural. By no means were Texas and California prisoners without racial identities when they entered the institutions that would hold them—race was, in Gramsci's language, common sense—but racial privilege and degradation would be even more deeply set when prisoners left.[13]

It quickly became apparent to all that white inmates generally enjoyed better opportunities, that officials saw light skin as a sign of reformability and dark skin as a strong indicator of incorrigibility. The rehabilitative ideal espoused by progressive penologists and prison administrators was, by and large, a matter of white privilege. African Americans would suffer the brunt of missed opportunities, bad food, and—even here—second-class treatment. Perhaps especially here. No one wanted to be at the bottom of the barrel, the lowest of the low. White prisoners made clear that they were men, white men—that though they were prisoners, at least they were not black or Mexican or Chinese. On the outside, where they lived on social margins, they might have been called white trash, Okies, or bums. But in the context of tightly packed, racially diverse prisons, they struggled to maintain white privilege, and claimed their place with pride as they denigrated racial others. When they did, they used working-class, and racially inflected notions of manhood to stake their claims. Yet if white prisoners seized their racial identities and the privilege whiteness entailed, so too did black, Mexican, and Asian inmates claim their own racial identities and masculinities, opposing their subordination to white prisoners or state authorities in racial and gendered ways. But prison guards—themselves hard-working poor white men—let prisoners of all races know who was boss, who superior to whom. Whips, clubs, rifles, and dogs made this brutally clear.

The argument in the chapters that follow operates at two levels. The first level posits that criminal justice functioned to control large numbers of Texas's and California's multiracial working classes, and predominantly working-class men, in a period of widespread economic crisis. Then as now, American prisons were deliberately instructive institutions, meant to impart lessons both to inmates and to free-world citizens.[14] As socio-legal scholar David Garland has written, punishment "teaches, clarifies, dramatizes, and authoritatively enacts some of the basic moral-political categories and distinctions which form our symbolic universe." It "communicates meaning about not just crime and punishment but also about power, authority, legitimacy, normality, personhood, social relations, and a host of other tangential matters."[15] Then as now, the vast majority of the imprisoned in the 1930s were poor and unskilled. The numbers of people behind bars who listed their occupation as "laborer" rose steadily across the decade.[16] Some, but not many, were clearly political prisoners: when the state of California sentenced labor radical Tom Mooney to die for the 1916 Preparedness Day bombings, when it kept criminal syndicalism laws on the books and imprisoned labor activists (or neglected to arrest corporate-paid goons who attacked strikers), it worked in obvious ways to limit working-class movements. But most prisoners were just poor, and not highly politicized. Across the nation, prisons controlled people who threatened wage-labor relations by finding ways to survive other than through wage work. Theft was the most obvious of these, and property crimes made up the lion's share of punished offenses in the Depression. The expansion of America's consumer culture of the 1920s led, perhaps unsurprisingly, to an increase in property crimes. As historian Elliot Gorn has observed, "A world of material goods, made more available than ever with the expansion of credit, raised expectations. Glossy magazines glamorized objects of desire, nightly radio programs dramatized the good life, advertising taught Americans about the things they needed to make their lives complete."[17] These desires, once set in motion, would persist. Desperation drove many to theft in the 1930s, and desire, just as surely, drove others. In 1937 more people in the United States were imprisoned for larceny alone than for all violent and sex crimes combined.[18]

Yet punishment entrenched hierarchies in complex ways. One can argue that nowhere was the unequal protection of private property and the state's rough treatment of the poor more blatant than in prison, its most repressive apparatus. In the 1930s widespread working-class movements emerged to fight for higher wages and a more equitable distribution of wealth. Workers demanded the state's protection from employers, the right to organization and collective bargaining, and support from the vicissitudes of an unstable economy. The New Deal, in its many forms and faces, promised succor for Americans down on their luck. From union halls to dance halls and from street parades to bowling alleys, radical, progressive, and multiracial movements grew.[19] In such a climate, prisons might have been particularly vibrant locations of radical proletarian politicization, where, in Marx's terms, the working class in-itself could become a class for-itself.[20]

When I first undertook this project, I was inspired by Michael Denning's book, *The Cultural Front*, which documented broad and multiracial working-class movements in the Depression years. I was driven in equal measures by the new social history's effort to unearth previously hidden perspectives on racialized capitalism, and by a Foucauldian project of finding transgressive spaces and subjects for critical insight into the workings of modernity. I suspected that border state prisons during the Depression might have been sites of multiracial proletarian class formation. After all, it was in this period—just six years after Owen wrote his commentary on the history of crime—that Georg Rusche and Otto Kircheimer, the Frankfurt School doyens of Marxian criminology, located punishment as being more closely related to political economics than to crime.[21] The Depression could have provided prime conditions for the development of a radical working-class politics, for inmates to find allegiance in similar conditions of poverty and stern treatment at the hands of the powerful. After all, New Left and Third World radicals would look to prisons for vanguard movements later in the century, and perhaps, I speculated, earlier forms might have existed.[22] Yet judging from the evidence I found—most of it state authored, to be sure, what Ranajit Guha called the prose of counterinsurgency—this was scarcely the case in the 1930s.[23] The civil rights and Black Power-turned-prisoners'-rights movement of the 1970s built on four decades of struggle, and came into fruition twenty years after global decolonization movements. But the Popular Front, as an opening volley in what some have come to call the United States' long civil rights era, scarcely penetrated prison walls. Fleeting moments of cooperation, of multiracial and even radical community, existed in the prison cultures of the Great Depression, and the forms of resistance and ambiguities that punishment produced will be discussed in detail. But far more records revealed antagonism. Denning convincingly argued that labor unions, libraries, public schools, and state funding for artists were key institutional components of the Popular Front as a social movement. In marked contrast, prisons in the 1930s were state institutions geared toward the *dissolution* of collective class behavior and the imposition of gendered, racialized antagonism that proved resistant to collective challenge. In prison, racial differences were quite literally set in stone. For authorities, this was no mistake.

At this second level of analysis, throughout the book I will argue that state punishment sustained a racially divided, masculinist, working-class population, and that the social forces prisons generated undermined the promise of radical working-class movements.[24] Yet state prisons did not passively reflect social hierarchies as they existed beyond the walls. Rather, throughout the book I argue that the penal state actively produced the multiple hierarchies of class, race, gender, and nation, born of slavery and the colonial conquest of the West. As inmates were classified by sex, by race, and sometimes by crime, the identification of those inmates in large measure conferred, rather than simply reflected, their identities.[25] Formal entrance procedures, labor and housing assignments, and opportunities for health care and education were structured by race and officials' perceptions of obedience. Prisoners confronted racialized hierarchies through the finely calibrated (if largely withheld) promises of citizenship and redemption, the tempered benefits of differential inclusion based on race and obedience, or social exclusion. The furthest limits of exclusion were near-permanent brandings of racialized criminality and, finally, death. Rather than sustaining cross-racial prisoners' and working-class alliances, white inmates frequently found greater promise in the wages of their whiteness. White supremacy remained foundational to American culture beyond the prison, yet its tenets were perhaps starker within the walls. White inmates collected their privileges through informal racial hierarchies that subordinated black, Mexican, and Asian and Native American prisoners, but also through formal mechanisms of retraining and the redemptive citizenship inconsistently offered. Nonwhite prisoners were broadly denied these opportunities, and had to scramble for the scraps that remained. Among the imprisoned, the cultures of punishment produced a racially divided working class in more finely grained ways, divisions they would take with them when their terms ended. Moreover, they would be less employable than before, and trained in rancor. Even though the term "the lumpen" is in use by some to describe a criminal class, it has the feel of heritable permanence rather than historicity. But as Edwin Owen argued, criminals are not born; they are socially made.[26] Prison made working people who had done wrong, worse. Many netted by the prison were guilty of minor crimes, but that would matter little. Many were surely innocent. Despite periodic nods to rehabilitative ideals, incarceration was, and remains, a destructive process for most who experience it, producing catastrophe, not correction, a struggle for survival from which few emerge unscathed.[27]

Entrenching racial hierarchies effectively kept prisoners turned against each other, but gender and sexuality were every bit as important, and perhaps more so. Women were incarcerated in Texas and California as in other states, but they rarely made up more than 2 percent of the inmate population.[28] Consequently, like the vast majority of histories of prisons, the pages that follow concentrate on the experience of male prisoners.[29] But *Doing Time* departs from much of that previous scholarship. Margot Canaday recently marveled at how traditional U.S. historians wrote political history without a conceptualization of the state, and we might shift the insight subtly to say the same of penal historians: most have written about men with little understanding of masculinities.[30]

Texas and California prisons held an overwhelmingly male population, but this hardly meant that gender was unimportant. Gender difference shot through the hypermasculine worlds of the male prison, for manhood itself was a conflicted terrain. Prison officials tried to remake varying male identities into a kind of respectable, heteronormative, self-controlled, middle-class manhood, thus mobilizing gender itself as a technique of social control. Officials did so through privileges offered or denied, through punishments meted out, and, on occasion, through invasive surgery. When officials offered better jobs to obedient prisoners, they constructed a labor ladder built on honorable masculinity. By disciplining themselves and their desires, inmates were instructed, they came closer to the free and independent manly citizens that they would one day be on the outside. Yet when prisoners opposed the terms of formal punishment, they mobilized their own, alternative, working-class ideas of resistant and antiauthoritarian manhood. Sometimes inmates expressed alternative manhoods through brotherly and supportive relation-ships. At other times, their alternative manhoods were expressed through love and consensual sex. On grimmer occasions, prison manhood found brutal expression as the capacity to inflict sexual violence on fellow prisoners who were symbolically feminized and, thus, degraded. Officials and guards sought to manage or eliminate alternative expressions of male gender and sexuality.[31] When it suited them, they exploited it.

Despite many similarities between these two border-state prisons, signifi-cant differences remained. Most prison histories assert a regional primacy to the story of punishment (usually the Northeast versus the Deep South), as setting normative imperatives for the practices of modern punishment. *Doing Time* contends that there has been not a single penal modernity but multiple penal modernities, which weave together but also diverge across time.[32] Analyzing the cultures of punishment in both Texas and California—border states of the southwest—brings the contours (and grim contribu-tions) of different regional penal modernities into better focus.

The Texas Prison System was predominantly agricultural, with one foot planted in the east Texas traditions of slavery, and another in the past of frontier violence. The Texas Prison System underwent a period of reform in the late nineteenth and early twentieth centuries. The convict lease system came to a formal end; hardened criminals were, in theory, separated from young first-timers; and a 1910 investigation led to new (if partial, and then rescinded) restrictions on the use of the lash. In the 1920s, women activists, after gaining the vote and the prohibition of alcohol, brought their moral authority to the task of bettering the plight of prison inmates. The reforms they championed, like others in the southern Progressive movement, were structured by race. "Progress" in the prison system, as in the increasingly rigid Jim Crow public sphere, attempted firm distinctions among black, Mexican, and white inmates, so that poor whites would not fall down the slippery slope of racial degeneracy and mix with people of color. Separat-ing whites from ethnic Mexicans and African Americans was arguably more important than segregating first-timers from violent recidivists, so that those whites could be redeemed into proper American citizens, while ethnic Mex-ican and black prisoners were contained and disciplined as the lowliest of workers.[33] The Texas prison's administrative center and largest building was at the Walls Unit in Huntsville, but prison farms and camps were scattered around the eastern part of the state, where slavery sank deep roots in the soil that sharecroppers still worked and where debt peonage remained. Here, prison farm managers ran penal plantations like small fiefdoms, and were more concerned with turning a bumper crop of sugar or sorghum than they were with reforming wrongdoers. On the farms, inmates were divided into different camps, organized by race, and categorized further by the threat they posed to the system. Texas prison farms may have appeared behind the times of modern penology, but, in fact, Texas prisons were highly modern. They were modern because segregation was itself a modern "solution" to the issue of racial management. Its labor regime might have been seen as archaic (indeed, it was redolent of slavery), but it was so to serve the modern end of absorbing as much labor and human energy as possible. The farms were modern because they were a spatial fix to the problems posed by contemporary capitalism.[34] Overfarming and subsequent ecological disasters; overproduction, mechanization, falling cotton prices; and then the displacement engendered by the Agricultural Adjustment Act—all were modern problems that contributed to mounting poverty and distress. The Depression was itself a crisis of capitalism, and therefore a crisis of modernity.

California's institutions at San Quentin and Folsom were more readily understood as modern, based on the "big house" prison model of large buildings, collective manufacturing labor, and individual cellblocks. Created shortly after the Gold Rush and statehood, San Quentin prison was founded in 1852, and Folsom in 1880. The California Prison System went through a brief convict lease period in the nineteenth century, but by the 1890s the state had effectively centralized control of lethal power and assumed responsibility for inmates' lives and labors in each institution, a West Coast version of Zebulon Brockway's Elmira.[35] A Board of Prison Directors, appointed by the governor, was responsible for each institution, though Folsom and San Quentin wardens had little call to consult with each other, and, not unlike prison farms managers in Texas, ran largely autonomous institutions. California inmates worked in large manufacturing ventures, like San Quentin's jute mill or Folsom's quarry, rather than on Texas's prison farms.

While I build on David Garland's articulation of punishment as a top-down process of "instruction" in broad cultural formation, I depart from his model by examining prisons as sites where diverse social forces and actors confronted and transformed each other. Multifaceted conflicts intersected at every level of punishment. These complex institutions were hardly monolithic, and countless fissures, the "defects of total power," as Gresham Sykes called them, shot through the formal bureaucratic hierarchies.[36] Prison reformers fought with hard-line wardens and guards; guards fought with prisoners; prisoners fought with each other; and prisoners manipulated corruptible officials. In this, prisons were sites where manifold forms of social power and difference were expressed and politics exposed. Borrowing from cultural critic Jorge A. González, I treat prisons as "sites or struggling 'arenas' . . . constructed though elaborate discursive work which traces the dynamics of situated conflicts and tensions." The cultures of punishment, as I call them, were created by inmates and keepers alike. Though guards lamented that convicts ran the prison and prisoners could bloody their fists against unyielding walls, the cultures of punishment reflected multidirectional efforts—some successful, others less so, and all dramatically asymmetrical—to shape the institutions to their own ends. The cultures of punishment must "be understood as complex structures of relations connecting institutions, agents, and practices." These are not just the domain of experts or elites; rather, they are made through "crucial dynamics with *social networks* in which non-specialists—families, folk, common people—read, interpret, interact with, and negotiate."[37] *Doing Time* examines the cultures of punishment from this multilayered perspective, tracing the agonizing conflicts and contributions that went into the making of punishment. From the knowledge produced by expert penologists about criminals to the music prisoners made; from forced labor on prison farms to debates in governors' committees; from sexual violence in prison dormitories to prison reform activists; from the phenomenological experience of time to the chilling control of space: each waking moment and every tormented sleep was born of conflict. Such was the culture of punishment.

Texas and California prisons concentrated intraclass and interracial antagonism among prisoners, and the resulting violence has been understood in different ways across the twentieth century. An early position developed under the traditions of Italian criminologist Cesare Lombroso has two variants. Its conservative, racialist dimensions—the criminal justice analogue to what political scientist Rogers Smith called America's nationalist inegalitarian ascriptive citizenship[38]—understand crime and violence as resulting from biological atavism, from people who are racially predisposed to wrongdoing and who must be forcibly controlled. Its liberal variant describes a pathological culture of poverty in need of softer social control by the police and what might be called ideological state apparatuses. Each naturalizes colonial capitalism as a social system and justifies controlling working people in terms of protecting elites and property and through condescending claims to protect the "good" members of subordinated populations from the "bad."[39] A second position developed in the 1950s and 1960s as part of anticolonial critiques and found expression in Frantz Fanon's book, *The Wretched of the Earth*. This tradition approaches theft and violence among subordinated populations not as biological deficiency or cultural pathology, but rather as the result of colonial dominance or capitalist exploitation. This position argues that people of color in the United States, for example, have been forced to contend with not just police brutality and an unjust legal system but also violence from within poor and subordinated communities. Acknowledging the validity of feminist, queer, and postnational critiques (not to mention the practical difficulties of identifying homelands to liberate) of late-twentieth-century "internal colony models," one might still argue that such violence is itself a symptom of internal dynamics within America's domestic empire. Violence coming from within poor or dominated communities and external state violence, then, exacerbate each other, and are the result of thoroughly dominating processes.[40] A third position on crime in poor communities grew with the new social history, and drew inspiration from the social movements of the late twentieth century. This position places analytical primacy on the agency and oppositional acts of subordinated groups. At the same time, however, it risks minimizing the less savory aspects of subaltern agency itself, or the intimate replication of structural violence. For example, in *The London Hanged*— which was an inspiration to my research—Peter Linebaugh brilliantly analyzed how acts and people challenging emergent British capitalism became labeled as criminal, and how those people able to live beyond wage labor were liable to punishment. Employers eroded workers' right to the scraps left over from production—scraps workers made sure were unusable to employers but not themselves—by criminalizing workers' acts as theft. Despite trenchant analysis, and unlike Fanon, Linebaugh found relatively little violence or theft among the working classes. London's poor were punished when they stole from their bosses, but not when they stole from each other.[41] The criminalization of acts and people by elites and state agents that Linebaugh described is a historical fact: the criminalization of black mobility in the convict lease era and the transformation of drug addiction from a public health to a criminal justice issue in the 1970s and 1980s are concrete examples of how the poor and nonwhite met the hard side of American law. Yet to examine processes of criminalization without the facts of violence is to tell only part of the story; it is to gloss over what Nell Irvin Painter saw as the "soul murdering" effects of slavery in one of slavery's direct institutional descendants.[42]

Doing Time incorporates the second two positions in a critique of the first: violence among the colonized and domestic working classes, and in this case, imprisoned populations, is real and cannot be minimized. To do so is to downplay one of the most insidious aspects of domination, in which indigenous, black, Latino, immigrant, and poor communities suffer from the reinforcing traumas of structural exploitation, and the double binds of state violence and state neglect. But unlike the Lombrosian criminological perspective, whose alternating liberal/conservative variations see violence or theft as primitivism to eradicate or a culture of poverty to correct, I argue that this violence results from and is exacerbated by ongoing traditions of domination. It is a symptom of the larger structures of racially gendered class rule. Labor historians have, at times, found the same: among canal diggers in colonial America, domination could be displaced onto peers, subordinates, or themselves. After all, for many working-class men, for whom the indignities of exploitation were compounded by traditions of racism, it could be easier to rob or attack a neighbor, a spouse, or a child than to attack the police, a boss, or a mob.[43]

Nevertheless, at rare moments and under certain circumstances, prisoners did work together against the institutions that held them. On occasion, such challenges might be absorbed by the system: Edwin Owen's historicization of crime was printed in a state-sanctioned publication, after all. Nevertheless, inmates used countless tactics to control their bodies and make their lives more bearable. They created new opportunities for pleasure and recreation; some, such as sporting events, were sanctioned, and others were not. The most successful of the illegal pastimes would evade detection, and leave no trace in state records. Less successful attempts would be duly noted in punishment logs as lashes struck, privileges lost, or parole dates pushed back. In either case, prisoners worked slowly or not at all; they sabotaged machinery and burned the buildings that held them. They cooperated in twos and threes to pull each other over tall walls; they brewed alcohol for mental escape; they had sex and found illicit pleasure in their own bodies. Some escaped their bonds through suicide and other self-destructive means—acts of troubling self-control that shamed prison officials and scandalized humanitarian reformers, and, for survivors, might have provided a few days of rest and decent food in the hospital. On the rare occasions when large numbers of prisoners worked together against the state, as in a food strike or labor stoppage, they became subject to overwhelming retributive violence. In the context of the New Deal, however, charges of state brutality could lead to reform. The whip was finally formally barred from use in Texas in 1941, and when news leaked about the harsh response to a food strike at San Quentin in 1938, it eventually led to the dismissal of the Board of Prison Directors. Inmates' activities, though rarely radical or directly linked with the Popular Front, would prompt institutional change. At times, it was change for the better; at others, for the worse.

The late twentieth century saw an increasingly sophisticated literature on the history of American punishment, in large measure responding to contemporary postindustrial mass incarceration. Much is based on the early modern period in the Northeast (roughly 1780–1820), on the convict lease period in the Deep South (1865–1910), or on the late-twentieth–early-twenty-first-century prison-industrial complex. In their periodizations, these works leave the middle years of the twentieth century unexplored, and thus unwittingly reproduce either progressive or rise-and-decline narratives in which the actual histories of punishment under the New Deal order remain uninterrogated. While Marxian narratives have predominated in the convict lease period of the New South, there has been a dearth of histories of punishment in the middle years of the twentieth century. The majority of writings on punishment in these years has been from sociologists, penologists, or criminologists, and save for rare examples, these scholars diminished the role that prisons play in class formation.[44] This might have been due to the increased complexity of class relations in the middle years of the twentieth century, when the naked coercion of the convict lease no longer served as a primary mechanism of securing working-class obedience. Or perhaps the Cold War limited midcentury sociologists' analytical tools.[45] Nevertheless, as Progressive Era politics incorporated the populist challenges of the late nineteenth century, and as expert efficiency came to rule in American political culture, capitalist reconfiguration meshed with new forms of regulatory government practice. Confronted with world war, managerial expertise developed in the Progressive Era bureaucratized and grew muscular; and these organizational processes came to full fruition with the New Deal.[46] In this period, expert-regulated programs meshed with new administrative capacities in what was to become the welfare state. The New Deal state sought to regulate economic cycles and to lessen the harshest edges of industrial capitalism, but not everyone benefited equally. White male industrial workers made the most gains, while women of all races, and black, Latino, Asian, and Native American men fared far less well.[47] Not only did prison populations increase in the Depression—one kind of state "fix" to unemployment and poverty[48]—but labor laws designed to protect (implicitly white) industrial workers—especially the Hawes-Cooper Act (1929) and the Ashurst-Sumners Act (1934)—restricted the ways in which officials could set prisoners to work. This gave rise to what historian Rebecca McLennan has called *postindustrial* forms of penal discipline.[49] Few scholars have attempted to place punishment within the new conditions of state formation and capitalist crisis in these years, or to broach the question of how punishment operated in the same period as the Civilian Conservation Corps, Social Security, and the National Labor Relations Board, or the growth of mass culture. *Doing Time* is a step in that direction.

Like previous works, it argues that punishment changes with political economic transformation. The models of brutal race and class rule prevalent in other periods of study, such as the convict lease period of the New South or early modern England, were appropriate for a period of industrial capitalist coalescence but are inadequate for analyzing the vagaries of punishment when an industrial society structured in racial dominance confronted deep economic crisis. Complicating factors included a shift from an economy of industrial production to one of industrial consumption, governed by an increasingly interventionist welfare state. Moreover, existing prison programs were challenged by active labor movements and overlaid with new mass-culture and media technologies.[50] Charles Bright's pathbreaking study of Michigan's prison system from 1920 to 1955 argued that there is a "deep interconnection between the constitution of the political realm and the construction of carceral regimes."[51] The stance has much to recommend it, but few of the federal reforms of the New Deal emerged at the carceral level. Indeed, the localism that characterized many state and municipal administrators' resistance to the New Deal was fortified in prisons. However, officials were by and large less willing to countenance scandal than they had been in the past. Early in the century, humanitarians joined prisoners in the fight for better treatment, more parole opportunities, vocational training, health care, and recreation. These new policies emerged as prison planners absorbed working-class protest against competition from inmate labor, as well as inmates' demands for pleasurable recreation woven into their prison routines. In California, some elements of progressive penology, which emerged in the early twentieth century, took root and strengthened. In Texas, however, the autonomous political structures of its prison farms, bolstered by a considerable localism and antipathy to New Deal programs, mitigated against substantive change. The weight of political economies pressed harder on prison systems than did the federal political realm. Cultural regimes beyond the walls—such as those of mass culture and consumption—penetrated more deeply than federal politics. As state capacities expanded to incorporate meager health care, entertainment, and even—on occasion for the best-behaved—vocational training, violence remained at the very heart of incarceration. The state's ability to kill or maim lay buried beneath consent-oriented policies and more subtly hegemonic power relations that absorbed prisoners' and humanitarians' protest.

Doing Time examines all of this through a close reading of what I call the cultures of punishment: the worlds that inmates as well as keepers made. Prisons are cloaked in secrecy—officials restrict knowledge of their institutions, and inmates are rarely more forthcoming. I attempt to broach the cultures of punishment through an examination of as many extant sources as possible. Prison ledgers, annual reports, board meeting minutes, inmate-authored and free-world newspapers, published and unpublished memoirs by prisoners and wardens, trial transcripts, investigations, punishment reports, pardon applications, execution files, medical reports, photographs, and sound and lyrics of recorded songs: all of these contribute to my reconstruction of these closed and grim worlds. The book's organization mirrors the experience of incarceration as I have come to understand it. Chapter 1 analyzes the demography of incarceration, but also the meaning and practice of arriving in each of these systems. It follows the paths inmates traveled to border state prisons, and the way their identities and bodies were reoriented by the new, cruel worlds that would hold them. The five chapters that follow reconstruct Texas and California prisoners' daily lives. Chapters 2 and 3 analyze the ways in which labor in each state system structured inmates' punishment and their differing experiences in the reproduction of gendered racial hierarchies. Though federal legislation in the Hawes-Cooper Act (1929) and Ashurst-Sumners Act (1934) circumscribed the uses of prison labor, officials still maintained that hard work was necessary to teach criminals a work ethic as productive citizens-in-training. Unlike the visible pedagogical function of early convict labor at public works, or the lease's hybrid place between slavery and emergent capitalism, labor served internal disciplinary and economic functions. Chapter 4 describes the braided overt and covert economies of cash, favors, contraband, sex, and sexual violence through which Texas and California institutions functioned. These connected to formal bureaucracies but also followed logics that produced hegemonic masculinities particular to each state. Chapters 5 and 6 assess the growth of mass culture as a new terrain of punishment and opposition, from radio programming to athletics and celebrations as new, "enjoyable" kinds of discipline. In this new era, consumption and leisure would join labor as a means of correction. Prisoners' cultural production in sport and music revealed fault lines in systemic emphases on racial hierarchies and universal antagonism. Music, sport, and entertainment worked as countervailing forces against the impositions of labor. They mobilized different meanings, practices, and feelings in inmates' lives. The final chapters examine the experience of leaving prison. Chapter 7 sheds light on departures through death and dying, through all-too-common disease or violence, or legal executions that, despite the federal failure to outlaw lynching, would replace the mob in this new historical formation. The final chapter interprets the way pardon or parole revived old forms of patronage in newly bureaucratized procedures. Leaving the prison, as much as entering it, reproduced region-specific hierarchies of race, sex, class, gender, and nation.

Instead of the worlds of boredom, violence, and alienation, progressive reformers and most prisoners would have preferred a consistently reforming world, where technocratic solutions actually limited violence, theft, poverty, or racial dominance. But prisons were, and remain, locations where beneficial change is elusive. Prison reform has scarcely worked to make things better. Prisons are sites where forms of power accumulate rather than replace one another. Michel Foucault famously argued that souls rather than bodies would be corrected in modern punishment, yet the history of punishment has shown the ongoing accretion of control technologies, without the dismissal of past forms of violence. Biopolitics of regulation and reclamation never existed without the ever more precise ability for states to kill, and to kill unequally by race and by class.[52] Modern forms of sovereign rule were laid bare, and the brutal sides of the New Deal order shone darkly for those who lived or died behind the walls. From arrival in prison to departure, either on parole or in a hearse, punishment in the 1930s seemingly did little to lessen suffering, while entrenching class hierarchies and exacerbating racial and sexual violence.

As we confront a new and massive economic crisis, more than two million people are behind bars and an additional five million are under some form of criminal justice surveillance, on probation or parole. The federal government is again offering Keynesian policies to regulate and thus save capitalism, and proposing new welfare measures for social protection. What this will mean for today's and tomorrow's state prisoners remains to be seen. The histories of crime and punishment, as Edwin Owen suggested from San Quentin in another Depression, are only beginning to be told.

1

Of Bodies and Borders

The Demography of Incarceration

In Robert Joyce Tasker's 1928 memoir, *Grimhaven*, the narrator describes his entry into California's San Quentin State Penitentiary:

> The official jerked his thumb towards a door. The very motion gave me the key to my position. I was merchandise, duly received and acknowledged. Henceforth I was to be an animated piece of baggage. And for that I was grateful, for it fitted with the least effort into my mood.
>
> The room into which I now passed was small—a mere recording office for the registry of new-comers. A convict rose from behind a desk and came to the counter that separated us. He asked my name, nativity, and age; later, my crime, and the county from which I was sent.[1]

After a bath, strip search, and shoddy haircut and shave, Tasker was disoriented and had lost his sense of place. "Somewhere in the bowels of the building behind me I had become confused in my bearings, and never again could I think of east other than as south. The whole institution had manoeuvred [sic] a quarter turn."[2] In *We Who Are About to Die*, his 1935 prison memoirs, David Lamson outlined similar feelings of detachment and disembodiment. As he described physically *entering* San Quentin and being discursively *entered* into its record-keeping apparatus, Lamson switched from the first person to the third. Wittingly or no, he effectively saw himself through the eyes of the other prisoners watching him (as he would soon be watching others) and the eyes of the authority surrounding him.

> The convict clerk produces a pen and a bottle of India ink and prints a number on the [clothing]—54761. He sprawls the same number on the undershirt; the drawers; each sock; inside the shoes. That number is the

man's laundry mark. It is his own mark. It is himself. For as long as he is in this prison, he is 54761. . . . So far as San Quentin is concerned he will be Fifty-four seven sixty-one until he dies.

The convict next enters a room full of typewriters. A young man in grey shirt and trousers

> runs a printed form into a typewriter and starts asking the man questions, typing the answers on the printed form. There are a great many questions—the familiar where and when born, home address, mother's name, address, age, birthplace, father's name, address, birthplace; and on down the line to education, religion, crime charged, plea, previous arrests or convictions. . . . He lights a cigarette, and tilts his head and squints his eyes against the smoke. These things give him an air of incurious detachment. It is as if he said, "I'm not asking these very personal questions out of curiosity, you know. I don't give a damn, really; I just work here." . . .
>
> Later, the new man will be brought back again to the fingerprint room in the rear of the offices, where he will be printed and have his Bertillion measurements taken. Later, he will be photographed again, this time in prison garb and with his hair clipped short. Later, he will be taken to the hospital for a medical examination.
>
> But for the present, his initiation . . . is completed. He has become a convict, following the road that all men follow in becoming convicts.[3]

Texas prisoner Benton Layman described a similar dislocation when he first arrived in Huntsville: "Made me kind of numb. It seemed like a dream—a bad dream."[4] Harry W. Jamison explained the feeling to prison investigators at San Quentin: "[W]hen I walked through these gates here it was like an empty feeling in your stomach."[5] Terrence Bramlett described the feeling in equally corporeal terms: "It took all the heart out of me. . . . Kind of stunned me, I guess. . . . I didn't come to my senses until I'd been in prison a while."[6] According to Texas prisoner Andrew George, his penal initiation was "burned into my mind as with a red-hot iron, never to be erased," part of a process that sociologist Erving Goffman aptly described as "mortification."[7]

Black prisoners were equally troubled by the transition to prison, redolent as it was with the histories of slavery—especially in the South. Blues and work songs immortalized Texas transfer agent Bud Russell and Black Annie, his 28-seat truck, which delivered 115,000 prisoners from county jails to the Huntsville Walls Unit over Russell's 39-year career. Armed with two six-shooters, two gas guns, brass knuckles, and a blackjack, Russell drove the truck with a submachine gun tucked between his knees.[8] Bud Russell took J. B. Smith in a coffle of prisoners from the Dallas County Jail to the Huntsville Walls Unit in 1938. Smith always thought that Russell was just a legend—there was a world of bawdy and blues songs about him—and was surprised to learn that the man was real. "He used to put a chain around your neck, and a lock, a Yale lock. Turn your collar up, and he says, 'All right boys get ready to put on this necktie,'" as he threaded the long throat chain through the whole line of prisoners. "Don't know what the 'Bud' meant," Smith recalled, signifying on the man's name, "but he was a rustler."[9] Another black Texan recalled a time before he was imprisoned:

> Everybody knew when they were going to pick up the chains. . . . The news was spread that Bud Russell was pickin' up the chains, because it was something to see. . . . He would have the guards lined up with machine guns. The convicts would come out chained by the ankles and by the necks and by the hands. Come out in what we call a "Chinese shuffle." . . . I never knew I'd be a victim of the same circumstances.[10]

Though seeing prisoners chained together was a spectacle for its residents—machine guns a show of force as much for the audience as for prisoners—as a young man, this prisoner had little reason to identify with the convicts themselves, whom he rendered as almost racially different, doing a "Chinese" shuffle. Russell's combination of the antebellum coffle with modern firepower made him into an effective contemporary Charon, ferrying prisoners across the divide from the land of the living to the grim prison world, where they were legally dead. He reportedly only lost one prisoner in all of his years.[11]

Once in the institutions, prisoners were subject to a battery of measurements and examinations—more explicitly modern in California than in Texas but still designed to humiliate as well as to impose finely tuned physical and even psychological surveillance. San Quentin chief surgeon Leo Stanley described the procedure. "Every man who comes to the prison is given a thorough examination. . . . The man's physical status is then thoroughly known and should he have any remedial defects he is slated for an operation or treatment as the case may require." A psychiatrist on staff also examined the incoming prisoner. "With these mental and physical examinations the prisoner obviously understands that his condition is known. . . . The prisoners realize that they would be unable to put anything over on the medical department and therefore they do not try. Malingering just does not exist in this institution."[12] If this biomedical knowledge of prisoners might prevent their playing sick and shirking hard labor, its ritual humiliations also helped break their spirits. "I have seldom seen one whose ego does not diminish under the preliminary medical examination." He continued that "[t]he dog-like shaving, bathing, medical testings [sic], robs the most defiant lawbreaker of bravado as it strips him of his clothes. It is not a grueling ordeal. But it makes the dullest criminal realize how firmly he is trapped, and, perhaps for the first time in his life, he quails."[13]

Prison officials needed ways to categorize their wards upon intake into their institutions. After the ritual degradation of arrest, trial, and sentencing, inmates entered the discursive and material spaces of prison systems when their bodies and histories were transcribed in record books. There should be little surprise that this dehumanizing process took place in rooms with names like the "fish tank" at San Quentin and the "bull pen" at Huntsville. Prisoners' bodies were categorized in different institutional forms, including convict ledgers, indices, and identification cards, all of which described inmates to better control them, and marked prisoners for the creation of institutional memories. Each of these processes created paper bodies to parallel the prisoners' physical ones. Moreover, they fixed complex, multiple, and contextual identities into a single, legally recognized person, recorded in text and mandated by the rule of law.[14] Sociologists have called this a kind of symbolic violence, a cultural practice that comes so naturally as to go unnoticed. It "tends to be taken for granted by virtue of the quasi-perfect and immediate agreement which obtains between, on the one hand, social structures . . . and, on the other, cognitive structures inscribed in bodies and minds." Symbolic violence operates "beyond—or beneath—the controls of consciousness and will."[15]

There were many versions of the prison and of the people who lived behind its walls: prisoners' own understandings of themselves, their views of each other, and the views of prison officials and the prisoners who served as their proxy. But the official version was especially powerful. It had the institutional and coercive ability to make its representations of prisoners' bodies into a material reality.[16] The visions of inmates' bodies described in institutional records operated precisely to this effect. Prisoners certainly saw themselves in specific and opposing ways to those of the state (though at times they overlapped), but the state had the ability to make its version of prisoners' bodies "real." When prisoners described feelings of disembodiment and disorientation on entering the institutions, of seeing and being seen, they articulated a phenomenon similar to what W. E. B. Du Bois called double consciousness: the dissonance between their own senses of self and the descriptions and controls that prison authorities and the state imposed.[17]

Yet who were the people arriving in Texas and California prisons? Where did they come from, and what had they done to be sent to prison? How did those populations change over the course of the Depression? Officials kept many records and tabulated much data, to better control their populations. Yet sociologists, statisticians, and demographers have had lengthy debates about changing prison populations: do increasing numbers of prisoners reflect more intakes, or longer sentences meted out for similar crimes? New policy priorities, at county or state levels? Growing fears of crime and thus increased arrests? Or do they reflect actual growing numbers of crimes committed and sentences handed out? Complicating factors appear in release decisions, not just entry: who gets to decide which prisoners are released, why, and when, questions of parole rates and decisions, the indeterminate sentence, and the uses of probation: all of these affect the size of a prison population, reflecting complex political priorities as much as if not more than the occurrence of criminal acts.

What is indisputable is that prison populations increased substantially in the Depression, even given the rapid growth that took place in the 1920s under the Volstead Act's criminalization of alcohol. San Quentin cells built for two people now held three, four, or five. Storerooms were converted into makeshift dormitories. Bodies packed Texas's tanks more and more tightly. Newspapers decried crime waves and criminals run amok, but prisons, increasingly overcrowded, were both a solution and a source of the problem.[18] Despite the ongoing contradiction, the trend was the same across the country. Despite some variations as to when their populations peaked—1934 in California, and 1938 in Texas—prisons grew across the Depression decade. They dropped sharply as war industries increased in 1940, and would continue to decline through the war years.[19] (See tables 1.1, 1.2, 1.3, and 1.4.)[20]

By the time the Depression hit, Texas and California had long been points of travel and arrival in overlapping migratory circuits. In the early nineteenth century, diverse streams of European Americans hailing from the Southeast traveled into Texas, frequently bringing enslaved African Americans with them. They met settled Tejanos along Mexico's northern frontier and Native Americans displaced from the central plains. These migrants, like those in the later nineteenth century, were harbingers of the expanding capitalist world system. California's Gold Rush and, later, its even more lucrative Central Valley agricultural industries drew immigrants from around the world. Multiple streams of Asian travelers sojourned east to arrive in these border-

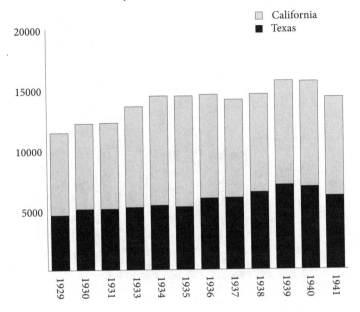

TABLE 1.1

Texas and California Prison Population, 1929–1941

☐ California
■ Texas

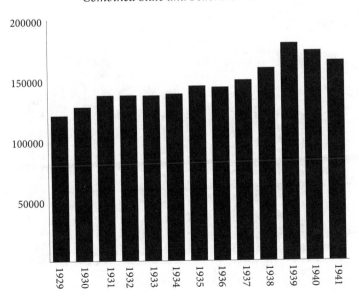

TABLE 1.2

Combined State and Federal Prisoners

TABLE 1.3
California Prison Population

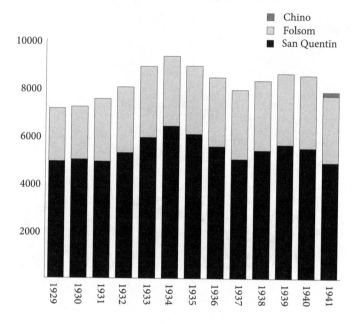

TABLE 1.4
Texas Prison Population

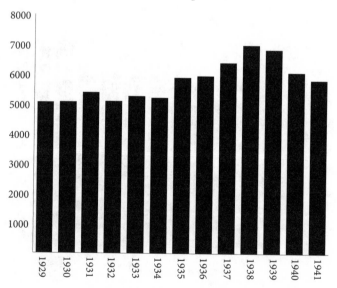

lands, displaced from homes by European expansion, capitalist development, and domestic political violence, drawn toward the colonial metropoles and centers of capital emergent in the western United States. Between 1850 and 1930, Chinese, Japanese, Filipino, Korean, South Asian Indian, Mexican, Italian, Portuguese, and Greek populations—and this is a partial list—streamed east, west, north, and south into the American West to work its booming (and busting) mines, fields, railroads, and factories. By the Depression years, "Okies" and "Arkies," as well as black southerners from the Southeast and European Americans from the Northeast, traveled into California.[21] Meanwhile, ethnic Mexican migrants displaced by revolution and enclosure movements and still permitted entry for agricultural labor under the Immigration Act of 1924, and black and white migrants from the American Southeast looking for new opportunities, had settled in Texas. At the same time, thousands upon thousands of black and white Texans moved from their rural homes into urban centers like Houston and Dallas. Mobility in and across these borderland states in the first decades of the twentieth century brought new and disparate peoples into contact with one another, making for new cultural opportunities and antagonisms. Many of the poorest of these people, and some of the most unruly, would find themselves behind bars.[22]

Traditional labor and immigration histories have demonstrated convincingly the ways in which racial hierarchies structured most segments of the economy from Depression to wartime. Even white transients in "hobo jungles" did their best to keep their favorite spots lily white.[23] But recent urban and cultural historians—especially of California—have found more substantial cross-racial interaction. Subaltern criminal economies were often racially diverse, though hardly egalitarian. Domingo Tomez (whom prison records marked as "Mexican") was arrested in San Francisco on January 29, 1938, with Charles Berg and Charles Young (for whom no racial markers were given), after robbing a garage owned by a Chinese American man and making their escape after locking him in a clothes locker. The 23-year-old Tomez had been born in Presidio, Texas, in 1915, moving with his family to El Paso and Cuidad Juarez, Mexico, until 1933, when he traveled and worked in transnational, multiracial labor circuits along the Pacific coast: in California, Washington, and Alaska. Indeed, it was in Alaska that Tomez first met his future accomplices Berg and Young. Berg obtained a gun from a Filipino man he had known in Alaska. Even after Tomez was at San Quentin, his father wrote from Cuidad Juarez, Mexico, to see if he could send some money to his son, maintaining transnational familial ties.[24] Tomez, Berg, Young, the Filipino man from whom Berg bought the gun, and the Chinese

American man they robbed were actors in multiethnic, if antagonistic, transnational communities of working-class migrants in the Depression years.[25]

California's prisoners came from an astoundingly large area. Tomez's father wanted to send him money, but when they could, prisoners did their best to post remittances to support their families. San Quentin inmate Quong Foo had the Bank of Canton, Ltd., San Francisco, convert fifty-two U.S. dollars to Chinese currency and send it to Lia Chung, his mother-in-law, in China, and many others did the same. Hajara Singh sent twenty-five dollars to settle an old debt in Punjab.[26] The largest number of inmates in each state had been born in that state, regardless of the year, but nevertheless, many had traveled widely before being imprisoned.

Prisoners by Nativity

Four hundred and two inmates received at San Quentin in 1929 were born in other countries, the largest number of whom (191) came from Mexico. They joined inmates already there to make up a total of 1,222 foreign-born prisoners, a quarter of the total San Quentin population. The number of foreign-born prisoners in California consistently decreased across the period, from 25 percent of inmates in 1929 to 12 percent in 1941. The decrease came predominantly from declining numbers of Mexican prisoners. Mexicans were expelled from the country en masse in the 1930s. As Mexican-born inmates' sentences ended or they were paroled for deportation, their numbers fell almost 13 percent to just 5 percent of San Quentin inmates. The geopolitical border, then, served as a preliminary deterrent for noncitizens during the economic crisis. Moreover, the legacy of Chinese exclusion meant that those born in China were but a fraction of San Quentin's population, with just eighteen received in 1929, and only four in 1940. There were fifty-six ethnic Chinese prisoners in prison in California in 1930 (for some had been born in the United States), and forty-six in the prison in 1940.[27]

As the border grew harder through Depression and deportation, travelers from America's domestic marginal economic regions, in search of better fortunes and the California dream, filled the gap. (See table 1.5.)[28] Consequently, percentages of California prisoners born elsewhere in the United States grew. Non-California-born Americans were a significant majority at 60 percent of the inmate population in 1929, but the number grew higher still to 67 percent in 1934 and 68 percent in 1939. Though much was made of the degeneracy and dangerousness of so-called Okies, they were only a small part of San Quentin's population. Oklahoma-born prisoners

TABLE 1.5

San Quentin Prisoners' Nativity

———— Total US (excluding California)
- - - - Total Foreign Countries
———— California

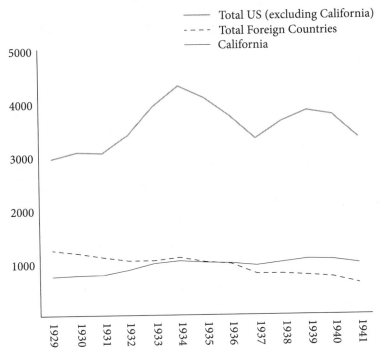

were just over 2 percent of San Quentin prisoners in 1929, and though the number grew steadily with Dust Bowl migration and mechanization, they peaked at 5 percent in 1941. Texas-born California prisoners were a larger number, increasing from 5.5 percent in 1929 to plateau at 8 percent in 1938. Despite common hysteria over Okie invasion, Oklahomans were no more likely to appear at San Quentin than migrants from Missouri, Illinois, or New York. Nevertheless, because "Okie" was a generic term for "poor white trash" or impoverished rural migrants from the Midwest or Southwest—and of these there was no shortage—anyone from Oklahoma, Texas, or Arkansas could be maligned as such.[29]

Nativity records in Texas were inconsistent; the categories that bookkeepers recorded fluctuated from year to year. Despite this, some patterns emerge. California prisons were largely populated by people born elsewhere, but the opposite was true in Texas. Nearly 68 percent of new arrivals in Texas in 1929 were born in Texas; 26 percent were born elsewhere in the United States, with the largest numbers coming from Louisiana and Oklahoma. One hundred and sixty three prisoners were born out of the United States, and 126 of these, 77 percent, had been born in Mexico. The rest came from a smattering of countries (nine from Germany, following Texas's long historical German migrant routes, and five from Italy).[30] In following years, percentages of foreign-born prisoners fell, from more than 6.5 percent in 1932 to just 3 percent in 1942. The vast majority of foreign-born prisoners were Mexican; their percentage of the prison population nearly halved, from just under 6 percent in 1932 to 3 percent in 1942. Only 28 of the 160 foreign-born prisoners in Texas in December 1942 were from nations other than Mexico. At the same time, percentages of American-born prisoners from outside Texas fell from almost 3 percent in 1930 to 2 percent in 1935, rising to 3 percent again in 1930, and falling to 2 percent again in 1940. As Mexicans were expelled from the nation and Texas in the Depression, their numbers fell from prison populations. As a result, the Texas-born increased as percentage of the prison population. In the same years, the numbers of Louisiana- and Oklahoma-born prisoners increased from around 250 in 1932 to around 350 in 1938 and 1939, having sought their fortunes in Texas, apparently perceiving that times were harder in their natal states. (See table 1.6.)[31]

What emerges from this picture is that Texas imprisoned peoples who were closer to home, or in the state's immediate economic or cultural orbit: the largest number of non-Texans at the outset of the decade were born in Mexico, but as their numbers fell, migrants from Louisiana and Oklahoma filled larger proportions of Texas prison walls and farms. In contrast, California imprisoned people from around the globe, but predominantly those people from America's Pacific and Latin American domains, drawn to dynamic metropoles like Los Angeles and San Francisco but also to its many factories in the fields. In each state, the largest number of prisoners came from the rapidly growing, largest urban centers: Harris and Dallas counties in Texas, and Los Angeles County in California. In both states, percentages of foreign-born prisoners halved across the Depression: from 25 to 12 percent in California, and from 6 to 3 percent in Texas. Economic depression and the expulsion or deportation of noncitizens hardened the international borders. Incarceration became a tool to control urbanizing domestic populations who could not be expelled.

TABLE 1.6

Nativity of Most Common Non-Texan Prisoners in Texas

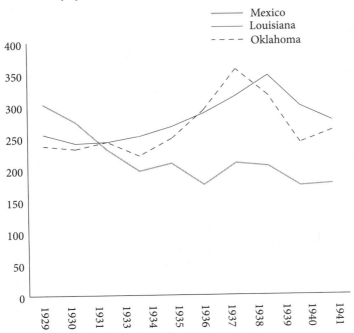

Incarceration by Occupation and Education

Regardless of where they were born or where they had traveled, the people who found themselves behind prison walls in each state tended to be poor, and listed their occupation as "laborer." The five most common occupations listed in Texas prisons between 1932 and 1941 were laborers, cooks and waiters, farmers, porters and janitors, chauffeurs and auto mechanics, and teamsters and truck drivers. In 1938, for example, 18.4 percent of Texas prisoners (1,287 of 6,989) reported being laborers. Fourteen and three-tenths percent (1,000) were cooks and waiters; 8 percent (570) were farmers; 7.5 percent (524) were porters and janitors; nearly 6 percent were chauffeurs and auto mechanics (410), or teamsters and truckers (408). Around 3 percent of Texas prisoners were clerks, bankers, or accountants. One might quibble at the grouping—clerks might run a small store for someone else and be better understood as waged employees, as opposed to bankers or accountants, who might have more managerial posi-

TABLE 1.7
Texas Prisoners' Most Common Occupations, 1938

Occupation	Number of prisoners (n=6989)	Percentage of total
Laborer	1287	18.4
Cook / Waiter	1000	14.3
Farmer	570	8
Porter / Janitor	524	7.5
Chauffeur / Auto mechanic	410	6
Teamster / Trucker	408	6

TABLE 1.8
Aggregated California Prisoners' Most Common Occupations, 1930–1941

SAN QUENTIN			FOLSOM		
Occupation	Number received	Percentage of total (n=13035)	Occupation	Number received	Percentage of total (n=6682)
Laborer	5211	40	Laborer	1336	20.0
Cook	1511	11.6	Cook	606	9.1
Clerk	1048	8.0	Clerk	351	5.3
Painter	630	4.8	Painter	319	4.8
Truck Driver	581	4.5	Mechanic	318	4.8

tions and salaries. Though we should hardly be surprised that white-collar crime also increased in the Depression, on the whole, the numbers of white-collar criminals were tiny compared to the aggregated plumbers and painters, stockmen and soldiers, bootblacks and barbers who made up the rest of the population. (See table 1.7.) [32]

California prisoners' occupations were generally similar, and inmates were overwhelmingly unskilled workers. Prisoners received at San Quentin were, in most common order, laborers, cooks, clerks, painters, and truck drivers. San Quentin arrivals across the period were almost five times more likely to be laborers than cooks, the second most common occupation. Folsom inmates received were the same: laborers, cooks, clerks, painters, then mechanics, followed by barbers. (See table 1.8.) [33]

Before 1933, San Quentin data is unavailable for prisoners' occupations, but if we take 1938 as a representative year, nearly one-third of all San Quentin prisoners were laborers (32 percent, or 1,710 of 5,377). Cooks were 7 percent (366 of 5,377), painters were 6 percent, mechanics 4 percent, and truck drivers 3 percent of the population. Because agricultural labor in California was done by migrant wageworkers (as opposed to Texas's tenant farmers and sharecroppers), farmers were just over 1 percent of San Quentin prison inmates in 1938. Farm workers, be they Okies, Filipinos, or Mexicans, of whom there were many in the Golden State, would have been listed as laborers. A handful of professionals found themselves behind bars that year in California—eleven lawyers and sixty-nine accountants, bookkeepers, and engineers of some sort—but as with Texas, their numbers paled in comparison to the combined sum of the mechanics, tailors, hospital orderlies, and pipefitters, who sat lower on the social scales of prestige and wages.[34]

In Texas, available data from 1932 through 1940 reveals that 23 percent of arriving prisoners were illiterate; 22 percent had "fair to good" educations, while 55 percent, with a "common" education, were somewhere in between. The largest numbers of illiterate prisoners arrived in 1932, but the count fluctuated from a few hundred in 1933 to almost a thousand in 1939. Those listed with "common" education ranged from 1,486 in 1932 to 2,337 in 1934, and dropped to 1,532 in 1940. Numbers of arriving prisoners with "fair to good" educations fluctuated wildly, with a low of 138 in 1932 to a peak of 1,015 the following year, with later drops and another peak (of 1,122) in 1937.[35]

Data from Folsom suggests that California's prisoners tended to be better educated than those in Texas. Eighty-four percent of inmates entering Folsom across the decade had some public school education, 12 percent of inmates entering Folsom between 1929 and 1941 had some college or university education, and the remaining 4 percent were evenly divided between those who were either self-taught and those who had no education whatsoever. Ninety-eight percent were listed as being able to read and write, while 2 percent could do neither. The number of illiterate inmates entering Folsom rose and then fell over the decade, from fifteen in 1929 to twenty in 1936, and down to just four in 1941.[36]

Incarceration by Offense

Crime data from Folsom and San Quentin is maddeningly inconsistent. However, the two institutions began recording comparable categories in 1935, and the period 1935–1941 shows that inmates were overwhelmingly con-

TABLE 1.9

San Quentin and Folsom Prisoners by Type of Crime, 1935–1941

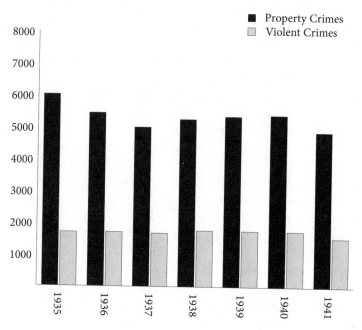

- ■ Property Crimes
- □ Violent Crimes

victed of property offenses rather than violent crimes. (See table 1.9.)[37] Crime wave reportage commonly portrayed criminals as highly dangerous threats to life and well-being, and though there was more than enough violence in the Depression, numbers of prisoners held for violent offenses remained remarkably steady. In 1935, 1,696 prisoners were behind bars in California for violent offenses. The number peaked at 1,764 in 1938 and dropped to 1,541 in 1941. Even in 1938, when California prisons held the largest number of violent offenders, they were still vastly outnumbers by those convicted of property crimes.

The same was true in Texas. People convicted of property crimes (counted here as burglary and theft) always dramatically outnumbered those convicted of violent crimes (here, rape and murder) in Texas prisons. Numbers of prisoners received in Texas for violent crimes remained relatively constant, while those received for property crimes rose substantially in the Depression, and fell once the economic recovery began. (See tables 1.10 and 1.11.)[38]

TABLE 1.10
Texas Prisoners by Selected Crime

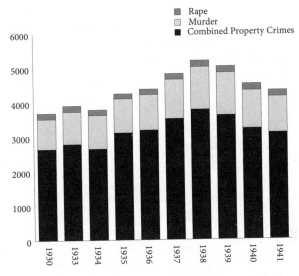

Property crimes here include theft of Auto, by Bailee, of Hogs, Horses, Mules, Fowls, from Person, and Misc Theft; Burglary, of Private Residence, of Private Residence at night, of RailRoad Car. Rape includes term and life sentences.

TABLE 1.11
Texas Prisoners Received, by Crime

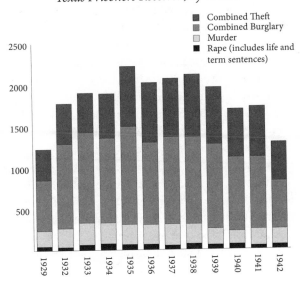

Incarceration by Race
California

Demographic data on California prisoners by race is ambiguous at best. Categories listed in annual reports changed from year to year; at times data was collected at San Quentin but not at Folsom. This is perhaps unsurprising, given that racial formations reflect political rather than biological differences. Racial difference, though lived as clearly and brutally real, was a social fact, not a biological fact. For this reason, the records, while useful, are also quite frustrating. One certainly wishes that the recordkeepers could at least have been consistent with their categories, for then the realities of penal racism could be mapped, even if the categories they used were historical fictions.

Prison inmates were predominantly working class and poorly educated, and racial disparities were salient in both states. California was an overwhelmingly white state in 1930. That year, the total California population was recorded at 5,677,251, with some 5,408,260 of those listed as white, a category that included Anglos as well as Mexican Americans. Thus, 95.3 percent of the California population was listed as white. The census also listed a total of 81,048 black Californians, who consisted of just 1.4 percent of the California population. At 168,731, those classified as Asian and Pacific Islander constituted nearly 3 percent of the California population. And Americans Indians, numbered at 19,212, were some 0.3 percent of the state population.

The prison populations reflected the preponderance of whites in the state overall. Whites were recorded as 89 percent of the San Quentin population in 1930. Those listed as Negro were nearly 7 percent of the prison population at San Quentin—almost five times their numerical representation in the state. Aggregated prison records also listed "brown" as a racial category. Though ambiguous, "brown" may have been coded to represent Filipino prisoners: the category disappeared the same year that "Filipino" appeared on the record books (also the year that "white" split into "white" and "Mexican"). If one combines the numbers of prisoners listed as brown, Hindu, Japanese, and Chinese in 1930—which would fit into the mélange category of Asian and Pacific Islander—there were some 169 Asian and Pacific Islander prisoners in California. Thus, they constituted 3.4 percent of the prison population—just slightly more than their representative population in the state. The thirty-seven American Indians at San Quentin in 1930 were 0.7 percent of the prison population, more than double their actual percentage of the state's population.

California's population grew significantly in the following decade, though it would grow even more quickly during and after the war. According to the 1940 California census, English-speaking whites were 89.5 percent of Californians. The black population also grew, from 1.4 to some 1.8 percent of Californians. Ethnic Mexican Californians (defined on the census as those who spoke Spanish as a "mother tongue") were estimated at 6 percent of the population. American Indians remained at 0.3 percent, while Asian and Pacific Islanders continued the long decline from the 1860s through a precipitous decline after the Chinese Exclusion Act to a low point in 1950. But in 1940, the Asian and Pacific Islander population was just 2.4 percent of California's population.

The California prison population again reflected the basic weight of these differences, though, importantly, people of color remained overrepresented and whites underrepresented. White Californians were some 73 percent of the San Quentin population in 1940, while African Americans were a solid 9 percent of San Quentin inmates. Ethnic Mexicans constituted 12 percent of the prison population at San Quentin. When we combine the categories Chinese, Hindus, Filipinos, Hawaiians, and Japanese, we see that they were 4 percent of the population at San Quentin.

However, also in 1940, we can see that the percentages of nonwhite prisoners at Folsom increased even faster than it did at San Quentin. The shift may have been due to administrative changes in the prison system as part of its proclaimed modernization. In 1936, San Quentin became the system's medium security institution and Folsom its maximum security prison. The white population at Folsom in 1940 was recorded at 77 percent of the prisoners, and whites were thus underrepresented among the maximum security prisoners; African Americans were 12 percent of the Folsom population in 1940, and ethnic Mexicans were 8 percent of maximum security prisoners. American Indians were 0.9 percent of Folsom prisoners, and Chinese, Filipinos, Hawaiians, and Japanese prisoners were 1.7 percent of its inmates. Ten Puerto Ricans were the last of the inmates to be accounted for.[39]

Texas

The general Texas population in 1930 was 85.3 percent white, with ethnic Mexicans and Anglos combining to make this category. African Americans were some 14.7 percent of the population in 1930. Yet the prison populations in 1930 were more varied, and there was little of the ambiguity about whether or not Mexicans were "white" in these institutions of direct control. In 1930, whites made up 49.6 percent of the prison population; African Americans were some 39.6 percent of the prison population; and Mexicans were some 10.7 percent of the prison population.

In the 1940 census, ethnic Mexicans were estimated at 11.5 percent of the Texas population, while Anglos were estimated at 74.1 percent. African Americans were some 14.4 percent of the Texas population. Not surprisingly, the prison population reflected its function as an institution of racial and social control, even in the new era of the 1930s. Whites were 48.2 percent of the prison population; African Americans composed some 39.2 percent of prison inmates; and ethnic Mexicans were 12.6 percent. This meant that in 1940, African Americans were imprisoned at rates that nearly tripled their statewide population. Imprisoned Mexican Americans more closely approximated their statewide population, while whites were dramatically underrepresented behind bars.[40] This might have been an improvement, however, given the prison's grim history. Between 1880 and 1912, black Texans, who dropped from 31 to 18 percent of the state's populations, generally made up between 50 and 60 percent of its prisoners.[41]

Discursive Marking, Racial Records

In the face of the complex ethnic and racial mix of travelers and itinerant workers in each state, prison officials demanded to locate the identities of their prisoners in clearly defined ways. Officials always wanted to know the individual identities of specific lawbreakers, to better link them to their criminal records. Despite this individuating drive, collective racial identifications were key to broader social controls.

Since the colonial period, discourses of morality and immorality have been linked to racial ideologies and connected to transgressions of the law. Following the Civil War and Reconstruction, the panoply of racist tags vilifying African Americans and colonized peoples the world over—indolent, childlike, violent, barbaric, sexually degenerate, and so on—were transferred onto criminals, now in an ostensibly color-blind fashion. In the 1890s, social-scientific discourse meshed with court reports and popular media representations to produce powerful new associations between blackness and criminality, justifying both new kinds of policing and control of nonwhites.[42] The very definitions of law performed ideological work, guaranteeing the sanctity of property relations and hiding historically contingent forms of bourgeois authority behind the seeming impartiality of the state.[43] Thus, all prisoners were immediately marked as racially and morally deviant. Nevertheless, the ideologies of racial hierarchy prevalent during the 1930s allowed for white-raced inmates (tainted though their whiteness may have been) to be potentially redeemed into mainstream society through putatively redemptive industrial labor, or through modest welfare or educational programs. However, progressive penological ideals gained meager traction in the class and state formations of the New Deal, and white prisoners were considered potentially redeemable citizens. Racial others, whose asserted claims to social equality were consistently marginalized, had far fewer opportunities for social redemption through "correction." For black prisoners especially, punishment remained the norm.

Racial categorization embodied in prison practice differentiated among groups as categories of humans but also eclipsed internal difference within those groups. Through the prison record-keeping apparatus (as one site in the construction of racial identities), state governments effectively distorted differences that heterogeneous groups knew prior to their incarceration—be they class, regional, linguistic, or ethnic. In prison as in the "free world," racial categories created difference among groups as well as the appearance of homogeneity among what were, in fact, heterogeneous communities. Through forms of record keeping, human beings with complex histories and identities were reduced to individual, administratively legible case files. This was a process in which prisoners' visions of themselves played little role at all. Indeed, the entire history of criminal record keeping aimed to remove all personal agency in controlling criminals' identity, which they might change in order to escape punishment.

California began the twentieth century using Bertillion files to record inmates' identities. The system was developed in the 1870s by Parisian police bureaucrat Alphonse Bertillion to precisely track and identify metropolitan French criminals. Bertillion cards first used in California had no photograph attached, but contained a great deal of biometric information. The right ear was measured, teeth and chin assessed, beard, hair, complexion, weight, and build measured, and place of birth noted, as a topography of bodies designed to concretely link subjects to criminal case files.[44]

As David Lamson's memoir suggests, biometric and racial information on prisoners was not recorded from on high by guards or wardens. The politics of record keeping in state prisons was more convoluted. Inmates were in charge of many of these administrative duties, and prisoner bookkeepers were generally the ones who made the notations of height, age, weight, race, and nativity. Like the inmate who admitted David Lamson to San Quentin, they smoked their cigarettes and probably did not give a damn about any of it. After all, they were just doing their job while they did their time, and were happy not to be working in the jute mill, the quarry, or the fields. The question of agency here—of *who* was the state—remains problematic, and this is a matter to be taken up again in chapter 4. Prisoners were the eyes of the state; their labor and their racial notations expanded the state's record-keeping apparatus. Despite the fact that these were prisoners, their vision was harnessed into the depersonalized, highly bureaucratic institution: in Marxian terms, these white prisoners' labor was captured and ossified into a technology of racial and state control. The ways in which prison book-keepers saw the inmates they entered into prison records became part of the prison's institutional memory, which would then be examined by other, similarly depersonalized prison workers and bureaucrats, and later still, by parole boards and prospective employers.[45]

California replaced its Bertillion books with identification cards to track inmates in a rationalized and accessible administrative space—possibly because inmate clerks, like Indians in England's colonial police forces, were not trusted to master the Bertillion system's complexities. The subsequent ID cards were still based on a rough anthropometry, but by 1930, San Quentin issued cards based on looser categories than Bertillionage, as its scientific accuracy in measurement had been called into question some years before.[46] These new ID cards relied more heavily on photographic visual imagery, but nevertheless maintained description of body types and recorded marks, scars, and tattoos, as well as fingerprint information. The cards remained consistent in form and use in San Quentin from 1930 through the end of the Second World War.

If cards remained largely consistent, the words used to describe inmates' bodies and, most importantly, their "color," did not. This inconsistency should come as little surprise, as the category "color"—combining disparate measures of nationality, race, and religion, and bearing little if any correspondence to the category "complexion"—adhered not to material bodies but rather to ideological representations. While the practices of determining someone's "color" and identity changed over time and in different political-economic contexts, once inscribed behind bars, they were quite literally set in stone. Identities would provide the basis for labor assignments, type of punishment, food served, and educational opportunities. Racial identities, in and out of prison, were the result of a complex matrix of forces, conflicts, and racial projects in the contemporary social formation. In this practice, distinctions between "folk" and "bureaucratic" definitions of race—commonly understood as race as everyday experience versus bureaucratic categorizations (like the census)—were wedded, and would have concrete effects on prisoners' lives. It would have made sense for an inmate to try to pass as white, given the opportunity. Better food and treatment would have been the result.[47] Ocie Hoosier, who served time in Texas, had been raised by his mixed-race grandparents. But Hoosier, who had light skin, was listed as "white" in record books, with red hair and a ruddy complexion, and was treated accordingly. This is not to assert that Hoosier was "really" black, but rather that racial identities are complex and contextual, and that Hoosier made a calculated decision to try to benefit from white-skin privilege, where being black was a serious threat to survival.[48]

In some of these cards, "Portuguese" was listed as a "color." So was "White," (capitalized), so was "Mexican," and so were "Jewish," "Chinese," and also "Canadian." Significantly, however, though record keepers were not totally consistent in this practice, the color "Negro" was typed in red ink. The color/racial designation "white" was always written in "normal," and normalizing, black script, while the terms "Mexican," "Chinese," "Spanish," "Portuguese," and "Filipino" could be written in either red or black.[49]

The symbolic significance of the red ink used in ID cards may seem trifling, but nonetheless bears further analysis. Each and every time a "Negro" prisoner was received at San Quentin, he or she was mechanically and consistently marked in the records and files, signifying the "special" and "different" status, as if the black prisoner needed to be watched more closely than the rest. When racial material was collected, a prison typist pressed the lever on the typewriter, raising the red ribbon and lowering the black one, as a special signifier of racial difference.[50]

A further note is that when the "marks" on a prisoner's body were recorded, prisoners' tattoos were also noted in red ink. Criminologists maintained a long tradition in recording prisoners' tattoos, and Bertillion himself found them fascinating. Furthermore, nineteenth-century Italian criminologist Cesare Lombroso (famed for seeking out biological criminality based on primitivism, thought to be visible through physical attributes) argued that tattoos were "a specific and entirely new anatomico-legal characteristic" that indicated better than any other the "born criminal."[51] Both the racial identity "Negro" and descriptions of prisoners' tattoos were printed on inmate ID cards using this different color. Through the use of red ink, these two discursive constructions of prison inmates were thus specially marked. Red, then, was a signal of stigmatized difference, as opposed to the relatively unmarked descriptions of a prisoner's height, weight, crime, place of birth, or numerical representation of fingerprints.

Both tattoos and blackness were identifications of people that the state felt needed particular attention and special control. Did the color red signal some perceived threat to the system? Was "blackness" or being racially "Negro" written in red because it was a threat, too? It was probably seen as such by prison clerks and officials in California, as a sign of inherent criminality, marking a criminal as beyond redemption into the New Deal state. Tattoos and blackness were marks on the body; they were on the surface of the skin. The difference, of course, was that tattooed prisoners got them of their own volition, as a performative statement and writing on their bodies. Among prisoners, tattoos were a form of bodily capital, a property and adornment that could not be taken away as punishment, when all other materials would be contraband, stored in a property locker. Prisoners used tattoos to mark themselves, and to use the surface of their bodies for writing themselves in ways that the state did not authorize. Indeed, giving tattoos at San Quentin was a punishable offense.[52] Conversely, blackness, like other dishonored racial identities, was hardly a matter of choice for the inmates so marked.

California authorities penned whole record books to keep track of "Other" prisoners considered dangerous or anomalous. Between 1922 and 1937, California kept ledger books identified by the titles "Black and Yellow #2" and "Black and Yellow #3." In addition, two other ledgers detailed specially marked prisoners: one was entitled "San Quentin Women #2," and the other specified inmates convicted of criminal syndicalism.[53] Each of these books contained photos and descriptions of prisoners—name, racial identity, crime committed, sentence, nativity, age, occupation, height, weight, complexion, eyes, hair, received date, parole/discharge date, and fingerprint information/formula. These books existed because the state classified and created "Other" racial, gendered, and political categories, while leaving "normal," normative identities unmarked.

Gender operated as another major regulatory and distributive category in the prison (and beyond). The "San Quentin Women" book was not structurally organized by race; it included images and descriptions of women of multiple ethnicities and markings. Thus, women were known first and foremost as *women*, regardless of race. They were then identified by race, as a secondary order of difference. Men, on the other hand, constituted the normative gendered category of prisoner (as well as citizen, thus indicating the key relationship between maleness and either positive or negative recognition—but recognition still—by the state). Male prisoners were segregated at the secondary bodily level of racial difference. No images of "white" prisoners graced the pages of the "Black and Yellow" books, which were solely devoted to documenting racial others. However, no Filipinos and few ethnic Mexicans were listed in these pages, either. Perhaps the complex colonial relationship between the United States and the Philippines and the Good Neighbor Policy between the United States and Latin America led to the contradictory ethnoracial and national status of Filipinos and ethnic Mexicans in California prisons.

These books are remarkable for the visions they produced and the way they show racial difference being marked as an explicit denigration. Prison bookkeepers wrote racial epithets next to the photos of the inmates. Thus Jas. Mori, alias Hajime Ota, convicted in 1935 of two counts of grand theft and serving one to ten years, was listed as a "Jap," the word written and underlined next to his name, despite the fact that he was born in Hawaii. Willie Williams, a 29-year-old musician born in North Carolina and sentenced for assault with a deadly weapon, was described as a "Coon," in underscored letters. Twenty-three-year-old Herbert Chan, born in California and convicted of violation of the State Poison Act, was listed as a "Chink," and Iasian Ali, a 41-year-old laborer convicted of assault with a deadly weapon, had the word "Hindu" written and underlined in bold letters across his photo. Some prisoners were listed as "Coon" while others were "Negro," one after the other. At times it seemed as if this might have been based on skin tone, but the markings seemed inconsistent, and the logic behind such demarcation, if such there was, remains opaque.[54] This should pose little surprise. The lack of any material referent for race would guarantee that the practices used to inscribe/describe race could not help but be inconsistently applied.

In the women's book, Cordelia McWee, born in Oklahoma and serving one to fourteen years for forgery, had the word "Cooness" written and underlined by her name, while Alice Halverson, a housewife born in Illinois who had passed bad checks, had no such marker, though her complexion was listed as "dark." Cassie Turner, a housewife from Modoc, California, served zero to ten years for manslaughter and was described as "Indian," with a "dark" complexion, "maroon" eyes, and "black" hair. Josephine Lee was a 23-year-old maid born in Louisiana, sentenced for forgery in Los Angeles County. Listed as a "Negress," she had a "brown" complexion, black hair, and "maroon" eyes. ("Maroon eyes" were frequently a marker of racial difference in prison categorizations.) Fifty-eight-year-old Maria Gonzalez was convicted of possessing a still in Riverside County and was described as "Mex" in the record books, with "dark" complexion, "maroon" eyes, and black hair. Interestingly, Rose Massucco, a seamstress born in Italy, with a "fair" complexion, had the word "Ital" written across her photo. Lest we think that this was purely a designation of her natal country, as according to the 1924 Immigration and National Origins Act, Lida Harden, a furrier convicted of receiving stolen property, was born in Holland but had no such stigmatizing mark in the book.[55] Perhaps conceived of as a "Nordic white" in the intraracial hierarchies of whiteness, Harden needed no marker, as did Massucco and other Italian or "Mediterranean white" women.[56]

Unlike Texas, which operated under a relatively stable ethnoracial definitional hierarchy, categories in California changed dramatically, and erratically, according to the arrival of a prisoner who might be difficult to categorize (such as the "Afghan" category, as well as "Malay," "Mongolian," and "Ethiopian"). Of course, much of this speaks to the ways in which these gradations may not have mattered too greatly in prisoners' lives—the difference between being described as yellow, Mongolian, or Chinese probably did not change the lived reality of racialization and its material consequences within the prison.

In all of these cases, prison authorities inscribed the bodies of their wards to categorize them in manageable ways, even if these categories, like the racial formations they furthered, were inconsistent and internally contradictory. Bodies and identities were administratively marked through a managerial, disciplinary, and technical practice to organize and identify prisoners in the bureaucratic record-keeping apparatus. In so doing, prison authorities reified the key discursive categories and hierarchies of the day. That these definitions were historically and geographically contingent made no difference to prison officials or bookkeepers, who, on the basis of these representational differences, arranged the bodies of their wards accordingly.

Spatial Organization of Punishment

Once prisoners' bodies were thoroughly and distinctly categorized, prison officials knew where to assign them within the prison systems. Managerial decisions based on representational differences thus had material and bodily ramifications, as prisoners were assigned to different locations and job assignments, where opportunities for education, vocational training, medical treatment, quality of food, and modes of punishment varied widely.

The geographic organization of the Texas Prison System was a sort of penal solar system in East Texas, a region whose dyadic black-white racial hierarchy and sharecropping economy made it the most "southern" of the state's varied social and economic geographies. The Walls Unit at Huntsville was the administrative center of this constellation, with a number of satellite prison farms literally scattered as peripheral sites. As the convict lease system came under Progressive Era humanitarian criticism, and as the cost of free labor fell to below the cost of leasing prisoners, the state gradually assumed control of prisoners and the potential profits they might make. The state, consequently, accumulated farm land where prisoners would be set to work. This model appealed to administrators for many reasons. First, it was relatively inexpensive, and prison farms needed little in the way of capital investment in the wooden buildings and bunkhouses known as "tanks." Secondly, the system was firmly rooted in forced, racialized agricultural labor. Forced labor was an easy fit, for the racially marked and the unfree. Food that prisoners grew could be used to feed themselves and other prisoners, and the cotton they picked would help finance a "self-sustaining" prison. This minimized the financial drain on state coffers and performed the ideological work that incarceration would "teach inmates a good work ethic"—long a theme of punishment in capitalist societies. Finally, it proved compatible with the legislated requirements passed in 1909 that strengthened racial segregation, even as it questioned the full whiteness of many convicts.[57]

Reformers in the 1920s tried to create a central prison colony based on more modernist big-house models, but the project died in 1928 in the wake of penal retrenchment.[58] As a result, the course of Texas's penal geography was set. It received the additional boost of scientific legitimacy in 1936, thanks to Laura Spellman Rockefeller–funded research into prison classification programs. Much to prison administrators' delight, the existing spatial foundation, rooted in the slave past of low costs and racialized agricultural labor, gained the imprimatur of modern penology. Texas officials joyfully learned that their geographically scattered system actually served the most "modern" classificatory and penological ends.[59] Refinements were made, however, though they were unevenly spread across the system. The 1936 classification plan suggested that "Negro" and "Mexican" prisoners should be segregated by race and age, and that first offenders should be kept apart from repeat offenders. This was hardly revolutionary programming elsewhere in the country, but the ideas were still somewhat novel in Texas. Young and first-time black and ethnic Mexican prisoners were also supposed to receive rehabilitative training, but in reality, their labor regimen was every bit as degraded as that of recidivists'. While black and Mexican prisoners saw meager classificatory differentiation, the white population was further classified into nine subcategories, all of which was lauded as progress:

More effective than any other single factor in advancing the prison system's plans of industrial progress is the program of inmate classification and segregation now in force here. This Classification and Segregation Program went into effect March 1, 1936, with the establishment of the Bureau of Classification at Huntsville prison, the receiving station for the entire system.

Negroes and Mexicans are segregated as to race[,] age [and whether they are] first offenders [or] recidivists. The white male population of the prison (the female group being too small to permit segregation other than as to sex and race) is classified in terms of the following groups:

1. Physically Defective.
2. Insane.
3. Feeble minded.
4. Drug Addicts.
5. Homosexuals.

1. Rehabilitative Group—composed of those not oriented in crime who have good prospects for adjustment after release; and segregated further as to:

A. those under twenty-five years of age, and
B. those over twenty-five years of age.

2. The Intermediate Group—including those prisoners with some criminal record and whose backgrounds indicate they are doubtful cases for rehabilitation; further segregated as to:

A. those under twenty-five years of age, and
B. those over twenty-five years of age.

3. The Custodial Group—including persistent offenders.

4. The Maximum Risk Group—including those who have indicated extreme viciousness or who may be expected to cause serious trouble, of [sic] those who have serious escape records and little regard for human life.

Nine geographically separate and distinct units are used for the segregation of the white male population. Agricultural units are reserved for classes 6, 7, 8, and 9, while two industrial units are reserved for the rehabilitative group. Rehabilitative measures, including apprenticeship, vocational training, etc., are concentrated on the rehabilitative group.[60]

Referring to the world outside the prison walls, historian David Montejano has written that the Texan social and spatial order of the 1930s revised the racial prejudices of an earlier period. "This was a new society, with new class groups and class relations, with the capacity to generate an 'indigenous' rationale for the ordering of people."[61] This new order tried to manage racial relations through spatial segregation, and drew on metaphors and meanings "remembered" from the slave South, but also drew on the agro-industrial Jim Crow order dividing Anglos, Mexicans, and African Americans into distinct social spaces. Each prison farm was thus effectively a plantation, but one broken into different camps. Under threat of the lash, prisoners worked from sunrise to sunset growing corn, cotton, feed crops, and other assorted vegetables in river bottom lands. In contrast, ethnic Mexicans arriving in Texas prisons would be sent to the Blue Ridge Farm, maintained exclusively for "Mexican"-raced prisoners. It, too, was divided into two camps, where prisoners picked cotton, corn, and vegetables on 4,505 acres. The Eastham Farm, however, was exclusively for "white" prisoners, who also worked all year round in agricultural fields.

These farms were for a particular race of inmates while others, such as the Central Farm, housed both Negro and white prisoners, but in separate camps. The Goree Farm was the only unit for women prisoners in Texas, and (like the "San Quentin Women" record book), it held women of different ethnoracial identities, though these were internally segregated. Lastly, Texas also had a farm specifically for "invalid" and tubercular prisoners, known as the Wynne Farm.

Francisco Serrano learned his way around the Texas Prison System over the thirty-odd years he was incarcerated. He was arrested for sodomy in Washington County in 1930 and was sentenced to three consecutive fifteen-year sentences. Though born in Cuba in 1900, Serrano was listed as "M," for Mexican, in the prison record books. Furthermore, the Huntsville bookkeeper recorded his complexion as "lt mex": light Mexican. There was no ethnoracial space corresponding to "Cuban" in the records. Serrano was, however, Catholic, married, and a tobacco smoker, but did not drink. He had worked as an auto mechanic, a boilermaker, and a common laborer prior to his arrest; whether or not he was employed at Huntsville as either of the first two remains unknown, though he certainly had more than his fill of field labor in the prison. Serrano had the letters "LM" tattooed on his forearm, and a heart on his upper arm, which he may have gotten while he served in the army or when he did time in a New Jersey prison. Though his tattoos were described in black ink, the Huntsville bookkeeper used a red pen to write the words "homosexual" and "marijuana user" across the top of his entry. Viewing him as a "sexual deviant," state officers also wanted to keep an especially close eye on him, for fear that he might infect others—syphilis and homosexuality were considered equally contagious in the penal context.[62]

Shortly after his arrival, Serrano was transferred to the Blue Ridge Farm. This was consistent with his identification as racially "Mexican," even though he was born in Cuba.[63] Officials would not have known where to put him otherwise. In his many transfers through the prison system (and after two different escapes, one lasting more than seven years), he was always returned to Mexican-raced spaces in the prison. The only time when he was not returned to a Mexican section of the prison was in 1946, when he was committed to isolation and demoted to being a third-class prisoner for "trying to force another inmate to homosexual activities."[64] As a sexually active and presumably violent prisoner, he was to be spatially isolated from others—for safety, for punishment, and to regulate sexuality in this all-male environment. By the war years, officials in Texas and California would try to police prisoners' sexualities through increasingly developed spatial segregation and labor assignments.

Asian American prisoners in California, too, were quickly located in the racial and gendered labor hierarchies at California's San Quentin, Chino, Folsom, and Tehachapi prisons. Male Chinese, Japanese, and Filipino prisoners were frequently transferred from one prison to another to work as cooks or gardeners in the institutions, as was the case when inmates Fong Suey Lung (52931) and Jo Lee (53645) were sent to Tehachapi "to work round the ranch house and to cook for the guards."[65] Prison officials preferred having these "Oriental" prisoners as house servants in their personal quarters. Leo Stanley wrote lovingly about his Chinese "houseboy." Because he was the institution's physician, "a house had been provided for us and one of the inmates, a young Chinaman, assigned as houseboy and cook." The servant took great care of Stanley's ailing wife, he wrote, "answering her every call and want with characteristic Chinese devotion. He is still a servant in my house, remaining after my wife's death in 1928."[66] Some, however, did not meet officials' expectation. Folsom warden Clyde Plummer sent "Chinese Prisoner No. 61580 George Yuen" back to San Quentin from Folsom because his services as "a house servant" were "unsatisfactory." Three different Chinese prisoners were sent "to work in the Warden's Residence as house servants" to replace him.[67]

The gender of Asian male prisoners was rooted in the feminized position of Asian men in California's political economy. Sucheng Chan suggests that in mid-nineteenth-century California, where there were so few women, any men willing to do "domestic" work, such as cooking or laundry—already dishonored and gendered as female—would be able to make a living. Thus because of the restrictions placed on so many Asians for their work (by "manly" and white union laborers, whose manliness and whiteness was largely produced in opposition to Chinese men), Chinese men found labor opportunities in the service sectors of laundries, restaurants, and households. However, work in the service sector was characterized as "inferior" through raced and gendered operations of power.[68] It must also be noted that black women prisoners were used as domestic labor for Texas governmental officials, including the governor, while black men could be used as domestic "houseboys" for select prison administrators.[69]

California's penal spatial organization followed a different definition of modernity than did Texas's scattered penal farms, organizing its prisoners in huge, centralized institutions based on individual cells and group, semi-industrial labor, known loosely as the "Auburn Plan" of penal architecture. In the 1930s and 1940s, the prison system expanded, centralized, and attempted to rationalize itself into a singular administrative bureaucracy, and this effort conjoined with ever more precise differentiations of prisoners. In 1934 California opened a new institution for women at Tehachapi (also segregated by race into supposedly homey "cottages"), and furthered inmate segregation by what wardens thought to be their rehabilitative potential. As a result, San Quentin became the intake and classificatory unit, as well as housing for medium security prisoners; the Chino Institution for Men was opened in 1942 as a minimum security institution; and Folsom became the prison for maximum security inmates.

Even within California's aesthetically "modern" institutions—centralized, capital intensive, and with individual cells (but doubled or even quadrupled due to overcrowding) as opposed to Texas's "tanks"—the link between race and space was apparent as well as essential to the process of incarceration. Records defining the spatial components are scattered, but nonetheless, there is clear evidence that black prisoners were segregated in different cellblocks than their white, Mexican, and East and South Asian counterparts. Unlike the legislated racial segregation in Jim Crow Texas, racial differentiation and spatial separation in California was much more a matter of custom than of law. Indeed, white inmates referred to "Dark-town" when talking about the "black" part of San Quentin—thus employing a metaphor from an urban landscape to explain modes of racial segregation within "The Walled City."[70] Folsom prison, too, saw racial hierarchy produced through formal and informal means, but especially by the assignment of black inmates to the least desirable cells—a virtual ghetto within the prison. The top two tiers of one of Folsom's cellblocks were known as the "Crow's Nest"—a name that obviously punned on the top of a ship's mast but was more pointedly a

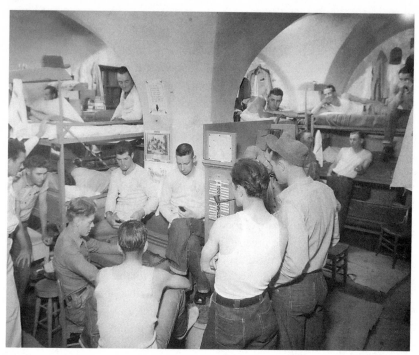

Most white inmates were placed in cells, but in May 1935, in the midst of considerable overcrowding, many were housed here, in a converted basement storage space beneath the New Mess Hall. Image 1925.006.005, Folder 6, Leo L. Stanley Collection, San Quentin Photographs, Anne T. Kent Room, Marin County Public Library.

derogatory and raced name for this part of the Jim Crow prison. Black prisoners complained that the tiers sweltered during the scorching central valley summers, when temperatures frequently topped 100 degrees. Furthermore, they were the last called to eat at mealtime, thus linking temporal with spatial segregation and the creation of honored and dishonored subjectivities.[71] Though prison records were relatively silent about the condition of ethnic Filipino, Chinese, and Japanese prisoners at Folsom, guards and investigators noted that there had been quite a "kick" from ethnic Mexican prisoners who protested being racially segregated and treated as subordinate to whites.[72]

California inmates' cell assignments and labor assignments were broadly influenced by race. But each prison's unstructured spaces, such

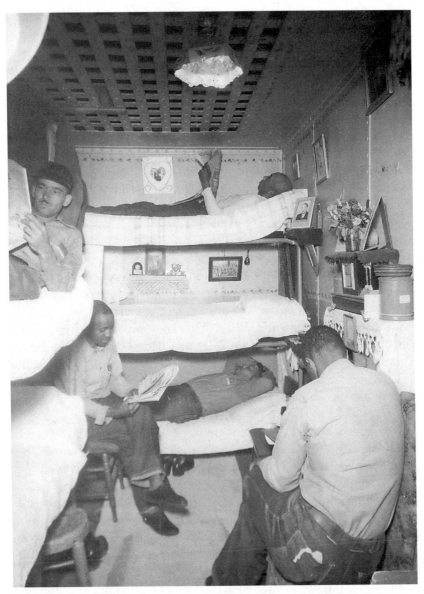

Five black inmates in a single cell: Tank Fifteen, in the Old Cell Block. While white inmates presented themselves playing dominoes, these black inmates' self-presentation was of literate reflection and dignified bearing in a cramped, yet domesticated space. Image 1925.006.007, Folder 6, Leo L. Stanley Collection, San Quentin Photographs, Anne T. Kent Room, Marin County Public Library.

as the main yard or the mess hall, were more fluid, and allowed for cross-racial collaboration or antagonism. There was plenty of each, when black, white, Asian, and Mexican prisoners gambled, traded, joked around, and even loved each other. A photograph of a crowd of inmates in the San Quentin main yard shows loose clusters of black, Mexican, or Asian prisoners gathered among the masses of whites, who are themselves clustered in small groups having conversations (see cover photo). Nevertheless, racial segregation became the norm in San Quentin and Folsom. White prisoners enforced racial spaces to delineate privilege and hierarchy. There was no formal rule about seating at mealtimes, but black prisoners could be booed (or worse) if they tried to sit and eat in the "white" section of the dining hall.[73]

When Joseph Blinsky stood with black, Filipino, Mexican, and other white prisoners outside San Quentin's cafeteria, guards harassed him for talking to a "kid"—a prisoner thought to be homosexual. In a letter to the warden, Blinsky complained that if black, Mexican, and white prisoners could intermingle, he should certainly be able talk to another white man, "kid" or not. "[I]f a white man can talk to a negros i think i can talk and line up with a white man if we don't do no rong. . . . [Y]ou know sir i have the right to talk and line up with a white man he is doing time like me."[74] Blinsky's desire for a white-only space available for homosexual contact articulated resistance to guards' authority, but also re-created a gendered racial hierarchy, while appealing to the warden as a source of just rule.

Regardless of where they had come from or even, to some extent, who they had been prior to incarceration, prisoners were entering a new world. They were nearly universally poor, and they were disproportionately nonwhite. Many had traveled great distances before they were locked up, and many, as we will see, would never leave. California's prison world was a harsher version of the multiethnic neighborhoods outside, where whites strove to reassert supremacy, and where administrators were generally happy to go along. Texas's scattered prison farms created a world that was more racially segregated than anything on the outside. Prisoners had to quickly reorient themselves to this new world, and to the regimes and hierarchies it imposed. Even once they were settled into new regimes and routines, disorientation remained. As one prisoner sang, "I don't know which side of the river / Oh boy, my home is on / Cause I been on this river / So jumpin long."[75] Times were hard on the outside, to be sure. But anyone sentenced to prison would learn that worse was soon to come.

2

Work in the Walled City

Labor and Discipline in California's Prisons

After new arrivals found their cells and met their cellmates, they negotiated bunk space and where to put any belongings they might have. They did not have long to do it, though. Soon enough they would be expected to make their way to their job assignment. Work mattered. From the San Quentin jute mill to the Folsom mess hall, from the bookkeepers' department to honor road camps outside the walls, work was a crucial part of prisoners' lives. It had always been. Behind bars as on the outside, work contained a range of meanings and practices that went beyond the tasks accomplished or shirked. It affected prisoners' health, their opportunities to get good food, and their chances for social interaction, prestige, or even early release. Prisoners' labor, moreover, allowed the institutions that held them to function. "The Walled City" contained a city's worth of work. Prisoners cooked the food and served it, sewed the clothes they wore and washed it when it got dirty, swept the halls, wrote and printed the prison newspaper, and ran the library. They also built furniture, assembled shoes, wove jute sacks, and pressed license plates—all of these could help the institutions recoup the costs of warehousing so many. As budgets tightened and the prison population grew, officials looked for any cost-saving measure. Prisoners' sweat cost nothing at all and, if properly managed, might even earn something for the state.

For this reason and others, a great many interests converged in prisoners' labor. In the 1930s, when as much as a quarter of the outside workforce felt the pain of unemployment, many on the outside wondered why convicts should have jobs while they had to scrape and bow to get anything at all. Workers in the Depression were hardly the first to despise competition with unfree workers; their sentiment contained elements that dated back to the Free Soil movement in the mid-nineteenth century and anti-immigrant movements in the late nineteenth century.[1] But when the stock market crashed in 1929, for the first time free workers had the benefit of federal legislation on their side. The Hawes-Cooper Act, passed in 1929, and the Ashurst-Sumners Act, passed in 1934, brought the power of the national government into the regulation of prisoners' labor. Following generations of organized labor's protests against competition with prisoners and the companies who could exploit them, Hawes-Cooper and Ashurst-Sumners restricted for-profit inmate labor and drove most prisons into a system of "state-use" only. It was a huge and symbolic victory for free workers, but prison officials predicted that their institutions would descend into bedlam if they could no longer rely on labor, that bedrock of penal discipline, and set prisoners to work however they wished. Nevertheless, by the 1930s prison labor no longer played the role in regional economies that it had during the northern private-contract period or the southern convict lease period.[2] Instead, labor comprised part of an internal disciplinary economy based in behavioral control and racial differentiation. It was, nevertheless, beset by corruption and pierced by inmates' and officials' varying definitions of manhood. Labor assignment in California prisons involved a range of controls, from physical punishment and the risk of injury in the worst tasks to the payment of wages and the extension of credit in the very best. California's labor systems in the 1930s modified existing progressive penological models.

Prison labor held disciplinary as well as financial appeals. A tired inmate was a docile inmate, officials hoped, but it went deeper than this. California's prison officials, firmly wedded to a modernist project of progressive penology, believed in the redemptive power of labor. A 1930 "Report on Prison Labor," authored by the California Taxpayer Association, succinctly voiced the ideology guiding prison labor since the Civil War: "Constructive employment is probably the most valuable means of leading a man away from criminal tendencies. To teach a man habits of industry and to impress upon him the dignity of labor will do much to restore him to useful citizenship."[3] The authors further described work's pedagogical and reformative aspects: "To the hardened criminal, the thought of work is repulsive. No doubt, this attitude has much to do with the fact that he has chosen a life of crime."[4] Young prisoners, they reasoned, could be reformed by learning the good habits of hard work, while hardened criminals would be punished by it. "The dignity of labor should be emphasized in the minds of prisoner employees and they should be allowed to acquire the habits of industry." They did offer a caveat, though. "Treadmill labor . . . cannot produce these results and would do more damage than good as a cure of criminal tendencies."[5] Hard work might teach criminals the Protestant ethic they supposedly lacked. Given the right training, officials reasoned, prisoners could even learn a trade that they could apply on release. Officials worried that such training would invariably provoke the ire of organized workers, but that bothered them less than not setting prisoners to work at all.

Prison labor held deeper disciplinary uses than physical exhaustion and went even further than instilling a work ethic. The work that prisoners did was highly differentiated. San Quentin and Folsom were, after all, massive institutions, whose complex economies required a multitude of tasks. And with difference came power, for not all jobs were equal. Work became indexed to the internal hierarchies of the prison and the broader hierarchies of American citizenship—replete with racial, class, and gendered implications. Some jobs were hard and dirty; others were cushy. Some were relatively rewarding and required some responsibility; others involved rote and deadening repetition. As one inmate reflected, "The 'Con' and the 'Con' only knows that the only thing that one cannot get used to; the only thing that the most adaptable of us has to fear, is monotony. . . . [W]ho can make light of the endless procession of days, each inimical to the other? Who but the 'Con' knows the torture of monotony?"[6]

Consequently, social hierarchy varied along with job assignment, and officials developed a narrative that gave disciplinary meaning to the work that prisoners did. Based on the traditions of free labor ideology and the ascendant notions of progressive penology, the formal narrative proclaimed that labor assignment reflected a prisoner's rehabilitation, and his or her upward mobility from less desirable to more desirable work. It rehashed Abraham Lincoln's classic story of free labor: the poor man who begins life as a wage worker will earn money and save it so as to employ others later, and those who languish at the bottom have no one to blame but themselves.[7] Labor assignment, then, worked in tandem with new systems to classify and differentiate prisoners and to set their sentences according to their supposed reform, and was sweetened by the promise of parole for the best behaved.[8]

While this was the theory, the fact of the matter was that California prisoners' labor was a coercive meritocracy of promotion and demotion geared toward social control and it mimicked many of the class and race structures of the state's political economy. At the same time, it was wracked by corruption. Though racial hierarchies could work at cross-purposes to putatively color-blind redemptive ideologies, in practice, racial hierarchy and redemption commonly interwove. Moreover, the association between masculinities and labor created a key tension in the struggle for officials to control prisoners' labor, and for prisoners to control themselves. Notions of manhood figured centrally in officials' justification of forced labor but also in prisoners' opposition to that labor. Prisoners, too, had their own understandings of the work they did. Only sometimes did they coincide with what officials intended.

The Bottom of the Ladder: Jute Mill and Quarry

San Quentin's jute mill and Folsom's rock quarry were the two institutions' worst job assignments. They anchored the bottom of the prisons' laboring hierarchies. Inmates were assigned there when they first arrived at each prison. As they demonstrated obedience and productivity—which officials would read as evidence of manliness, diligence, and rehabilitation—they could be promoted up the ladder of labor assignment. Other jobs, from the mess hall to the laundry, furniture, and barber shops, sat somewhere above the mill and the quarry: work was quieter, safer, and at least marginally more interesting. The apex of the work system was the outside honor camp, where prisoners built roads or, later, worked in forestry or harvest camps. At outside camps, they earned small wages, which they could save in a prison account, use to buy commissary goods, or send home to their families. If they did, they might reclaim the prestige that accompanied patriarchal support (and control) of wives, children, or parents. Inmates who had been promoted but who were found guilty of rule breaking would be demoted back to the prison. As San Quentin warden Clinton Duffy explained, "If we get a convict ring . . . we break up the ring by . . . moving them around to other jobs where there are not so many privileges . . . or send them to the jute mill or quarry."[9] Obedience was rewarded and recalcitrance punished through assignment to harsher labor.[10]

The jute mill was far and away San Quentin's largest labor assignment. It also was the prison's most lucrative industry. In 1936, a typical year, the jute mill employed more than one thousand prisoners, some 20 percent of the San Quentin population, and netted $420,803 for the prison system—nearly half of the total money earned by the prison.[11]

Despite earning money for the prison, the jute mill's workers received no wages, and the work's degradation was more than symbolic. It was numbing, loud, dusty, crowded, and dangerous. Prisoners arrived at 7:00 a.m. and worked among the hundreds of clanging machines until their tasks were completed. They could take occasional breaks, provided that they accomplished their tasks. The work was repetitive and boring. Workers would thread the cop end of the jute through a shuttle, lock the shuttle, and fit it into the box, and then push the starting lever over. When the shuttle misfed—and it did so often—it needed to be resituated correctly or it risked tearing up the warp, which would then need to be refed with string.[12] Jute mill superintendent E. F. Zubler claimed, "I have seen strong men cry like babies as they labored despairingly to complete impossible tasks. Punishment for failure to make the required yardage was severe and certain. No excuses were accepted. Broken looms, rotten jute strings, defective equipment took not a yard of cloth from a man's stint." Zubler continued, "I can operate any machine in the mill as expertly as the best, but even I could not make task under those conditions. I have seen loom tenders, and cob winders spend more time tying knots in rotten twine than operating their machines."[13]

The mill was opened in the 1890s, and by the 1930s, its aging equipment was in tatters. Much of the equipment and tools used were, in fact, made by prisoners.[14] Their inventiveness, driven by the hope of avoiding punishment, allowed the jute mill to run. Time spent repairing machinery ate into the time necessary to make their daily task, but there was no other option.

Inmate Donald Lowrie's 1912 autobiography, *My Life in Prison*, described the jute mill in terms that would ring true to poet William Blake's ideas of both dark and satanic mills.

New men get caught in the machinery or in the belting through inexperience or lack of proper instruction and caution as to the danger. There is not a single shield [protective device] on any of the cog mechanisms that I ever saw on the hundreds of machines in the jute mill at San Quentin—certainly not on the looms.[15]

Thirty years later, another prisoner said the jute mill was

something to give you nightmares. It is a madhouse of bedlam, a half-century old, one-story contraption, with a cement floor—cold! It lies very close to the San Francisco Bay high-tide level, and is ever damp—and cold! It is dusty, and some men suffer jute-poisoning. Jute-poisoning is something that breaks the skin, festers, eats at the vitals. Some men that catch it never get well.[16]

Officials were wont to dismiss such stories as inmates' predictable griping. But as San Quentin's chief surgeon, Leo Stanley—hardly a sentimental advocate of prisoners and charged with identifying malingerers—could not. His work forced him to treat those prisoners "mangled and torn by accidents in the jute mill."[17] Dwight Myers was one such prisoner. Meyers was accustomed to forcing open gear box doors to work on a malfunctioning rover, and his hand was crushed by moving gears when a door opened unexpectedly. He had three fingers amputated in the prison hospital.[18] Not only were hands mangled in the jute mill, but it was also a breeding ground for respiratory disease. According to Stanley, "Bad ventilation of the jute mill caused the air to be full of fine particles of dust, which injure the air passages, leaving a fertile field for tubercle bacillus."[19] The danger to inmates' health that the jute mill posed was neither accidental nor incidental to its significance in laboring hierarchies—the threats to health proved functional to its place as a means of punishing recalcitrant inmates. In this sense, the jute mill offered productive labor on two counts. First, the bags woven and sold to California's grain growers made money for the prison. Second, the suffering it caused anchored the prison's use of labor as a systematic form of discipline.

Prisoners understood this, and resented it. George Boston Gray, received at San Quentin in June 1934 for petty theft with priors, clearly did. In November 1935, he was punished for "deliberately breaking [a] shuttle in the jute mill," a classic mode of resisting forced labor. Getting caught in his sabotage of the means of jute production, a form of labor that served as a means of control, a means of repression, cost him three months of his future six months on parole.[20] Alfredo Contreras, convicted on a narcotics charge, was punished "for continually neglecting his work in the Jute Mill and making bad spools after repeated warnings."[21] Such punishments were common for prisoners at the jute mill, for whom sabotage was an oppositional practice that thumbed its nose at prevailing conceptions of self-discipline through labor.

The ideology of upward mobility, whereby one could work one's way from the jute mill to other positions, tended to work more easily for white prisoners than it did for black or Mexican inmates, who were constantly disrespected and shuttled across a series of subordinated jobs. By and large, black prisoners worked in the worst jobs in the California Prison System. Like most prisoners, they were initially assigned to the jute mill, but unlike many whites, they were less likely to be promoted out of the jute mill and into other positions.

Edward Brown provides a case in point. Brown, an African American man, was born in Wilmington, Delaware, and had worked as a chauffeur in Los Angeles. He was first received at San Quentin in July 1933 for second degree burglary, after he and an accomplice were charged with stealing food from a Pasadena grocery store. At San Quentin, Brown worked in the jute mill and was then switched to the position of janitor in the Educational Department and the Department of Public Works (internal to the prison), then made a yard sweeper, and then assigned to the New Road crew (also within the prison grounds—not a road camp). All of these—jute mill worker, sweeper, and janitor—were subordinated positions in the official economy of the prison.[22]

White inmates frequently began in the same way, but moved into more varied positions in the prison hierarchy of labor roles, such as in the shoe shop, the laundry, and the tin shop, or into positions of greater authority, such as on the newspaper or in the clerk's office. If they held a valued skill, the transition would be easier still. Frank Kelley had been a steel worker prior to his imprisonment. As the captain of the yard later explained, the white, Kentucky-born Kelley "was a steel worker when he came in; being a steel worker, I assigned him to the Department of Public Works, where he could be used."[23]

Officials periodically responded to complaints about the jute mill, to much self-congratulation. In 1933, a new roof was installed to stop the existing leaks, and a ventilator would draw at least some of the ever-present jute dust out of the air. "Great changes have taken place in what was once an infamous place of torment. But even greater changes are in prospect. A new, modern building in which working conditions will be of the best is to be erected in the not far distant future." Lest anyone think that this was better than life on the outside, the author wrote, "San Quentin's Jute Mill is far from being a pleasure resort. . . . A man who puts in a week's work there will know that he has been working. . . . [C]onditions in the Jute Mill have improved, and . . . intelligent management not only makes tasks easier, but increases output tremendously."[24]

Despite the warm words used to describe the jute mill's improvement, the 1939 California Industrial Accident Commission counted some 283 cases of unsafe working conditions in San Quentin. By far the majority of these were in the jute mill, with seventy-seven cases reported.[25] Moreover, a 1939 Special Crime Study Commission reported that inmates learned nothing useful from their work.

> The jute mill at San Quentin in no way qualifies as a desirable correctional industry. Its machinery is so old that few useful vocational skills can be learned therefrom. There is no jute industry in California or the West in which the inmate could capitalize on whatever experience he may acquire while assigned to the mill.[26]

The jute mill was San Quentin's most profitable but least desirable job assignment. Among the tightly packed and generally unsafe machinery, a sign reads "Don't Clean Machinery While Running/No Limpien Maquinas Cuando Estan Corriendo"—suggesting a need for constant yet dangerous upkeep. Image 1925.009.004, "Jute Mill—San Quentin 1936," Folder 9, Leo L. Stanley Collection, San Quentin Photographs, Anne T. Kent Room, Marin County Public Library.

Stories like these countered the progressive narrative in which inmates would become "men" though their hard labor. But perhaps it made sense of one kind: if the jute mill was punishment, there should be little redemptive possibility or manly reward. That was reserved for those prisoners who labored (or connived, as will be seen in chapter 4) their way out of the mill and into better positions, where their manhood would be recognized, and cultivated, through official channels.

An article about the prison furniture shop in the prisoner-authored San Quentin *Bulletin* made the connection between labor and manhood explicit. More than a place for constructing fine furniture, the author bragged, the furniture shop was "a builder of men." "Men and boys . . . are encouraged, trained and made into master craftsmen." These were men, it was presumed, who would not want for work on their release. Anyone who examined the furniture produced at San Quentin would see "not merely a display of things but . . . a reflection of manhood rehabilitated behind prison walls to take again an honorable place in society."[27] The manhood produced in the furniture shop, as well as the ideology linking manliness with craft production, was rooted in Victorian notions of self-control, prestige, and self-directed labor. That the artisanal production of furniture was defunct in an age of mass production mattered little to prison labor boosters, whose nostalgia for manly competency was ill suited for this era of industrial capitalist crisis.[28]

Nevertheless, relatively obedient prisoners could benefit from this system. Inmate author Robert Joyce Tasker was one, and his description of the furniture shop revealed something more than satisfaction with building a nice desk, something better even than a respite from boredom while serving time. Tasker took the gendered aspects of labor a step further than officials intended. After a passage lamenting the absence of women, he turned toward his machine for thinly sublimated erotic pleasure. "I could not deny that part of me was crying out for tenderness," he wrote.

> Amazingly, affection began to surge up in me for my machine. . . . It began to respond to me like a young hound learning to hunt. I played a symphony upon it, my ear attuned to the least vagrant vibration; then an indefinitely small turn of a pressure-bar screw, a jamming tight of bed-bolt— and the hum again. . . . The purring hum of the machine I was beginning to love. At work I was content. I had a mistress.[29]

Another much-vaunted labor site was the laundry, where racial and sexual identities and hard labor came together. Asian prisoners were often assigned to the laundry room, but so too were effeminate whites. *Bulletin* authors celebrated the laundry's advanced facilities, which, they proclaimed with requisite fervor, not only provided a necessary service but "also represents a forward step in the rehabilitation program." Replete with the most modern washers, dryers, and presses, it was a heavy industrial laundry plant, and could wash up to sixty-five thousand pieces of clothing per week. Employees' families' clothes were also laundered, and were of special note—their different colors stood out from the drab tones of convict attire. When one inmate writer wrote that there were even eleven ironing boards for "fancy work," he used code intended for other inmates—but that free-world readers would miss—signifying that this was a job for prison queens.[30] A laundry supervisor at Folsom believed that "the boys with a little lavendar in them make better ironers, and I have a considerable lot of so-called lavendars."[31] Because openly effeminate prisoners and those convicted of sodomy were directed to the laundry, it developed a reputation for being a place for illicit sexual encounters. As a result, it would come under special scrutiny in the 1940s.

Even if few prisoners at San Quentin found erotic pleasure in their workplaces, all who could were glad to leave the jute mill. Yet prisoners rarely valued the jobs that officials offered simply because they adhered to a formal narrative of upward mobility, or because they conferred traditional masculine, bread-winner producerism. Instead of promises of patriarchal manhood, in which docility earned them a good job and the possibilities of a wage (which they could use to consummate their manhood by making consumer purchases at the commissary or sending money to family members), prisoners sought self-control. Unlike the official ideology of upright respectability, inmates valued jobs for the degree to which they might use them to connive, steal, trade, or gamble. Jobs themselves meant little to prisoners' hierarchies. "It isn't the job," one inmate reported, "but the privileges attached to the job" that made it valuable.[32]

The official narrative of masculinity regained through labor assignment was countervailed by a prisoner-authored narrative, which inverted the masculinist stories of earning a living through obedience and subservience to prison officials. Sociologist Donald Clemmer referred to a "con ethic" that demanded an "anti-administration attitude."[33] The attitude was articulated in the language of gender, based fundamentally on a sense of masculinity. Clemmer quoted a prisoner who told a story about one guard, trying to get prisoners to obey him.

> He [the guard] said, "If I were a prisoner here I'd keep all the rules. I'd work harder than I was required to work. I'd gain the goodwill of the guards; I'd shine their shoes if that would help, and I'D HELP THE OFFICIAL BY REPORTING TO MY OFFICER ANYONE WHO BROKE THE RULES. Now, will you promise me to do that?" The prisoner was well aware that he could be dismissed without punishment if he promised, but he merely said, "Deputy, I can't do that." "Why not?" the deputy yelled at him. "Because," said the red-headed lifer, "I'm a man." The inference, of course, is that the deputy was lacking in manhood and the deputy did not fail to draw it.[34]

According to Clemmer's informant, obsequiousness was a sure ticket to better assignments and to avoiding punishment, but the "red-headed lifer" was more deeply invested in his own countervailing masculinity.

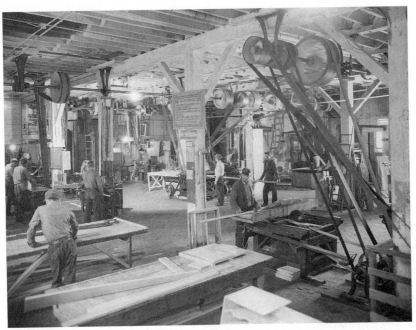

Prisoners assigned to work in places like San Quentin's carpentry shop had more physical space and relatively more autonomy than those assigned to the jute mill. A sign explicitly forbade making contraband, washing clothes, or playing games—which meant that prisoners here had the opportunity to do each of these. Image 1925.008.007, "San Quentin—Carpenter Shop," n.d., ca. 1935.

But others saw opportunity in servility, and enjoyed better working conditions as a result. Obedience was rewarded as much as—if not more than—good work and a clean record. John C. Hurst had been in jail or prison for much of his life, in San Quentin, Folsom, and the Oregon state prison. Hurst had worked in the jute mill and at other locations, but by becoming an informant, he was given better work opportunities. The information Hurst gave to officials proved very useful, if not to officials then at least to himself, even if it proved risky to give that information. A San Francisco probation officer noted that Hurst was "open to attack while in jail by inmates; as a result of this he was given a fairly decent job." He became a trustie and chauffer at Folsom, driving guards and the warden outside the walls. And after he was transferred to San Quentin, he became the con boss in charge of the Department of Public Works office inside the walls in 1940 and 1941. In numerous letters to San Quentin's Warden Duffy, Hurst claimed to be "obedient and submissive" and "loyal and cooperative." Hurst disclaimed the world that the cons made in favor of the beneficence of the prison administration.[35]

The Concentration Camp: Folsom's Rock Quarry

At Folsom prison, the rock quarry served the same punitive role that the jute mill did at San Quentin. Work was hard, dirty, and dangerous under the blazing central valley sun. Prisoners consigned there understood that their job was meant to be harsh and degrading. Their name for the quarry—"the Concentration Camp"—said a great deal.

Though the quarry and the lower yard were the worst of Folsom's assignments, they were not sites of absolute racial segregation—the open spaces surrounding the derricks would have mitigated against complete spatial differentiation. Black prisoners were commonly sent to the worst jobs, but they also worked with the worst of the white prisoners while they were there. Disobedient white prisoners were consequently racialized, and black prisoners, in turn, were forced into the most degraded and violent conditions, with the most dangerous inmates.

There were approximately 470 prisoners working in Folsom's lower yard on the No. 2 derrick in the Depression and war years. Conditions were crowded, and prison workers were divided into the "house gang," the "breaker gang," the "roustabout gang," and some "car loaders," each of whom had specialized jobs in the quarry. Some worked in the mornings and others worked in the afternoons.[36] Donald Clemmer described the quarry at the prison he researched in the early 1930s. While conditions certainly differed from those at Folsom's quarry, his description is at least suggestive. And though Clemmer was generally silent about race in prison, he did note that black prisoners were frequently assigned to the dirtiest and hardest assignments—such as the quarry. Being black and being among the most dangerous criminals were ideologically, spatially, and behaviorally conflated in a liberal vision of race, crime, and reformability. In addition, from one-quarter to one-third of the members of the six different quarry gangs at Clemmer's prison were black.[37] According to Clemmer,

> The quarry process includes the removal of the surface dirt by hand shovels, dynamiting (done at noon when the men are at dinner), "making little ones out of big ones," that is, breaking the dynamited rock with 30-pound sledge-hammers and chisels, wheelbarrowing, loading the broken rock

The Folsom quarry was a hot, dirty, and dangerous assignment. In James A. Johnston, *Prison Life Is Different* (Boston: Houghton Mifflin, 1937), opposite p. 42.

into the small, cast-iron cars which are on a track, pushing the cars to the stonecrusher where it is ground or pulverized according to what is needed. The inmates have various jobs. Some are "shovelmen," some are "hammermen," and some are "pushers." The work is heavy, hard, and dirty.[38]

Even within the conditions of deliberate degradation for quarry prisoners, there seems to have been at least some racial segregation. White prisoners were assigned to skilled jobs, even here. James H. Freeman, a white Arkansan, had been living and working on ranches in the Central and Imperial valleys since he came to California in 1936. Trained as an auto mechanic and as a tractor operator, Freeman had been picking cotton and living in a cotton camp in Hanford when he was arrested as a recidivist for grand theft. On his arrival at Folsom in July 1941, he was sent to work as a blacksmith on the lower yard, where his "Arkie" status was probably superseded by a starker whiteness in this multiracial location.[39] Clifton Longan, a white coal miner born in Missouri in 1903, was sentenced to Folsom in 1937 for petty theft with prior convictions. Longan had previously served time in Kansas for auto theft. Like James H. Freeman, Longan worked in the lower yard as a blacksmith—a skilled position in the worst assignment.[40] But it was still better than working in the gravel pit, or doing pick and shovel work, as many black prisoners did.

A black Folsom inmate named W. Mills complained about this in a letter to the Governor's Investigating Committee in 1943. "Our servitude here is limited to inferior work. The only work that is given to Negroes is such as porter work, digging in the ground and breaking rock or what ever else the white inmates don't want to do."[41] Among the most powerful testimonies offered to racial segregation in the California Prison System came from Wesley Robert Wells, a black prisoner who contested the conditions of prison Jim Crow, and whose death sentence for throwing an ashtray at a guard became a rallying point for civil rights and radical labor advocates in the 1950s.[42] Wells explained that racism abounded in the California Prison System when he arrived there in 1928. "There was a lot of jimcrow [sic] stuff in Quentin in those days—just like there is now. Then you were constantly addressed as a 'n——r,' you got the worst jobs, and if you objected you were a marked number."[43] Wells refused to be treated as a second-class citizen, even within the prison. "I know this—I don't and never did want more than the next man—I just don't want to be pushed around. I never took it."[44]

Wells believed that racial segregation—and especially segregation in prison labor—was the core of its continued social inequality. This was most pronounced when he was returned to Folsom in 1941 for the theft of a car battery, after spending several unsuccessful months in Los Angeles looking for work. Wells asked for assignment to a road camp, "where I could do a job and be treated decent."[45] Wells saw learning a trade as the key to his social redemption, but this path toward social and economic—if not political—citizenship was denied him less by Folsom's Warden Plummer, whom Wells portrayed as a reasonable (though still racist) official, than by white prisoners and shop supervisors. Wells requested assignment to the welding shop, but Plummer refused, explaining, "it would disrupt work to bring a Negro down there. They're all white workers." He received the same response from the Trade Department—no blacks wanted. Prison officials conceded to white supremacist prisoners (and it seems officials needed little convincing) that prestigious labor should remain among the benefits of white-skin privilege. The white workers' protests were the equivalent of the hate strikes that plagued war industries and maintained a racially and sexually segmented labor market, efforts to which Folsom's warden was all too willing to concede.[46] After being denied access to a job whereby he might learn a trade, Wells was eventually assigned to the rock quarry, "making little ones out of big ones."[47] Throughout his sentence, Wells despised the insults he received, including, among others, being called a "black skunk" by warden Larkin, Plummer's predecessor, or by white prisoners or guards. "I was young and I held my head up. I didn't take no stuff from prisoner, stoolie, or guard. As a result, I got it bad. I got the strap, the rubber hose, the club, the curses."[48] Wells was effectively made into a recalcitrant prisoner through racist treatment. He responded to racial insult with protest; his protests were read as recalcitrance and punished accordingly.

Robert W. "Cannibal" White, an African American prisoner sent to Folsom's quarry after his second burglary conviction, complained to the warden that reform was nearly impossible. Because the most violent and recalcitrant prisoners were sent there, it was very difficult to stay out of trouble. He also explained that "I don't have an easy time trying to go to school" from the quarry. In other words, it was difficult to manage the few reformative offerings at Folsom while dealing with punitive hard labor. White requested that he be sent to work in the mess hall, or in the laundry, rather than in the quarry. Redemption was difficult, if not impossible, where "there is a lot out there that gose [sic] on out there that you dont [sic] know."[49]

White prisoners also complained about their assignment to "the Concentration Camp." Albert Ellsworth Jackson Jr., a white man born in 1907 in Milwaukee, had been arrested for forging checks nine times between 1927 and 1935. Jackson returned to the California state prison system in 1938, for violating his parole by writing another bad check. When he was returned to the prison after being a parole violator for fourteen months, he was sent to the rock quarry as punishment. He complained about this in a letter to Warden Plummer: "Captain Ryan assigned me to work in the Ranch Rock gang, known as the 'concentration camp.'" Jackson felt that this assignment was unjust because regardless of the bad checks he had written on the outside, within the prison "my conduct record is spotless." Jackson proposed instead that he be assigned to work on radio installation for Folsom, as he had previously owned a radio-making business.[50]

Jackson felt that he did not belong in the rock quarry, not only because of the contribution he could make to the institution elsewhere but also, equally as importantly, because of his education, behavior, and, more than likely, his race and class status: "I am a more or less harmless individual and I do resent being made to work and associate with the men of the institution who are continuously in trouble—assigned to the 'concentration camp' for possession of a knife, fighting, or general misconduct." Jackson strove to convince the warden that he belonged in the prison's white-collar world. Though it is unclear whether or not he was assigned to the radio installation after pleading to the warden, Jackson later received a prized harvest camp job, where he could earn a wage and connive some goods for himself. Indeed, it seems likely, especially from an intercepted November 3, 1942, letter (which told in code how to send checks and postal money orders to other prisoners), that Jackson became a well-connected conniver himself.[51]

In every case, labor assignment to privileged or denigrated positions in California prisons offered or denied a sense of self-control, and expressed either an officially sponsored sense of patriarchal manhood or a working-class, oppositional sense of masculinity that grew out of the "con ethic" and prided itself on self-control, and opposing prison administrators and the state.

California's Honor Camps: Coercive Cooperatives

If the jute mill and the rock quarry were the bottom of California labor hierarchies, its outside honor camps were the much-vaunted peak. One researcher of the day claimed that California's road camps "made a distinct contribution both to the solution of the prison-labor problem and to penology."[52] The Prison Industries Reorganization Administration, a New Deal agency investigating the expansion of state-use prison labor, lauded California's road camps as exemplary and called for their expansion.[53] Camp disciplines were far more sophisticated than any of those involved in the main institutions, because inmates earned money for their work. From available evidence, it appears that wage payment tried to harness inmates' aspirations and desires for financial self-control. Inmates labored alongside free workers, doing work esteemed as highly masculine and rugged. And though physical controls diminished, economic surveillance intensified. Guards only played a modest role in direct supervision. Instead, highway officials rather than prison guards directed their labor. If road building workers oversaw their labor, commissary clerks surveilled their consumption habits. In the end, these clerks proved to be the camps' most important agents of control.

California prisoners had worked on roads in the immediate vicinity of their prisons since the 1890s, but the work expanded dramatically as road camps became wedded to progressive penological ideologies. The California legislature, inspired by success in Colorado's prison road camps, founded road honor camps in 1915 as part of a raft of progressive reforms. Western road camps were radically different from the southern chain gangs. In Georgia, for example, chain gangs presented racialized rituals of brutality and public shaming that developed the state's infrastructure while honing the visible spectacle of the local constabulary's authority.[54] California's were meant to confer honor (among lowly convicts, to be sure) rather than racialized degradation, and legislation passed in 1923 and 1927 permitted prisoners to earn meager wages in addition to good time toward release. The difference was fundamentally a function of the racial populations of western prisons, institutions that, in the first half of the twentieth century, were predominantly geared toward reinstituting class control.[55] Road camps and inmates' public works put inmates' labor to "state use," allowing a promising avenue for prison labor into the Hawes-Cooper era.[56]

Honor road camps were spatial locations and labor assignments toward which prisoners could strive, part of a graded system of labor and classification based around a narrative of literal progress in behavioral and economic responsibility.[57] From 1915 to 1936, prisoners built more than five hundred miles of road, stimulating segments of California's economy, from lumber to tourism, in the once-remote parts of the state.[58] California's much-vaunted national parks, including Yosemite, would not be what they are without convict labor. The number of camps grew from three to six in 1923, expanded to eight in 1925, and then decreased to six again in 1933. Those camps remained in operation and their populations remained relatively steady even as prison populations swelled. Assignment to road camps became increasingly difficult for most prisoners across the Depression. Though the use of road camps declined in the war years, forestry and harvest camps grew in their place and would expand at war's end.[59]

For the time being, though, most prisoners could only aspire to camp placement. The camps were outside the prison walls, offered payment, and were characterized by less supervision and, from available evidence, by less harsh punishment. They were intended as a transitional ground between prison and the "free world." Because prison labor was not supposed to impinge on the rights or wages of nonimprisoned workers, honor camp prisoners were to receive wages "at the going rate" (though no prison officials or employers of prisoners addressed the many repressive measures designed to limit workers' wages).[60] In addition, penologists reasoned that neither road nor forestry work could impinge on the rights of free workers since the roads and forests protected were far from the places where free workers lived, or where unions could rail against the use of prison labor. Organized workers did protest against using prisoners in "skilled" jobs like bridge building, however.[61] Moreover, the scarcity of labor in these mountainous locales would have allowed those few workers available to demand a higher wage than road contractors would have desired. At the same time, prisoners would contribute to an expanding "good roads" movement across the region. And finally, it was hoped that prisoners would have trouble escaping from remote locales.[62]

Early experiments with road camps were only marginally successful. Despite the privilege of working in the road camps, one investigator found the "convicts wasteful, dishonest, and neglectful of their work."[63] The California Highway Commission listed some shortcomings:

> The atmosphere of the camps is charged with secretiveness, sullenness and silence. Conversation is in low tones. No laughter or song is heard. There is always something to kick about. The desire to be efficient is absent, for there is no reward for same. The convict does as little work as possible and is as extravagant with all materials as possible.[64]

Yet this changed in 1923, when the new law, authored by prison reformer Julian Alco, offered inmates a wage for their road camp work and financial interest in camp administration. The new road camp regime created highly sophisticated mechanisms of internal and external control. They were remarkable, in fact, for using the same sort of compulsions inherent in wage labor beyond the prison. Early on, reformers realized that wages were a means of developing road camp workers as self-regulating prisoners. After wages were introduced, one official opined, the "prisoners [were] more satisfactory in every respect."[65] The combination of good time earned, wages, and outside work sustained a sort of coercive cooperative that more closely approximated life outside. The camps involved the long-standing belief in the purifying power of "wholesome outdoor life and intimacy with nature," characteristic of America's visions of the West, to redeem the denizens of the corrupt city.[66] According to a 1933–1934 biennial report,

> From the standpoint of rehabilitation, these road camps are the most effective part of the prison system. The opportunity . . . to do constructive work in wholesome surroundings, to become self-supporting, and to make some small contribution to the support of their dependents who would otherwise be a public charge, has made these camps invaluable.[67]

The 1923 law specified that prisoners would be paid no more than $2.50, while the state highway department, which actually paid the wages, determined that inmates would earn $2.10 for each day worked. Inmates paid for their own incarceration from the money they earned: guards' salaries, food supplies, bedding, shovels and picks, pots and pans, knives and forks. Accountants also tabulated depreciation reserves, which prisoners paid to replace major camp equipment.[68] Consequently, deductions mounted quickly. Despite regulations determining that prisoners could bank no more that seventy-five cents per day worked, that ceiling proved largely unnecessary. In 1932 the Highway Division reported that convicts' average net earning between 1923 and 1932 was 27.6 cents per working day.[69] Still, most thought it was better than nothing.

Application to work on the road camps required significant effort and a good record.[70] Applicants needed to meet an extensive list of qualifications and gain endorsements from prison officials. No formal mechanisms existed for selection, and the problem of choosing prisoners for assignment to honor camps mirrored the general problem of classifying and segregating prisoners. Researchers continually sought scientific means for this classification, but it proved elusive. Instead, road camp prisoners were selected on the basis of the "unfettered discretion" of prison officials, including the captain of the yard, the warden, the dentist, and the physician, who offered their recommendation or denial based on their feelings about the inmates' suitability. While physical able-bodiedness was significant to the hard work prisoners did, more important was official perception of the inmates' docility. Until a scientific basis to determine risk could be established, advocates thought this to be quite satisfactory.[71] Importantly, race, according to investigator Milton Chernin, was not a determining factor in assignment to road camps. In his study of San Quentin road camps (Folsom officials refused to cooperate with his investigation; the racial regime at Folsom was grimmer than at San Quentin), Chernin found that road camp populations roughly reflected San Quentin's populations.[72] Perceptions of docility might have proven more important than total white supremacy in this context.

The camps were set in remote and mountainous parts of the state, often along rivers, which served both as a boundary and a water supply. Fences were put up around the camps, though one investigator reported that these were to prevent citizens from entering rather than to keep prisoners from leaving. Prisoners slept in lumber and tar-paper bunkhouses or sometimes in tents, arranged in a semicircle around the sergeant's quarters. Some bunkhouses were small, and held just eight prisoners, but at times larger ones were used. In any case, there were no bars on the windows or doors. Camp sizes varied according to the labor requirements that the Highway Division set, but ranged from fifty to one hundred prisoners. Two or three guards typically were responsible for custodial control of the prisoners, though, as these were "honor" camps, the guards constituted more of a symbolic than a military impediment. Guards typically carried no weapons, though some were locked in the office in case an inmate did escape. The guards' main task was to administer a morning and an evening count. According to Chernin, a visitor to a California prison road camp "might well complete his stay without realizing that he was among convicts."[73] Perhaps that would have been true, but the same could not be said of the convicts themselves.

The food was far better at the camps than it was at San Quentin or Folsom. Because prisoners paid for their own food from their income, operators were willing to spend more on supplies. Organized by the Highway Division rather than prison officials, the rations were geared toward satisfying free workers instead of prisoners. In fact, prisoners ate in the same mess hall as the free workers, though who sat with whom is hard to know. Prisoners cooked and served the food as well as washed the dishes, under a commissary clerk's supervision. In addition to a cobbler and a tailor, some prisoners worked as barbers, and others still looked after the camp grounds. They worked eight-hour days and a six-day week and observed holidays.[74] Recreation was provided (including movies and athletic facilities) from the Prisoners' Fund.

Prisoners were duty-bound to obey a strict set of rules. While "honor" was the key word, the capacity for state violence was ever present. Prisoners knew very well that though they might elude the few guards on duty and escape, the likelihood of permanently evading detection was slim. For this or any camp violation—and there were many proscribed activities—on return to prison, they could face stiff new charges in addition to serving the full remainder of their existing term. If a prisoner had a complaint, he could not raise it among other prisoners—that sort of lateral organization might lead to collective action. Instead, he must bring it directly to a camp official, ensuring vertical rather than horizontal alliances.[75] Griping to other prisoners would probably have been considered "agitation" and been subject to punishment.

Productive work on the highway camps was overseen by Highway Division officials rather than prison guards, who, in any case, had no expertise in directing road work. Prisoners wore common overalls, and according to Chernin, "cannot be distinguished from the free laborers working at their side."[76] Their tasks were varied, but generally involved the least skilled aspects of highway building. The original 1915 legislation secured organized workers' consent by guaranteeing that skilled tasks, including any bridge building or heavy machinery operation, was reserved for free workers. Instead, prisoners cleared brush and timber, built retaining walls, and dug ditches for drainage. "Grading involve[d] drilling rock in preparation for blasting, hauling materials into fills and moving surplus earth and rock to one side. Standards and specifications adhered to are equal to those prescribed under free labor contracts."[77]

The inmates' relative freedom, their physical and conceptual proximity to nonprison workers, and, especially, the wages they earned were the means of their discipline. Wages offered a complex foundation of control. Road camp payment signified not just money—for inmates did not earn much— but rather symbolized a form of respect, and tied them into emergent forms of desire for consumption and independence. But as road camp designers understood, that sense of independence was to be founded upon literal debt. It was an age of expanding credit for wage workers on the outside, too.

Parole board members estimated that a prisoner needed to work for eight months at a road camp to "earn sufficient money to pay for their clothing, blankets, tools and other equipment which the law states must be supplied and charged to them." Prisoners were extended credit for the use and consumption of these necessary goods. Until they had paid for their tools, clothes, and blankets, as well as for ongoing board and camp maintenance, they were considered in debt to the state and were ineligible for release or parole.[78]

Debt was the centerpiece of the road camps' discipline. The controls were effective primarily because they eschewed physical compulsion in favor of the workings of the market, participation in which, as gendered workers and consumers, signified prisoners' successful behavioral reincorporation. Officials believed that criminals would finally be set straight not only as workers but also, importantly, as consumers. "[A]fter spending from one to two years in a highway camp, these men . . . learn to work, and, what is equally important, adjust their needs to their daily wage."[79] If they did not learn how to spend as well as how to work, they could be punished. Commissary clerks looked into prisoners' bank accounts, meager as they were, and prisoners had to demonstrate financial savings. If they did not save enough, they could be sent back to prison, with loss of good-time credits. This would be taken into account when parole decisions came up. According to the superintendent of prison camps, "The prisoners realize that failure to show a saving after being at the camp a reasonable length of time will mean a denial of parole, and . . . therefore they make every effort to economize."[80] The debt that they worked off—to pay for tools, bedding, and the administration of the camps—was only a first step. Officials admitted that many prisoners came to the camps only interested in the good-time credits they would earn. But, one report suggested, perhaps idealistically, "as deficits for transportation, clothes and other necessities are eliminated and their credit balances begin to grow they take an interest in honest labor and its fruits. When this point in the prisoner's road camp career is reached . . . the start towards the new life is begun."[81] Because inmates paid the camps' operating costs, they had a monetary interest in their efficiency.

Despite these controls and the risks of punishment, prisoners used the relative freedom of the camps for their own ends. Roy Salgot and Earl A. Harrison were caught brewing liquor at a road camp in Big Sur in October 1935 and were sent back to San Quentin, with their parole dates rescinded.[82] Wasting materials, feigning sickness, trading with free people, loafing, or agitating would all lead to an immediate return to the prison.[83] And despite the many desires that road camps provided and the sophistication of its controls, prisoners escaped in considerable numbers. Nearly 5 percent of honor camp prisoners were punished for attempted or successful escape, though they were also recaptured in large numbers. Of the 519 escapees that Milton Chernin counted, 420 were recaptured.[84] Detailed information on the reasons for road camp prisoners' escape is sketchy for the 1920s and 1930s, but they were probably similar to reasons given by those escaping—or taking temporary leave—from wartime or postwar camps. Many gave no reason; some were trying to visit a girl. Many escapees were only gone for a few hours; some returned of their own volition, but were drunk when they got back.[85] Some were gone only overnight, others for years. Adam Hinostro and Walter Kneller escaped from a road camp in Junction City in October 1934. They presumably sought complete escape rather than just temporary leave, but were recaptured three and a half weeks later. Each had his parole rescinded, lost his good time, and had his sentence reset to the maximum—ten years each, for theft and forgery.[86]

Prisoners had a vested interest in preventing other inmates' escape, since their own income was affected by a mandatory two-hundred-dollar deduction from camp funds for each attempt. Chernin noted that prisoners commonly reported on each other to ensure their own continued privileges.[87] But one can imagine a greater likelihood to report on those attempting permanent escape than on those who promised to be back before the next count, especially if they would bring a little whiskey back with them.

Nevertheless, the complexities of reward and punishment in honor camps were muted by the paeans to the prestige they provided, which cast prisoners as the state's agents, engaged in an epic struggle to tame nature. Inmate writers described the masculine battle that road camp workers waged:

> Working over terrain exceptionally difficult for highway construction these men are building a monument that will endure time. Fills of gigantic proportions, tunnels and cuts through solid rock, bridges over streams that become torrents in the spring, retaining walls of concrete to prevent slides, adequate drainage and a surface as smooth as a show-room floor, are the results of their work. The corners of mountains have been reshaped to build this highway. Done by prisoners. Truly, it is a mark of honor to the men of San Quentin.[88]

Inmates' labor in California served multiple and contradictory ends. Labor was guided by the administrators' long-standing belief that forced labor would teach criminals the ethic and habits they lacked but needed in order to return to free society. At the same time, the ideology behind prison labor suggested that assignment to different positions would replicate gendered hierarchies, where the best would control themselves and their labor, even earning a wage to confirm their masculine ability to participate not only as producers and consumers in the market but also as patriarchs contributing to their families' well-being. Obedient prisoners would be rewarded by promotion through these hierarchies, becoming part of what officials identified as a meritocratic system but that must be understood as a coercive meritocracy, wherein material benefits and punishments were associated with obedience or recalcitrance. Even reward was a means of control, founded on a system of credit, wages, and debt.

Yet the conditions of labor differed from the ideological ideals. Labor assignments were frequently structured by racial hierarchies and de facto if not de jure racial segregation, especially at Folsom. The best jobs were reserved for the most highly skilled, the best behaved, and often for white prisoners, many of whom found real pride in their labor, and a respite from boredom and the alienation of not working. Black, Mexican, and the worst-behaved white prisoners were generally assigned to the most degrading assignments in each institution—Folsom's quarry or San Quentin's jute mill—while Asian prisoners and effeminate men were commonly assigned to gendered positions in the laundry, or as "houseboys" for prison administrators. Young black or Mexican prisoners, and especially seemingly obedient ones, were more likely to ascend hierarchies at San Quentin than they were at Folsom, but each institution's labor hierarchy was structured by race.

Prisoners nonetheless claimed alternatives meanings for their labor. Many subverted the official gendered hierarchies with their own alternative masculinities. For many, obedience signaled weakness, and recalcitrance bespoke a powerful masculinity. Prisoners constantly sabotaged the tools of production, slowed down work, and were impudent and mutinous. In every case, gendered and racial hierarchies wove through disciplinary and oppositional techniques. Labor, as a tool of economic production as well as social control, proved a tense front through which social conflicts were fought but never resolved.

From Can See to Can't

*Agricultural Labor and Industrial
Reform on Texas Penal Plantations*

When you go down Old Hannah,
Don't you rise no more.
If you rise in the morning,
Bring Judgment on.
I ain't tired of livin',
But I got so long.

—Ernest Williams and Group, "Go Down Old Hannah,"
Big Brazos: Texas Prison Recordings, 1933–1934

In the California Prison System, labor assignment mimicked the race-blind coercive meritocracy through which American society and liberal capitalism were supposed to function. And while California officials hoped that income from prisoners' labor might help offset the costs of running the institution, they scarcely believed they might actually turn a profit. Things were different in Texas. Since the prison was situated on more than seventy thousand acres of fertile agricultural land, officials saw no reason why it shouldn't make money. After all, the traditions of slavery and the convict lease system loomed large, and setting black, Mexican, and poor white men to hard labor in cotton fields almost went without saying. Labor assignments in Texas prisons were geared toward self-sustaining agricultural production and cutting costs to the bone. As Texas prison general manager Lee Simmons announced to inmates shortly after his appointment to the position, he would run the prison first and foremost "from a business standpoint."[1] We might take him at his word. Antebellum plantations were businesses, too.

Yet this business standpoint, which emphasized running the prison at low cost, could have conflicted with the ideology of labor as redemptive, a belief that even southern prison administrators had to reckon with. Simmons saw no contradiction, because he also identified himself as a "humanitarian." "You may not agree with me," he told the gathered prisoners, "but when we keep you at work, *and this means work*, we are helping you. . . . [W]e are rendering you a service because we are preparing you to go out and hold a job." If this was a business, it was one that would brook no workers' voice. When inmates cheered Simmons for saying he would ensure they got enough food—here was his humanitarianism—he silenced them. "Boys, you are forgetting that I told you I did not want any demonstration of any kind."[2] Later, when prisoners demonstrated by refusing to work, they would be driven by pitchforks, baseball bats, whips, and guns. Simmons's hard labor regime, underwritten by violence, would be celebrated by later criminologists as "control penology." It dominated Texas prisons for the next fifty years.[3]

Lone Star prisons claimed increased efficiencies over the Depression decade. Economies of scale may have played a role as the prison population grew larger, but more effective systemic exploitation of prisoners' labor was a likelier foundation of those savings. Cotton farming was the backbone of prison business ventures, and it would remain so for most of the twentieth century. The cotton that its prisoners planted, cleaned, harvested, and ginned became the cash officials used for daily operations.[4] Cotton bolls were rolled into bars, bullets, and the wages in guards' pockets. Between 1928 and 1940, the Texas Prison System devoted an average of 16,990 acres to cotton production each year. Moreover, forcing inmates to grow their own food—which Simmons called a "live at home plan"—also led to considerable savings. In 1933, prisoners produced more than four hundred thousand cans of vegetables to feed prisoners and to sell to other state institutions.[5] Six years later, prisoners would grow nearly 1.2 million pounds of Irish potatoes and sweet potatoes, and more than 1.5 million pounds of vegetables, providing food for themselves as well as for other state institutions.[6] In 1940, more than forty-five thousand acres of cropland were under cultivation, and this was just 62 percent of the prison's holdings.[7] Between 1929 and 1935, per inmate costs fell by 27.5 percent from the previous decade, and between 1935 and 1939, costs fell by another 12.5 percent. By 1939, per prisoner operating costs had fallen more than thirty dollars below what they had been earlier in the decade. Despite this, the prison still ran at a deficit, and officials looked for many ways to cut costs or increase productivity.[8] This meant working prisoners harder, in more diverse crops, or in more profitable industries.

By this reasoning, prison officials, and especially the more liberal members of the prison board, sought new manufacturing opportunities and tried to link labor assignment to classification and reform. They imagined that they might employ a system similar to California's coercive meritocracy, placing the best prisoners in the best jobs. Movement from farm to factory or from one labor assignment to another would become part of promotion or demotion, according to a progressive ladder of upward mobility for obedience and downward assignment for recalcitrance. The worst assignments were on the numerous farms scattered in the eastern part of the state, though these, too, were supposedly structured by redemptive and punitive possibilities. Indoor work on the prison farms was far more desirable than working outside in the sun. Reformist investigators explained the logic behind various assignments in the Texas prisons:

> The Board has adopted a policy of promotion from unit to unit on the basis of work and conduct record. For example, men assigned to Retrieve Farm as intermediate prospects for rehabilitation can work up to Camp No. 2 at Harlem or Camp No. 2 at Central; men from Harlem or Central can be promoted to industrial jobs at the Walls (or Central Farm when industries are developed there). Farm jobs are considered hardest, and it is felt that shop assignments should only be received after men have taken their turns in the fields. Conversely, men assigned to the units which enjoy greater privileges can be demoted for cause and transferred back to a more restricted unit.[9]

Prison officials boasted loudly of the system's few industrial ventures, and reformist board members consistently sought additional programs. Because they already had a highly spatially segregated prison system to divide prisoners into types, they believed that industrialization would provide the best inmates training in cutting-edge technologies and labor skills, and prove the full modernization of the Texas Prison System. An author for the Texas Historic Commission and the Texas Department of Criminal Justice bragged that when "industrialization [came] to the Imperial State Farm, Texas penology entered the modern era."[10] For southern prisons no less than southern boosters, industry equaled modernity. Yet by this equation, the benefits of modernity were reserved for whites only, and even then, only a small number. In 1936, six of the ten "industrial" programs in the Texas Prison System were based at the Huntsville Walls Unit. The others were located at the Central Farm, which was in the process of expanding as another main industrial unit. The industrial units at the Central State Farm remained fully and formally for whites only until 1968.[11] General Manager O. J. S. Ellingson understood this in terms of predilection rather than in terms of systematic white supremacy. Even though increasing numbers of prisoners of all races hailed from cities and had no farming experience, a "greater per cent [sic] of the Negroes and Mexicans are content to do farming than the whites."[12] It is unlikely that he asked anyone's opinion.

Furthermore, there is little evidence that transfer ever became a common way to deal with poor or positive behavior. Texas prisoners were frequently punished—whipped, put in the dark cell, or physically tortured by other means—for insubordination or laziness without any transfer taking place. Rather, when prisoners worked too slowly or when guards felt disrespected, the behavior was treated as a problem of labor control. In December 1937, Joel Denley, a black prisoner at the Clemens Farm Camp 1, was made to "Stand on the barrel" for three hours as punishment for "laziness." In August 1938, he was given "20 lashes for [being] lazy and stubborn." The whipping was "executed in full," but he was not transferred.[13]

Farm labor needs and racial hierarchies, then, trumped penological or rehabilitative priorities, and this version of penal modernity—with white privilege and black and Mexican subordination—had roots going back to the late nineteenth century and the slow demise of the convict lease.[14] As one farm manager wrote to his supervisors, "[Sugar] Cane season is fastly [sic] approaching and I would appreciate some more negroes if you can possibly let me have them."[15] Seasonal agricultural cycles and markets set the pace of life and the distribution of labor in Texas prisons. Select white prisoners could find themselves in the privileged industrial jobs. Though these jobs were relatively few in number—just 7.5 percent of prisoners were assigned them—they represented the apex of formal labor assignments.[16]

Industrial Programs

Scholars have rightly stressed the plantationlike nature of southern prisons and their reliance on cotton farming; the Texas prison's roots, like those of Mississippi's Parchman Farm and Louisiana's Angola, were clearly based in the slave past. But Texas's Depression-era prison administrators' desire to modernize by expanding prison industries was more than just idle talk or a sop to liberal northern penologists. Even Lee Simmons recognized that industrialization was also a fiscal plan, and a diversified prison economy would be better able to weather literal and metaphorical storms. Floods and droughts, flea hoppers and boll weevils could ravage prison cotton crops. In years when they did, which were often enough, the sales from license plates, shoes, and printing constituted significant portions of the prison's income.[17]

Nineteen thirty-four was one such year. Total income amounted to $1,322,179. Of this, $486,439 came from combined manufactured output, while cotton and cotton-seed sales netted $509,763.[18] That same year, the thirty-seven thousand pairs of shoes that inmates made earned $35,643 for the prison.[19] And the license plate factory, in its first year of operation, pressed 2,800,000 plates.[20] When the brick-making plant opened at Harlem Farm in 1935, another so-called industrial opportunity (and source of income) loomed.

Beyond supplementing funds from cotton, industrial ventures provided many of the goods necessary for the prison to run. After all, prisoners endlessly trudging through muddy fields wore through a lot of shoes. While the brick plant was understood in terms of "vocational training" and as a potentially profit-making venture, its primary benefit was in providing building materials for the prison itself. Brick buildings gave a more convincing appearance of modernity than the wooden structures on most farms. Not least in importance, brick walls would make it harder for inmates to burn the prison down. In 1929, a large corn-crib at Ramsey Farm was set ablaze, and tubercular prisoners at the Wynne Farm set a fire that completely destroyed the main barracks.[21] After the disastrous 1930 fire at the Ohio State Penitentiary, which killed 320 and badly injured another 144, this was especially pressing. A month later, the Texas state fire marshal reported, "the Penitentiary Plant, as a whole, is the worst fire hazard coming under my observation." He urged "speedy correction" of its many problems "before a disaster occurs."[22]

The majority of the industrial assignments were at the Walls. Inmates lucky enough to get these jobs provided goods necessary for the prison system to function as the massive, dispersed plantation it was, and to house and feed the many thousands of prisoners and guards who worked there. Workers in the machine shop, the electrical shop, the power plant, the ice plant, and the garage all kept the physical structure and the means of production/means of control in good order.[23] Among their other tasks, woodworkers in the construction shop built wagons and furniture for the prison system (and later, for other state institutions, like schools). The print shop produced annual reports, the inmate newspaper *Echo*, and other documents used within the prison system, and also made envelopes for mailing license plates. The mattress shop made the thin bedding on which prisoners got their meager rest, and women worked in the Goree clothing shop, making clothes for all prisoners, as well as their discharge suits.[24]

The license plate plant was another of the industrial ventures, valued primarily because it provided a consistent source of income. In 1940 the plant consumed 1,511,860 pounds of steel, and 16,490 gallons of paint. Using heavy machinery, inmates cut, punched, stamped, and painted an average of thirty thousand plates per day, totaling 3,455,700 for the year.[25] The job held an additional perk for its workers—scrap metal could be smuggled out to make knives.[26]

Conditions in the shoe shop drew more on manufacturing techniques than on heavy machinery. A white inmate named Harry McAdams described the Fordist organization of the shop, where around seventy-five prisoners repeated their tasks throughout the day. A leather inner sole was nailed to a wooden last, before the upper was connected. Next, the shoe went to the lasting table, where other workers tacked the upper around the last and onto the inner sole. Different workers had already cut the uppers from a standard pattern, and these were then passed on to others who sewed the uppers together. Next, the shoe moved to the welt table, where inmates hand sewed a small strip of leather around the edge of the inner sole. The shoe was then treated with heavy glue and put in a dryer, after which it was placed in a machine where another inmate sewed the heavy outer sole onto the inner sole. Finally, it moved to the finishing table, where the outer sole was retrimmed, the heels attached, and the shoe polished, shined, and laced. If it was one of the rougher, lower-quality shoes, it was ready for prisoners to use. If it was of somewhat better quality, it could be sold to other state institutions or used as a "going out" shoe. In 1938, McAdams and other shoe shop workers made nearly thirty-six thousand pairs of shoes, averaging around 140 pairs per day.[27]

Central State Farm, formerly known as the Imperial Farm, housed approximately eight hundred, mostly first-term, prisoners on fifty-two hundred acres of land. Managers there attempted to develop industrial ventures, so that the system would not need to buy as many manufactured goods as they had previously. When administrators actively pursued this in 1930, they chose the farm because of its proximity to Houston.[28] By 1938 there were forty-two hundred acres in cultivation, where prisoners grew cotton, corn, feedstuffs, and vegetables. Farm manager Captain Flanagan described the organization of this unit:

There are three camps of white men and one of negroes on this farm; our agricultural units are Camps No. 1 and No. 2, and part of No. 4; our dairy unit is Camp No. 3; here we have a small group of trustees housed; No. 4 is our industrial unit and is called "STATE FARM INDUSTRIES."[29]

Hardly the vocational training officials claimed it to be, the shoe shop remained a privileged assignment for Texas prisoners. 1938 Souvenir Rodeo Program, p. 45. 1998/038-404, Folder "Rodeo Program 1939." Texas State Library and Archives Commission.

Camp Number One was for young black prisoners, while Camps Two, Three, and Four housed young white prisoners. Camp Four was also occasionally called "the New Unit," or "the Industrial Unit." This housed 350 inmates operating a canning plant, where, one piece of prison propaganda lauded, a "large ice plant and a modern Diesel-equipped power plant here furnishes trade training for a number of Central inmates."[30] The canning plant was seasonal work only; prisoners worked in agriculture for the rest of the year. The canning and meat-packing plants were both located at the Central Farm. They produced and prepared foods for the rest of the prison system. The canning plant used sixty workers; the meat-packing plant used thirty.[31] "For ten hours a day our men work hard, but they are well fed and clothed, and eventually we can say that they are well housed; as we will soon have under construction at Camp No. 1 a modern dormitory building which will replace two of our wooden, fire-trap structures that have outlived their usefulness."[32]

Assignment to "vocational training" jobs at the Walls, at State Farm Industries, or elsewhere, offered a narrative structure to reward supposed good behavior. The ideological foundation of existing formal labor hierarchies was that inmates would learn a valued skill through their assignment, much as they did in California. But the vocational training opportunities clearly remained an ancillary goal to the financial health of the prison itself. While not formally classified as an industrial assignment, construction was understood as a vocational, and thus privileged, job. The general manager's report in 1937 explained that "construction work has been a beneficial vocational outlet for the abundant supply of labor; and it has assisted materially in the establishment of vocational training, an integral part of our educational program."[33] Prisoners were set to work at necessary tasks (building expansion or repair, making inmates' clothing, making bricks for new structures, cooking for the lines or canning food for inmate consumption), and these activities were then labeled as "vocational programs."

Charlotte A. Teagle, who chaired the Prison Board's Welfare Committee, was especially pleased by the vocational training prison cooks received. In addition to the other vocational programs described in a 240-page paean to Texas penal progress, she explained that aspiring inmate chefs learned their craft from the U.S. Army Cook Manual. According to one farm steward, "cooking is a fine art and embraces the preparation of foods, sanitation, serving, balanced diets, methods of cooks, food values, the preservation of calorie content, and the proper handling of food."[34] Army privates and prison inmates may have been surprised to learn that their cuisine was fine art, but nevertheless, cooking was one of the few "vocational" courses offered to a variety of prisoners, regardless of race or the farm they were on. This should come as no surprise: every farm needed cooks, and this allowed for putatively vocational training to overlap with the system's custodial needs. One can see why prisoners would like the job. They could work inside rather than in the sun, and cooks with quick hands would have the first choice of available food, for themselves or for their friends. Prisoners who worked in the fields—and these were the vast majority of Texas prisoners—had to make do with whatever they could get.

Prison Farms: Hell on the River

Prisoners on farms worked, in the old phrase, from sunup to sundown, from "can see to can't," or, as some prisoners put it, "can shoot to can't shoot."[35] Inmates at Huntsville's shoe shop or license plate factory worked according to the industrial rhythms of their machines and the clamor of the factory. But for Texas prisoners who lived, worked, and, too often, died on farms, seasonal and daily farming imperatives set the timing of their days, their weeks, and their years—crop schedules mattered more than timetables of bells or whistles. Growing cotton was a year-round job. Prisoners plowed fields in January and planted cotton in February and March; plowing and hoeing continued through June. They harvested crops from late summer through December. They also tended garden vegetables and the foods prisoners would can and eat themselves, or sell to other state institutions. This was in addition to the livestock they raised, butchered, and canned. When they were not planting, weeding, pruning, or harvesting food or cash crops, they cut down trees to clear land for more crops or firewood, tore up brush, and built roads.[36] They did it without machinery, for, with a hoe in their hands, they were like machines—but cheaper. "This lowland Brazos," J. B. Smith sang, referring to the river adjoining the Ramsey Farm, "is a burnin hell."[37]

The Ramsey Farm was the largest unit in the prison system. It held black and Mexican prisoners throughout the 1930s and 1940s, though they were housed in different camps. Incorporated into the prison system in 1912, Ramsey was named in honor of William F. Ramsey, Texas Supreme Court justice and head of the Texas Prison Board. Ramsey oversaw the purchase of the 8,000-acre farm, which was a phenomenal boondoggle for Basset Blakely, the farm's owner, who nearly tripled his money on the land he had bought just two years earlier.[38] By 1934, the administration had purchased adjacent farms, and Ramsey covered more than fifteen thousand acres of farmland along the Brazos River. Its four internal camps, where 738 prisoners slept between bouts of hard labor, sat along Oyster Creek, which ran through the farm.[39] Nearly 60 percent of the farm was under cultivation in 1934, with prisoners tending more than six thousand acres of corn, sixteen hundred acres of cotton, and just under twelve hundred acres of garden crops and feed. Some 350 mules, 288 horses, and 21 oxen worked alongside the prisoners, while seventy-five dogs were on hand to chase anyone who tried to swim the Brazos. That year, Ramsey's inmates turned a profit of $43,713.62 for the prison that held them.[40]

The organization of work on prison farms was hard to know during the 1930s, and few records survive. Nevertheless, an October 1927 farm manager's report gives a snapshot of how work and prisoners were distributed at Ramsey. In the week of October 8–14, 1927, 323 prisoners, out of a total of 567 on Ramsey, picked some 119 bales of cotton, while twenty-four prisoners ginned 145 bales. Corn was heavy in the fields in this fall week, and twenty-seven prisoners gathered 7,617 bushels, about a third of the corn they had thus far gathered in the season. While the majority of imprisoned workers at Ramsey picked cotton or corn in this time of year, twenty-two mule skinners hauled the cotton, corn, and other materials from one part of the farm to another. Nine building tenders enforced order in the different camps and the various wings of different tanks. Four men tended hogs, four others chickens, seven were dairy workers, and two more tended the stock. Nine worked in the Ramsey Farm's version of a hospital under four hospital stewards; there were twelve each in the laundry and in the kitchens, and six "houseboys" worked at the manager's and the assistant manager's residence. Five worked full-time just repairing the huge sacks prisoners filled with cotton. Four tended the guards' quarters and five more were the guards' waiters, while there were five headwaiters for the rest of the prisoners. Four full-time blacksmiths sharpened and fixed tools that were probably damaged with alarming frequency; ten loaded cotton and cotton seed at the gin, and ten more tended the wagons that delivered water to prisoners in the fields. These were the "water boys" sung to and about in so many prisoners' work songs. Other prisoners did work with obscure names—there were eleven "lot men" and thirteen "Flunkies" and "Helpers"—but there were also pump and power plant men, ox drivers, collar makers, mail wagon and commissary men, barbers, clothes patchers, messengers, a carpenter, and a bookkeeper.[41] This was a fully functioning plantation, designed to be as productive as possible.

The guards who oversaw line prisoners—the high riders, the dog sergeants, and others—tended to be uneducated white men from rural backgrounds, with deep ties to the prison and abiding loyalties to each other. The guard force existed within a tightly knit patronage network that lasted through most of the century.[42]

Despite a 22 percent increase in field guards' salaries between 1935 and 1938, they remained poorly paid. Board members advocated for higher wages for guards, which they hoped would improve the personnel and decrease guard turnover.[43] But salaries were just part of what guards received from their employment. They had access to cheap prison-grown vegetables, syrup, and meat. This was hardly something to scoff at during the Depression; the food significantly extended their wages.[44] When farm managers reported the provision requirements for inmates, they were sure to include their own and the assistant manager's food needs. Moreover, farm managers and assistant managers were assigned convict "houseboys" as domestic servants. In the nostalgic South, unfree black workers bestowed significant status on the masters of the households, and "houseboys" were seen as a precious benefit.[45]

While cheap food and the potential of a black servant were important nonwage considerations, the psychic pleasure of being armed and in control of other men surely had its own appeal. Most working people in the Depres-

The Texas Guard Force. Abundant violence, firepower, and speed on horseback (to extend violence) were key means to control prisoners in Texas's open agricultural spaces. 1938 Souvenir Rodeo Program, p. 59. 1998/038-404, Folder "Rodeo Program 1939." Texas State Library and Archives Commission.

sion were subject to the whims of the economy, and so were Texas prison guards. But sitting on horseback, gazing down on men who were legally subject to their control—the power of life and death was in their hands. They took this power to extremes. They were quick to resort to leather, lead, or more creative measures to drive prisoners. Even Lee Simmons, who never shied from brutal punishment, acknowledged that some guards were "pretty bad eggs." Muckraking reporters wrote about guard violence on the farms, but the same habits could spill out when they left the prison. Off-duty guards were sometimes written up for shooting up "Negro dives" in Houston's red light districts. At times they even shot at each other.[46] In 1937 the prison board made a modest effort at professionalization, and began giving oral and physical exams to prospective employees. Members hoped the new process would "greatly improve the character of our personnel,"[47] which said something about how guards could behave.

Whether they behaved violently or not, guards were more than just workers. The food that sustained them and their families came from the prison; the respect they felt each day came from the lethal power they wielded. Their very senses of self were wound up within the prison, and their managers demanded unswerving loyalty. If this were not enough, silence over prison conditions even became official policy. By the end of the decade, employees were expressly prohibited from supplying information or giving interviews to reporters.[48] Such policy hardly seemed necessary, but it was there nonetheless.

Line prisoners awoke before sunrise. They climbed from filthy, lumpy mattresses, which had been made by prisoners. The rancid latrines they used, if they were cleaned, were cleaned by prisoners. The clothes they pulled on were made from cotton that they had grown, and that was ginned by other prisoners and sewn into recognizable shapes by women at Goree. The lunky shoes their sore fingers quickly laced had been made at the Walls by prisoners luckier than themselves, and were sturdy but of a quality deemed appropriately low for convicts. They filed into the dining area under the eye of convict building tenders to eat the food that convict cooks had prepared. It was food that prisoners had grown, which other prisoners had canned. They had only a few minutes to eat, for there were miles of cotton and vegetables to pick that day, and every day thereafter. Guards did not hesitate to beat anyone who was late.

Prisoners ran to and from work, miles in the morning, miles back to sleep. They were often too tired even to eat. At work in the fields, prisoners were driven hard, with little or no rest. Yet they would be whipped for working a mule too hard, because the mule might get injured. They worked long days outside under pounding sun, oppressive heat, in cold or rain, as crops and market dictated. Though the heat and dehydration was a constant threat to life, one prisoner remembered the bitter cold: "Stand out in the field and eat your dinner. Be raining hard . . . like a cow pissing on a flint rock, wash the beans out a your plate. You got to keep working. Rain didn't stop you, cold didn't stop you."[49]

The high rollers, the picket bosses, and the line guards watched prisoners work and made sure they did not escape. But guards also employed some of the quickest workers to drive the others. Two of the fastest, called the lead and the tail row, worked at either end of a line of prisoners. They set the pace that the rest were supposed to follow; if anyone lagged too far behind, another prisoner, one of "the biggest and roughest guys in the squad," would threaten them. Guards rewarded the lead and tail with special privileges, but they could also be punished if the line did not pick enough. A former prisoner named Lawrence Pope said they were "enforcers. Like in—under slav-

Texas prisoners filling a trench silo. 1941 Souvenir Rodeo Program, p. 36. 1998/038-404, Folder "Prison Rodeo Program 1941." Texas State Library and Archives Commission.

ery." They were not armed, but they could, and did, beat slower workers with the full sanction of guards.[50]

Inmates on each prison farm were broken into smaller teams, called hoe squads, and assignment to different squads was often based on the speed at which prisoners could work. At times, prisoners invested their own masculinity in their work and found a modicum of pride in their skill and strength. An inmate who was assigned to the fastest team, "One Hoe Squad," reflected,

> After a while it becomes a challenge. You get kind a get a little team spirit more or less, you like to be in One Hoe. I mean, you work harder and faster, but you're better than those pull-dos [slow workers]. You know. Just like a guy that can drink more whiskey than somebody else. It's ridiculous, but it's that way.[51]

One Hoe workers also got other perks from their guards—sometimes tobacco or a drink—in addition to the masculine pride associated with muscular exertion. Yet that pride and those privileges were founded

The crops prisoners picked stretched to the horizon. 1938 Souvenir Rodeo Program, final page. 1998/038-404, Folder "Rodeo Program 1939." Texas State Library and Archives Commission.

on denigration of less able-bodied workers, who they then lambasted as effeminate. The less able suffered. Even the strongest prisoners could be beaten down by the sun, and collapse, or "fall out" from exhaustion. If they did, they risked punishment. By law, prisoners were not supposed work more than ten hours per day. But exceptions were permissible, and indeed, widespread, at farm managers' or guards' discretion. One guard earned the nickname "Sundown" for his habit of working prisoners past dark.[52] Work on farms was much more likely to extend beyond the ten-hour day than it was in industrial projects.[53]

When overwork took its toll, prisoners might help each other. A former inmate from Harlem farm told an investigator that once, he was sick and too weak to work, "but managed to keep up by holding on to the shirt-tails and belts" of the prisoners in front of him. If a prisoner collapsed on the turn-row, he might be "picked up by four of the stronger men and carried for a distance, after which they hand him to four others, and so on—the squad is not even slowed down."[54] This was crucial for line prisoners' individual and collective survival, because guards would "test" stricken line prisoners. As an inmate recently told historian Robert Chase,

If you fell out, the first thing they'd do is the guard would ride over there with his horse and try to get the horse to step on you. If the horse stepped on you and you moved—you were in trouble. You weren't hurt—you were faking. If you didn't move, well you got stepped on, and then they'd have the water boys come over and get you and drag you over by the water trailer or somewheres and wait till the pick-up come down.[55]

For those accused of impudence, laziness, or breaking their tools—any accusation would do—the whip awaited them. Remaining punishment records offer insight into how prisoners opposed the terms of their labor and their incarceration. There were some thirty-seven different official whipping orders executed in April 1930 alone. Of these, nearly half (eighteen) involved punishments specifically geared toward forcing prisoners to work. These involved "laziness," "refusal to work," and "refusing to thin corn right." Other punishments were directly in response to attacks on guards or on state authority, such as "mutiny," an "Assault on Cap't Baughn and Guard Woulverton," "destroying state property," "destroying crops," and "impudence." April 4, 1930, saw eleven prisoners at Ramsey Farm punished for mutiny. Each received twenty officially sanctioned lashes; informal punishments, of course, were not recorded and remain beyond the official historical record.[56] The whip was sometimes called "the strap" or "the bat," but on occasion a wet rope dragged through the sand would do. Texas prisoners risked whipping for myriad reasons.[57] Looking back at his time in the fields, inmate A. L. MacDonald recalled, "The leather was the worst of all, I guess. You never knew when you were going to get it, and then when you got it, you never knew what for." In what passed for Texas progress, official whippings were limited to "twenty licks." "But they used to give you a hundred if they felt like it. And you got as many whippings as they wanted to give you."[58]

In the face of relentless work, overwhelming degradation, and the constant threat of violence, most prisoners struggled just to make it through the day. Black prisoners, who sang in the fields as they labored, drew upon an African diasporic tradition to lighten their burden and voice suffering in bondage.[59] Most importantly, work songs allowed black prisoners a means of crafting a space of their own within isolating systems of punishment and labor.

Prisoners' work songs voiced terrible lament through beautiful sound. They expressed existential suffering that went beyond the productive process. Most of the songs were characterized by longing, want, and distance from loved ones and family. Prisoners lamented the duration of their imprisonment, often with tragic irony ("My buddy got a hundred / I got ninety nine / Now weren't I lucky / When I got my time"). Multiple cadences based on the driven timing of the axe or hammer, harmonies and intonations, and calls and responses all set prisoners' bodies in motion to the time of music. The songs were characterized by some degree of improvisation within the cadence of the work, and drew on previous songs and folk tales. Singers reworked received lyrics into new combinations, adding new ones and discarding others on the basis of their feelings, the moment, or their sense of humor. The convicted black workers swinging axes or hoes performed work songs for each other, for the guards when they were nearby, and, on very rare occasions, for recording machines. Their rhythms communicated timing for work, so that they labored in cooperation, rather than under the suspicions and antagonisms that the prison's radical coercions yield.

Music formed a tense negotiation among line prisoners, the guards, and convict drivers. The slowest prisoners, often the aged or the infirm, could be whipped for moving too slowly. Prison work songs were a vital part of that negotiation, satisfying guards—almost lulling them into compliance—with the pace that prisoners wanted to work. Albert Race Sample, in his recollections of being a prisoner on the Retrieve Farm, described how the sound of music drew guards onto terrain that prisoners set. "Every axe hitting in rhythm. Boss Deadeye sat on his horse contented, 'When them ol' nigguhs is sangin, ever thang's awright.' With a shotgun laid across his arm, he listened as we sang and sang."[60]

As a negotiation over the pace of labor, singing assured steady progress through the day without taxing the workers beyond their physical endurance. Setting the pace of work allowed prisoners some control of the productive process, as opposed to the absolute dictation of their lives and labors. It allowed workers to move themselves to the music and not focus on the sun, the armed guard, their aching shoulders, or their blistered hands and feet. Work songs functioned as a politics of forgetting and remembering: forgetting the torture they were undergoing and remembering other times, other places. No less than with industrial workers staging an assembly-line slowdown, these songs were a slowdown of the productive process. The ability to dictate the pace of labor, and to seize moments for rest, was a crucial way that the different space and the different time of prison music were literally crafted by prisoners.

A prisoner named Bama explained that when prisoners sang, the time just went better. Another inmate commented on the temporal acceleration that work songs provided: "When you listenin how the song run, the day just go by mo faster . . . and befo you know it, the sergeant or the driver is hollerin dinnertime."[61] Other songs, like "Go Down Ol' Hannah," were almost prayers to the sun to fall more quickly, so that prisoners could get some rest.[62] Thankfully, another day of their sentence would end.

Prisoners sang work songs when they chopped down trees for firewood or to clear land for more crops. These "cross-cutting songs" functioned so that the eight or ten men standing in close quarters around a tree, each of whom was swinging an axe, would time their strokes so that no blade would fly out of control and maim another. Music provided the rhythm through which prisoners timed their labor, and this made for efficient work, in a relatively unalienated way. One said, "You take [prisoners] around a tree and they'll sing it down, they'll sing down in harmony[;] . . . when you workin' in union and singin' in union, it makes it a lot easier all around."[63] By singing their way through hard labor, prisoners shifted the ground of their incarceration. According to one visitor to Mississippi's Parchman Farm, the sound of the music "could almost take you off of your feet."[64]

In "Let Your Hammer Ring," song leader Big Louisiana set the timing for the prisoners' work, but he also invoked the gendered feelings of sexual loss. In California, men invested gendered meanings into their work, and Big Louisiana's verses did much the same thing. In particular, he mourned his separation from his spouse, Berta, who, according to the song, he saw in a dream. In this and other songs, the singer's spouse is left at home or in the courthouse, begging the judge for leniency. And the singer despairs that Berta might find another man.

> Well I believe I spied Berta . . .
> In my midnight dream, boys . . .
> She standin' ahead of my bedside . . .
> In a negligee . . .
> Well big leg Berta . . .
> Well I left my woman . . .
> She's in the courthouse cryin', boys . . .
> "Well Judge can't you help my man" . . .
> Well I'm going away to leave you gal . . .
> But I'll be back home gal . . .
> Don't let nobody . . .
> Tear my playhouse down, gal . . .
> Well Berta don't you love me, gal?[65]

Yet, more complex still, work songs also allowed for a nurturing and supportive male voice in penal farms, one that might have otherwise not been permitted in the codes of masculinity that scorned weakness. Prisoners could show genuine concern for each other, despite the alienations of this punitive world. Just as some might carry fallen prisoners, one leader sang, "Watch my buddy / Buddy he start to fall / Help that boy / Won't you make it long."[66]

Songs allowed for expressions of masculine potency, and these helped fulfill male prisoners in a situation that attempted to render them powerless, and thus, according to dominant gendered meanings (heightened here), symbolically feminine. In versions of "Let Your Hammer Ring," the leader says that his hammer (axe) is on fire—because it is so powerful. The hammer serves as a phallic symbol, an extension of the singers' masculine power. The axe (variously called a hammer or a diamond) often took on supernatural powers in songs.[67] It is on fire as it bites into the tree he is felling. The hammer, though, cannot be cooled by the waterboy's water. He takes it to the Brazos River (itself symbolic of freedom, according to folklorist Bruce Jackson), but it still will not be cooled. Nor can it be sharpened by the guards. In the song "Alberta," the hammer "rings like silver and it SHINES LIKE GOLD / Price a my hammer, boys, AIN'T NEVER BEEN TOLD." The workers claimed value in their labor and pride in their physical strength. Using images of diamonds, precious metals, and highly valued goods, they valorized the tools they were forced to use. Needless to say, their unwaged labor was not highly esteemed by the state that cared little for them, their families, or their lives. Their music represented the struggle to survive in horrific circumstances wrought by racialized status in a capitalist economy, and by the degradation of this unfree labor.

Yet still, within the very material context of prison farms, work songs allowed for prisoners to circulate knowledge of guards' habits, weaknesses, and indulgences. In the 1960s, a long-time prisoner recalled, "when the penitentiary was kind of rough they used to sing songs about the bosses, sergeants, lieutenants, whatever they think about them, that's what they'd sing about them."[68] And while they magnified the power of their hammers, prisoners would sing a guard's shotgun into a "derringer": a very small pistol. "That's what we call 'down talkin'" it," one man reflected, "makin' it small."[69]

References to guards were often coded in complex ways. Texas guard Carl Luther McAdams, who went on to become a particularly despised warden, was sometimes called "Beartracks" by prisoners, for the size of his feet as well as for his ferocity. He was reputed to be able to beat just about anyone in a fight with his bare hands—he wasn't dependent on a shotgun or badge for violent authority. Though he was despised, prisoners also positioned McAdams as a masculine antihero of near mythic proportion, much like Stagolee, an uncontrollable bad man who celebrated nihilistic defiance of black and white norms of behavior.[70] In one version of the song "Grizzly Bear," listeners were warned, "Oh don't let that Bear catch you, man, GRIZZLY BEAR . . . / Well he will catch you and he'll kill you that GRIZZLY BEAR."

But in another version the singer follows the grizzly bear down to the Brazos River, the river that irrigated the vast majority of Texas penal farmland. "You know I ain't scared a no bear GRIZZLY BEAR / Because the workin' squad they killed him there, GRIZZLY BEAR."[71] In this version, the working squad kills the bear, signifying their communal overpowering of the guard. Unlike other versions of this song, and unlike the trickster Brer Rabbit stories, this is the group's—rather than an individual character representing the group's—revenge.

Yet for all of their power, work songs did not topple the force of the prison, or of the guards on horseback. That was not their purpose. Rather, the songs allowed black prisoners the ability to survive; in one prisoner's words, "to make it, make a day."[72] In a system that cared little if they did, that was enough.

White and Mexican prisoners left far fewer records of their reflections on penal farm life and labor than did black prisoners. Mexican border ballads and western swing music critiqued conditions of poverty and the unfairness of the law, but if white or Mexican prisoners sang these at work on prison farms, no records remain.[73] Nevertheless, white country singer Merle Haggard, who served time at California's Folsom prison, sang about planning an escape from Texas prisons; farm labor was one reason why: "My hands don't fit no chopping pole, and cotton never was my bag. / The Man better keep both eyes on me, or they're gonna lose ol' Hagg."[74] But despite the relative paucity of white prisoners' perspectives on labor in Texas prison farms, white prisoners also opposed the terms of line work.

Many prisoners threatened violence against their keepers, though given the odds of survival, this was understandably rare. Inmates told stories about hiding rattlesnakes in their lockers, to surprise guards (or anyone else) who might search their belongings.[75] While this may or may not have been true, fabled escapes by Clyde Barrow's gang, as well as mass escapes at other times, bespoke the failure to fully contain inmates on farms. On June 22, 1937, three prisoners tried to escape from the Eastham Farm, a farm for white recidivists. As they worked about a mile east of the Eastham Camp No. 2, a guard on horseback carelessly allowed prisoners to work closer to him than they were ordinarily permitted. As the guard rolled a cigarette with his shotgun across his lap, one inmate distracted him while another grabbed the shotgun. Once the guard was disarmed, they stripped him and donned his clothes, shaming him while trying to hide their identities as marked by their convict uniforms. After they made their escape, no other guards chased them. Though three prisoners participated in the break, twenty-one others did not, preferring their chances on the farm to life on the run.[76] A fugitive traded the violence of prison for the loneliness of the road. The need for quick mobility, coupled with paranoia, left little room for loved ones. As Haggard put it, a lover would "only slow me down, and they'd catch up with me." The choices were stark: "outrun the law, or spend my life in jail."[77]

Prisoners across the system opposed the terms of their labor and their incarceration in grimly self-destructive ways. Workers at San Quentin's jute mill may have had their fingers crushed in gears of industrial machinery, but prisoners in Texas mangled their own hands to get out of the fields for a short while. Many were the prisoners who cut their Achilles tendon or who severed fingers in order to avoid working while they convalesced on the Wynne Farm or the hospital at the Walls.[78] In 1938, Senator Gordon Burns voiced his disappointment at these prisoners on the radio, as he proposed an expanded clemency plan.

> [L]ately there has been a good deal of maiming going on amongst the inmates. Prisoners—some of them—have been injuring themselves to keep from working. And no man guilty of this could ever obtain his freedom through clemency under the terms of my bill.[79]

Self-mutilation was all too common a part of the Texas Prison System, a deeply troubling way for prisoners to escape the harshness of forced labor and to get some rest in the hospital for a while. There were many reasons why Texas authorities hated that prisoners injured themselves. Perhaps the clearest was economic—prisoners could not work when they were injured, and became drains on the prison's budget. In addition, self-mutilation disgraced the system by demonstrating its inherent violence, when officials, as we will see, claimed that theirs was a care-giving state. Lastly, self-mutilation was a way for prisoners to claim their own bodies, even if it was literally self-destructive. But it was nonetheless self-motivated action.[80] As a result, prisoners who severed their Achilles tendons lost good time, and their action was seen as almost as bad as an assault on the prison staff.

Prisoners' self-destruction demonstrated limits to the historiographical notion of heroic agency in this hyper-alienated environment, and to some extent confounds interpretation through many established tools of historical analysis.[81] However, this does not mean that we cannot attempt to understand the meaning of self-destruction. Prisoners who destroyed their own bodies did so as an expression of what others might understand as madness, laziness, or irrationality. Certainly this is what many officials believed. Prisoners hurt themselves even though they risked further punishment. But self-injury was also an attack on the authority of the system, and of the prison's control of their bodies. Much as it had a century before, self-mutilation demonstrated the fallacy of slave owners' (and now prison officials') fantasies that they were firm but benevolent patriarchs. It showed that this was a regime founded on violence, regardless of the stories that officials told themselves and others. But not all officials responded with shame or embarrassment. When one journalist asked Lee Simmons what he intended to do about prisoners who maimed themselves, Simmons replied, "Give them more axes."[82]

Anthony Sayers, a white prisoner on the Retrieve State Farm, wrote a letter to Governor Coke Stevenson explaining how maltreatment and brutal work regimes made prisoners into "mad dogs" rather than citizens or men, and drove self-destruction and more:

> In the hearts of those men that are classified as incorrigibles and placed on these camps is a livid hate and when they get loose they are called mad dogs by an indignant public who never stop to wonder what made them that way. They have been made to come out of their barracks with tear gas and bullets and herd them to fields and tried to force them to raise crops. They worked—Yes—they worked hard and sweat rolled off in torrents as long as the guards had their eyes on them but the moment their eyes were turned they destroyed with vigor that which they were forced to do.
>
> They have burned their barracks and they burned their barns filled with feed. They have sabotaged every piece of machinery they have had chance to. They have killed thousands of Dollars worth of stock; they have mutilated themselves in groves of protestation. . . . They are not Mad Dogs and they can be turned into useful citizens and they can be lead [sic] to pull their own weight while they are doing their debt to society.[83]

Sayers argued that benevolent treatment would be far better suited to Texas's prisoners than continued brutality. Otherwise, they would continue to burn and destroy their prison, and remain lost to society. Hardness would be met with hardness, he reasoned, and brutality with brutality.[84]

Opposition to domination, as a form of semi-autonomous expression of life and desire, could perhaps be of three fundamental types. The first was a direct confrontation with the mode and method of oppression—in Texas, this might mean the Barrow gang's spectacular escape, or attacking a prison guard who had the authority to kill. A second type was more subtle than direct confrontation: prisoners might break the tools they worked with or otherwise sabotage the means of production. Because the prison treated them as little more than tools themselves, this might also include self-injury. This was virtually impossible to prevent. But in addition to physical pain and the possibility of long-term impairment, self-destruction, like sabotage, and like rebellion, risked punishment. A third kind was that of black prisoners' work songs—it moved onto a new terrain than the one set by the dominant form of power, in a maneuver that changed the direction of the conflict. Work songs did not provide an external escape from the prison, but rather folded new senses of time and space into the prison itself. The first kind of resistance was more easily understood, controlled, and repressed (though never fully) by overwhelming violence: Bonnie and Clyde were, eventually, gunned down in a summary execution orchestrated by Lee Simmons. The second form of resistance was merely a cost of the Texas Prison System being run "from a business standpoint," but it was a nuisance, to be sure, as well as a source of shame for liberal Texans that would eventually prompt some reorganization. The third, the work songs, were incorporated into prison labor assignments while also materially transforming the work regimes themselves. All three oppositional forms met on Texas prison farms, where agricultural labor extraction and guards' demands for submissiveness sustained a brutal regime. They overlapped when all prisoners were subject to universal degradation as convicts, and through what male prisoners felt to be their emasculation through forced labor, disrespect, and lack of control.

Inmates' labor in Texas and California served different and contradictory ends. In each state, labor was guided by the long-standing ideology that hard work would teach criminals a good work ethic and the habits of industry. At the same time, the ideology behind prison labor suggested that assignment to different positions would replicate raced and gendered hierarchies throughout society, where men could control themselves and their labor. Obedient prisoners would be rewarded by promotion through these hierarchies, becoming part of what officials identified as a meritocratic system, but which must be understood as a coercive meritocracy, whereby there were material benefits and punishments associated with obedience or recalcitrance.

Yet the conditions of labor departed from these ideological ideals. Labor assignments were structured by racial hierarchies and de facto, if not de jure, racial segregation. The best jobs were reserved for the most highly skilled, for the best behaved, and always for white prisoners. Black and Mexican prisoners, and the worst-behaved whites, would be given the worst and most degrading assignments, to the fields and farms throughout the Texas prison world. This clearly recalled Texas's plantation heritage, but administrators' desire to diversify the system's productive capacities gave a sense of looking forward rather than solely looking to the past. California prisoners might ascend its industrial and bureaucratic apparatus through good behavior, or, as we will see, through good connections. In Texas, the updated traditions of slavery allowed some prisoners, especially building tenders, to advance through the ranks by doing the guards' bidding. The gains they made came at a cost to others.

Shifting Markets of Power

Building Tenders, Con Bosses, Queens, and Guards

Bull was a long-time building tender, appointed by guards to keep order in the "tanks"— dormitories where inmates slept on Texas prison farms. Dumpling was a new young inmate, and even though he should have been sent to a unit for first-termers, he was assigned to the Retrieve Farm. When the transport dropped Dumpling off, the captain paraded him before the farm's building tenders, or BTs, who hollered obscene remarks about the newcomer and begged the captain to let them have him in their tank. The captain made a half-hearted attempt to settle down the BTs. Perhaps in consolation, he offered to let Dumpling choose the tank that would be his new home, and, consequently, which of the BTs would control him. Dumpling said that it did not matter, so the captain taunted, "You mean it don't matter who fucks you in yore ass?" Building tenders' rape of other prisoners was no secret. When guards and building tenders collaborated in dominating weaker prisoners—and all prisoners were weaker than the BTs—they created what passed for good order in the Texas prison.[1]

Bull, armed not just with knives but with recognition as a state agent, forced Dumpling into sexual servitude. Eventually, Dumpling fought back. He found a razor blade, and one night, while the two were in Bull's bunk, Dumpling cut off Bull's penis. Bull, as building tender, had respect from one and all around him. But when he stood naked, wounded and pleading for help, the guard yelled at Bull to quiet down and quit spraying blood on the floor. Bull was no longer the building tender, but just "this ol' nigguh wit his dick cut off." On the phone with his superior, the guard asked, "Cap'n, kin ya'll hurry? This sonuvabitch is ableedin all over everthang."[2] Disgraced, disarmed, and emasculated, Bull was worthless to the guards. Although Dumpling was punished and lost good time toward release, from then on, other inmates left him alone. He had proven himself in blood. He was no longer a "galboy" and had "earned his right to sleep in hell."[3]

Power and authority in Texas and California prisons in the Depression wove together overt and covert networks, relationships that ensnared the guard, Bull, Dumpling, and the rest. Select prisoners played lynchpin roles in each state. Building tenders like Bull were the key figures in Texas, but in California, prisoners called "con bosses" were the most important. As the heads of prison departments and managers of productive processes, con bosses cultivated political and economic relationships to their personal advantage, often to the detriment of other prisoners. Building tenders and con bosses linked the official productive forces of the prisons to their informal economies, where markets of economic, sexual, violent, symbolic, and bureaucratic capital combined in dense networks of authority. Each of these systems undermined the possibilities of inmate solidarity, as prisoners frequently found themselves pitted against one another, rather than against the keepers of their institutions. To this end, the BT and con boss systems undermined the "con ethic" that midcentury sociologists identified and romanticized, which suggested that prisoners supported each other against their keepers.[4]

The BT and con boss systems were effective because, at their core, they appealed to prisoners' masculinities, expressions of difference and power that were arguably more important to inmates' lives than class or even race, or their shared status as prisoners. Consequently, these markets of power and violence, steeped in masculine identification, came from "above" as well as from "below," from the state as well as from the domestic sphere's foundational form of inequality.[5] Prisoners inhabited a welter of masculinities, which were indexed in multiple ways to work, race, violence, sexuality, wealth, and self-control. The range of masculinities that male prisoners in Texas and California embodied overlapped with each other and with those on the outside, though as historian Regina Kunzel convincingly demonstrated, American prisons constantly "queered" commonsense understandings of gender.[6] Yet the specific conditions in Texas and California prisons gave rise to different configurations of masculinity, with different forms emerging as hegemonic, and dominating alternative forms.[7] Yet there was some room for maneuver, especially in California. There, queens—men who glamorized and traded on their effeminacy—managed an alternative fund of power to negotiate the Depression's penal economy.

The con boss and BT systems came into crisis at the end of the decade and in the war years, when inmates' actions led to a round of penal reforms. In 1939, San Quentin prisoners staged a series of food strikes. Subsequent beatings prompted official limits on guard violence. A second round of California investigations in 1943 and 1944 grew around the con boss system. Con bosses came under scrutiny, but so did prison queens, whose sexuality officials feared almost as much as the con bosses' power. Reform efforts in Texas were anemic compared to those in California, but concern over homosexuality and self-maiming led Texas officials to rethink their system. Each state tried to impose a rational order that would regulate the unkempt markets of sex, violence, and commodity exchange within a modernizing capitalist regime.

Building Tenders: Sexual Violence as Statecraft

After the largely failed 1928 reorganization of the Texas Prison System (which restructured the highest levels of the prison administration but left everyday conditions largely unchanged), the Texas Prison System's administration was a hierarchical structure with the state prison system's general manager at the top. The general manager reported to the State Prison Board, whose members exercised minor obligations, produced innocuous reports, and occasionally met with legislators but left the general manager firmly in charge of daily operations as well as significant long-term planning. The various prison farms within the system were run as individual and largely autonomous entities, with a warden or farm manager responsible for daily operations, crop rotation, and discipline. If managers ran a productive farm without much public complaint, they were pretty well left alone. If there were escapes or a surprising number of deaths, they might be investigated. Imperial State Farm manager Buck Flanagan ran the farm as if it were "his own private kingdom, and for many years it appeared to be."[8] On the farms, managers delegated authority to their well-armed guard corps, who oversaw prisoners at work in the fields and on the roads. Perched on horseback, they drove prisoners to work harder, run faster, chop more cane, or pick more cotton. When not overseeing labor, guards were stationed in central hallways between the tanks where prisoners slept. But guards could not see into the tanks. Rows of bunk beds lined the walls, obscuring the views of the guards and, thus, of the official representatives of the state.[9] Even the newly built dormitories, constructed from Harlem Farm bricks and thus a proud sign of modernization, were quickly overcrowded in the Depression, with "double-deck bunks . . . placed so close as almost to touch each other."[10] This was no panopticon. Guards generally oversaw work in the fields, but building tenders controlled the tanks. This basic administrative structure existed on all prison farms, regardless of the race of prisoners or their status as repeat offenders or first-timers. As reformers would complain, prisoners in the tanks could do as they wished.

Prisoners could argue over who was the strongest or fastest worker, and physical labor was one component of hierarchical masculinity. But the tanks were the crucial domain where prisoners battled for positions of control. The capacity for violence, and especially violence that was linked to sex, fostered gender as a relational mode of domination. On average, 5 percent of those who died in each state prison were killed by other inmates—stabbed, clubbed, or killed by some other means.[11] Violence became linked with Texas's hegemonic masculinity, and violent hypermasculinity became one form of currency, along with cash, tobacco, and sex, operating across subaltern prison economies and hierarchies. When folklorist Bruce Jackson interviewed long-time black prisoners in Texas, they said there "was a lot of killing," and not just by guards. Much violence arose "over petty debts, petty thefts, money, hustling money to gamble."[12] The BTs were the masters of that violence—among prisoners, at least.

The building tender system might be understood as an "officially unofficial" delegation of authority that dated back to the Reconstruction-era "subboss" system.[13] Before that, surely, were the slave drivers. There was little in the way of classificatory science behind the selection of BTs; guards relied on gut instinct to choose them from the most brutal prisoners. Despite the measures of trust involved, guards were rarely disappointed.[14] For their part, BTs knew that their position depended on guards' support. If they lost that support, they could lose their status. If they lost their capacity for violent rule, as Bull did, they could lose guards' respect. If prisoners organized against them, they could lose their lives.[15]

In theory, building tenders were similar to other trustee inmates and were given moderately more responsibility and unsupervised work than mainline prisoners. A BT's official task was to look after the internal workings of his tank, making sure that it was clean, that prisoners had bedding, and so forth. In formal hierarchies, this was a privileged labor assignment. They also received additional "good time" credits: in 1929, head BTs received three hundred overtime hours each month, and assistant BTs received 250.[16] They had access to better food than most prisoners, and, in managing the day-to-day upkeep of the tanks rather than picking cotton, had an easier work assignment. Moreover, later in the century, BTs would be permitted to run their own commissaries. In this, they operated as something of a franchise within the formal commissary system, profiting from other prisoners' deprivation by providing the infrastructure for the for-profit distribution of goods.[17]

BTs' responsibilities were far more substantial than just looking after the sleeping quarters. Though not officially charged with maintaining violent order, that is precisely what they did. One contemporary investigator and critic reported that building tenders' violent rule, though patently illegal, had existed "for many, many years, with the full knowledge and consent of the management." Officials would "deputize prisoners to control the dormitories and allow them to arm themselves with clubs with which they brutally beat fellow-prisoners for alleged rule infractions."[18] In his memoirs of life on black Texas prison farms, Albert Race Sample called BTs "the policemen of the tanks." BTs, in Sample's words, "received preferential treatment and were privileged to possess overt weapons." Furthermore, "Under the guise of enforcing the 'rules,' their brutal behavior was tolerated by the officials."[19] Another former prisoner validated the claim: "Building tenders . . . are extremely brutal. These men are really agents of the captain and placed in the tanks to beat up other convicts the captain wants punished."[20] Evidence is limited from women at the Goree Farm, but female BTs could be equally violent. Unbeknownst to officials, Melba Newton George, an investigative reporter, had herself sent to Goree. On her first day, she complained to Matron Heath about rough treatment. The captain scolded her for her attitude, but a BT named Clara took it a step further. "It's a good thing I wasn't there when you sassed Mrs. Heath. I'd have clawed your eyes out."[21]

This violence could take specifically gendered inflections. Women might scratch at eyes and male BTs might beat prisoners with fists and chains, in a fight understood as one between men. But male BTs also raped. In the highly gendered domain of Texas men's prisons, sexual violence became the foundational form of control. Sexual violence was more than the pain of beating or assault, because it "unmade" the victim's identity as a man. Sexual violence forced victims into servitude as a "galboy" or a "punk," a subordinated, feminized manhood. As feminist scholar Susan Brownmiller persuasively argued, rape was (and is) used to politically and physically dominate women. But it was also used to dominate men.[22] When BTs raped other men, and when the threat of rape terrorized others into compliance, the state benefited. Consequently, as Sample testified, the BT's "gang rapes, beatings and harassment of the weaker cons were ignored," because they helped the prison operate. Prisoners' experience bore out the analysis. Two Louisiana prisoners recently reflected that prison rape had little to do with homosexuality or pleasure. It was about "violence, politics, and an acting out of power roles."[23] When the rapist was a state agent, rape became a tool of statecraft.

Inmates arriving in Texas prisons needed quickly to orient themselves to the world in which they were embroiled. And though prison rape became almost cliché in popular culture in the 1970s, the sexual violence came from an all too powerful reality among Texas prisoners. There were glints and intimations of consensual sex among Texas prisoners, and we can say with some confidence that prisoners on Texas farms practiced a range of sexualities.[24] But among remaining records, rape was more prevalent. R. Craig Copeland conducted an interview with a prisoner who described his arrival in the tanks at a Texas prison farm:

> The day I got to the farm the Warden looked at me and said "number two wing." That is all the warden said to me until he transferred me out. When I walked into Number Two Wing, a convict who was about twenty-five years old named Billy the Kid walked up to me and told me, "As long as you stay in this wing I take care of you." I did not know what he meant at first, but I later found out. The first night he came to my bunk before the lights went out and bragged about the fights he had had, and showed me his weapon. It was a piece of lead and was rolled to fit the inside of his hand. He carried it in his pocket all the time. About two weeks after the Kid had been playing with me, he came to my bunk one night after the lights were out and said, "Let's go," and just walked away. I didn't go with him and when I looked up I noticed the Kid and the Building Tender had exchanged bunks and the bunk had a sheet draped over it, like a tent. The Kid came back and cursed me, hit me in the back with his fists, and told me he meant business. I followed him because I was afraid of what he might do. That night he committed an act of sodomy on me and from that night on I was known as "Billy's Punk."[25]

This description might have come from a number of midcentury prisons; it was hardly unheard of in other prisons for a "wolf" or a "jocker" to con an inexperienced prisoner into being his "punk" through promises of protection.[26] But what was different in Texas was the degree to which the building tenders' ability to dominate was enhanced through their official position, the ways in which this form of masculinity became hegemonic through state support. Billy the Kid was not Number Two Wing's building tender, but it was nevertheless clear that Billy and the BT's "exchange" solidified a reciprocal relationship. As a result, the BT agreed to let Billy sexually dominate this prisoner. And every bit as significantly, the prisoner who was subject to this violence had little interaction with official state representatives. He only met the warden on his first and last days on the farm—other than that, he was largely in the hands of building tenders, their allies, or the lesser guards in the system who directly oversaw his labor.

Sample recounted numerous stories about building tenders. In one, a BT named Big George engaged another inmate in quiet conversation, which Sample suspected contained a sexual proposition. The man replied, "I don' play that shit." Later, Big George attacked and beat the same man, for turning him down. Big George then took the prisoner to the guard under the pretense that the prisoner created a disturbance. "Since it involved a Building Tender, no questions were asked."[27] To the extent that this prisoner was officially disciplined (for example, if he was whipped, was hanged by his handcuffed wrists, or lost good time toward parole), in addition to the beating Big George gave him, Big George used official state mechanisms for his own sexual domination.

Perhaps as a result, not all prison officials were comfortable with the building tender system. Perhaps their discomfort is reflected in the scarcity of references to BTs in official minutes or annual reports. The Prison Board rarely mentioned building tenders—they seldom surfaced at that level of administration, operating at a nearly invisible level of state authority. However, in 1937 some of the more progressive members of the Prison Board moved that BTs should no longer be armed with "dirks and other knives," though they would still be permitted to carry clubs.[28] This change hardly mitigated the violence meted out by building tenders on other inmates. After a 1938 grand jury investigation of the death of L. C. McBride, a young, black first-timer on Darrington Farm, the foreman of the grand jury lamented the "condition within the prison that permits acts of brutality between the prisoners and building tenders. It is our hope that this condition can be improved and such acts as unnecessary beatings by the tenders can be stopped or at least lessened in brutality."[29]

The effort, weak as it was, was part of a broader movement to limit violence in the prisons. Reformers had argued against whipping (and especially whipping white men) ever since a failed 1911 investigation under the Colquitt administration. The whip was reintroduced in 1915. The most success that investigation could claim was to regulate the size and shape of whips guards could (officially) use. The latest protests were spearheaded by humanitarian muckraker C. V. Compton, a Kentucky-born lawyer and civic activist, and a consistent thorn in the prison administration's side.[30] Much of his prison work was documented in two self-published exposés, *Deep Secrets behind Gray Walls* in 1940, and *Flood Lights behind the Gray Walls: An Exposé of Activities*, released in 1942. A relentless and media-savvy advocate of progressive penology and a critic of the lash, that "relic of Southern Barbarism," Compton offered to pay prison officials two hundred dollars in cash and another one thousand to charity for every time they were willing to be whipped.[31] If officials believed that the lash was a reasonable and modern punishment, they should be willing to show why. None accepted the offer, but the point was made, and in February 1941, the bat was finally abolished as a legal punishment.[32] Prison Board member S. M. Lister had prophesied to the Dallas *Morning News* that the decision to stop whipping would be disastrous: "If you pass this law, [convicts] will be thumbing their noses at us before the week is over."[33] But by the end of the year, he changed his tune, and even had the board take credit for this reformist vision. Rather than an invitation to chaos, Lister called the decision "the most progressive step toward rehabilitation ever taken by the Texas Prison Board."[34]

Despite success in the de jure diminution of state violence, the truth of the matter was that suffering hardly lessened. In 1942, a recently released prisoner told Compton that, yes, "the lash has been abolished," but inmates were still carried off and "beaten by another convict, with a club furnished by a dog sergeant." Another explained that conditions were "just as brutal as before they abolished the lash."[35] Guards retained a panoply of means of punishment. Prisoners would be starved and sleep deprived in overcrowded "solitary" cells, and guards would again pick up whips later in the century—if indeed they had ever put them down.[36] Even without whips, making prisoners "stand on the barrel" was a favorite. They could (and did) hang prisoners from handcuffs attached to the ceiling, or cuff prisoners' hands to bars high up behind their backs, so that their circulation was cut off and their fingers turned purple and black. Guards would squeeze and "milk" prisoners' fingers, and screams would echo through the tanks. The Texas Department of Public Safety trained officers in a similar technique.[37]

The 1938 grand jury foreman's hope would remain unfulfilled. Beatings and maimings continued along with the low budgets of the Depression. In 1940, fiscally conservative members of the prison board even considered replacing field guards with rifle-toting trustees, to the cut costs associated with already-low salaries. Members of the board toured Louisiana, Arkansas, and Mississippi prisons, where, they said, arming prisoners was "in vogue." Despite the Texas attorney general's opinion that such a practice was illegal, the board remained split.[38] They finally elected not to give inmates rifles, but the BT system persisted. Carl Luther "Beartracks" McAdams, the guard who would become a warden in the postwar period, championed the BT system. "[T]he building tenders is the only way," he opined. "In other words, the inmates know how to impose on one another."[39] Wardens and guards alike were content to let that cruel order, based on sexually violent masculinity, remain. After all, few Texas prisoners rebelled, and, with low guard-to-prisoner ratios, operating costs decreased.

Yet reform movements persisted, driven by the scandals of inmate self-maiming. Violence reached shocking levels during the war, when military service and better-paying wartime industries lured the best guards away (and recall previous board statements about concern for the quality of the guard corps) leaving only the most inept in charge of the prison. Demands on prisoners' labor remained high, and brutalities abounded. Moreover, and as C. V. Compton had publicized, prisoners were maiming themselves in droves to protest the conditions of violence, the overwork, and the lack of medical care. In 1944, the Texas Prison Board solicited Austin MacCormick, a nationally renowned progressive penologist, to investigate its prisons and recommend systematic reforms.

MacCormick released the sobering results of his investigation in 1947. Guards were often drunk and prone to violence, and inmates responded by maiming themselves or trying to escape, each of which led to a new round of ineffective but grim punishments. MacCormick thought the problem was clear: rather than being a matter of overwork or endemic cultures of state-sanctioned violence, "most of our troubles [are] due to the whole life in the tanks."[40] Communal life in large dormitories, MacCormick argued, bred and led to the contagious transmission of what he called "perversion," a term, in his usage, ambiguous enough to encapsulate consensual homosexuality, building tender rape, and self-mutilation. Tightly packed bunks allowed prisoners to crawl from one to the next without alerting any guards. His understanding of perversion did not distinguish between rape and consensual sex between men, for he understood them to be not only equally dangerous but also similarly contagious. "The problem of perversion," he wrote, "is always present in dormitories." Without the sanctity of individual cells, the "free mingling of varied types" of prisoners caused perversion to spread. "Perverts" he continued, "get their weaker, more suggestible, or more impulsive fellows into trouble."[41]

MacCormick linked inmate self-maiming with these perversions. Countless prisoners injured themselves to avoid work in the fields, but MacCormick understood self-destruction less as a desperate form of resistance than as a disease. Self-mutilation had "attacked Texas like a peculiar tropical disease; it is as contagious as can be." Inmates who maimed themselves tended to be those who were physically weak, subject to stronger inmates who "made" them do it, or those who were physically strong enough to work but so morally debilitated as to prefer injury to labor.

As a modern liberal penologist, MacCormick identified problems that fit the mold of issues he already understood. In his vision, architecture would better separate and differentiate inmates from one another. Until cellblocks with individual cells were built, Texas prisons would continue to reap a harvest of brutality, self-mutilation, and deviant sexuality. While the Texas legislature would appropriate money for cellblock development in the post-war period—an extension of the architectural modernization undertaken in shifting from wooden to brick buildings in the 1930s—they would not spend the money to build a Big House prison, like Sing Sing, San Quentin, or Folsom. But the fears of inmate "perversion," be it consensual sex or violent rape—for they were indistinguishable in the MacCormick report—were crucial to architectural and penal modernization. The future would remain bleak, however, and the reform efforts of 1947 were thorough failures. New cellblocks would heighten rather than diminish building tenders' violent power for the next thirty years.[42]

Masculine Markets in Honor, Commodities, and Violence

California's prisons shared many features prevalent on Texas's prison farms, but the overt and covert markets of power that bound inmates and the state together were fundamentally different. If the roots of the BT system grew from the slave plantations Texas farms so closely resembled, California's con bosses were managers and entrepreneurs at home in the factory setting. Moreover, the sheer scale of California's Big House prisons, the range and development of their industries and their wide-ranging demographics, seem to have made for a broader spectrum of masculinities and controls, where a different state formation led to differing opportunities and dangers. Masculinity was still linked with power, and capacity for violence was still important because it remained the principal means of protecting masculine honor. But violence was just one among many ways in which power and manhood were linked—money, bureaucratic power, and reputation mattered, too. At the apex of penal hierarchies, they mattered more.

California inmates struggled to maintain prestige, honor, and respect. Prisoners fought over what seemed like trivialities to outsiders: an insult made years earlier; a few dollars' gambling debt—as in Texas, any of these could lead to blood. Mike Carden stabbed and killed Lee Watts, his 29-year-old San Quentin cellmate, due to one such slight. "Well," Carden explained, it was pretty straightforward. Watts "borrowed the sack of weed off me about a month ago. . . . I asked him for the sack about two weeks ago and he told me to go fuck myself. So I stuck a knife in him today." An investigator pointed out that tobacco seemed a small thing to cut a man for. "[I]t wasn't the tobacco," Carden clarified, "it was the thing he said to me when I asked him for it." Watts, it seems, had not understood what was at stake. Before he died, he asked an inmate carrying him to the hospital, "Can you imagine a man doing this to me for one sack of weed?"[43]

Official investigations into inmate deaths solicited prisoners' testimony to prosecute offenders and impose control, and inmates were typically loath to testify against one another. Yet the "convict code" was less a form of subaltern solidarity than an understanding that the state was irrelevant to righting insults to their honor. These were stains, most felt, that only blood they spilled could wash away.[44] Raymond Boyd was stabbed near the San Quentin book counter in the old library, on a January afternoon in 1933. Before he died, guards asked him who did it. He refused to say, and told them "he would care for the matter himself."[45]

Racial difference could exacerbate existing tensions. Folsom inmate Wesley Robert Wells described a fight between black and white prisoners that started because a white prisoner named "New York Red" owed Emory Hudson, a black prisoner, some money. It rapidly turned into what Wells called a "free for all," in which Hudson was stabbed and killed, and for which Wells—himself black—was punished.[46] On another occasion, a white, Georgia-born prisoner named Grover Garrison stabbed Jack Young, a black prisoner, for "shoving" him. "This morning, when we were on our way to the quarry," Garrison later told guards, "I accidentally—sorta stepped on this nig—this man's foot. He shoved me. I'm from Georgia and I ain't taking no shoving from a Negro. That's all!" At work alongside black men in the quarry, Garrison surely felt his southern whiteness was already in question. Jack Young refused to acquiesce to Garrison "accidentally—sorta" stepping on his foot, further affronting the white man's sensibilities; violence was the only salve to his honor.[47]

Prisoners gambled, stole, and traded for goods behind bars. Gambling was forbidden but rampant, and most guards found better things to do when they heard dice clicking off a cell wall or saw a card game among bored prisoners. Just as numbers bankers in cities might base the winning numbers on certain digits of the days' clearinghouse numbers, so too was the prisons' unofficial economy based upon the official order.[48] They used tobacco, tooth powder, shaving soap, matches, and safety razors as goods to gamble with.[49] In his 1940 study, Donald Clemmer argued that "[l]ike physical courage, gambling skill is a value held in considerable esteem."[50] Prisoners played poker, coon-can, and rummy. They played dice when they could, either smuggling them in or making their own, ingeniously fashioned out of various materials. Goods changed hands, but masculine prestige was also on the line: "Men gain status," Clemmer wrote, "by being known as shrewd gamblers."[51]

Robert Tasker detailed the exchange rates at San Quentin, and their connection to the official economy of the commissary. Indeed, it was not long after he arrived in San Quentin that Tasker had been "initiated into the art of conniving," participating in the prison's covert economy.

> The chief medium was tobacco. Soap and toothpaste were common tender; one bar of soap or one tube of dentifrice commanding two sacks of weed in exchange at all times. Writing-tablets brought the same. A pack of envelopes—one sack. Those staples, with a few others, formed the nucleus of our fiscal dealings. Tobacco was the inflexible standard—the gold in reserve.[52]

At other times, prisoners bartered with pens or candy. Writing under the name Roark Tamerlane, another prisoner explained, "Gambling and conniving were once so widely rampant that it was not safe to walk through the Big-Yard with candy or other eatables. . . . Pen sets were formerly the medium of exchange for the element that call themselves 'sports.'"[53]

If prisoners could not win something they wanted through luck or skill, they might be able to buy it outright—if they had the cash. Most worked in the jute mill or at other unwaged tasks, so the cash economy remained beyond their reach, unless friends on the outside—family members, especially, with money to spare—could help. This shifted much of the burden of incarceration onto prisoners' wives, girlfriends, and families, who were forced to subsidize their incarceration. Of course, not all prisoners were lucky enough to have people on the outside to support them.

Though cash had been a useful medium of exchange—risky because it was contraband—food was also valuable. A Folsom prisoner explained that "[t]he hill gardens inside the walls could be a continual source of food for the main line. Instead of this, however, they are all private enterprises. Melons, onions, lettuce, and so forth, are raised by the ton and sold by the inmates to other inmates."[54] Illegal, "black market" exchange was very much the norm. In point of fact, a transaction only became "corrupt" when it was identified as such by investigators, or by the prisoners who were cheated or violated in the process. Otherwise, this was simply how the penal world operated.

Some guards tried to develop their own systems for preventing prisoners' conniving, but it was an uphill battle. A notably agitated Joseph H. Fletcher, captain of the yard at San Quentin, went so far as to make his own stamp to put on his documents. But prisoners made copies of his stamp.

> They can make anything. Stamps don't mean anything. Signatures don't mean anything. Keys don't mean anything in the prison. You can go in there and lock something or other, and in half an hour there will be a dozen keys just like it.[55]

Fletcher also described drinking, gambling, and sex:

> Well, of course, so far as gambling and degeneracy and drinking home-made hootch is concerned, in my opinion, as long as we have jail houses like this, we will have that going on. We can do everything that we can to prevent it, but at the same time, we know that it goes on.[56]

Clearly, guarding prisoners was endlessly frustrating. Guards knew too well that corruption was rampant within the prison, and that some prisoners did all too well for themselves. Prisoners who controlled the kitchen could get their friends an extra steak while mainline prisoners had to eat what they called "jute balls" instead of meat balls because so little meat made it into their diets. One prison worker testified that the milk Folsom's mainline prisoners drank had a lot of the "American River in it."[57] California's penal economy allowed for certain inmates to emerge as skillful manipulators of the prison market. Those prisoners, thanks to their political acumen, charisma, personal connections, or job in the prison, developed and exploited conceptual maps of penal power structures for their own gain. When they did so, it was often with the collusion of the prison system itself. If building tenders were masters of violence and sexual violence, con bosses were the masters of penal commodity markets.

Con Bosses: Politicians, Productive Economies, and Personal Gain

Violence among California prisoners was relatively common, but physical strength was not the core of overt and covert power networks. Instead, the most important prisoners in California's prisons, known as con bosses, drew their authority from their position in the prison's productive economy. Con bosses managed prison shops at San Quentin and Folsom, such as the shoe shop, the clothes shop, or the jute mill. Instead of trading blows, they traded shoes, steaks, cigarettes, and good time toward release. Control of labor processes and commodity markets, then, became the defining feature of California prisons' covert markets, and its hegemonic masculinity.

In a 1933 publication, one San Quentin prisoner defined a con boss as "an inmate at the head of a department . . . usually appointed for superior knowledge and experience. . . . [a] man who watches over all the work."[58] Con bosses maintained control of productive processes on the state's behalf, earning a degree of personal control in the process. Like building tenders in Texas, they worked at the state's behest. W. H. West, a free worker in charge of the laundry facility at Folsom, explained how the con bosses fit into the industrial mechanisms. It just made good sense, he reasoned, to delegate authority to certain "key men."

> Well, I will tell you: running a gang of men like this, is more or less the same as running them outside. . . . In any laundry, every department has to have somebody that you have to hold responsible, and once you get a crew that you have a little amount of dependence in, you will have a pretty smooth working crew, because they will keep the others working, and they will keep the stealing down to a minimum.[59]

Con bosses would keep theft to a minimum—or more likely, regularize it under their control and therefore make production predicable. Nevertheless, many keepers felt that theft in the prison was inevitable. "As far as theft is concerned, there will always be theft. You can't stop it."[60] In a dominating system that relied on the obedience of selected overseers as well as on the repression of other, creative people, subversion would be contained as much as possible into manageable paths.[61] This was the sort of give-and-take between free personnel and inmates that Gresham Sykes described as a "defect of total power"—some rules needed to be bent for the prison to run smoothly.[62]

Though con bosses worked directly under guards and paid managers, they had considerable independence, which connoted—in prison as elsewhere—masculine status. Occasionally con bosses could come to understand the extent of their authority and their importance in the prison system, and get out of control. Laundry manager W. H. West testified about Big Slim Hale, a Folsom con boss who became too powerful for the good of the prison:

He has practically built this institution. He has been a con boss all his life around here. He is very capable. . . . Some 22 years I think he has been around here, in and out, and I would say that he was an exceptionally good pusher, as we call them, but I do think that at times he got out of hand. I had to step on his hands several times, because I thought he was going too far, and he always calmed down and got right in place again.[63]

This was the sort of power sharing and negotiation perhaps typical of hegemonic relationships, but it was all too clear that Hale's "pushing" ability did little for the inmates beneath him. Bosses who pressed too hard might upset the tense equilibrium of consent, fear, and boredom. When they began to "push" against guards, they provoked antagonism and crisis within the system itself.

Folsom's power structures came to public light in an investigation beginning in 1943 when outside reporters learned that Lloyd Sampsell, a prisoner assigned as the cook at the Straloch Farm harvest camp near Davis, had been making weekend trips to see his girlfriend in San Francisco. Much like the bracero program, prison harvest camps at Straloch and elsewhere were developed to address California's wartime agricultural labor shortage. As the scandal developed, Folsom warden Clyde Plummer made (and surely regretted) numerous glib excuses for Sampsell. According to the warden, Sampsell was merely taking "French leave" from the camp for the weekend. More important, he suggested, Sampsell was always back to work by Monday morning. Plummer handled the politics of the incident too lightly for his own good, but the media were also taken by Sampsell's charisma. He was already known in the press as the "Yacht Bandit." While other famous robbers would capitalize on fast automobiles and the interstate highway system to evade capture, Sampsell earned the moniker because his gang traveled and hid out on a boat during a series of robberies along the West Coast.[64]

Over the course of the investigation, in which the public learned about harvest camp prisoners' access to alcohol and the ease of their mobility, it became clear that Sampsell was a powerful man at Folsom. According to Albert Mundt, a disgruntled former Folsom clerk, Sampsell had been able to ingratiate himself with the warden. Eventually he became the con boss in charge of the education department, an office from which he gained "freedom of the institution." No guards ever confronted or challenged Sampsell, Mundt believed, "because he was known as one of Plummer's men, and came and went as he pleased."[65] Sampsell's authority was charismatic, but also came from his ability to organize and locate himself in covert networks of favors, gifts, and punishments.

Though Lloyd Sampsell was powerful, Mundt called Burroughs McGraw Folsom's "con king." According to Mundt, McGraw could "subject guards to his control and to his orders, and guards were definitely fearful of McGraw's influence."[66] Perhaps an indication of McGraw's power was that Sampsell, rather than McGraw, became far better known in the 1943–1944 investigation. It was reputed that McGraw could even get an early release for prisoners. However, in confidential testimony to the Alco Investigating Committee, a former guard named Osborne suggested that "McGraw is just a tool" for another prisoner named Sheldon, the con boss who ran the print shop.[67] The webs of deception, interpretation, understanding, and misunderstanding rendered the actual functioning of power opaque, and members of the investigating committee were unlikely to get to the bottom of it.

Burroughs Madison McGraw had a long history in the California Prison System. Described as "an expert forger" by the Los Angeles *Times*, he was arrested in 1923, when he was nineteen.[68] He was in and out of the prison system through the 1940s, and, like Sampsell, ascended to a high rank at Folsom. He was reputedly "arrogant in his contacts with the free personnel, and impulsive and overbearing with the prisoners" while assigned to an outside camp—itself a privileged position in the penal system. McGraw "constantly posed as an intimate and personal friend of the Warden and has sold the idea to the prisoners to such extent that many of them believe[d]" that he could—and did—acquire good time credits for prisoners. "And he has more or less substantiated his claims by exhibiting many letters of an extremely friendly and personal nature, purportedly from the Warden."[69] Whether these were forgeries or originals mattered little; in either case, they boosted his prestige.

But McGraw's professional skills also placed him high in the official prison economy. In late 1942, after being returned to San Quentin for a parole violation, McGraw requested to work in the prison's administrative office. W. H. Baxter, the San Quentin accountant, looked on his request favorably, and reported to Warden Duffy that "McGraw is a high-class accountant who worked several years in the Accounting Office at Folsom and is familiar with every phase of prison accounting." Baxter further explained that McGraw's "industry and conduct while working in the Accounting office at Folsom was highly satisfactory." He closed his letter to the warden by pleading, "I assure you I am very much in need of experienced accountants."[70] But McGraw was not to stay long at San Quentin. He quickly was transferred to Folsom, quite possibly at Clyde Plummer's request. McGraw received trustee status as soon as he arrived.[71]

Folsom's Warden Plummer and Burroughs McGraw had a close relationship. Plummer reportedly played cards with McGraw weekly, had him over for meals at his home, and once gave him a five-dollar hat as a gift.[72] Prison officials have long used prisoners as their private labor, and Plummer was no exception: McGraw did Plummer's personal taxes. In a detailed letter he sent from San Quentin, McGraw explained Plummer's various options for shuffling his reported income along with his wife's to lower their tax payments. He closed the letter on a friendly note: "Sorry it wasn't possible to give you a hand this year. We can't always do what we'd like to do. How are you feeling?"[73]

Not only did McGraw have connections with the highest levels of the Folsom prison administration, but he had a following of his own. Though many despised him (inmate Daniel Forsythe complained he'd been double crossed by McGraw because Forsythe had conned him some eight years earlier in the Los Angeles County jail),[74] Lyle Egan explained that "McGraw was a man that stuck up for the inmates a lot. McGraw was for McGraw, first and always, but he stuck up for the inmates. . . . [H]e was kind of a front man"—at least for those who paid him.[75] McGraw's authority, then, combined elements of business acumen, formal appointment, and personal charisma, which extended upward to the warden and downward to those below him.

Indeed, prisoners like McGraw and Sampsell, who knew how to operate within the system—and were bolstered by their official bureaucratic positions—could make out relatively well for themselves. This knowledge of the prison elevated some con bosses from being a sort of middle manager into what others called, disparagingly, but also with admiration, a "politician." Prisoners outside their networks ate the worst food and drank river water instead of milk. And if prisoners knew the right people, and had some capital to bargain with, they could even shorten the length of their sentence. With a few dollars, one prisoner wrote, the official hierarchy could be upended.

> If I decide I want a cell move, and I put $5 into the hands of the right people, I get the move. Otherwise, either I stay where I am, or get another filthy cell. The same thing applies to getting a job. A little money in the right place will buy any job in the institution. It makes no difference whether I am capable or not. I can also buy my way out to a forestry or harvestry camp.[76]

Lyle Egan, the Folsom Classification Committee clerk, thought McGraw was one of those people in the right place. Egan never could quite figure out how McGraw rigged credits, but he was sure McGraw was up to no good. "Well, it is a hard thing to put your finger on any one thing, but I felt that . . . if anybody wanted credits McGraw could get them a month or so. I think I know the method in which he operated, because he used it all the time." Egan suspected that a prisoner would request a letter from a work supervisor—from Mr. West in the laundry, from Mr. Daseking in the mess hall—that would ask for the prisoner to be given a month or six months' worth of credits. It was unclear whether McGraw forged the letters or exerted pressure or offered rewards so that the supervisors would write them. In any case, "McGraw was smart," and he would have the letter on file in case he was challenged, Egan said.[77]

Egan admitted that he had no hard proof about what McGraw was doing. Nevertheless, he reported, "I am sure of it in my own mind." Egan became suspicious when he saw a prisoner who had maintained a perfect record serving a full ten-year sentence. With a perfect disciplinary record and earning good time toward an early release, he should have served six and a half years and been eligible for parole. But he served the full ten years.

> And I said "It is a shame when anybody can go out there and work, and nobody pays any attention to him, and they don't get anything, and these other guys,—the politicians,—get everything," and that is what made me boil over . . . the poor fellow probably didn't know where to apply, . . . while the other fellows,—if you are a friend of the con bosses, they will be sure that you apply.[78]

If the man had been "in the inner circle, he would have gotten the credits. That is the way I feel about it."[79]

The power that con bosses, and especially politicians, wielded and the patronage networks they mobilized, based on their positions in the prison's productive and administrative economy, was entirely about benefiting themselves. They did little for those prisoners who were not well connected or had nothing to offer them. In this, even the subaltern networks of prison authority were complex and contradictory: they simultaneously undermined official state power while stratifying prisoners according to their positions in the political, racial, monetary, and sexual economies. For all this, they allowed the prison to function as a complex institution. For prisoners and state representatives at Folsom, all of these were encapsulated in the term "politics."

Even guards were frustrated by this system. Martin Eng, who began his stint as a guard in 1929, was infuriated by prisoners' lack of respect for him. "Well," he complained, "it is getting to the point where a guard almost has to take his hat off for an inmate."[80] Moreover, patronage was prevalent among the guard force, and not just among prisoners and con bosses. A few years earlier his shift had been changed to the second watch. This was effectively a demotion. Eng testified that a guard who was not "in" had no authority at all. Like many of the lesser guards in Folsom's patronage regime, Eng felt relatively powerless. Yet guards could find ways to recoup that sense of control.

Prisoners' Collective Action and Guard Violence

If guards were frustrated by the con boss regime, prisoners had it worse. The whole of the institution was, of course, designed to make them suffer. According to inmate Robert Tasker, imprisonment generated a seething, universal hatred. "I, too, hate my fellow convict, and am, in turn, cordially hated. It is not because of any particular blemish in my body or character, but because I am irrevocably an integral part of the prison." He continued,

> The convict must hate prison and all in it; therefore, he cannot bring himself to throw in his lots with those he hates. There can be no unity in prison, but merely dissension. There will be no organized attempts for unlawful freedom; riots will come only when the indignities transcend the individual's natural prejudice against those with whom he must join forces.[81]

With feelings of alienation deeply etched into the walls and culture that surrounded them, it was rare for inmates to ever join together.

Nevertheless, at the end of the decade, San Quentin prisoners began a modest collective movement against their keepers. In May 1938, five hundred prisoners undertook a "Folded Arms Strike," demanding the restoration of merit-based "rest periods" that had been lost through an administrative change.[82]

Inmate H. Buderous von Carlshausen described other actions at the Walled City. Early in 1939, he said, there had been a

> series of strikes by inmates in protest against being denied the privilege of enjoying the very few minutes in sunshine, after work and before entering the dining room for lunch—and later—supper. Prison routine calls for

sixteen hours daily inside their cells for the greater part of the population. Orders were issued to march from the shops direct to the mess halls. . . . The strikes followed. The orders were withdrawn.[83]

San Quentin's prisoners were successful in their collective action to see the skies before lunch and supper. On February 1, prisoners mounted what the press reported as an "ominously sullen hunger strike," demanding less corned beef hash, or "corned willie," as they called it. Four thousand prisoners refused to eat that evening. Fifteen hundred of the strikers gave up when Warden Court Smith promised that none of the strikers would be punished, and they would eat spaghetti and meatloaf rather than hash for lunch the following day.[84] More than a thousand continued the strike for another day, and despite being locked in their cells and put on bread and water diets, 133 maintained their protest for a day longer.[85] Vic Johnson, a Marine Fireman's Union member imprisoned during strike battles with Standard Oil, said San Quentin was ripe for unrest in 1939. "[T]he general conditions and atmosphere got so bad over there that something just had to let go."[86]

Tensions remained high in the wake of the February strike. Rumors that jute mill prisoners would demand shorter hours circulated through the prison and made the outside newspapers. "We're ready to handle it," administrators reported. "We've got extra men on the job."[87] On March 21, perhaps emboldened by earlier successes, sixteen hundred prisoners staged another food strike. According to von Carlshausen,

Rumors had circulated that a "food-strike" might take place. The general agreement among the men was to obey all rules, use no violence, perform all required work, but to consume no more of the unsavory, dirty, repetitious meals. The apparent success of the small strikes perhaps gave birth to the dream that more improvement could be gained with a large demonstration.[88]

Von Carlshausen's narrative is worth quoting further:

One hash-day-noon—this hash was but half-cooked during previous weeks sent hundreds to the hospital with stomach complaints—when the whistles blew for line-up, about one hundred men grouped themselves in the center of the Big-yard . . . bordered on three sides by the fortress-like prison blocks, with the two joining mess halls to the west—and silently desisted efforts of guards to join the remainder. There were some tense moments during which thousands in line looked uncertainly at us few, and then, miracle of miracles, like droplets from icicles, the lines melted away, the little group grew like a whirlpool. The only voices raised were those who cheered the fellows joining-up. The guards were baffled. There was no way to shove hundreds that grew to thousands in but a few minutes. There was no violence. Then came a storm of laughter—the laughter of relief and redicule [sic] too, redicule [sic] for vein [sic] efforts to move this body. Every man felt like a brother to the strangest "fish" in the yard. Just a few hundreds ate lunch—there are tories in every clime.[89]

In von Carlshausen's description, the ever-present antagonism subsided in the process of their protest. Indeed, the strike itself generated a feeling of community and solidarity through the male-gendered fictive kinship of "brotherhood," joining old-timers with the newest and strangest "fish." As the prisoners united against their keepers, von Carlshausen reflected that laughter and the refusal to comply were their most powerful weapons: non-violent, disarming, aural, and communal—an assault on guards' and state authority by way of humor. The laughter bespoke their fear and relief and their community as prisoners in protest.

As we waited in the yard, wondering what would happen to us, expecting machine guns to cut loose any minute from the cat-walks above where the half-dozen guards grew to a half-company, a wild rumor was born and spread: *For the first time in the history of his regime*—according to the "Old Timers" . . . *[t]he then warden would talk to us en masse in the Big-Yard, to learn our wants*. More guards joined the rails, armed with gas bombs, masks, riot guns and other armnament [sic]. . . . Then, surrounded by another dozen guards and officials, the former warden actually entered the yard and made some nervous promises of better food. Meanwhile, a number of men suspected of being organizers of the strike (they weren't) disappeared from our midst. We heard rumors that they were on the "shelf" or in the "hole." The tempo of the men was for continuing the strike until their fellows were released from this special punishment. . . . Many did not go to work, and, as evening came, only a handful actually entered the dining rooms. From that night on, for nearly a week, very few men left their cells at any time, although many did go to work. Meanwhile, and while the Big-Yard still swarmed, news-planes flew low over the institution to take pictures, for, I understand, the warden would not allow a single reporter within the reservation to learn what was going on.[90]

A guard named Richardson later gave his recollection. In the investigation that followed, Governor Olson asked him, "What was the riot? Where were they rioting? What was done in the yard?" Richardson explained, "Well, it really wasn't a riot. They just refused to go to work." Olson continued to question him:

Q: What did they say?
A: Well, they said the food was bad, and they wasn't going to work until they got to see the Warden or the Captain.
Q: And then they were taken to Siberia?
A: Yes. Well, we took them to the Captain first.
Q: Is that substantially what you mean when the reference has been made to a riot; that their food was bad and that they wouldn't go to work until they could see the Warden or the Captain?
A: That is right.
Q: And that is all they did?
A: Well, they all got in a big crowd and wouldn't go to work.[91]

Forty-two prisoners were identified as the ringleaders and brought to "Siberia," the solitary confinement area at San Quentin.[92] The ringleaders, according to Warden Smith's secretary, Barnett House, were immature "jeer leaders," with nothing more substantive than a grudge against officials. They were, House suggested, "young hoodlums, mostly in their 20's, reform school graduates and small-time robbers and auto thieves. There isn't an old 'con' or a mature mind among them."[93] Most of the strikers' case files have been destroyed, and consequently, it is impossible to know the races, ages, or sentences of most of the strikers. But it does seem that they were low within prison hierarchies. At least ten of them worked in the jute mill, the prison's worst assignment.[94]

Located on the top floor of the North Cell Block, the west side of Siberia was used for solitary confinement, and the east side was the Condemned Row for prisoners sentenced to death. Guard W. G. Lewis, the officer in charge of Siberia, ordered the strikers to strip and had the inmate barber shave their heads. Strikers were given shoddy clothing, ragged underwear, or no underwear at all, and doubled up in the solitary cells. Afterwards, all the prisoners were made to stand on "the spot," gray circles painted on the floor, some twenty-two inches in diameter, and commanded not to move or shift their weight for eight hours. If a prisoner lost his balance or moved, he would be beaten.[95] "The spot" functioned exactly as did "standing on the barrel" in Texas.

Shortly after the food strikers began their time on the spot, captain of the guard Ralph H. New, known in the prison as "rough-house New," told them that they would spend the next six months in solitary. Upon hearing this, the strikers disobeyed and sat down. Lewis called for reinforcements. Prisoners were ordered back into the solitary cells; they obeyed. One at a time, Lewis ordered them out and onto the spot. Guards beat them, one at a time, across the head, arms, torso, and legs.[96] They used an assortment of homemade weapons: clubs; a rosin-coated rubber hose filled with buckshot, with a jute-wound handgrip; and a heavy, metal spring sewn in leather.[97] Prisoners offered no resistance, though they doubled over to protect themselves as best they could.[98] When one guard tired, another took his place. After all of the prisoners were systematically beaten, Lewis heard a prisoner talking to his cellmate. "This man hasn't got enough," Lewis shouted. "Come back down here and hit him a few more." The guard, obeying his superior's orders, hit him four or five more times.[99]

A guard named Trafton also participated in the beatings, which he maintained were necessary, "for the safebeing [sic] of the prison."[100]

If those men had gotten out of hand, and continued to defy the rules and regulations, and so on, the men in the yard—they have ways of finding out what had been done, and they would have soon figured "Well, we have control of the prison now." Consequently they would have rioted, and various other things. I know that the men on the walls would have suppressed the rioting. It would probably have meant the lives of a good many prisoners, and probably some of the guards.[101]

In other words, some prisoners needed to be beaten, so others would not be shot. For Trafton, as well as for others who participated in the beatings, nothing less was at stake than the prison itself. In the face of emboldened prisoners, they believed that the strikers needed to be broken as individuals and as a group, and the guards saw no other option than concentrated violence. But such violence on behalf of the state was also highly personal violence, among people whose bodies touched, who breathed the same air and each others' smells. For reformers, it was the intimacy of the violence that troubled them.

Indeed, when guards whipped prisoners, they thought they were protecting the prison from chaos. But more than institutional order was at stake: Lewis and other guards beat strikers to reinscribe personal authority and teach a lesson in violent mastery.[102] They were hardly alone among the nation's prison guards. As others said of prisoners, "You can never trust any of 'em; they'd cut your throat and never give it a second thought." Another testified that if "a con" got surly, "we'd . . . whip him until there was no fight left in him."[103] The beating that Lewis gave was not the bloodless force of an abstract state. It was a highly personal, intimate performance of power. Lewis struck Donald Harris not just with kicks and blows from a club; he also "gassed him with a pyrene fire extinguisher," leaving him unconscious for hours.[104] Another guard asked a prisoner if he had had enough, if he was broken and would submit. The prisoner answered "Yes." The guard then "hit him two or three times; and he [the guard] says 'can't you say 'Sir.'"[105] After answering "Yes, Sir," he was placed back in his cell. Mere submission was insufficient: the prisoner was made to call his aggressor "sir," to affirm the guard's authoritative, personal masculinity, to end the beating.

In the midst of the investigation that followed, Culbert Olson, California's sole New Dealer governor, charged the Board of Prison Directors with tolerating egregious violence. In the 1939 investigation, Olson inverted the conventional order of good and evil. Prisoners were figured as victimized workers organizing for dignity and humane treatment, attacked by zealous and irrational guards wielding batons and lead-packed hoses. In the progressive moment of the late New Deal, this sort of state violence was to be curtailed. Interpersonal violence should be minimized in favor of rational planning and reorganization. Though the guards' and the Prison Board's defenders argued that violence was necessary, Olson claimed the moral high ground. Mr. Olshausen, the attorney representing the state against the Board of Prison Directors, quoted Penal Code Section 681, which prohibited any corporal punishment, into the testimony, and reiterated,

> If the punishment is cruel, it is forbidden. If it is corporal, it is forbidden. If it is unusual, it is forbidden. In other words, the Code Section without any qualification forbids all forms of corporal punishment in prisons or in other State institutions. . . . [T]he mere argument that punishment may be justified by circumstances is excluded by the language of the Code section itself.[106]

Invoking the classic modernist and progressive narrative of punishment gradually becoming less brutal, Olshausen referred to corporal punishment as "forms of old-style punishment" entirely inappropriate to a modern penal system.[107] While critics charged Olson with political maneuverings in reorganizing the prison board, he clearly intended a reformed and less violent institution. In fact, the very first action the new prison board took in 1940 was to abolish the practice of making prisoners stand on the spot. In a short time, Clinton T. Duffy, who replaced Court Smith as warden, dismantled all the locks and doors in the part of the prison formerly known as "the Dungeon."[108] Equally symbolic, Olson dismissed the entire Board of Prison Directors for complicity after the fact in the beatings, and for permitting such a system to exist. Reflecting on a regime that would allow these punishments, inmate von Carlshausen said, "The word justice seems sheerest mockery. The claim of reform violent hypocrisy."[109]

Queens: Sexual Capital and Reformist Fear

Capacity for violence was a cornerstone of manhood for guards and prisoners alike, but some prisoners could sidestep that kind in favor of a different sort. California officials and inmates alike wrote about queens, the flamboyantly effeminate men among them. At times they wrote with humor and affection, at others with fear and disgust, seeing queens as a source of contagious disorder. In either case, queens were as important to the sexual and political life of California institutions as the con bosses or the guards. In 1943, reformers would find them as troublesome as con bosses or violent guards had been.

"We know them the minutes they step through the front gates," wrote San Quentin physician Leo Stanley. "They are known as the 'Queens,' the 'Fairies,' the 'Queeries,' and by other names. Many have decidedly feminine characteristics. A peculiar twist to the hips, a sly smirk, and other motions and mannerisms betray them. . . . The 'old wolves,'" Stanley suggested, "show a furtive interest."[110] Stanley couched his own spectatorship in the language of scientific observation, but his eye for men was as keen as those of any of the "wolves."[111]

The long traditions of California working-class men's relative openness to homosexuality, from the Gold Rush through the 1940s and beyond, allowed for relatively overt expressions of men's effeminacies on the outside and behind bars. Effeminate men's prominence emerged from the queer and drag cultures that grew in the Golden State and especially San Francisco's bars and clubs. The prewar sexual culture George Chauncey analyzed in New York was perhaps even more expansive in "wide open" San Francisco, where sailors, hobos, and other working-class men might have sex with fairies or queens and find no reason to consider themselves as anything other than normal, "real" men. This tradition, driven underground in San Francisco in the 1920s but reemerging in the 1930s, ensured that a range of sexualities remained an acceptable part of male inmates' lives. At least the inmates thought so.[112] Officials confronted a more vexing issue. As agents of moral stringency, espousing fears of medical and behavioral contagion—and with their own masculinities at stake—they strove to contain male prisoners' sexual being.

Queens validated rather than undermined the otherwise dominant masculinities that most self-identified "straight" prisoners felt. As historian Regina Kunzel recently demonstrated, as long as prisoners maintained (or claimed to maintain) the "masculine," penetrating role in sex rather than the "feminine," receptive role, their self-identities as "normal men" were secure.[113] The all-male world of the men's prison heightened that sensibility.

Queens drew on a different source of authority than either con bosses or building tenders, but they were no less a part of the prison's covert markets. Prison queens' capital was sexual, and came from their male femininity.[114] Queens—who assumed feminine characteristics and roles in sex and behavior—could exchange sex for favors, sometimes operating as sex workers but also, at times, fulfilling the role of wife or long-term partner. Queens set themselves against the dictates of more commonplace dominating masculinities that stressed physical power, control of labor, and so forth. By celebrating and emphasizing their femininity, they developed a significant measure of agency. Often just a few visual cues were necessary. Fairies did not "betray" themselves, as Stanley suggested. They actively cultivated the signs their ever-attentive audiences would see. Many went further than a "peculiar twist of the hips," despite the limited resources available. Bleach from the laundry room could lighten hair, chalk could be crushed into face powder, grime rubbed from iron bars could become eye shadow, and red tomato-can labels, soaked in water, made rouge.[115] If performance was a key aspect of fairy interaction with men and with each other, San Quentin offered countless opportunities for much-appreciated display. The main yard was ideal: prisoner Malcolm Braly recalled that "the queens had been free to swish around the yard," even going so far as to "carry on open love affairs."[116]

For all of their openness, queens' authority operated within covert forms of power, and especially commodity exchange. For their affections, queens enjoyed a "continued flow of favors that come their way."[117] Their sexuality conferred capital in the form of fine clothes or commodities. Moulin, "one of our noted queens," according to Folsom's laundry man, used his sexuality to better his life behind bars. The laundry man marveled over Moulin's silk-lined suit, which, he guessed, must have cost at least two cartons of cigarettes. Indeed, Moulin's suit was "much better . . . made, [with] . . . all silk linings, and . . . an outside label on it, . . . it looked like an outside suit," nothing like the ordinary, rough-hewn and ill-fitting prison garb.[118] Clothes connoted status as well as comfort; it was hardly surprising that inmates would prize the subtle or not-so-subtle distinctions that would differentiate them from the rest.

Moulin may have had sex with multiple partners, or he may have been involved in a longer-term relationship with another man, his "husband" or a "jocker." Each had its appeal to effeminate men, and not least, according to officials, were the economic benefits—"from the commissary, and the protection that comes with it, and all that."[119] Nevertheless, though they speculated about it, officials were loath to acknowledge the possibilities of pleasure or the importance of intimacy—rarities in prison life—which queens and their partners might develop. Specific records on the nature of these emotional attachments are slim (perhaps unsurprisingly, given that sodomy remained a punishable offense and permanently marked an inmate's case file). Yet Leo Stanley at least partially recognized the commitments that queens and their partners shared. A photo from his collection identifies a besuited man and queen in drag as "A. Watson, Negro, Lover of C. Washington, Negro homosexual."[120] Letters later confiscated by San Quentin officials gave insight into the depth of some prisoners' feelings. "I have known a lot of queers," one inmate wrote to his partner, "but I never fell in love with them as I have with you." Another finished a letter to his inmate wife by confessing, "I love you with all my Heart."[121]

Queens' effeminacies allowed them to avoid some kinds of violence. By validating rather than threatening other prisoners' manhood, they posed little threat to masculine status. Because they presented themselves as fairies rather than as men, an accidental bump in the hallway or the mess hall would be unlikely to escalate into a fight. This was an important tactic, but it might not always work. Queens might be understood to be fair game for a man to claim, and they were not always wooed. As a result, queens could and did fight when necessary, even against guards when called to.[122]

When they partnered with husbands or jockers, queens could have a source of protection, and someone to fight on their behalf. Later inmates testified to the sense of well-being this could afford.[123] From the husbands' perspective, the control of a queen publicly validated their manhood, along with offering the solace of intimacy and the comforts of something that might be recognizable as home. But this, too, could come at a price for the queen. If a queen paired up with a "man," the queen could become the man's property—much as wives or girlfriends were on the outside. Men's jealousies could lead to murder. The familiarity of such domestic violence led some officials to realize just how similar these relationships could be to those on the outside.[124]

While jealousy led some men to beat their prison wives, control over queens also led men to fight each other. Folsom's Captain Ryan believed that two-thirds of stabbings at Folsom occurred when a prisoner lost possession of "his" queen. "We had a cutting scrape only two or three months ago," Ryan explained. "A fellow named Morgan and a Mexican named Garcia,—it was over . . . Evalsizor,—both of them were cut, and it was over this queen."[125]

Queens or not, prisoners were adept at making spaces for sex. There were certain areas where prisoners were relatively safe, and which they might make sites for illicit pleasure. Strategically draped sheets could make some privacy in a cell, but might also call a guard's attention. Folsom's baseball alley was popular for a while.[126] The bath house and the laundry were also identified as likely venues. Guards were posted there to watch for illicit sexual acts. But Captain Ryan had heard rumors that prisoners could buy privacy from guards and use the woodshed. So, to circumvent guard complicity, he had the shed knocked down.[127] But closed spaces were not the only ones available for homosexual contact. Guard O. L. Jensen caught two prisoners having sex one morning in the Folsom Upper Yard. A small, off-set space next to a building afforded some privacy, but it also meant the partners could not see who was coming. Jensen reported, "neither inmate could see me approaching." While Jensen took them away for punishment, one swore, "Dam it, here goes all my good time[,] and I had such a good record."[128] An important source of pleasure, sex was also a punishable offense. The ambiguities of prisoners' sexualities, a seemingly inescapable part of the prison world, would provide one foundation for massive prison overhaul in the 1940s.

It was hardly uncommon for inmates otherwise understood by officials as heterosexual to be caught having sex. "They surprise you around here sometimes," explained Captain Ryan. "Sometimes I think a fellow is O.K., and he is caught in an act of degeneracy." Officials like Ryan saw same-sex sex as a threat made worse by its unpredictability.[129] Even an "okay" prisoner could turn out to be "in danger" of becoming homosexual, and consequently, a source of danger to the rest. In the context of such uncertainty, prison officials may have actually been glad that some prisoners were recognizable queens, who might be managed through punishment, segregation, or work assignment. At least queens were forthright about their sexuality. Officials thought they understood these "true" homosexuals. But when apparently "real" or "normal" men began to have same-sex sex, officials were shocked and confused. Their understandings of sexuality, which increasingly demanded well-defined lines between male/female and homosexual/heterosexual, were inadequate to the world before them.

Prison officials have always been vexed by prisoners' sexualities. They were confused as to where and how to draw the line between homosexual and heterosexual prisoners, but drawing those lines, and asserting a firm definition between normal men and "degenerates," became an obsession in the Depression and the decades that followed. Prisoners, for their part, constantly revealed the ambiguities. Confused and contradictory understandings about the nature of sexuality in and out of prison made controlling inmates' sex a failed effort from the start. Beginning in the 1930s and continuing through the coming decades, prison officials and sexologists around the country developed a differentiation between "situational" and "true" homosexuality. Situational homosexuality was understood as a "normal sex perversion" in which heterosexuals would engage in same-sex sex to satisfy "natural" urges and needs, because there were no members of the "opposite" sex available. This was in contrast to "true" homosexuality, which, they believed, reflected either psychoanalytic manifestations of psychosis or other illnesses.[130] Shoring up the boundaries of men's sexuality was an anxious project when unemployment undercut men's earnings. It would become even more urgent in the 1940s, as men left home to live and fight in close quarters, as women increasingly left home and entered the waged work force, and in the context of increased racial interaction and geographic travel.[131] By the war years, California prison officials would do their best to cordon off homosexuality among male prisoners. Just as stopping "perversion" would be a goal of reform in Texas tanks, preventing sex between men was central to the creation of the California Department of Corrections.

A New Deal for Prisons: Regulating the Economies of Sex, Violence, and Commodity Exchange

By the war years, widespread reform movements were afoot in each state. In California, the 1939 food strike and subsequent Olson investigation, followed by the 1943 Alco investigation of the con boss system, led to the demise of the California Prison System and the formation of the Department of Corrections. Widespread violence, escapes, and scores of self-mutilating prisoners in Texas during the war led, in the immediate postwar years, to another massive investigation and substantive transformation. While there were significant differences between the 1939 investigation at San Quentin, the investigation at Folsom in 1943–1944, and investigations in Texas in 1947, their commonalities point to emphases among prison reformers. In each case, reformers were concerned with the reassertion of governance over markets, bodies, and politics out of control. The interpersonal hierarchies and markets, steeped in violence, sexuality, and commodity exchange, were made by prison guards, wardens, and inmates alike. The indeterminacy as to who the state was and how it operated was increasingly unpalatable for reformers, who saw rational planning and bureaucratic administration as the panacea to social ills. California reformers understood guard violence and con bosses' authority as illegitimate. Prisoners' consensual sex was equally confounding. Texas reform efforts were more muted. Investigators, be they muckrakers or official appointees, identified the dangers of the building tender system, and the systemic propensity for violence and sexual violence. In the end, their solutions proved to be none at all.

If out-of-control guards had been the problem in the 1939 Olson investigation, con bosses and queens emerged from the 1943–1944 Alco investigation as the scourge of the prisons. Most reporting in California newspapers focused on con bosses Lloyd Sampsell and Burroughs McGraw and on the lax conduct in the harvest camps. The public face of prison reform was the need to eliminate the corrupt con boss system. Governor Earl Warren called con boss Lloyd Sampsell's ability to leave harvest camps "the most outrageous thing I have ever heard of in prison management."[132] Moreover, he decried that "the authority of the Con Bosses has often been greater than that of the Captain of the Guard."[133] Predictably, the scandal and public reform centered on the dangers of inmates running loose, a narrative that led, in turn, to an unveiling of the con boss system. The internal politics of the investigation, however, revealed queerer sides to the story. The desire to control queens, and thus eradicate prisoners' sex, was the secret of reform.

California prison officials commonly strove for mastery over space as a way to control sexual behavior and maintain their version of good order. This was the foundation of modern prison policy, after all: control of bodies in space would eliminate the need for the lash. Yet individual officials ran up against a system that was nearly as convoluted for them as it was for prisoners. Even high-ranking officers found the complex institutional formation of the Big House surprisingly difficult to manage. When some tried to regulate inmates' sexuality, they found themselves fighting against the con boss system itself. Prisoners, despite all official efforts to the contrary, continued to have sex.

K. L. Buchanan was the Folsom turnkey. As such, he was in charge of inmates' cell assignments, and was particularly well suited to enforce the policy that no "known homosexuals" be permitted to share a cell. But cell assignments involved much more than a simple administrative decision. As he explained to the Governor's Investigating Committee in 1943, "You have the power to move them around to a certain extent, but you can't move everybody around as you like. If you interfere with the steward's help, he will come out with a complaint against you for moving his men around. And if you move any of the office forces, you have the office force to contend with. If you don't put them in the cells that they want to be put in, you will have trouble with the other departments, and you will get a call from the Warden, or somebody else."[134]

Buchanan related the context of his frustrations. Inmates in the kitchen crew had been celling together and having sex, and in order to break them up, he needed to move a group of prison clerks from their cells. But the clerks did not want to be moved, and started a petition against him. He explained, "There are certain cells around here that they want, and if they don't get them, they just put the heat on, and you just leave them alone." Senator Deuel asked, "They put the heat on from what source?" Answer: "From the front office." Deuel: "From the Warden's office?" Buchanan: "Yes."[135]

Because the inmate office staff had a direct line to the warden, even the turnkey was constrained. Moreover, the alleged connections between Warden Plummer and prisoners who had sex proved a powerful line of attack for those who wanted Plummer's ouster. Plummer was vulnerable because he had a relatively laissez-faire attitude toward prisoners' sex, which he understood as specific to the penal context. Captain Ryan, who was one of Plummer's most consistent detractors, and was invested in his downfall, told investigators about a conversation he had with the warden about prisoners' sex. "Oh, Hell," Ryan reported the warden saying, "I don't blame them. . . . You would do it up here." To which Ryan responded, "Like Hell I would." Plummer, Ryan believed, just "didn't seem to care much about it."[136]

Albert Mundt, another of Plummer's critics, agreed. Mundt saw inmates' sexuality as a disease run rampant, and he used Plummer's seemingly lax attitude about same-sex sex to attack him.[137] Mundt accused Plummer of permitting homosexual "degeneracy" to persist because, Mundt suspected, Plummer believed "it was not harmful and most probably because it was or appeared easier to permit such activity." Mundt also alleged that Plummer discouraged guards from enforcing prohibitions against sex by instigating a new policy. Whenever a guard caught prisoners "in an act of sodomy or other compromising position," the officer was to take a smear from the convict's penis to be introduced as evidence at a hearing before the warden. In other words, the guard is required to . . . personally wipe off the inmate's penis. The guards have taken the position that they will not perform such acts and have recognized the order for what it was apparently meant to be, namely, an order not to arrest convicts for degeneracy.[138]

The fact that men had sex with men might have challenged some guards' sense of their own masculinity, but then again, it might have validated their "normal" manhood and presumed desire. Some, like Lt. W. E. Kamp, shared Plummer's views and were not overly concerned with men's sex.[139] Others were outraged. Guard J. J. Solberg complained that "you can't get no backing" on homosexuality charges.[140] When he brought charges that were not then enforced by superiors, his own prestige was diminished, because prisoners no longer respected his authority to punish. Moreover, taking a swab would require a guard to touch another man's penis, queering him in the process.

Plummer, unsurprisingly, had a different opinion. He explained before investigators that there had been a number of cases where guards accused men of sodomy without evidence, and, when the case came to the trial board (which included Plummer and the captain of the yard), the inmates would "out-talk the guard, and the guard would get confused, and he wouldn't know whether he saw what he thought he had seen." Having worked on the Los Angeles vice squad, Plummer said he was accustomed to the need for evidence before going to court, but guards, who never needed proof to punish their wards, took exception to such a burden. Moreover, according to Plummer, guards "resented the proposition that an inmate's word is worth anything at all. . . . Evidence is evidence, and most of the guardline have never had to appear in court, and they don't know what evidence is." Plummer continued, "I have been on a police force long enough to know that police officers make mistakes."[141]

From Plummer's perspective, the policy on wipes was imposed not to prevent guards from policing inmate sex but rather to replicate the contours of a trial (with himself as judge, of course). Plummer believed that guards had been framing prisoners under the predecessor Larkin administration, and he wanted this stopped. The prison, Plummer thought, should be a place where inmates and guards would argue their cases when an inmate was charged with an infraction. The implication that guards were fallible, and that inmates might need to be listened to, offended many guards.

But Plummer's case was further undermined when his detractors accused him of homosexuality. He was only the most recent official whose career was undermined through such insinuations: Thomas Mott Osborne and Miriam van Waters's careers were ruined on similar accusations.[142] He was not charged outright, but Albert Mundt told investigators that Plummer spent time with sexually questionable prisoners. The warden, he reported, employed a prisoner named Baker—a known associate of homosexuals and member of the weightlifting and tumbling team, no less—as his personal masseur. And, Plummer reputedly took massages at his personal residence. Plummer also reputedly assigned Baker to supervise the children's playground at the Folsom reservation. Mundt indicated that he stopped the assignment from taking place, but when he left Folsom, it did go through.[143]

The damage was done. With the public investigation charging widespread corruption, and the internal investigation charging sexual degeneracy, Plummer's tenure was over. The scandal afforded the long-time anticorruption activist Earl Warren the opportunity to overhaul the California prisons. Plummer would be replaced, and the California Prison System would be fundamentally restructured into a single administrative unit, renamed the "California Department of Corrections." New architectural features would be used, and more stringent segregation would be enforced to cordon off inmates charged as homosexual from the rest. This would include not just the queens but also, increasingly, the masculine-identifying men caught having sex. Clinton Duffy had been doing just this since his appointment at San Quentin, with special jobs and housing assignments to quarantine identified homosexual prisoners from the "normal" population. "[S]ome play the male role, some the female," Duffy opined, but "all have one thing in common. . . . They are deviates."[144] The strict enforcement of heterosexuality and nonparticipation in any sex was the dream of penal reform and bureaucratic reorganization. Prison reform at Folsom was a highly sexualized—or antisexualized—process. The modern California Department of Corrections emerged from the reorganization in the wake of the investigation. It was a child born of sex between men.

Guard violence and prisoners' sexuality were both anathema to the rational visions of elite state reformers, as violence was sexualized and sexuality overlapped with power and frequently expressed domination. Yet guards—the representatives of the state on the ground and behind bars—frequently saw sex as deviant but violence as necessary, especially when they felt their own personal gendered authority at stake. Guards knew all too well that their best defense, and perhaps the only thing that prevented them from being killed or beaten—or, in their worst nightmares, raped—by rebellious prisoners was their symbolic authority as representatives of the state, bolstered by physical violence. Without that violent capability, guards felt themselves emasculated and physically threatened. This was precisely why the old-line guards resisted elite reforms and why Lee Simmons, Texas general manager from 1931 to 1935, could still advocate whipping as late as the 1970s. This is also why Clinton Duffy, the progressive warden installed after the 1939 investigation, would meet stiff resistance from his guard lines. The guards who demanded continued access to personal violence would have been the last to note the sexual and gendered elements of the foundations of their authority, or to have acknowledged the phallic properties of their clubs and whips. And it was no coincidence that they were among the most vocally opposed to male prisoners' consensual sex. Their opposition to men having sex with men increasingly understood this sex as an abomination to be destroyed rather than a disease to be managed, as did elite reformers and advocates of therapeutic correction.[145] In California, queens would no longer validate "normal" manhood, but threaten it. In Texas, some may have disdained BT violence and rape, but for mainline guards, who used BTs as extensions of their own power, there was nothing wrong with the system at all.

Building tenders and con bosses were invested with and took hold of different types of authority. Con bosses' power grew from their bureaucratic and economic position in the prison hierarchy—they were typically the heads of departments and had access to paperwork and to the prison's productive capacities. Therefore, the hegemonic masculinity in California was of a managerial sort. Texas's building tenders' power was less properly bureaucratic (in the official hierarchy of performing rationally administered tasks, organizing production, and mobilizing labor), though it was sanctioned by wardens and guards. Building tenders' authority came from their unofficially sanctioned violence, and especially sexual violence, and their charge of controlling the spaces of the tanks. BTs were armed by guards, but their presence as keepers of a violent order was decried by the more liberal elements of the penal elite. While California prisons underwent numerous investigations and reform movements in the mid-twentieth century, Texas prisons saw few substantive challenges to the sexually violent regime. Indeed, BTs continued to maintain "order" until the 1980s, when the liberal vision of how punishment should function gained a tenuous, temporary hold in Texas under enforced federal judicial oversight.

Guards occupied a contradictory position as the working-class representatives of the state, whose authority was challenged by prisoners and sometimes undermined by their superiors. They found themselves intertwined in confusing networks over which, despite their formal rank and their state-issued batons, they had little control other than their own capacity for violence, or the symbolic authority that they could muster as representatives of the state. When reformers tried to make the prisons less violent, guards lost the material and symbolic foundation of their authority, which were inextricably tied to notions of masculinity.

Suspended in the networks that the con boss and BT systems made, mainline prisoners remained thoroughly alienated, often seeing each other as potential threats or as victims. Only rarely could they be friends or lovers, and if they did form these relationships, they risked punishment. When prisoners fought with each other, they embodied a certain type of penal disorder. But that disorder was itself useful, because it meant that prisoners were divided among themselves—they were not fighting guards. The surprise was not that prisoners fought so much but that they ever worked together and shared the moments of humanity that they did.

In rare moments when prisoners overcame nearly universal antagonism to protest the conditions of their incarceration, they came up against guards—or their proxies—who knew that violence was the foundation of their authority, and who believed that keeping prisoners pitted against each other was the key to their own safety. Yet in the early years of the New Deal order, reformers decried this personal violence, and aimed to reorganize the structures of authority into impersonal, clean, and bureaucratically regular hierarchies. Despite the omnipresence of violence, both symbolic and material, officials in each state sought to present a more beneficent, caregiving, and unified front. Thus, prison officials tried to intervene in shaping public perceptions of punishment. To do so, they would draw on mass culture as both a new disciplinary tool and a means of public relations. These are the subjects of the following chapters.

Thirty Minutes behind the Walls

Prison Radio and the Popular
Culture of Punishment

At 10:30 p.m., on March 23, 1938, four chimes sounded on Fort Worth Station WBAP, and listeners heard words that in other circumstances would have struck them with terror: "We now take you to the grounds of the Texas State Prison." But instead of the sound of a gavel strike or the word "guilty" from a jury foreman, there was pleasant music. No judge spoke to declare a sentence; rather, listeners heard a radio broadcaster's smooth intonation, with music playing softly in the background.

Good evening, Ladies and Gentlemen. . . . This evening through the facilities [of] WBAP, Texas prisoners make their air-debut in a series of completely original weekly broadcasts authorized by the Texas Prison Board expressly to acquaint Texas with the excellent talent behind these walls, as well as with the modernized program of rehabilitation recently adopted by the Administration. It will be the purpose of these programs to vividly illustrate what is being done by the Prison Board and the Management to adequately prepare the inmates to reestablish themselves in organized society after their release. It is the sincere wish of the Board, the Management, WBAP, and the prisoners that you find these programs entertaining as well as enlightening.[1]

Texas governor James Allred strode to the microphone after the professional radio announcer. He told listeners far and wide that their exciting new radio program, *Thirty Minutes behind the Walls*, would allow prisoners to speak directly to the listening public on the still-new medium of radio. This, he made clear, was a bold experiment in penology. But the governor was less than wholly forthright, because *Thirty Minutes* was also a bold experiment in public relations on behalf of a prison system beset by scandal. Nor did

135

the governor mention the hope that *Thirty Minutes* might offset the public's troublingly persistent fascination with crime and gangsters.[2] Through their conjoined efforts, a commercial radio station and the Texas State Prison broadcast new penological messages over the airwaves, along with music and comedy, to instruct listeners in the Jim Crow order of Texas law.[3] Their message, broadcast from 1938 through the war years and carried by WBAP's 50,000-watt clear channel broadcast, spread far. Two years into the broadcast, prison officials estimated that some five million listeners tuned in each week, and some estimates would range as high as seven million. A year later, more than 221,000 fans from forty-two states in the United States and abroad signed letters supporting the program that "boys and girls in white" performed each Wednesday.[4]

At its inception, *Thirty Minutes behind the Walls* was unique in featuring convicted felons as entertainers, though other prison systems, including California's, soon followed suit. *Thirty Minutes behind the Walls*, like San Quentin's *San Quentin on the Air*, followed a classic variety show format. A typical program might include a warden's description of a new rehabilitative plan, an interview with a prisoner, perhaps a poem or a comedy sketch, and a letter written from a fan. But the majority of the show was dedicated to music— the music of the Texas working class. The eight-odd songs played each week ranged from gospel and spirituals to blues and hot jazz, from western swing and country to *canción-corridos* and rumba. The music was the hook. People listened to a staid Texas Prison Board member's speech because of the music and the prisoner interviews that surrounded it. And what listeners heard may have been different than what broadcasters intended.

Radio broadcasts emerged as a new element of American penal discipline in the late Depression. As inmate labor was increasingly circumscribed by New Deal–era labor laws, such as the Hawes-Cooper Act (1929) and the Ashurst-Sumners Act (1934), prison radio meshed with other popular cultural forms, including baseball leagues, rodeos, literary magazines, and newspapers, to retrain prisoners in recreational activities appropriate to the welfare state and a Keynesian economy. At the same time, these popular cultural events instructed the free world audience in the risks of breaking the law. The programs were as much for audiences outside the prison as they were for inmates on the inside. The citizens that these broadcasts aimed to create, steeped in the liberal ideologies of consumption, leisure, and athleticism, were at every step consistent with broad transformations in American society.[5]

Scholars have long examined public punishments as a form of state-directed theater, orchestrated to instruct the condemned and the free in the power of the law. Early modern subjects would know the majesty of the law when they saw a man gibbeted or shown royal mercy, just as slaves, their masters hoped, would learn obedience from the final lessons offered on the gallows. But as liberal reformers came to recognize and as scholars have since noted, public spectacles in the early republic allowed unruly crowds to gather and gave them opportunities to learn lessons of brutality, rather than the restrained but efficient power of the law. Worse still, reformers feared that those who gathered to watch a hanging or see prisoners working in public might misinterpret their lessons and challenge the government's authority. Punishments would be carried out away from public view, behind prison walls.[6]

As a result, scholarship on modern punishment commonly stresses the removal of criminals behind prison walls, but *Thirty Minutes behind the Walls* worked against these penal traditions. In examining the importance of prison radio programming, this chapter makes three related arguments. First, *Thirty Minutes behind the Walls* was a cutting-edge form of public punishment, much as legal hangings, public labor, and even lynchings had been a generation before. As a kind of public punishment, *Thirty Minutes behind the Walls* capitalized on the economy of mass media, and by stressing correction for select prisoners, was very much a product of the New Deal era's expanding reformist impulse. *Thirty Minutes*, after all, was entertainment, not torture. Yet its entertainment masked the violence that remained an intrinsic part of incarceration.[7]

Second, *Thirty Minutes* helped enforce Texas's modern racial and class hierarchies. This was the case not just because it justified Texas's prisons, which, like Mississippi's Parchman Farm, was a bastion of Jim Crow law.[8] This was true enough, but *Thirty Minutes behind the Walls* also worked in more subtle ways. When prison officials spoke on the program, they proclaimed their system's benevolence in ways that belied the actual experience of incarceration. Further, when white working-class male prisoners described their lives in interviews, they were portrayed—and portrayed themselves—as men who could become good citizens, if they obeyed the rules of the prison and took advantage of its new rehabilitative programs. In contrast, black and Mexican men, and all women prisoners, were denied these opportunities on the broadcast and in the prison system itself.[9] Black and Mexican men, and all women prisoners, could serve as entertainers on *Thirty Minutes* but were rarely portrayed as potentially redeemable citizens who might regain the public's trust.

Third, like earlier displays of the condemned, the show's actual effects could be unpredictable. Spoken words, such as officials' speeches and inmate interviews, literally broadcast the state's ideology of respect for the law, of a kind prison system, and of firm racial hierarchies. Yet the music inmates performed existed in tension with the words themselves. As George Lipsitz has shown, music and song were sites of racial hybridity as well as cross-class community formation.[10] Music sustained affective pleasure and dignity for prisoners and listeners alike. Prisoners' music was put to the state's use, but elements of that music remained beyond the state's control.

Precisely for these reason, *Thirty Minutes behind the Walls* was not a univocal production by state and broadcasting officials, though it was intended as such.[11] While racial hierarchy remained a central goal of social control, the very conditions of incarceration and, especially, prison radio broadcasts, ensured that people from Texas's multiracial working class would be brought into contact. As the spoken words of *Thirty Minutes behind the Walls* overtly legitimized the ideology of class and racial hierarchies, the music it carried valorized black, white, and Mexican working-class men's and women's lives. Though the pedagogy of prison radio starkly defined racial difference, the very music it presented was a hybrid of raced musical styles. The music expressed numerous working-class concerns, and these messages operated differently than the state pedagogy of the program. But the music—arguably the most important component of the program for listeners and performers alike—is also the most elusive.[12]

Cultural historians have turned their attention to the middle years of the twentieth century to hear voices otherwise ignored, but scholars of American punishment have not followed suit. Radio programs, baseball games, rodeos, as described in chapter 6—these are hardly the images that come to mind when one thinks of Texas prisons, of spectacular or mundane punishment in American historiography. Instead of chain gangs, we have jazz musicians; instead of the lynch mob or whipping post, we have minstrel routines and audiences gathered around radios in their living rooms; instead of cotton fields, we have baseball diamonds. Of course, this imbalance of imagery is due to the persistence of violent racial domination in American punishment from slavery to the present.[13]

After the Wednesday evening count to make sure no one had escaped, performers changed from their coarse white duck cloth uniforms into their "Sunday Specials." They tuned their instruments, and a WBAP employee adjusted the balance and positioned the musicians to get the best sound. They timed and adjusted each song and segue to fit the half-hour format, ate what nervous stomachs would allow, and held a final rehearsal at 8:30. By 9:15, members of the public streamed into the prison, entertained by inmate vaudevillians or the military band until the broadcast began. With five minutes until showtime, the WBAP announcer warmed the crowd up and "instruct[ed] the audience in the manner of their applause."[14] At 10:30, the show went live. Four chimes rang, and *Thirty Minutes* traveled to Houston by wire, where it was sent by transmitter to the big broadcasting antenna in Fort Worth. From there, it traveled across land and sky and into people's homes, where families gathered around radios for their weekly trip behind the prison walls. When the prison orchestra opened the first show with Teddy Wilson's "You Can't Stop Me from Dreaming," they simultaneously stressed the limits of state control in their lives while they expanded the prison's influence through mass media.

If Robert Burns's 1932 film *I am a Fugitive from a Chain Gang!* critiqued southern punishment by suggesting that down-on-their-luck whites might be unjustly punished and turned from respectable men into criminals, *Thirty Minutes behind the Walls* used popular culture to legitimate penal practice.[15] Officials used the radio show to dispel the conception that the prison system was badly run. They surely understood that listening to the radio was one of America's favorite pastimes, and how politically effective Franklin Roosevelt's "Fireside Chats" had been.[16] With the access to listeners that radio delivered, officials could broadcast their version of prison life directly to the public, and, with some luck, replace the widespread allure of bandits like Bonnie and Clyde with a certainty that the law would prevail. As Governor Allred indicated on the first program, *Thirty Minutes* would "prove to be not only *entertaining* but *instructive* as well."[17] San Quentin's reformist warden Clinton T. Duffy agreed, and celebrated his institution's *San Quentin on the Air*:

> The public relations that the prison has put out in this manner has been one of the things that has enlightened the public as to prison conditions. . . . I think it has been a marvelous thing. We have had thousands and thousands of letters approving the broadcast, and I haven't read one yet that has been against the thing.[18]

Prison inmates, of course, used *Thirty Minutes* for their own ends. On the show, inmates presented images of themselves to counteract the conservative political notion of all prisoners as irredeemably criminal, dangerous, and deserving of harsh treatment. Inmate writers for the prison newspaper *The Echo* believed that *Thirty Minutes* would show the public that prisoners were basically decent people who, in moments of weakness, had done wrong.

Thirty Minutes would present "the radio public with prison life as it is lived by the prisoners, not as it is written into fiction by clever novelists."[19] Prisoners could portray themselves as ready to return to society once they had paid their debt and served their time. They hoped that on release, *Thirty Minutes* would lessen the stigma of being an ex-con. Thanks to *Thirty Minutes*, an inmate author wrote,

> people outside are gradually drifting away from the influence of publicity which condemns the lawbreaker too harshly. . . . [T]hey are coming around to the broader point of view that there is good and bad alike in all of us, and that no man . . . is utterly without some redeeming feature.[20]

Allred's successor, Governor Pappy O'Daniel, himself a radio personality, lent the weight of God and the governorship to the *Thirty Minutes* project, with which parole-hungry prisoners surely agreed.

> Before the advent of radio, prisoners were exiled. Citizens outside paid little attention to them. But now you hear them talk; you hear them sing; you find out they are sons and daughters of good mothers. You find out that they made mistakes, thus proving that they are human; and thus recalling to our minds that He who gives us the radio, and everything else that we have, is the same One who gave us the assurance and the hope of redeeming our souls after we had made even the greatest mistakes. And if the Great Benefactor . . . can forgive the most terrible sinner spiritually, isn't there some reason in believing that we as human beings should find some method of permitting men and women who make mistakes to redeem themselves and reestablish themselves among us[?][21]

Interviews with prison officials and with prisoners themselves—known as "human interest" segments in the broadcast—became the primary mode of "informing" the public about the "realities" of Texas prisons. Prisoner interviews would "present to you a picture of the man in prison—to bring out his viewpoint, his attitudes—to show the various effects of prison upon the man." Nelson Olmstead, WBAP representative and primary interviewer for *Thirty Minutes*, explained the interviews' rationale in bucolic terms:

> We believe that we will be better able to convey to you a picture of prison life as it is lived now in the little world, walled in among the rolling, pine-clad hills of East Texas. And, as you become acquainted with the advanced

plan of rehabilitation employed by a prison system modern enough to authorize these unusual broadcasts, we should like you to feel that you are personally acquainted with the prisoners who plan and present them.[22]

This was hardly an unmediated introduction. Almost without exception, the prisoners who spoke on the radio were carefully vetted by officials. Most were trustees—prisoners who had earned good jobs, status, and bureaucratic privilege through many years of good behavior. These prisoners would represent the institution in the most positive light. If they did not, they risked losing the modest privileges they had accrued. Few would take this chance. Nevertheless, their "life stories" were censored, and as an *Echo* writer noted, "A crime-does-not-pay theme predominates."[23]

Nelson Olmstead guided prisoners through their interviews with leading questions. Thanks to Olmstead's heavy hand, a number of themes, all highlighting respect for the law, were evident. Time and again prisoners stressed the regrets they had for breaking the law. Time and again they told listeners that crime, quite literally, did not pay. Following Olmstead's prompting, George Young—serving a fifty-year sentence for a holdup netting sixteen dollars—calculated that since his conviction, the robbery paid him "less than 2 1/2c a week so far!"[24] Interviewed prisoners also testified that the prison was better "now" than it had been "then." And thanks to the firm kindness of the prison system, upon release, they would commit no more crimes.

Within the crime-doesn't-pay theme, a number of different genres emerged from the weekly interviews. First among these was what might be called the "old-timer" interview. Consider Olmstead's conversation with James L. Warner, who arrived at Huntsville in 1923:

OLMSTEAD: Warner, what was your impression of the prison in 1923?
WARNER: Bad. It didn't take me long to realize it was pretty doggone tough, especially on the farms . . .
OLMSTEAD: Warner, you've seen the good and the bad of it . . . tell me, what do you think of the improvement that has been made in the prison system as a whole since 1923?
WARNER: They've made great improvements since I came here. . . . It's more comfortable on the inmates, and they can live a lot better now than they could then. . . . Oh, it's a whole lot better . . . in every respect. One thing, they used to just try to keep you from getting' away. Now they try to make somethin' out of a man if the man'll let 'em.[25]

C. C. Johns, superintendent of the construction crew, underscored the point in his interview. Describing conditions when he first began work in the prison, he explained,

> They worked many of the prisoners on lease to the plantations, coal mines and railroads. The Prison received a dollar a day for each man. But the System was a poor one, and the treatment was bad. Of course, I wouldn't want to go into that . . . it is all past.

Yet Olmstead asked him to go further; the contrast would be more instructive as a result. Back then, Johns reflected, "they had the dark cell and the strap. And then the prisoners were kicked with boots and spurs, and they were whipped with a wet rope that had been dragged through sand." Thankfully, "Conditions are much better now . . . a great deal." The on-the-job training Johns offered, which included blacksmithing, painting, and carpentry, could rehabilitate prisoners into men as they built an ever larger and stronger prison system.[26]

The "working prisoner" interview became another key genre, and underscored the point of modern vocational training rather than just punitive or for-profit labor. In these segments, select inmates gave a short description of their job in the prison and explained that they were being trained for a productive, wage-earning life on the outside. Like the "old-timer" interviews, these advertised the Texas Prison System's benevolence as well as the way these prisoners could be reintegrated into productive society. Though the Texas Prison System was overwhelmingly rural, and though most prisoners worked on farms, nearly all of the prisoners who described their work were engaged in some sort of manufacturing or construction. And, importantly, save for very few exceptions, they were all white. Thus, the sounds and imagery of the prisoner who learned a trade and was ostensibly being reformed by the state was a white, English-speaking man, whose prison-based labor became his vocational training. Agricultural labor (still the mainstay of the prison system), and black and Mexican prisoners (who disproportionately filled its walls and fields) were rendered invisible and silent in the redemptive narrative of progressive prison reform and training.[27]

John Adamek spoke in one of the prisoners-who-work segments, and told listeners that he was learning a trade. Since he began on the construction crew, Adamek said that he could set between seven and eight hundred bricks in an hour. "On foundation work and jobs like that I can easily lay two thousand bricks in an eight hour day." Adamek's story served the prison well, because it conflated the architectural control of ever growing numbers of prisoners (which might as easily have been narrated as a social failure) as part of a humane and progressive state. The message was clear: at the same time that the Texas Prison System built modern facilities, it was also rebuilding prisoners into hard-working men.[28]

Nearly all the inmates interviewed about their work labored in prison industries or construction, but Mona Bell was an exception. Bell spoke because he won many events in the widely publicized Texas Prison Rodeo. Nevertheless, Olmstead asked him about his work in the prison. Bell answered, "I'm working in line—regular farm work." Olmstead suggested that "[p]erhaps that accounts for your excellent physical appearance—I'm going to guess your height and weight: You're six-feet-two and weigh two hundred."[29] According to Olmstead, work on the prison farms *created* Bell's impressive physique, a claim that characterized forced agricultural labor as masculine and constitutive of strong bodies rather than as destructive, enervating, and deadening. Of course, Olmstead never pointed out the injured prisoners broken from farm work, the many who fractured their arms and severed their Achilles tendons to get out of this labor, or the legislation sponsored by the Prison Board to make a prisoner's cutting of his "heel string" a felony offense.[30]

In addition to uplifting if misleading stories of white male prisoners' labor, WBAP's audiences were treated to descriptions of women prisoners' work. On a few occasions, *Thirty Minutes* took listeners to the women prisoners housed at the Goree State Farm, a few miles from the Walls. Reable Childs, a white inmate who performed country music with "The Goree Girls" on *Thirty Minutes*, explained the women's work regimen: "Every inmate must work ten hours a day at something fitted to feminine abilities. . . . We cook, keep house, raise flowers, do light gardening, milk cows, raise chickens, sew . . . just the usual farm life for a woman." In addition to making their own clothes, they also made "all the clothes worn by convicts in the system . . . their discharge suits are tailored here. . . . We make pillow slips, sheets, in fact, everything in that line that is used by the prison is made here." Childs made clear that the work regime for women prisoners was gendered toward labor seen as "feminine" and as "the usual farm life for a woman."[31] At Goree, Olmstead also interviewed Julia Brown, who, judging from the transcription of her voice, was black.[32]

Olmstead asked, "What kind of work do you do here, Julia?" Her response: "Well, sah, Ah's done ever'thing here 'cept the bookkeeper's job—but right now Ah's herding watermelons." Brown's field labor seems to have

The first broadcast of *Thirty Minutes behind the Walls*. 1938 Souvenir Rodeo Program, p. 24. 1998/038-404, Folder "Rodeo Program 1939." Texas State Library and Archives Commission.

hardly been the "light gardening" that Childs described. Indeed, southern black women have consistently done "men's" work in the fields, while white women—if finances allowed—were expected to be both more domestic and "feminine" in their labor.[33] The prison, it seems, was little different.

The pedagogical narrative of Texas as a benevolent state came through in "errant youth" interviews, a suitable opposition to the "old-timers" so frequently featured on the show. If old-timers demonstrated systemic improvement from the past, the errant youth might show the promise of the future. Johnnie Carpenter was one such youngster. In his interview, Johnnie explained that he got into trouble shortly after his mother left his abusive father, when he stole jewelry from a house his mother cleaned to give her as a gift. From there, he descended into vagrancy and petty crime. Though John-nie suggested that childhood poverty led to his law breaking and ultimate incarceration, Announcer Byrne suggested that Johnnie's crime was better understood in familial rather than class terms. Byrne lamented that "[m]any of the inmates inside the penitentiary are products of broken homes and lax supervision," and, in so doing, he revitalized the common belief that much crime was the result of a crisis in the home—caused by ungiving patriarchs and by working mothers who, by necessity or dereliction, left their children untended to earn a wage.[34] This "crisis" of the patriarchal family, certainly underway during the Depression, would be exacerbated during the war years, when fathers were at war or in industries, and mothers were increasingly in the waged work force.

In the interview, Byrne wondered, "Didn't you try to get a job, Johnnie?" Johnnie: "I don't know no kind of work. . . . I never had no job." Byrne, in full pedagogical swing, asked, "Don't you want to be a credit to your government?" Johnnie, perhaps ignorant, or perhaps playing an assigned role, asked, "What is a government?" Byrne's response rang with condescension: "We'll let that pass, Johnnie." With that, the interview shifted to the educational and vocational opportunities Johnnie might find in the prison: "[T]he officials told me I can go to trade school and learn how to get a job. Maybe I can get a job and be rich."[35]

And the interview ended on this hopeful note. Here, then, was the answer to Johnnie's question: *what is a government?* It was the Texas prison, the stern but fair system that would teach him to do right. Such, at least, was the message of the program. But the promises made were little more substantial than the ether that carried Johnnie's voice across the land. Education for prisoners was minimal, the vast majority of prisoners did either backbreaking agricultural labor, whose free-world wages were almost nil, or unskilled construction or repetitive factory production. The few who learned trades in the prison, it seems, were those white prisoners who already had some economically valued skills that overlapped with the jobs themselves—the educated worked as clerks or in the print shop, the trained mechanics worked as mechanics, the plumbers as plumbers. The unskilled worked chopping cotton and hoeing roads; the uneducated, and the racially subordinate, dug ditches and planted crops. Like Julia Brown, they would not work in the bookkeeper's office.

The ability to speak proved to be a crucial measure of how *Thirty Minutes behind the Walls* structured racial hierarchies, and thus how the program, as a disciplinary event, aimed to influence the listening public. In terms of format, *Thirty Minutes* was primarily divided into musical numbers and the "human interest" interviews described above. And this division consistently mapped with a differentiation between nonwhite and white inmates. In other words, musical numbers could be played by the Rhythmic Stringsters, who were white, by the Hot Jivers, who were black, or by the racially designated Mexican Stringsters. But almost without exception, Nelson Olmstead only interviewed white prisoners in the self-described "human interest" section of the broadcast. Race was the fulcrum on which social reintegration or continued exclusion turned, even on the radio.

Interviews with prisoners, such as Johnnie Carpenter or John Adamek, showcased the progress select inmates made toward their return to society as skilled workers and productive citizens. Their bodies were never explicitly marked, nor their voices transcribed in any dialectal way, thus indicating that they were white. The message was clear enough—white, English-speaking men who practiced respected trades were the subjects of interviews and the beneficiaries of rehabilitative programs—limited as they were—and social redemption. In contrast, black and Mexican inmate musicians were consistently denied speaking roles on the show, and were thereby excluded from this form of symbolic equality. Women of any race rarely spoke, and when they did, it was never to demonstrate their vocational training but rather their enforced domesticity. Perhaps both measures were unsurprising. Just as black and Mexican men were commonly denied jobs in the prestigious industrial sections of the national economy, so too were they relegated to the prison's dishonored and brutal agricultural fields. Symbolically, on the radio, and materially, in the everyday prison world, black and Mexican inmates could perform music but would not perform as beneficiaries of correction. Women were located in a domestic sphere, and occasionally as entertainers. Such was the fate of women and people of color in the New Deal era, sacrificed in the political compromises of the day to protect the tenuous status of white men.[36]

However, on the rare occasions when black or Mexican men were able to speak, announcers did their best to contain and alienate them. Such was the case in Candelario Salazar's interview. Olmstead begged the listeners' forgiveness on Salazar's behalf, as Olmstead condescended to struggle with the foreignness of Spanish. "[B]ecause he neither reads nor writes English, and speaks it only with the greatest of difficulty, we are going to ask you to be patient whenever he seems to stumble or falter in answering the questions we shall ask him. Now: Do you mind if we use your name?"

SALAZAR: No—I do not. . . . It is Candelario Salazar.
OLMSTEAD: I promised to spend all of last week learning to pronounce that
name—Candelario Salazar . . . is that right?

When Olmstead asked Salazar about the work he did prior to incarceration, Salazar undermined Olmstead's claims to his implicit foreignness (and his inability to speak English): "Oh, I just do anyt'ing—farming—work in a foundry—and I fight in the World War, too!" By referring to his service in the U.S. military, and as a veteran of the Great War, Salazar made claim to American nationality, valor, and patriotism.[37]

Candelario Salazar was one of a very few Mexican prisoners permitted to speak on *Thirty Minutes behind the Walls*. And this very fact might encourage us to take cultural theorist Gayatri Spivak's question literally: can the subaltern speak?[38] On prison radio, they could typically only do so with their instruments. Consider the following moment, when harmonica player Ace Johnson was about to perform. According to the announcer,

> And here's another of our Negro entertainers—Ace Johnson, a strapping, six-foot Darky with an educated harmonica. *He says the little instrument does everything but talk.* But be listening, Folks, in case it does do a little bit of off-the-record speaking. Okay, Ace—we're ready for that demonstration you promised us.[39]

The following song was listed in the transcription as a "Harmonica Novelty." That Johnson's song lacked a formal name implies that it was probably one he composed. Whether this song was part of a collective repertoire or was his own, this was an important moment for black representation in prison radio. Johnson, one of *Thirty Minutes'* most featured musicians, was not permitted to speak for himself. His musical skill allowed his presence on the air, announced him as a skilled human being, and had the potential to communicate subtle messages. But even in this very public case, Johnson was forced to acknowledge that his harmonica could not speak in ways that were recognizable as such.

Black prisoners were rarely allowed to speak on *Thirty Minutes*. Announcers consistently represented black prisoners with a mix of opprobrium and condescension, while still emphasizing their musical skill to listeners. Announcers went to significant lengths to ensure that listeners understood when they listened to black, as opposed to Mexican or white, musicians, in order to minimize the chance of listeners' confusion. Announcers actively identified black musicians as a homogeneous group on the air; time and again they were called Negroes or "Darkies," united by skin color, who played music from "the cotton fields" or "darkyland." But the diverse styles of music black prisoners played revealed a range of identifications. Though the Hot Jivers and the Negro Choir were equally marked as black, their musical performances of jazz, blues, or gospel signaled the different strategies and cultural affinities (be they spiritual, secular, rural, urban, classed, gendered, or some combination) that helped black prisoners survive. The subversions and strategies expressed through music had different effects than did, say, food strikes or work slowdowns in the fields, but nonetheless expressed that different black prisoners claimed a number of ways to do their time. Though their effects are hard to gauge, gospel, blues, and jazz all provided grounds for different communities to coalesce according to stylistic predilection and the subtle politics, as well as contradictions, embedded within them.[40]

Consider also the episode on November 1, 1939: Charlie Jones and Louie Nettles had performed as clowns at the prison rodeo. Both Jones and Nettles were black—one doing life and the other, ten years. After numerous fan letters requested their appearance, they performed under the names "Fathead and Soupbone" on *Thirty Minutes*. Their routine was perhaps typical of radio blackface popularized by *Amos 'n' Andy*—exaggerated "Negro" dialect, buffoonery, malapropisms, clever wordplay, and so forth. One example was particularly important:

FATHEAD: Looka' here, Soupbone. Did I tell you what happened to me out dere at de Rodeo grounds one Sunday?

SOUPBONE: Go on, Fathead, tell me whot happened to you.

FATHEAD: Well, you see I was a clowning out dere befo' all dem milluns o' white folks, an' wuz actin' kinda smart and graceful you know. When all of a sudden one of dem big Brahma bulls broke loose an' started toward me.

SOUPBONE: He did, an' whot did you do Fathead.

FATHEAD: I started to gittin' away from there in a hurry. I made a big razzo fo de fence, and I busted right into one o' dem big men whot was wearing one o' dem big hats. Well, I hit him so hard I bet he thot it was dat Brahma Bull instead of me.

SOUPBONE: I'll bet yo' got into a jam, did'nt yo'?

FATHEAD: I sho' did, but I come out of it alright.

SOUPBONE: How's dat, Fathead?

FATHEAD: Well yo' see, I gets up off de top o' hem and he gets up an' we both brush de dirt from our clothes, an' he sez . . . "Look here, don't you know who I am?"

SOUPBONE: Whot did yo' say then, Fathead?

FATHEAD: I sez no I don't know who yo' is . . . an' he sez, "I'm the governor, that' who I am."

SOUPBONE: Lawd have mercy on you! I bet yo started runnin'.

FATHEAD: Oh no, I didn't. No No!

SOUPBONE: Well whot in de world did yo' do then, Fathead?

FATHEAD: I jes' sez in de mosest sweetest voice I knew how, "Pardon me Governor."[41]

Here, then, was a comic story offered by two black inmates who had worked as rodeo clowns, and as such were trickster figures as well as objects of racial scorn and emblems of white bigotry. But their status as clowns enabled them to tell a story in which a black convict knocked down the very figurehead of state authority. In the story, "Fathead" dirtied the governor on the ground, and as they dusted themselves off, each stood in relative equality. When the governor attempted to reassert social hierarchy, Fathead verbally turned the tables, and, through his pun—the foundation of radio slapstick— tried to trick the governor into freeing him through an inadvertent pardon. By assuming the racialized, mass-mediated voice of blackface minstrelsy, Fathead broadcast upstart humor, usually a hidden transcript, far and wide, mocking his keepers in such a way that listeners heard it across the land.[42]

The problems of racial representation cut deep. Indeed, the only way for a black prisoner to speak in the public sphere of the radio, in the performances of the excluded but redeemable members of the body politic, was to perform a blackface racial ventriloquism. Black inmates Louie Nettles and Charlie Jones had no public voices, but as the minstrel characters Fathead and Soupbone, they did—just as Ace Johnson's harmonica could almost, but not quite, speak. From this, it seems that there were two ways to be a public black prisoner. One was to perform the stereotypical modes of blackface minstrelsy. The second was to be a skilled musician playing the blues, spirituals, or jazz that WBAP producers and prison officials saw as useful in marketing their disciplinary message. By playing these roles, inmates created the popular culture of punishment, displaying and celebrating a penal system rooted in traditions of slavery, centrally organized around forced labor, and attempting to contain the contradictions of a global economic system in crisis. But prisoners also circulated messages alternative to the prison's.[43] Through humor and through music, black prisoners expressed their self-worth and dignity in a social formation that asserted they should have none.[44]

For all of the pedagogy of spoken words on *Thirty Minutes behind the Walls*, and despite the human interest in prisoners' selected life stories and even humor, the allure of the program was its music. Prisoners' music appealed to listeners for many and diverse reasons, but surely Angela Y. Davis is correct when she writes that musicians "gave their life experiences as an aesthetic form that recast them as windows through which [listeners] could peer critically at their own lives." These songs, sung by prisoners trying to make good, offered listeners "the possibility of understanding the social contradictions they embodied and enacted."[45] Methodologically, however, understanding the effects of the music is among the most challenging aspects of the program, as in most cases, the closest that we can get to the music played on *Thirty Minutes* are the names of the songs themselves. The only recordings of the show were destroyed by WBAP.[46] The lyrics and style of each arrangement, the riffs, variations, flourishes, surprises, harmonies, dissonances, and blue notes dissipated as soon as each song ended. Though many surely continued to play for their families, it seems that few of the musicians went on to continue their musical careers on the outside, preferring, apparently, to forget that part of their lives.[47] Though music was perhaps the most important part of the program—if only because most airtime was dedicated to music—the music itself is largely inaccessible.

Yet traces of the music remain, and if they indicate the quality of the music played on *Thirty Minutes*, it was high indeed. Jack Purvis directed the prison orchestra for *Thirty Minutes*. Purvis was an accomplished jazz trumpeter as well as an occasional smuggler, pilot, and, by some accounts, mercenary and chef. Purvis toured the United States and Europe with numerous swing groups, among them the Dorsey Brothers, Fred Waring, and Charlie Barnet, and also worked in radio orchestras. Purvis had a history of arrests—including one in Los Angeles for playing his trumpet in the middle of a busy tunnel (he told the police that the acoustics there were perfect), but a 1937 robbery in El Paso landed him in the Texas prison. Purvis's style, according to jazz critic Scott Yanow, mirrored his life: "full of fiery bursts, unrealized potential and some crazy chancetaking." Few white trumpeters were as unashamedly influenced by Louis Armstrong as Purvis, and this certainly shaped his performance on *Thirty Minutes*.[48]

While Satchmo-inflected big band swung the show, less popular musicians made their appearances, contributing to the program's great appeal. Some of these musicians even left musical recordings. On their 1939 southern tour, folklorists John and Ruby Lomax recorded a few of the *Thirty Minutes* performers playing songs listed on the transcript. The Lomaxes were interested in prisoners' work songs and spirituals rather than the more popular tunes on *Thirty Minutes*, and as a result, their archive contains a tiny sample of the musicians who performed on *Thirty Minutes*. Nevertheless, Ace Johnson, the "harmonica wizard," recorded a few songs, and the Lomaxes also set out their machine for "the blues singing Negress" Hattie Ellis, accompanied by "Cowboy" Jack Ramsey, a white prisoner, who recorded two tracks together. One, "Desert Blues," was composed by Ellis; the other, "I Ain't Got Nobody," was a popular tune that Ellis made into a blues number.[49] The Lomaxes also recorded black gospel singers performing "Ride on, King Jesus," "Great Day," and "When the Gates Swing Open," an almost doo-wop, four-part a cappella gospel whose title surely signified the day when the prison's steel gates opened, as much as the pearly gates of heaven.[50]

Hattie Ellis rose above the other performers. Celebrated as the prison's "Ella Fitzgerald," Ellis made almost weekly appearances until her conditional pardon in 1940. She performed a wide range of material, from popular tunes like "Somewhere over the Rainbow" to "St. Louis Blues" and racier songs like "Sugar Blues" and "Dedicated to You." Though the market differentiated between sacred and profane music, Ellis's repertoire blurred distinctions between the genres. Like other blues singers, male and female, Ellis could sing sexually suggestive blues, show tunes like "Franklin D. Roosevelt Jones," and also the spiritual supplications of "Swing Low, Sweet Chariot."

Hattie Ellis's life was the stuff of blues. Known as a "bootlegging sister," Ellis lived in the hard space available to black women in urban Texas.[51] In 1933, the eighteen-year-old Ellis was arrested in Dallas, where she sold bootleg whiskey. One evening a drunken group of women came to buy a dollar's worth of liquor, even though Ellis and one of the women, Henrietta Murphy, had recently fought over an outstanding debt. Ellis didn't sell them any whiskey, and Murphy and the others left. But before they did, Murphy urinated on Ellis's floor. That night, Ellis drove to Murphy's house, and the argument continued. It ended when Ellis shot and killed Murphy, but only, according to Ellis, after Murphy had pulled a razor.[52] Ellis was sentenced to thirty years. One inmate thought that this was an unusually long sentence and that Ellis would have gotten a shorter term if she hadn't "sassed the judge when he brought her boot-legging activities into the murder case."[53]

When Ellis sang on *Thirty Minutes*, the voice she sassed the judge with carried across the land, and if it brought her fame, little fortune came her way. Though the prison capitalized on her talent and notoriety to publicize its messages of benevolent control, the music she sang remained her own, and appealed to other listeners. When Ellis sang "I Ain't Got Nobody" for the Lomaxes and for *Thirty Minutes*, many, in prison and out, could surely understand:

> Now I ain't got nobody, and there's nobody cares for me,
> 'Cause I'm sad and lonely—
> Won't somebody come on and take a chance with me.[54]

It seems that plenty of people were willing to take a chance on Hattie Ellis, and wrote in to let her know. Captain Heath, in charge of the women at

Goree Farm, told the Lomaxes that she received *three thousand* fan letters in a single week.[55]

Other prisoners received similar accolades. The Goree Girls, one of the first all-female country and western acts in the United States, received candy, money, flowers, and even marriage proposals in their fan mail.[56] While this attention was surely a treat, the alienation of incarceration, as well as the ongoing violence never portrayed on the program, made the sadness and longing in the country music they sang all the more relevant.

Ace Johnson, another featured musician, recorded four songs with the Lomaxes, and "Rabbit in the Garden" was a version of a harmonica tune he played many times on *Thirty Minutes*. "Rabbit in the Garden" referenced the classic Brer Rabbit trickster story, and, like much black music, expressed different meanings on different levels. Johnson repeats the following lines a few times throughout the song.

> Rabbit
> Got a mighty habit,
> Goin' in my garden,
> Eatin' up my cabbage,
> Rabbit,
> Get up in the hollow,
> *Catch 'im* [shouted]
> Get 'im.[57]

"Rabbit in the Garden" was an instrumental, vocal, and thematic frolic, and its music conveyed dramatic tension between repetition and variation. The song is structured by a rapid cycling of low- and midrange notes, including bent notes, that are the foundation of blues harmonica, but he plays them much faster than most blues harmonica tunes. Unlike the longer repeating structure of a twelve-bar blues, such as Ellis's "I Ain't Got Nobody," he plays the same few notes over and over again in rapid succession and a seemingly endless cycle.

Just as Nikolai Rimskij-Korsakov's "Flight of the Bumble Bee" buzzes and hums like an insect, the combination of variation and repetition in "Rabbit in the Garden" describe the travels of a mischievous rabbit. Notes scamper and dash like the rabbit through the garden before Johnson returns to the spoken words. The musical phrase repeats time and again, but Johnson also moves up the scale and stretches the harmonica's highest note, which squeaks like a rabbit and whistles like a farmer calling his dog. Dutifully, in response to the whistle, Johnson uses his voice to bark and holler like a dog, chasing the escaping rabbit out of the garden and up the hollow.

"Rabbit in the Garden" continued the slave trickster story tradition, which, as historian Lawrence Levine argued and Fathead and Soupbone made clear, endured in this twentieth-century prison.[58] Like its forebears, "Rabbit in the Garden" referenced the weak overcoming the strong but was also more ambivalent than a straightforward heroic story because Johnson's song signified from multiple perspectives. The most obvious came through the spoken words, and is the farmer's complaint of the rabbit "goin' in my garden, eatin' up my cabbage." The farmer calls his dog to protect his property from this thief. It may seem odd for an imprisoned musician performing in the black tradition to invoke the position of the farmer—analogous to the slave master or prison guard—but rural Texas audiences could surely understand the need to protect family food plots from animals, especially in the Depression. Even urban Texans, most of whom had only recently moved to the cities, weren't so far removed from the country, or from urban tricksters and thieves. Second, the barks and howls Johnson intersperses in the song represent a farm dog chasing down an escaping bandit. Though free-world listeners may not have known this, the bloodhounds used to track escaping prisoners figured powerfully in black prisoners' work songs, as symbols of power, prowess, and fear, which Johnson surely knew quite well.[59] Lastly, the music—the notes Johnson played and the manner in which he played them—opposed the dog's barks, the spoken words, and the farmer's position. They enacted the rabbit's perspective, stealing from and then eluding more powerful opponents in an ecstatic flight. This is part of the trickster's widely celebrated history of symbolic subversion. All of these perspectives resonated in prison culture, and across Texas, in the 1930s and 1940s. None of these meaning was mutually exclusive, none could be reduced to the others, and what listeners took from "Rabbit in the Garden" must remain speculation. But it is clear that the pleasure of the song, for listeners and musician alike, offered something more than the prison could control, even as it put that music to its own use.

In contrast to the pedagogy of the spoken word in prisoner interviews, which broadcast messages of white redemption and black and brown exclusion from the New Deal state, the music that Texas prisoners performed demonstrated the unstable potential of the prison broadcasts in mediating racial difference. *Thirty Minutes behind the Walls* crafted a space in which working-class, polyracial music floated over the airwaves. The space of the thirty-minute program was very much racially integrated—*despite but also because of* the prison's efforts to maintain racial difference. More critical still, the very music itself provided territory for cultural exchange and fluidity. In his cultural history of the 1940s, George Lipsitz argues that black and white music "had always grown through creative fusions" with each other. White country musicians like Gil Tanner and the Skillet Lickers played Dixieland jazz numbers, just as African American bluesmen like Blind Willie McTell brought country songs into their repertoires.[60] Historian Edward L. Ayers refers to polyracial musical roots in simple terms when he writes that "[t]he genealogy of Southern music is tangled."[61] It is even more tangled in the Texas borderlands.

Musical production on *Thirty Minutes behind the Walls* was a deeply hybrid assemblage of musical styles and genres, where rampant stylistic borrowing, love and theft occurred, where prisoners-turned-musicians listened to and learned from each other.[62] This learning and contact was by no means unidirectional; black musicians played with and surely learned from those identified as white and as Mexican, just as whites appropriated black and Mexican musical styles. Musical aesthetics interpenetrated behind the walls, just as they had long done in the oustide world. Music provided a location where identities became fluid and could intermingle—though never without numerous elements of power being expressed. The cultural exchange of the Texas borderlands was always laden with power and conflict, but also with transgressive potentials of communication and community formation.[63] The performances of raced music among a multiracial, working-class, inmate population blurred the boundaries of identity even in the context of a location that enforced those identities with the rule of law, and performed them as technologies of social control.[64]

On *Thirty Minutes behind the Walls*, Spanish speakers sang in English and English speakers sang in Spanish; the Mexican Stringsters played the nineteenth-century-Austrian-patriotic-march-turned-western-swing-hit "Under the Double Eagle," and black prisoners sang "white" pop tunes at listeners' requests.[65] Ace Johnson, who had typically been relegated to playing songs labeled as "harmonica novelties," also played with the white Rhythmic Stringsters, as when he joined bass player Happy Weeks and guitarist Woody Stansberry to play Euday Bowman's "Twelfth Street Rag."[66]

The "Mexican tenor" Humberto Boone joined the Rhythmic Stringsters to sing "Mexicali Rose," which the announcer identified as "a beautiful Borderland tune."[67] So too did Herman Brown "forsake . . . his native tongue" to sing in Spanish. "Herman's fellow inmates tell him he sounds almost too natural" the inmate announcer reported, "but you decide as he offers—'El

Rancho Grande.'"[68] Brown's voice thus gestured toward Spanish while the announcer made clear that this wasn't his "natural" language. Nevertheless, Brown clearly felt some longing to perform in Spanish. This surely combined both the deleterious appropriation of Brown's popular-culture-mediated images of Mexicanness as well as his own sincere desire to perform in Spanish. That other white inmates ridiculed Brown for sounding "too Mexican" also bespoke the persistent racism that coupled with Brown's sentiment.[69] To be sure, music on *Thirty Minutes behind the Walls* did not create a utopian and egalitarian space in which racial power disappeared. We invalidate the concept of hybridity if we evacuate it of the power relations that were reconstituted in Herman Brown's performance, and in his peers' ridicule.

Two performers particularly embodied the racial contradictions and fluidity manifest through musical production, and presented cases where the bounded sounds of race overlapped and had to be actively policed by prison announcers. First, consider Ocie Hoosier, one of the oft-featured harmonica players. Hoosier was from DeQuincey, Louisiana, and had been a laborer and a truck driver prior to his 1936 arrest for burglary and the theft of a hog and a car. Official records listed him as white, with a ruddy complexion, blue eyes, and red hair. Despite occasional punishments for lesser and greater infractions (stealing coffee and sugar form the Huntsville dining room on one occasion, and stealing the Harlem Farm manager's shotgun, rifle, and state vehicle on another), he remained on all-white prison farms and assignments.[70] Time and again, *Thirty Minutes* announcers stressed his light complexion and his hair: on one show he was introduced as a "red-head—with a harmonica in one hand and the blues in the other, this Dallas boy, Ocie Hoosier, blows hot and cold in a novelty number: 'Deep Elm Blues'": a song about the mostly black neighborhood and red-light district in Dallas.[71] Hoosier, like Ace Johnson, played blues, or at least blues-inspired music, and played it well. Perhaps Hoosier had spent some time in the black neighborhood known more widely as Deep Ellum.[72] What Hoosier's relationship may have been with the black-raced spaces of Dallas is open to conjecture, as is his own complex racial identity, and his use of blues music to express his sense of who he was, and who he was perceived to be. On occasion, he also performed as supporting member of a minstrel show.[73]

On another show, the inmate announcer introduced Hoosier by his hair color and freckles. But in addition to the tropes used to establish his whiteness, the announcer marked Hoosier with some of the same signs of blackness that other announcers used to describe Ace Johnson, the Negro Choir, and many other black performers. Hoosier had "a wide smile and a happy disposition—and plenty of ability on the harmonica. Show 'em, Ocie!" Despite the formal recognition of his whiteness, these tropes of blackness— the performance of happiness in incarceration and musical skill—marked Hoosier as if he were black, and content in his unfreedom. This indicated Hoosier's indeterminacy as a racial figure, as not being of quite the same quality of whiteness as the inmate announcer.[74]

It was in cases such as Hoosier's, and especially due to his performance of "black" music on the harmonica, that the firm boundaries of racial identity imposed by the prison revealed a looser foundation. The constant resigni- fication of his "red hair" and his spatial location on the white Harlem State Farm reasserted his whiteness of a different sort. The need to do so spoke to the very indeterminacy of his racial performance. In point of fact, Ocie Hoo- sier was something of a racial trickster. Though known as white to officials in the prison system, Hoosier was of mixed ancestry, and he was raised by his mixed-race grandparents. Prison officials must have not known this, and in fact it may have been something Hoosier denied in everything, save perhaps his music.[75]

Humberto Boone's presence as "our Mexican tenor," but also as the leader of the "Cuban Rumba band" similarly complicates matters. Born and raised in Del Rio, Texas, Boone himself had been a professional singer prior to his arrest, and performed on the radio in both Del Rio and across the border in Villa Acuña, Mexico. By playing rumbas, Boone participated in the limited space that the market allowed for Mexican musicians—and this meant that he was to play "Latin music." In the late 1930s and early 1940s, the limited market for Mexican music guided many musicians into the growing mar- ket for "Latin" boleros and rumbas, which were increasingly popular with a "general" audience.[76]

Humberto Boone's band played the popular and marketable Latin sounds of rumba, associated more with "the islands" and "Cuba" than with Mexico or ranchero, or corrido, or even *corrido-canciones* styles. The representation of Boone as Latin rather than Mexican showed some of the interrelation of these identities but also distanced him from the more racially degraded sta- tus of "indio" (or Indian) within Mexicanness. Like the difference between gospel and jazz among black prisoners, the stylistic differences between Boone's rumba and the Mexican Stringsters' ranchero articulated a range in the infrapolitics of identification. While ranchero valorized rural, working- class, ethnic Mexican lifestyles, rumba was far more urban, cosmopolitan, and socially prestigious. As a result, Boone was at different times identi- fied as "our Mexican tenor" but also as "our golden voiced Latin," with all of the racial meanings variously associated with and articulated by class performances.[77] Boone's elite-oriented, marketable music may have effectively "lightened" his aural complexion, locating him as a Latin musician, or perhaps a Mexican American, rather than consistently as a more racially degraded Mexican.[78] Thus, while Ocie Hoosier's racial indeterminacy performed the subordinated blackness of Dallas's Deep Ellum, Boone's was one of upward mobility toward the centers of racial and economic prestige.

Time and again listeners were told, "This is YOUR show." Through the "educational and entertaining" elements of *Thirty Minutes behind the Walls*, officials aimed to craft an audience that was amenable to state disciplinary messages, and used numerous techniques to generate this positive publicity for the prison system. State officials made full use of the era's emergent audience surveillance techniques. From these, WBAP officials estimated the numbers of listeners and strove to make the show more appealing, and thus to more effectively broadcast their messages.[79] Announcers pleaded with listeners to send letters to the *Thirty Minutes* staff. "We're anxious to know whether you like us or not; whether our old friends are sticking with us; and, whether new ones are being added to our audience."[80] The letters served multiple purposes, certainly, but prominent among them was that prison officials might learn more about their listeners and thereby tailor the show to appeal to the largest number of consumers. This would be the most effective way to market *Thirty Minutes*, generate good public relations for the prison, and disseminate the ideologies that guaranteed racial and class hierarchies through the rule of law and the threat of incarceration.

Sending and reading fan mail was a crucial part of radio programming in the Depression years. Listener participation in 1930s radio enlivened "national rituals that helped to constitute a revitalized sense of national identity." Shows featuring "'average Americans' provided a series of compelling performances of who 'the American people' were, what they sounded like, and what they believed in."[81]

Regrettably, few of the hundreds of thousands of letters sent to *Thirty Minutes* remain. The only ones that do were those selected by prison staff to be read on the air, or those reprinted in *The Echo*, the inmate-authored newspaper. Letters read on the air—more specifically chosen than those in *The Echo*, as they found a larger audience—were clearly selected for the ways they supported the prison system's message. Letters selected by *The Echo*'s inmate staff more commonly applauded the musicians and the prisoners themselves. It is impossible to know with certainty how many people wrote to applaud the state's new forms of punishment and how many wrote in to cheer the prisoners, whose music they enjoyed. The reasons were surely as varied as the listeners, and probably combined elements of all of these. Nevertheless it is very suggestive, as noted earlier, that Hattie Ellis received three thousand letters in one week. And one might suppose that those were letters from *her* admirers, rather than fans of the prison system.[82] Despite the selection of remaining letters by the broadcast staff, we can know something about the actual listeners of the show, as well as the listeners that the *Thirty Minutes*' planners hoped to create. These letters were, by definition, exemplary.

Letters read on the air came from an astoundingly large area, as officials celebrated the very distance that their spectacle of the condemned traveled. Listeners wrote from as far away as Hawaii, Colombia, and Canada. A listener in northern Manitoba explained that two families traveled forty-five miles *by dogsled* each Wednesday to hear the show on a friend's radio set. Nor was this sort of community gathering (and community formation) around the radio uncommon in Texas. People from all over Denton came to H. J. Jones's house to listen to the show, because he had the only radio in the neighborhood.[83]

Many who wrote in testified to *Thirty Minutes*' effectiveness as a pedagogical tool, and broadcasters particularly selected letters from people in authoritative positions. Mr. O. E. Enfield, county attorney in Arnett, Oklahoma, congratulated Texas prison officials for their progressivism:

> We . . . enjoy to the fullest, your weekly programs and are sympathizers with . . . the aim of your institution, that is, the rehabilitation of persons committed there. Almost a century ago, Enrico Ferri, an Italian criminologist said "The time will come when we will correct wrongdoers with no thought of punishing them, whereas, we now punish them with no thought of correction." To us it appears that the spirit pervading your institution is to that effect.[84]

Schoolteachers and church leaders also played the show for their wards. Oklahoma teacher Emma Flood used *Thirty Minutes* as an example to her students "to impress them never to make mistakes in life that will land them behind the walls."[85]

While some writers applauded broadcasters' disciplinary intents, others expressed their pleasure at the inmates' music. Dorothy L. Pinnick of East Gary, Indiana, wrote to cheer them on.

The Rhythmic Stringsters are one of the most talented I've ever heard . . . and that Original Blues song [played by the Jive Trio with Hattie Ellis] was swell; the way the musicians jammed it, really, it sounded like some of the big swing orchestras. . . . Oh heck, I could go on and on, but I'm trying to get over that your broadcast is so good, it's one of my Wednesday night programs from now on.[86]

Few were read, but a great many letters were mentioned, that requested favorite performers get more airtime. Pinnick's letter was one of countless flooding WBAP with requests for pianist E. S. Shumake's Jivers to play "Original Blues" again, or listeners who sought consolation in more gospel or spirituals. Letters like these had little to do with the show's disciplinary intent, or with the legitimization of state authority. They had more to do with the pleasure of the music, and its broad working-class appeal. Tom Iron Cloud, from Oswego, Montana, was heartened by the *Thirty Minutes* performers, and his letter was reproduced in *The Echo*. "Way up here in Montana we look forward to your broadcasts on Wednesday evenings. It is wonderful how cheer and happiness comes out of a place of confinement." Mrs. Clarence A. Johnson of Puposky, Minnesota, was "sure that your songs have brought happiness to many a weary heart."[87]

Others, familiar with isolation, found solace in the program. An ex-convict working as a night watchman in Chicago wrote that the show had "deep meaning" for him, and a trapper "twenty miles west of the Quebec boundary and five hundred and twenty-five miles north of Toronto" wanted to hear "Somebody Stole My Gal" to help him "forget it all." Sixteen hospital attendants at the Tennessee State Penitentiary in Nashville reasoned they had special insight into the *Thirty Minutes* performers' lives. "We are brothers under the skin and for this reason find more surcase [sic] from the cares of the day than the ordinary John Q."[88]

But John Q. Public and others wrote in large numbers. Inmate statisticians calculated that 75 percent of the letters came from married couples. Of the remaining 25 percent—excitingly for the male performers—20 percent were signed "Miss." Two percent (judging from the letterhead) were professional men and women. If 2 percent were professionals, the vast majority, we might infer, were ordinary people, without fancy letterheads or stationery.[89]

Such listeners were certainly swayed by guitarist and print-shop worker V. J. "Lucky" Rousseau's down-home attitude. When asked about his ambitions on release, he said, "I want to be a musician . . . a *good* musician." The announcer complimented, "I'd say you're a good one now, Lucky." Rousseau responded, "Aw—Thanks! But I want to be really good. . . . I don't mean high-brow—I just want to play music that ordinary folks understand and love, but I want to be so good at it they'll be happier for having heard me play."[90] Rousseau proclaimed little interest in catering to elite tastes and espoused a white working-class ideal to make other working people happier. This was perhaps the sensibility that historian James N. Gregory described as "plain folks Americanism" among working-class whites in the 1930s.[91]

Yet when a black woman sent a letter asking if "the black vote" counted in support of a special hour-long anniversary broadcast, announcers snubbed her. Unlike other letters read on the air, and especially those that championed the prison system itself, this woman's name was never read, nor her hometown mentioned. The announcer, however, assured her that her vote would count, and, "by way of saying 'Thank You,'" to this unnamed black supporter, "a talented 19-year old Negro singer . . . dedicat[es] his song to our colored listeners. . . . 'Old Folks At Home.'"[92] As a reward for her letter in support of the inmate performers and the institution that housed them, one of its many black inmates sang a blackface minstrel song nostalgically recalling plantation slavery. "The collusion of coercion and recreation" in *Thirty Minutes* was rarely more evident.[93]

Despite such popular support, the reality of prison life constantly threatened to peel back *Thirty Minutes'* pleasant veneer, which required constant servicing. In July 1946, officials pleaded with the Board of Pardons and Paroles to delay the Wednesday night execution of L. C. Newman, a black man from Polk County, because it would interfere with the broadcast.

> Last Wednesday evening we had 373 outside visitors in the auditorium for the program, and . . . will probably have more than that for the broadcast tomorrow night. We do not have sufficient means to notify the public of any change or cancellation of the program. And too, the "gloom" among the inmates is always "heavy" on execution nights.

The emergency stay of execution was granted; Newman was sent to his death the next day.[94] This was show business, and the show must go on.

Thirty Minutes behind the Walls signaled a new mode of state formation and a new spectacle of the condemned. It was quite different from the lynch violence of previous years or public legal executions and convict labor, and was in fact supposed to be good fun, entertaining as well as instructive. But like previous displays of legal authority, *Thirty Minutes* expressed the pedagogy of white supremacy, the sanctity of property, and respect for the law that guaranteed them both. Prison radio underscored the contours of inclusion and exclusion in the national imaginary, and masked ongoing violence within the prison system.

While the broadest theme of prison radio was to present the state as a benevolent, modern, and paternalist entity, it was more than this. It presented a progressive vision of prisoners as potentially redeemable members of society. Yet from the structure of interviews, the format of the program, and the musical numbers, listeners learned that it was *white* prisoners who might be brought back to the fold of respectable citizenry, worthy of education and vocational training. It was predominantly white prisoners who were interviewed and given voice in the structure of the program. Black and Mexican prisoners had far less voice, though their musical presence complemented but was never reducible to the state-sponsored messages. They could sing—and singing mattered—but they could not speak. Many years after her release from prison, Mozelle McDaniels Cash, one of the Goree Girls, recalled, "No one thought we could sing, but we did. We sure damn did. At least we did that."[95]

Thirty Minutes behind the Walls' appeal to diverse audiences was unmistakable. Few listener responses remain, but it was almost certainly the quality and variety of the music that made it so popular. And the general mood of the Depression was one in which many listeners knew that they, too, could fall on hard times and wind up behind bars. Like the lonely Kansas nurse who wrote in, and whose only son was in prison, many surely felt that the show "makes the harsh nights softer."[96] If they did not have a relative in prison, it was a possibility they could imagine, and listeners wrote in to say so.[97] Much popular culture in the 1930s and 1940s celebrated working-class values, in the explicitly politicized Popular Front, but also in the multiracial class appeals of blues, gospel, western swing, hillbilly, jazz, and *canción-corridos*. Working-class listeners could hear the music of people just like themselves, across an age and racial spectrum. This appeal wasn't strictly white or black or Mexican but evoked a multiracial, working-class hybridity at the same time that black and Mexican inmates were marginalized as mere purveyors of musical talent. And though its producers intended *Thirty Minutes* to legitimate a penal system guaranteeing racial hierarchy and unequal property relations, this was by no means the totality of the show's significance: it also gave some prisoners modest voice and celebrity status. It broadcast messages about expanding parole, which prisoners certainly supported. It made prisoners human (whites more than African Americans and Mexicans), and sonically returned them to the communities from which they had come. The networks of power in which inmates performed were as multidimensional as the airwaves themselves, and prisoners struggled to shape their lives within the institution and the society that confined them. In the next chapter, we will explore the complex dynamics of inmates' performances in different venues, before live audiences ranging from just a few to many thousand spectators. Texas Prison Rodeo and the San Quentin baseball leagues championed fair play and obedience to the rules, and celebrations commemorating the Fourth of July or even Juneteenth celebrated the nation that held the prisoners captive, while making money for the institutions themselves.

6

Sport and Celebration in the Popular Culture of Punishment

Though understood as "play," prison sports were serious business. For inmates, athletics and the celebrations that went with them were a means of pleasure and recreation, and personal and collective fulfillment. Sports allowed prisoners to move their bodies in ways that were profoundly different from the exhausting or numbing tasks of hard labor, or the deadening monotony of inactivity. As a result, prisoners took every opportunity to engage in this play, and loved the holidays when they could rest, relax, eat different foods, and either participate in or watch sports. Boxing was always a favorite, and it featured prominently among prison athletics. On Texas's Fourth of July celebrations in 1935, there were four fights on the day's card, and each linked muscular masculinity, violence, and a working-class aesthetic of powerful performance to racial difference and hierarchy. As in the rest of the country, no boxing matches between whites and nonwhites had been permitted since Jack Johnson pummeled Jim Jeffries in 1910 (also on the Fourth of July). Nor would black and white boxers meet again until 1938, when Joe Louis fought Max Schmelling and Americans decided that they would rather see an African American as world champion than a Nazi.

An early fight on the card was between Don "Kid" Hamic and Ed "One Round" Evers. Hamic knocked Evers out and broke two of his ribs in a fight inmate writers described as having a lot of "class." Here, "class" signified the boxers' style and panache, the intelligent, self-controlled fighting that appealed to the inmate writer's aficionado eye. In another fight Tony Garza, listed as Mexican, beat Mike Gabriel, described as Syrian, after three rounds. The newspaper reported that "[b]lood streamed during the last round. Both men refused to quit until the fight was finished." The flowing blood was a show of stoic manhood that appealed across racial difference—violent performance through pain signified a "universal" and certainly working-class manhood as the "Mexican" and "Syrian" boxers met in the ring. It was only permissible for "Mexican" blood to mix with that of the comparably raced "Syrian," however, not with that of a "white" or a "Negro" boxer. The last fight was between black athletes: "Lightning" Perry and Herman Hilliard. *Echo* writers explained, "Perry has ruled as King Pin of the entire colored realm in the walls, having beaten them all until Hilliard was imported to take his measure." Hilliard had been promised a job at the Walls if he could beat Perry, which he did, "using extremely clever tactics" and landing a knockout uppercut "directly on the 'button.'"[1]

As a highly structured sport, with strict time limits and in a delineated space, with obedience to rules and the referee's authority, and with permissible and prohibited moves, boxing showcased a self-disciplined masculine aggression. Though black and white prisoners could not face each other as equals in the ring, male prisoners of all races could and did watch each other fight, appreciating clever tactics, well-placed blows, and the ability to persist through pain. That, surely, was something all prison inmates could identify with. As Elliot Gorn described in his history of working-class men's prizefighting, such descriptions recalled the talents of the independent artisanal laborer, crushed by industrialization and, now, Depression.[2] Moreover, when prisoners watched or read about sporting events, they behaved much as their counterparts did on the outside, participating in the ascendant consumer and leisure culture of the day.

Prison wardens, too, were strong advocates of sport. In a speech to inmates in the early years of baseball at San Quentin, Warden James A. Johnston "compared the game of baseball and the game of Life, and assured us all [the prisoners] that by playing both games on the square we could win the reward that is sure to follow honest endeavor."[3] In 1935 San Quentin Warden Holohan told the *Bulletin,* "no better influence could be brought to bear upon rehabilitation of the men than participation in contests of fair play and skill." Holohan, moreover, was "a firm believer in physical recreation as a stimulant toward a healthy mind—and realize[d] that at no time is this so important as during incarceration."[4] Court Smith, Holohan's replacement, continued the tradition. He cut to the heart of the matter and proclaimed that a "healthy body" was the "foundation for good citizenship."[5] It is hardly surprising that wardens would feel this way. In charge of warehouses full of mostly young and energetic men, officials looked for ways to expend the energy of their wards. Beginning in the Progressive Era in the Northeast, but emerging in home-grown forms throughout the rest of the country, athletics grew as field of penal discipline when inmate labor was increasingly circumscribed.

Prisoners and their keepers cherished sport and holiday celebrations, though for quite different reasons. Athletics, as another component of the popular culture of punishment, nurtured a hegemonic formation based on the key features of labor discipline, sublimated aggression, gendered notions of sportsmanship, racial hierarchy, and national belonging. While keepers intended instructive messages, as with prison radio, prisoners claimed valued senses of themselves and their relationships with their audiences, which authorities could not fully control. Sporting events provided narratives structured by ideas of collective, often masculine, and national heroism, and replicated the foundational structures of modern bourgeois society: self-control, competition, muscular masculinity for men and subdued, racially inflected femininity for women, respect for authority, and adherence to spatial boundaries.[6]

But organized prison sport was not the result of studied forms of new discipline by elite prison planners. Rather, the first recorded sporting events came in the 1890s at New York's Elmira penitentiary.[7] Inmates had "freedom of the yard" on special occasions, and they used this time to put together the first recorded organized prison sporting events. Authorities were quick to see the disciplinary appeal, and tried to harness the spirit of competitive play. Zebulon Brockway, the noted New York prison reformer, developed institutionalized prison sports in order "to foster self-control and team spirit." Historian Blake McKelvey has suggested that this new focus on sport during the late nineteenth century "was to prove one of the most popular of the reformatory's contributions to prison discipline in the next century, although only a few institutions were able to derive other than entertainment value from it."[8] Whatever the proclaimed benefits of sport as a device of behavior modification, officials were glad for the innovation and understood athletics as a way to fill inmates' time with activities other than productive labor, when organized workers protested competition with prison industries. According to McKelvey,

> organized sport was . . . to make life in prison more tolerable, and its welcome was doubly enthusiastic because the lax industrial activity was failing to occupy the full time and energy of the prisoners. The wardens, through cautious experiments with their first graders, had discovered their ability to control men in masses. . . . [A]thletics opened a new horizon in correctional therapy.

He continues,

Grandstands were erected, indicating that the recreational possibilities of athletics were to be sacrificed to the entertainment feature of league games; the wide introduction of the movie a few years later, and of the radio later still, further emphasized the transition from the recreational program of the reformatory, with its educational motivation, to the amusement program of later prisons, seeking to keep their inmates contented.[9]

McKelvey lamented a decline from what he saw as the rehabilitative potential of sport to that of "mere entertainment," but he misinterpreted the importance of "entertainment" as a technology of social control. Playing sport, watching others play and reading about them, watching movies, and consuming mass culture were new disciplinary forms developed under the nascent progressive and welfare state, and signaled the interpenetration of mass culture and governance.[10] These disciplinary reforms were concomitant with the growing emphasis on mass culture, sports, and media in and out of prison in the New Deal years, and the resuscitation of capitalism. Sport became part of the transition in American culture from emphasis on forms of manly production to forms of masculine consumption, and the development of what Warren Susman and others have identified as the twentieth-century American culture of leisure.[11]

Prison sports were well suited for imposing class-based hegemony, insofar as sport offered a pleasurable recreation for and of labor in the working classes. Athletic training made for healthy prisoners, who were intended to understand the benefit of adherence to the rules and respect for authority. In San Quentin, the prison baseball league was organized with the captain of the guard as the league's "Commissioner."[12] Furthermore, athletics helped to structure prisoners' sense of time. Prisoners would labor in the daylight hours and were only permitted to play in the evening, on weekends, and on state holidays, once work was done. Writing in the San Quentin *Bulletin*, inmate Hal Eble glowingly described the disciplinary model, combining aspects of capitalist labor and capitalist leisure. "Work has always been the panacea for men's ills and nowhere is this so strikingly evident as in San Quentin. Relaxation follows." Of the pastimes, he continued, "Baseball is unqualifiedly the most popular."[13]

Officials liked sport because it allowed prisoners to develop, express, and resolve antagonisms. Sports aimed to channel the aggression created by captivity against other inmates (rather than their warders) through sanctioned means. Texas general manager Lee Simmons recalled that shortly after baseball games were begun, "Rivalry between prison-farm teams grew hot. The hotter the better, thought I."[14] Competition made for good baseball, Simmons believed, but more importantly, intraprisoner rivalries displaced aggression from the conditions of incarceration and spent pent-up energy.[15] Indeed, athletics and other forms of play constituted a common disciplinary strategy of the period: Japanese internment camp managers in California and Nazi ghetto administrators deliberately used sports and leisure in this manner.[16] One publication from San Quentin proudly publicized, "At times the rivalry reaches white heat but the sportsmanship is surprisingly good—during the past year no fan or player has been compelled to leave the game."[17] Prison sports were intended to develop competitive rivalry but also sportsmanship—the manly self-control that would hold it in check.

Sport's value to administrators was clear. As a result, one might be tempted to emphasize sport as disciplinary containment: an ideal Foucauldian technique through which self-control and social control conjoined. But to inmates, sport was more than this. Their experiences of bodily pleasures exceeded, in complex ways, the networks of prison control.[18] They gained access to behaviors and allegiances that drew as much from civil society and mass culture as they did from the state, embodying valorized notions of class-based and raced identities, masculinity and femininity, and American nationalism—and of self-mastery in the face of competition, fear, and pain.[19] Prisoners gained pride and prestige from athletics, but by no means was this inimical to the desires of prison authorities. Prison officials adopted and appropriated multiple elements of working-class life within an expanding prison world, which they saw as kinder and more benevolent than its predecessor. It was the very success of this hegemonic formation, its tensions and countervailing forces, that allowed it to persist across and beyond the twentieth century. We must take ideas of pleasure and experience seriously, because they offer alternative, if not contradictory interpretations of prison sport, and the lives that people made in these deeply repressive locations.

San Quentin Sports

With its Big House prisons at Folsom and San Quentin and a foundation in progressive penology, California developed sporting events earlier than did Texas. As early as 1913, inmates at San Quentin and Folsom played baseball, had boxing matches, and participated in patriotic celebrations featuring sport.

A few years later, a reporter for the Atlanta *Journal* argued that baseball "is the greatest single force working for Americanization. No other game . . .

teaches the American spirit so quickly, or inculcates the idea of sportsmanship or fair play so thoroughly."[20] Prison administrators agreed. As "America's
game," baseball was freighted with messages for how inmates should behave
in order to return from the pen as American citizens. Officials stressed
the necessity of teamwork, cooperation, perseverance, clean living, and
sacrifice.[21]

The basic structure of prison baseball in California mirrored the raced
and classed imperatives of play in the major and minor American baseball
leagues. At one level were the internal prison leagues, in which teams from
different units played against each other. In the other league, an assortment
of the best players (predominantly white, with perhaps a few ethnic Mexican
inmates) from the prison would form something of an all-star team, to play
against outside, minor league or semipro teams in the area. These leagues
were prioritized by the days that they played—the "minor league" games
were played on Saturdays, while the "majors" played on Sundays. The Sunday
games were consistently given more attention and drew the most talented
players from the prison community.[22]

The Sunday games against outside teams had official scorecards made in
the prison print shop, with the date and time of the game listed, along with
the name of the visiting team and the roster and batting order for each team.
The San Quentin All-Stars frequently played against squads from nearby
army bases, the Southern Pacific Trainmen, and other corporate-sponsored
teams, and also against Pacific Coast League semipro clubs. In games against
corporate teams, the growing tradition of anti-union company welfare met
prison welfare leagues, as each made use of "cultural" tools and leisure activities to nurture both community and compliance.[23]

Though at times San Quentin fielded racially segregated teams (there was
a Chinese-only baseball team in 1915)[24] in the early Depression years, the San
Quentin All-Stars' roster showed a mélange of different "ethnic" names—
an imperfect (but the best available) measure of the team's makeup. A man
named Jefferies played catcher, while Juarez was the shortstop. Goode batted
clean-up and played left field, and Garcia played right field. Brook was at
first base, Griffin at centerfield, and Farrell at third base. The pitching staff
consisted of inmates named Roy, Conchola, Stoponski, Stern, Tennant, and
Paulsen. On the bench sat Martinez, Cusak, Torrez, Adams, Pittman, Key-
rose, Johnson, and Sokoloff. In addition, the Southern Pacific team had a
similar mix, with Italian-, German-, Spanish-, and Eastern European–sur-
named players.[25] Given that black, white, and Latino players could compete
on the same teams in the California semipro and professional leagues, it is

conceivable, but as yet unverified, that black inmates might play for the San Quentin All-Stars. Black players participated in the largely white teams at Folsom early in the century.[26]

The high point of the San Quentin sports calendar came with the San Quentin Track and Field Day, also known as the Little Olympics. The Little Olympics were in large measure the creation of San Francisco's Olympic Club, an elite men's club founded in 1860.[27] In 1913 the Olympic Club began the event as a kind of late Progressive Era philanthropy. San Quentin warden James A. Johnston was a club member, which certainly helped in gathering financial support and in formulating the idea of their sponsorship.[28] "For a month in advance of the day," Johnston wrote, "the prison hums. Expectancy is in the air."[29]

Like other sporting events in New Deal–era prisons, sportsmanship was the key to state pedagogy. Warden Clinton Duffy explained, "At first, it was probably surprising to outsiders to learn that true sportsmanship exists in prison—that fair play in athletics is the rule rather than the exception. Sports play a major part in rehabilitation." Duffy lauded the Olympic Club, as well as the inmate athletes and prison guards, for their good work at the Track and Field Day. Thanks to them, the Field Meet "has won recognition all over the country as the outstanding prison athletic attraction."[30]

Teams for the day were structured by labor assignment. Attempting to create a sense of team solidarity based on work, prison guards and managers rooted along with prisoners against other teams, guards, inmates, and managers. This might have created a vertical sense of solidarity linking prisoners and guards, rather than a horizontal sense of prisoner solidarity—possibly against their keepers. Though there are no records from prisoners to suggest their feelings one way or another about solidarity with their guards in relation to sports, we might surmise that prison athletes did feel some allegiance to their "coach" and that he, too, would feel connected to "his" players and offer them privileges when possible. In the 1930 event, the "Mess Hall" team brought in prisoners from the General Mess, Library, Hospital, Gardeners, Yard Men, Dental Department, Cell Tenders, Quarry, Cottages, Outside Gatekeepers, G.Q. Construction, Officer and Guard Mess and Barbers, and Waterfront. The "Shops" team consisted of workers in the Print Shop, Tailor Shop, Furniture Shop, Patch Room, Laundry, Carpenter Shop, Paint Shop, Machine Shop, Blacksmith Shop, Tin Shop, White Wash Crew, Scavenger Crew, New Road, General Construction, Shoe Shop, and Plumbing Shop, as well as the Administration Building staff. The "Mill" consisted of people in the jute mill, still the largest single productive operation at San Quentin.[31]

The day began with a parade of athletes and entertainers. Early parades were relatively sparse, with athletes marching behind the military band. Clowns cavorted; four black men in cassocks, crowns, and armbands carried a white performer in a swan dais, while inmates of all races laughed from the stands.[32] The procession became more ornate over the decade, as prison populations grew. The increasingly bedecked floats boasted flags and patriotic messages. Across the decade, team members carried banners proclaiming "the Mill" or "Shops," or their specific assignment.[33]

By the war years, the Field Day's parade was a venue for inmates' attempt at national inclusion, based in nationalist opposition to foreign and racial others. The parade was replete with floats advertising for war bonds, ridiculing the Nazis, and making a racial attack against the Japanese. One float read, "Buy 4 War Stamps a Day, Put the Japs Away." Another showed the inmates' desire to participate in the war through their labor: it read "Keeping Our Shops Working for Victory." This image, too, displayed some of the materials made in the San Quentin shops. Significantly, a photo of one such float showed a black man standing and holding an American flag along with white coworkers and prisoners. This degree of wartime racial liberalism, validated by an executive order requiring fair wartime employment (though hardly limiting racism in Richmond's Kaiser Shipyards across the bay or preventing racist violence culminating in the Zoot Suit riots in southern California and across the country), was laudable, but it was hardly something that all Americans were included in, given the many struggles of the war years themselves.[34]

Track and field events were among the day's main attractions. There were one- and two-mile races, a 100-yard dash, hurdles, a relay race, and longer sprints, too. Along with the formal events were silly ones: sack races, an old man's race, a centipede race, a lifer's race, and a crawl race. Field events included a sixteen-pound shot-put, standing broad jump, running broad jump, standing and running high jump, running hop-step-jump, pole vault, baseball distance throw, and fungo batting. Records were duly kept, listed, and broken each year.[35] Prizes were donated to the winners—"entirely in the form of permitted merchandise"—and ranged from "bags of peanuts to typewriters and fountain pens."[36]

The tug o' war was the single most important event of the day. According to historian Kenneth Lamott, "The tug of war aroused such passion that old-time guards remember that sometimes it took as long as twenty minutes to pry a contestant's hands loose from the rosined rope."[37] There had been segregated black, white, and Japanese teams in 1930, but by the 1940s black and

The tug o' war at the 1930 Little Olympics. Image A.1925.001.014, Folio 8, 1930 San Quentin Field Meet Album, Leo L. Stanley Collection, Anne T. Kent Room, Marin County Public Library.

white inmates could compete together. In remaining images, men strained with all their might. One image shows what competitors looked like after the event: collapsed, arms splayed and legs akimbo, while other prisoners caringly massaged their hands.[38] Clearly, bags of peanuts were less important a part of the contest than the pride and bragging rights associated with victory, or the volumes of tobacco or contraband bet on the event. According to a caption accompanying a photo of inmates in the tug o' war, in the Olympic Club scrapbook, "More than $10,000 is wagered on the outcome [of the tug o' war]; in candy and tobacco, that is."[39]

In one of the earliest historical assessments of San Quentin's Little Olympics, Kenneth Lamott characterized the event as a "modern parallel to the Roman saturnalia, when slaves were treated like masters, [and] the usual prison rules were suspended" for inmate revelry.[40] His conception of the event as ritual inversion was perhaps apt, especially considering the ways in which transgressions verified imposed order for the rest of the year. Men's bodies displayed a gamut of masculinities on this day: from lithe, muscular (and barely clothed) tumblers to effeminate and slender queens; from hulking shot-putters to participants in the "old-timers' race."

Set in motion for competition and pleasure, their bodies communicated their skill, speed, agility, and all of their associated erotics.[41]

Perhaps most transgressive was the queens' proud display in the parade and in the day's stage shows. There were many, many men in drag. These were not the athletes, though they played a key role in the day. For example, a well-dressed black man and queen were featured in a number of photographs in the Olympic Club's scrapbooks: he, in coat, tie, and boater's hat; she, in a long dress. In another image the same couple pose: she stands coquettishly as he stands behind her, and appears to be smelling her cheek and neck. As photos progressed in documenting the day, the photographer was clearly taken with her performance (which seemed to have included a sort of strip tease and fan dance). In the last of a progression of images, she proudly stands in a bikini, displaying her beauty with the fan held at her legs. Hers was only the most striking of the displays of performers in drag. Some, such as the inmate described above, took their femininity seriously and tried to look beautiful according to an aesthetic of slender builds, hairlessness, made-up faces, and scanty clothing. Others were deliberately ridiculous, making no attempt to hide hairy or flabby bellies. One such balding white man wore a grass skirt and bikini and had darkened his skin, doing a "Hawaiian" dance on stage as four musicians and two shirtless white men (wearing trousers and leis) looked on and laughed. This second performer made a mockery of both sexual and racial difference. He was clearly an obese, hairy, white man, blacked up and in drag, which "playfully" underlined his whiteness and masculinity. Nevertheless, this performance in race and gender was clearly desirable both to him and inmate onlookers in eroticizing racial otherness. Furthermore, as inmates in this homosocial world, these men knew that gender differences were frequently less rigidly biological than many on the outside understood.

Inmates looked forward to the event each year—the change of routine, the foods available, and the transgressions it allowed. Inmates at Folsom enjoyed similar events, calling such celebrations "a grand elixer [sic] serving to sweep the cobwebs from minds that dwell within themselves."[42] But for all of their acclaim and the much-vaunted benefits of prison sport, these were private events. Only prisoners and members of the Olympic Club or sponsors could attend. They were publicized by the prison staff, to be sure, but only to inform free-world people that they existed, not to bring large numbers of free people into the institution. In Texas, the opposite was true.

Sister Kate, a favorite at the Little Olympics. Image 1925.013.004, Leo L. Stanley Collection, San Quentin Photographs, Anne T. Kent Room, Marin County Public Library.

Texas Spectacle

Prison sport in Texas shared something with sports in California and elsewhere. Inmates in Texas played baseball, they boxed, and they even had volleyball. While black and white athletes might play together in the San Quentin or Folsom baseball leagues, this was unthinkable in Texas, which sponsored firmly defined white and Negro leagues. But penal sport in the Lone Star State had a peculiar twist. Rather than private affairs, prison sports and celebrations became massive, public spectacles.[43]

The Texas Prison Rodeo, originally billed as the "Fastest and Wildest Rodeo in Texas" (later expanded to "the World") was first instituted in 1931 as a self-proclaimed progressive reform. Lee Simmons, who claimed the rodeo as his brainchild, thought a rodeo would be cheap entertainment for prisoners and guards. It was this and more—the rodeo ballooned into a huge public relations success and a source of considerable income. Audiences grew from just a few hundred in 1931 to tens of thousands by the end of the decade. The prison stadium was built, expanded, and rebuilt to hold the overflowing crowds, thousands of whom were regularly turned away for lack of capacity. According to prison official Albert Moore, the first Sunday's rodeo in 1939 drew "the largest crowd ever to witness a rodeo in the United States."[44]

The rodeo drew from Lee Simmons's invocation of the slaveholding tradition of forcing captives to celebrate. Its form was of an imagined Texas frontier past. A radio advertisement hyped the event, where "one hundred and fifty daring inmate buckaroos will clash with outlaw broncs, vicious brahma bulls and steers, which have been brought in from the outlying reaches of the vast farmlands and river bottom pastures of the System. It's a case where outlaw meets outlaw! And there will be action such as you have never seen before."[45]

Baseball may have been America's game, but rodeos held a special place in Texans' hearts. The rodeo accessed a different form of nationalism and state-mediated identity than baseball did. Like baseball, the rodeo was notable in the way that it structured the temporality of the prison year, and in the way its creation of "leisure" validated the existence of "labor" as an organizing force of life. But unlike baseball, the Texas rodeo was based in an Anglo-Texan memory of the American West, steeped in the lore of the open frontier. On the introductory page of an Annual Rodeo Souvenir program, the prison's general manager, O. J. S. Ellingson, wrote,

Crowding to buy tickets to the 1938 Rodeo. 1938 Souvenir Rodeo Program, p. 22. 1998/038-404, Folder "Rodeo Program 1939." Texas State Library and Archives Commission.

Right here let us turn the clock of time back to the days of the great ranches of the Old West. . . . When the season's work was over; when the cutting and branding was done, it was the custom to make sport of the rangeland routine that made up the cowboy's work-a-day world. And as the rodeo of bygone days grew out of the cowboy's desire to play at his work, so did this rodeo grow out of our desire to provide a period of recreation for the prisoners after the principal work on our vast farmlands had been done. In the years since the inauguration of this feature the annual prison rodeo has become a tradition.[46]

Ellingson invoked a memory of the West that, like many such invented traditions, would legitimize contemporary social practice. It took just eight years for the rodeo to become such a tradition, valorizing the Anglo-Texan memory of a white ranching past, an idyllic time of masculine labor in the open range. In the thick of the Depression, the image of the independent cowboy roving the range embodied the freedom that so many white men (all men, really) desired, while in truth, they were financially dependent on wage-labor jobs. Moreover, the Anglo memory of the West largely occluded the presence of Mexicano/as or African Americans in Texas's history, and of Native Americans as anything other than obstacles to orderly progress.[47] A few black and Mexican inmates did participate as contestants in the rodeo, but more provided secondary entertainment. Some did comedy routines, and the "Cotton Pickers Glee Club," black men in tidy white uniforms and black bow ties, performed from the back of a flatbed truck. Simmons outlined the place of black men in the rodeo—a side joke to the main event—in his memory of frontier Texas:

> We had one 385-pound singer who had an unusually powerful voice of wonderful quality. As stage props for his entry, I had the boys rig up an old one-horse wagon, to which we hitched a large and angular mule that had not been sheared in some time. Under the wagon we tethered an old hound. The wagon contained a few old quilts and like plunder, while on the side next the grandstand we hung a skillet, a coffee pot, and a lantern.
>
> The instructions to our big singer were to drive into the arena about midway of the grounds without looking up until he got opposite the grandstand. Then he was to halt his equipage, stand up in the wagon and sing "Goin Down Dat Lonesome Road." He knocked them over—he really did. And I got as big a kick out of it as anyone.[48]

While many white spectators were warmed by the memory of Texas's frontier past, they were thrilled by the threat and spectacle of seeing spilled blood. The audience's interest was aroused with the following description of a Brahma bull, quoted from the prison's Souvenir Rodeo Program: "No more savage beast has ever crossed a rodeo arena than a mad Brahma bull. More often than not, having thrown his rider, the bull will turn and charge him, sharp horns lowered for the kill."[49] Indeed, the danger was a vital part of the performance, when spectators thronged to see inmates—sometimes in explicitly degrading convict stripes, sometimes not—risk dismemberment and chance glory before an ebullient crowd. Given that inmate rodeo riders had violated the laws of the land, the injuries they received could even be seen as one element of their punishment.

Consider this description of the "Mad Scramble," a rodeo event said to be too dangerous to exist in outside rodeos:

The mad scramble combines thrills, spills, chills, and action into one of the most comically spectacular of all rodeo events. All chutes are flung open simultaneously. Contestants are mounted on wild bulls, saddle broncs, bareback broncs, wild cows and mane-hold horses.

These animals, chosen chiefly because of some freak trick of bucking, are selected from the prison's herd of wild rodeo livestock. Wild bulls are ridden with a belled loose rope; saddle broncs are contested according to association rules; bareback broncs are ridden with a surcingle, just as in the regular bareback event, and riders drawing a mane-hold horse are allowed only a firm hand hold on the wild animal's mane. This last is really fun!

Sometimes a rider manages to maneuver his mount into a clear and less dangerous spot in the arena but this is usually impossible. Animals used in this event simply ignore the performer's wishes and seem drawn toward each other as if by a magnet. This adds danger as well as spice to the contest, for occasionally there is a head-on collision and riders, as well as their mounts, go down in a heap. Almost all of the inmate performers clamor to take part in the mad scramble, however, even though only a limited number of them may do so at each performance.[50]

The "danger and spice" of the rodeo was alluring precisely because prisoners were represented as every bit as desperate as the animals they rode. As one program boasted, "nowhere will you find a more dangerous athletic contest."[51] Competition, danger, and crowds of cheering spectators were crucial ingredients. Manly individual competition and ticket prices combined to make this lesson in turbulent market capitalism a metaphor for life in the Depression.

In 1941 Mary Waurine Hunter penned an article entitled "No Holds Barred: Best Possible Morale Builder Is Bone-Cracking Prison Rodeo" for the magazine *Texas Parade*. In it, she explained the draw for the crowds: "*Action* is what brings them here, *action* is what they get—raw, unadulterated, kicking, goring, bone-cracking action." In a caption accompanying a photo in the article, Hunter wrote, "Jack Williams, a 25-year man, drew a tough critter. After falling on his rider, the bull rolled over, got to his feet, and gored Williams."[52]

This was bloodsport, to be sure, but blood and danger made men. As Aaron Snyder, a rodeo cowboy prior to incarceration, explained, "I go in for everything that's rough! Bareback bronc riding, wild cow milking, wild mule racing and wild horse racing and of course I will be in on the mad scramble which is the big opening event on the program." Snyder particularly relished the mad scramble, which he called "the wildest, roughest, toughest and fastest event known to the rodeo world."[53]

With resounding bravado, Morris Hager explained that danger and risk of injury were all part of the fun: "It wouldn't be a rodeo if some of them didn't get hurt. That's what puts spice into the thing—the danger there is in it. We like it that way. I don't imagine any of the boys would want to get into a tame rodeo. Wouldn't be any fun."[54] Mona Bell, another rider, said that danger was "all in the game. Nobody takes a hand in it unless he wants to—I mean, he isn't forced to ride, or anything like that."[55] For Snyder and Hager, the allure of the rodeo was the prestige and the performance of potent masculinity and skill, the braving of danger and death in a battle of "man" against "beast." As an anthropologist of rodeo would later write, it demonstrated the riders' ability to conquer fear and pain.[56]

The terrible thrill of seeing a man get gored was the core of much rodeo advertising. But it was hardly the entirety of what spectators felt. If prisoners believed people came only to see them suffer, they would scarcely have joined in the numbers they did. Instead, audiences heaped adoration on prisoners who took part, and especially those who performed with grace. A fine play on the baseball diamond brought prestige for the player in front of other prisoners, keepers, and the free-world audience, but style was perhaps even more important for rodeo riders, because the stakes were so high. Moreover, because style resided in inmates' bodies and communicated directly with cheering fans, it exceeded prison officials' control.[57] "The crowd roars loudest over the bronc forking and the wild bull riding. When Bob Campbell came plunging out of the chute this year to fork a mean bronc named Sky Rocket to a finish, every spectator came to his feet, yelling encouragement. When wiry Raymond Cameron kicked his wild Brahma into a frenzy, the crowd worked itself into another. For a little cigaret [sic] money these boys were risking their very lives."[58] The crowds loved it. When an inmate reached these heights of performance, he could create what Gena Caponi-Tabery described as "a point of unity between audience and player that occurs when a player . . . performs . . . with exceptional ease, grace, and flair, taking a risk while maintaining control."[59]

The phenomenology of play was crucial to rodeo riders. The rodeo engaged prisoners' bodies in ways that became tremendously powerful: the intensity of its experience was a radical departure from the mundane. This perspectival focus on the experience of sport mitigates the top-down model of prison athletics as solely an embodiment of nationalism, capitalist leisure, or the process of inculcating a repressive masculinity in the maintenance of prison control.

The rodeo required profound focus beyond the prison or even the large crowds, and allowed moments of dangerous exultation.1998/038-390, c 1935. Folder 8, Texas State Library and Archives Commission.

When prisoners entered the bull ring or walked onto the pitcher's mound, they might experience what later-day athletes would call going into "the zone." The semicontrolled danger that inmates described was different from that which they faced each day from BTs or the high roller guards on horseback: this was a matter of self-control and public celebration rather than survival. In this ritual event and public performance, inmates rode dangerous animals, but they also straddled the line between controlled and uncontrolled event, before an enormous audience of the free and the imprisoned—all this must have heightened rodeo riders' experience and the contortion of spatial and temporal boundaries. Sport anthropologist Alan Klein describes entering the zone as a spatial transformation, "hyper-remote" from the location and environment of which a player was a part. An athlete told Klein that once he got into the on-deck circle, "I couldn't even hear the fans."[60] Though evidentiary material is thin for Depression-era prisoners—beyond their willingness to participate—one can specu-late that unalienated athletic production could temporarily transform the bounds of the prison, which then made its impositions more bearable until that next, sought-after moment arrived.

One can imagine what it felt like for prisoners to ride broncs in front of tens of thousands of cheering fans, to be seen and have their names known for their bravery, masculinity, and style. Imagine the nervousness and anticipation of a rodeo ride for a prisoner who has seen a previous rider fall—hard. Imagine a prisoner mounting a bull in the chute, the intensity of this experience drowning out the roar of the crowd, the pain of a previous injury now gone, focusing down to a hand pinched tight under the rope around a Brahma's back, the musk of its sweat and coarse fur, the other hand in the air for style, feet and spurs on the bull's shoulders, looking for a perfect ride. Imagine the gate swinging open, and the thousand-pound beast taking off. One can imagine being a young man playing baseball, knowing that there are members of the "fairer sex" in the audience watching his every move, but then having even that knowledge fade into the background as he steps to the plate, hefting the weight of the bat and waiting for the pitch. After a hit, a run, anything, consciousness would return—to the crowds, and the public recognition of his accomplishment. J. H. Bird, a Texas prison rodeo director, speculated as to why prisoners risked life and limb in the rodeo. It was, he believed, one of very few moments for a prisoner to be recognized as a worthy person. For some of these men, he suggested, having thousands cheer for them may have provided a life-long memory.[61] But surely the intensity of the experience, the danger and the spice, and the validated manhood were as much a part.

Though Mary Waurine Hunter suggested that prisoners risked their lives for a little cigarette money, it was more likely that they did it for the moments of glory, for the intensity of their celebrity and their physical experience—that they did it to be seen in public. When Raymond Cameron worked the crowd into a frenzy and Bob Campbell rode Sky Rocket to the finish, they heard cheers and felt the celebration of thousands of women and men, a public validation of their mastery of fear and pain. Those fleeting moments needed to last for the rest of the year, as they labored in drudgery and obscurity, invisible and socially ostracized. The rodeo thus accessed for the prisoners who were permitted to participate a celebrated, working-class masculinity, fundamentally based in self-control. Rodeo participants visibly overcame pain, fear, and danger, understood to themselves and to the crowds through the myth of the American West. While a handful of black and Mexican prisoners were able to ride in the rodeo and gain its prestige (increasingly so in the postwar years), the rodeo, like the narratives of Texas and western history, relegated racial others to the status of minor characters in the background of white redemption.

Despite the fact that prison athletics were decidedly not a form of wage labor—and this was much of their appeal to both managers and prisoners alike—this does not mean that the rodeo had no economic value. The first rodeo netted some six hundred dollars in admission fees, but in later years, it garnered tens of thousands of dollars each October. Time and again, listeners on *Thirty Minutes behind the Walls* were told that their admission charge (fifty cents for adults, twenty-five cents for children, free for police officers, guards, and their families) would go toward the Educational and Recreational Program of the prison system, which the legislature refused to fund. As one official explained,

> Many of our listeners would like to know just what the money taken in at the Rodeo is used for, so here are some of the things purchased with fifty cents admission: Musical instruments for the large Military band, and for the various string bands over the System, fiction, biographical, technical and vocational books, magazines, hymn books, religious tracts, Sunday school lessons, Bibles, radios, loud speakers, and moving picture equipment were paid for out of this fund last year. . . . So, while you are attending the Prison Rodeo and enjoying the action in the arena, you are also assisting the Prison Board and the management in carrying out an educational program that is reformative and rehabilitative, thereby making better men and women out of the unfortunates who have fallen from society and are now inmates of the Texas Penitentiary.[62]

In essence, then, prisoners worked as entertainers, earning money for the maintenance and "modernization" of the prison system, while spectators paid covert taxes toward the recreational, educational, and rehabilitative programs that the Texas legislature would not support. As both producers and consumers, working-class Texans supported the prison system financially, as it circulated entertaining messages about crime and punishment, and about the beneficence of the state. All were exploited in this scheme of a "fiscally conservative" government, at the same time that they had fun.

The rodeo was king among Texas's festive sporting events, but it was hardly alone. Texans also came to see the Fourth of July celebration, replete with boxing, baseball, and music, akin to festivities elsewhere. More striking was Texas's Juneteenth celebration, held in the prison stadium. If the rodeo and the Fourth of July championed Anglo-Texan historical memories, Juneteenth did much the same, now contorting the memorialization of black emancipation from slavery.[63] Thousands of patrons, mostly black, came to the festivities. Writers for the *Echo* explained that "a greater part of the colored population of this part of Texas . . . [was] here in all their glory," presumably a reference to the finery worn on this special day of celebration.[64] The Juneteenth celebration became a location for the proud expression of black culture in the thick of Jim Crow segregation, despite its location behind prison walls.

Juneteenth shows began with a selection of music by black inmates—the 1939 event featured blues, jazz, and spirituals. There were also comedy numbers, and music featuring the "popular novelty song team" of inmates Simon Toldon and Ocie Lee Lewis. "But the main attraction," one official explained, was the "ball game between the Prison Black Tigers and the Riverside Hardhitters," a Negro minor league team based fifteen miles northeast of Huntsville.[65] The Black Tigers and the Riverside Hardhitters developed something of a rivalry over their years of play. While the Huntsville Tigers (the "white" team) had more frequent games against local semipro and company teams, the Black Tigers' schedule was more limited. Nevertheless, in 1939, the Black Tigers beat the Hardhitters in front of the "largest crowd ever to witness a holiday ball game in Tiger Stadium." "Fast Black" Toldon, who had previously played for the Negro League's Odessa Black Oilers, pitched eight innings, and, according to *Echo* writers, his "burning fast ball held the visitors well in hand through most of the early innings."[66] Though it rained for most of the game, this neither stopped play nor dampened spirits.[67]

Simon "Fast Black" Toldon was repeatedly the centerpiece of the stories, and must have been quite a showman. Through his play on the field and as part of the "popular novelty song team" mentioned above, Toldon made himself into a celebrity in this Juneteenth context. His remarkable talents made him into a very visible prisoner, and this was rare indeed. His masculine athleticism made him acceptable, and even admirable, to white inmate newspaper sportswriters whose racism frequently marred their stories. His personality as an "entertainer" who sang "novelty" numbers was unthreatening enough for prison authorities to allow him access to the stage. Toldon performed a strategically permissible black masculinity that was desirable to prison authorities. It allowed him public presence at Juneteenth, and enabled him to represent himself as a skilled agent rather than a submissive prison inmate, thereby joining a black public sphere alternative to, but overlapping with, the public sphere sanctioned by the Texas prison.

Juneteenth at the Walls became an important event for black Texans in Walker County. According to writers for *The Echo*, "All in all Juneteenth this year is going to be a wonderful celebration, Huntsville will be the hub of

Walker County Juneteenth celebrations, and [the] Prison Stadium will be the hub of Huntsville as thousands of colored folks throng to see the big annual affair which the prisoners stage each Juneteenth."[68] Literally thousands of black Texans came together in the prison to celebrate. While the prison's Juneteenth event incorporated the celebration of black emancipation into itself, at the same time, black Texans in Walker County shaped the prison system to their needs. Where else could they find a venue that would seat thousands of people? Walker County Juneteenth had been celebrated in local churches and open spaces, but in reality, the prison stadium may have been one of the very few locations replete with seats, bleachers, and entertainment that would allow this number of black Walker County residents to congregate.[69] Perhaps it was because this space was so heavily fortified, and already so very raced as black, that this Juneteenth celebration was allowed.

Doubtless, too, African American prisoners and viewers inscribed their own messages into these events, and transformed them from celebrations of the carceral state into part of an alternative, black public sphere. Just as African Americans throughout the country celebrated the Fourth (sometimes Fifth) of July in their own and oppositional ways, so too did black prisoners make Juneteenth their own—all the more so because of its sedimented history of opposition to racial injustice.[70]

The Gender of Women's Athletics

Women, too, participated in athletic culture in Texas and California prisons, but their physical training was less focused on competitive sport than on recreating commonsense understandings of womanhood. Clara Phillips, writing in *The Bulletin*, described the "Physical Culture" class at San Quentin. Phillips informed readers that Spartan women had trained as athletes so that they might bear healthy children. This, too, was part of her goal at San Quentin, or at least after release. There were numerous methods for achieving such healthy womanhood. On one occasion, their Physical Culture class played a record by Walter Camp, the turn-of-the-century college football coach, a founder of the NCAA, and, according to historian Mark Dyreson, "a major public figure in the cult of the strenuous life."[71] As Phillips described the Physical Culture class, "fifty women follow their leader through the most intricate and difficult of setting-up exercises. No real gymnasium costumes; just anything that happens to be handy to jump into—so that the Physical Culture class in the Women's Department resembles a flower-garden in a high wind when it goes into action."[72] She continued,

Under the direction of the State, and the supervision of an inmate teacher, the class for physical development meets regularly. The teacher has some knowledge of the exercise needed for certain bodily corrections, and also the importance of a balanced diet.

Not only must healthy bodily organs be kept in perfect functional order by the essentials of fresh air, rest, proper mental and physical exercise, but the healthy mind must be given the chance to function in the healthy body.[73]

It is also significant that the women's Physical Culture class engaged primarily in noncompetitive activities, such as dance or gymnastics. Indeed, there was a long belief that white women, especially, ought to participate in sports that maintained an emphasis on feminine moral purity rather than competitiveness.[74] Nevertheless, on special occasions, women at San Quentin did play baseball, and enjoyed it a lot. Phillips even suggested that the fans got as much exercise as the base runners, from their jumping and cheering. "The women play this game well, and the teams are so evenly matched that the event is always a time of wild excitement." They, too, thrilled at competitive games that, unfortunately, were played only occasionally. Nevertheless, Phillips continued,

All this brings life and color into what would otherwise be a drab existence. Through these exercises, we keep our strength and health in the midst of cramping surroundings, and preserve that "salt of youth" which has been found a blessing to "justices, and doctors and churchmen," as well as to imprisoned women.

Through exercise, which always tends to put the mind into a clearer state, and stimulate it to function more brightly, do we strengthen and add to our capital of virtues, and the aptitudes we have received. There is no better insurance against the advance of years than a regimen of regular exercise, resorted to conscientiously every day.[75]

Phillips spoke very well to the new forms of care of the self, the belief in mental clarity drawing from physical discipline and bodily training. She spoke to the desire to stay "young" in a place where life ebbed away—especially relevant considering the gendered imperatives for women to appear youthful. The San Quentin Physical Culture class was more than a "fun" pastime; it was also a way to train prisoners in new forms of citizenship—healthy, vibrant, flushed with victory or defeat, paying allegiance to rules and to authority figures, and structured by gender conventions. The athletic games permitted at Tehachapi during the Second World War included tennis and shuffleboard, hardly the bracing activities of baseball, football, or boxing.[76]

In Texas, at the Goree Farm, "white and colored" women played sports on racially segregated fields. One photo in the Eleventh Annual Prison Rodeo Program shows a group of black women in the midst of a softball game. It seems as if competitive athletics, like hard labor, was permissible for black women but generally discouraged for whites. Where Mexican women prisoners and athletes (2 percent of the Goree population in 1941) stood in this race-gender system is difficult to know.[77] Women prisoners in Texas also had athletic programs, though they were less developed than the Physical Culture class for women at San Quentin, or later at Tehachapi.[78] Goree did offer some informal opportunities for women to participate in sports, such as softball, and there were two teams organized for play. They also went swimming on a few occasions.[79]

But more common than organized athletics, and far better publicized, were the periodic "Dance Nights" held at Goree Farm. The dances were the closest that women came to having an organized athletic program, a pleasurable engagement of bodies, a privilege and discipline that was both entertaining and fun. When men had baseball games or boxing matches to commemorate national holidays such as the Fourth of July or Juneteenth, women at Goree danced.[80] Thus the engagement of male bodies in competitive and sometimes bloody sport signified a masculine public sphere and national celebration, conflating maleness with competition, the public, and the nation itself. Conversely, women's leisure celebrations took place inside, in a version of the domestic sphere.[81]

Nearly all the women at Goree loved the dances. They offered a literal change of pace, a respite from work and a chance to listen to the Rhythmic Stringsters put on a special show. When asked if she enjoyed the evening events, Lovie Blackerby responded, "I'm having a grand time—all of us are! These dances are the real thing to us, and some of us just live from one to the other almost!"[82] The pleasure of dancing made Blackerby look forward to the next dance, the next month, and provided a temporality of punishment that was different from her daily labors and helped break up her sentence. This was literally time-consuming, helping inmates check another month off the calendar. Moreover, dance, like other forms of play, could conjure other worlds into existence, worlds that were more real for participants than the painful one they were forced to endure. This bodily activity—self-directed, and claimed for pleasure rather than labor—became a process through which prisoners of different genders and races could claim their bodies and themselves, if only temporarily, as the liminal space of the dance allowed transgression of some, but not all, categories of power and difference.[83]

First and foremost, Goree dances both recreated and subverted gender norms. In this homosocial world, who, we might wonder, danced with whom? And who led, when two women danced together? In this all-female environment, it seems that it was quite literally whoever wore the pants. Clothing proved to be a key feature of gender differentiation and female masculinity at Goree. Two women writers described the 1935 July Fourth dance in *The Echo*. "Part of the ladies were dressed as men," they told readers, and served "as escorts to the remainder." Blending the genres of gossip columnist and society reporter (as most inmate writers did, in one form or another), they explained that

> Dot dressed handsomely as a Gigolo, [and] seemed to be the prize that was sought by all of the lady-fairs, however, she had nothing for them but a cold shoulder, she was more interested in finding a cool place to rest her weary bones. "Pee-Wee" was one of the main attractions, with all the others enjoying the event immensely.

The writers continued, "some danced until they were all but 'out on their feet,' and resorted to staying in the building the next day to recuperate."[84] In a special *Thirty Minutes behind the Walls* radio interview held at a different dance, announcer Nelson Olmstead was surprised to see several women wearing trousers rather than skirts. Olmstead said to Fannie Burnett, "Listen, I see you're wearing trousers—in fact, I notice a number of the girls wearing them. Is there any special reason for this?" Burnett responded, somewhat shyly, "No suh—no special reason. Ah just likes to be different, I guess. Jus' makes the dance seem mo' real." Olmstead asked, "Are you enjoying the dance tonight?" Burnett replied, "Yes, suh! Ah sho' am. I always enjoys these dances!"[85] The transcript clearly marked Burnett as a black prisoner. For Burnett, and presumably for her partners throughout the evening, gender difference was expressed in the erotically laden atmosphere of the dance through performances of masculinity and femininity. Wearing trousers and performing sexual difference through bodily contact and physical motion made the dance *more real*, and more pleasurable. Dot and Pee-Wee were besieged with partners for the evening, but in order to maintain the demure nature of the newspaper's report, the handsomely dressed "Gigolo" offered nothing more sexual than a cold shoulder to suitors. Scheduled dances like these reproduced the controlled leisure and pleasure of slave regimes, yet in prison as under slavery, women claimed their bodies through dance in covert ways, and wove in the latest (and lewdest) dances from the outside. The Goree matron and captain did not permit dancing beyond dance nights, but there were many rules that the women flaunted. As a group of women taunted in song, "We don't care what the Cap'n won't 'low / We gonna fish-tail anyhow"—but they would have to do it on the sly.[86]

Though all the women said that they had a wonderful time at the dance, and thus verified gendered norms of pleasure in dance (if in an admittedly unconventional way), Reba Nawlin confounded Nelson Olmstead's gendered expectations when she told him that she would much rather compete in the rodeo than dance at Goree. Indeed, Nawlin had been a professional bronc rider before she went to prison. When asked if she would rather dance or be in a rodeo, she gave an emphatic "I'll take the rodeo every time!"[87]

Though gender identities were both demonstrably destabilized and confirmed in Goree dances, racial categories in the Goree dances were enforced around a black-white binary. Prisoners at the dances were segregated by race, with white women on one side of the auditorium and black women on the other. No mention was made of where Mexican prisoners stood in this Manichean world. When asked if they always administered the dances in this way, dividing the space of the room racially, matron M. V. Heath explained, "Yes, that way, we're able to give more dances. And that's what the girls want. We haven't another auditorium—and if they had to alternate, they wouldn't get to dance as often as they do."[88] While it was permissible for women in drag to dance with women, according to Heath, the spatial crossing of racial barriers was unthinkable. In this prison official's imagination, there was no alternative other than spatial separation. Thus racial intermingling was more threatening than that of same-race, homoerotic contact among women prisoners.[89] Perhaps that was why black and white prisoners could not dance together, for fear that white women might dance with masculine black prisoners like Fannie Burnett, even in drag.[90]

Athletic programs developed in the Texas and California state prison systems grew from small programs to large-scale organized events and celebrations from the Progressive Era through the New Deal years. They originated as part of the progressive impulse in the Northeast, where sports filled gaps in the disciplinary program opened by organized workers' protests over competition with inmate labor. Penologists quickly came to see the utility in these athletic programs, whose intended pedagogy including teaching keen competition, fair play, sportsmanship, respect for authority, and rule compliance—all practices that inmate would do well to internalize in order to satisfy their present keepers and future bosses. Prison authorities drew from the expanding pool of mass culture and leisure practices in the United States to retrain inmates in proper behavior, as productive laborers with good work ethics as well as consuming citizens whose buying would stimulate economic growth as well as national, and individuated, identity. All of this was part of the popular culture of punishment.

Prison sports were very much structured by the social imperatives and class relations of the day. Baseball was segregated by race, especially in Texas, delineating anew the privileges of whiteness and denigrations of blackness. The national meanings of inclusion and exclusion performed in baseball and women's athletics, as well as through Juneteenth, the Fourth of July, and California's Little Olympics, demonstrated how racial hierarchies, further structured by gendered identities, were remade for prisoners and for the publics who saw them play. But prison sports were this and more. Prisoners found new value, meaning, and pleasure for themselves in athletics. Unlike deadening labor in Texas's cotton fields or in the San Quentin jute mill, sports were socially prestigious, pleasurably gendered activities. And women's dances, as well as other sporting pursuits, also gave prisoners new, if temporary joys that could sustain them in memory or be withdrawn for noncompliant behavior. Prisoners claimed themselves and their own priorities through their bodies. Whether they did so by imagining themselves as peers with their free-world competitors on the baseball diamond or the rodeo arena, through the crowds that cheered for a fine play, or by concentrating on a game they had money riding on, they expanded the boundaries of their prison. When an inmate boxer stepped into the ring, he strove to assert himself into the multidimensional and conflict-ridden culture of the prison, where these members of the mobile working classes had been gathered for their crimes. The liberal aspects of disciplinary spectacle and entertainment were often intended for a broad public audience, while brutal displays of prison violence, still the foundation for the penal order, remained hidden. Violence, the material basis of control, was well known among inmates. In this juxtaposition we can interpret how different audiences were understood and "instructed" through state practice, from pleasure to work to the infliction of pain. The many forms of violence, and the death that punishment could bring, remained a secret known only to prisoners, and, obliquely, to their families. It is to inmates' experiences with death that we now turn.

A Dark Cloud Would Go Over

Death and Dying

There were many ways to die. From the capitally condemned to the tubercular to the overworked to those stabbed in fights, prisoners developed an intimacy with death. At San Quentin, they called it "going out the back door" or getting a "backdoor parole." The condemned to hang would "do the air dance," those sentenced to the gas chamber would "sniff the eggs." In Texas, black prisoners spoke of death as a dark cloud. The dead could walk for some Texas prisoners, who might call on them for strength to keep living, as they worked on these haunted grounds. Augustus "Track Horse" Haggerty called out in song, "Oh just wake up dead man, help me carry my row." Another song called Mississippi's Parchman Farm a "murderer's home," and Texas prison farms were no kinder.[1]

Death was always proximate: random or targeted violence, accidental deaths or deliberate killings—there was not always a distinction. Grasping the nature of prison life requires that violence—always an amorphous concept—be defined beyond the ordinary sense of a knife, a fist, or a bullet. For a full accounting, violence, in the prison world, must include a microbe, forced labor under a scorching sun, putrid water, new and "humane" forms of execution, and even a rope used to hang oneself. Death was perhaps a bit less proximate in the 1930s than it had been in each state's convict lease era, when even the pretense of concern would have been an improvement. Prisons heightened the immanence of violence—state violence and interpersonal violence—as well as the chance of dying from disease. These were structural impositions—institutional ways of death and life. Inside America's growing carceral facilities—the underside, and thus a foundation, of the modern regulatory state—prisoners died by means that ranged across a spectrum of medical, legal, and illegal concerns: from state sanctions like capital execution to diseases like pneumonia; from "accidental" drowning to gunshot wounds; from inmate stabbings to sun stroke. Some were recorded as deaths from "natural causes," others as violent illegal killings, others still as executions fully approved by the state. Too often, scholars have misunderstood these deathways as analytically and politically distinct.[2]

Yet the line between these kinds of death was not always clear, and decisions as to where officials drew it were subjective. In fact—and this insight extends beyond the prison—there is no such thing as dying of "natural causes." Death is a condition of life, but belief in death from natural causes is based on an understanding of nature as a precultural, nonpolitical state of being. All lives, and their ends, are invariably shaped by cultural practices, the power relations of which are always historical, and always political.[3] When three black men died on a single day from "the heat" on Clemens State Farm in 1930, the Texas Prison Board determined that these deaths could not have been avoided: "The evidence show[s] that the utmost care was taken to prevent these unfortunate circumstances, and that the death of these three men is not the fault of the employees of Clemens State Farm."[4] In extant records, the deaths were attributed to "heat exhaustion" rather than human action, and to circumstances as uncontrollable as the weather.

These men's deaths at everyday labor under state control reveal the prison's function in institutionalizing a zone of indistinction, a threshold space between life and death.[5] It also reveals a shift from nineteenth- to twentieth-century modes of state formation. In the nineteenth century, racist lynch violence bolstered a relatively weak state, while the convict lease system worked countless black prisoners, often to death, in the interest of an expanding capitalist infrastructure and political economy. Punishment in the Depression differed in many respects; indeed, modernizing and New Deal states would protect and extend subjects' lives in innovative ways. But they would continue to permit degrees of death for unruly and racially degraded criminals, as crucial Others to the category of the citizen, who would be more closely protected.

A growing historiographical, anthropological, and philosophical literature has developed around the meaning and ways of dying. Michel Foucault's conceptualization of biopower as the modern governmental regulation of life rather than sovereign rule through death is but one element of this. New histories of southern lynch mobs have convincingly argued that as the modern regulatory state emerged across the South, the prison system, and particularly its private and technocratic death penalties, suppressed racist lynch violence.[6] More people were executed in Texas and California in the 1930s than ever before. The same decade that saw the long-overdue curtailment of southern lynch rule and the expansion of the welfare state also saw a dramatic spike in capital execution. In fact, capital sentencing rose nationwide in the Depression, peaking in 1935, when 199 people were put to death. Then as now, Texas was a leader in lethal punishment. The twenty men who died in Huntsville's electric chair in 1935 made up 10 percent of all executions for that year, and Texas accounted for 7 percent of the nation's total executions between 1930 and 1942 (148 of 2,065 total executions). Texas legally executed 158 people between 1929 and 1942, and California citizens sanctioned the killing of 144 people in the same period.[7] These numbers dramatically outpaced previous decades of capital punishment. Progressive Era movements against capital punishment had withered. Only six California legislators supported an anti–death penalty bill in 1933, while thirty-three voted against it.[8] Though abolitionist pockets remained, a 1936 Gallup Poll found that 68 percent of Americans supported execution.[9]

As prison officials wrote their own histories in annual reports, they downplayed executions (if they were mentioned at all) but stressed the increasing concern shown to prisoners and the expansion of medical facilities. This was in large measure true: the 1930s did see an improvement in prisoners' health care. The availability of medicines, of hospital wards, of tests and treatments for syphilis and other ailments were welcomed by prisoners—especially if they could get some decent food, time away from prison fields or the jute mill, and a bed with clean sheets. Yet for all this, few recall that one of the first outbreaks of the 1918 global flu pandemic took place at San Quentin, perhaps because so many people and so many bacteriological materials from around the world were gathered in its dank walls.[10] Penal modernity would bring new dangers.

If incarceration can be understood as a form of social and civic death, actual biological death was all too real a possibility. Death is a difficult matter to analyze, for, as Claudio Lomnitz has put it, "dying is the experience of slipping beyond the social world of affects and signification."[11] But for the historian as well as for the family members of the incarcerated, the actual conditions of death were especially opaque—doubly so when the circumstances of death were suspicious, or for people who had reason for skepticism as to whether or not policemen, prison guards, or wardens would tell the truth about what had happened to their kin. Even for those inside, death, and its threat, enforced a veil of silence. A black Texas prisoner once explained that talking about how someone died might itself be dangerous. As in so much else, speaking in code was necessary.

You actually can't tell how nothing happened. You got to go on the side with them if you want to live a long time. . . .

You may be cuttin' wood and they say, "He was cuttin' wood and a tree fell on him." All the rest of the guys say, "How'd he get killed?" Say, "He was cuttin' and got trapped by a tree."

You can never tell. Things I actually seen here and things that actually happened—you got to lie, you got to lie. You tell just how it happened, a dark cloud will go over you, and nobody never know what became of you. You runned away. "Did he get away?" "Yeah, he got away."

He got away in a shallow pit grave somewhere, in them woods somewhere. Ain't nobody can come back here and tell a report but *them*. So that's the way that goes.[12]

Medical Death, Violent Death

Keeping prisoners alive was not always easy in the Depression's underfunded and overcrowded institutions. Many years after his release, Skip Lankford recalled with no small gratitude the role that doctors played when he was behind bars. Most prisoners, he said, suffered from some degree of malnutrition. Only when the doctor intervened would a prisoner get a full meal per day. "A thousand men woulda died if it hadn't been for that doctor."[13] Prison physicians' roles meshed disciplinary and caregiving functions. One of their tasks was to prevent inmates from malingering. The other was to keep prisoners back from the edge of death. The doctors defined the bottom threshold or baseline expenditure below which the prison should not go, unless it would countenance the widespread loss of life. Liberal democratic states like California, and even illiberal ones like Texas, were unwilling to cross far below that line, but neither would they dedicate the funds necessary to rise much above it.[14]

In the late nineteenth and early twentieth centuries, the most sophisticated medical facilities available in the Texas Prison System were at the Huntsville Walls Unit, though investigations lamented that these were antiquated and inadequate.[15] Doctors employed by the prison were to make weekly tours of the numerous farms where prisoners, then leased to private and state farmers and railroad builders, lived, worked, and died in conditions that were both putrid and violent. As the convict lease system fell into public disrepute and free-world wages dropped low enough to make the lease undesirable, the state assumed control of those farms, but medical care on these scattered sites remained inferior to that available at the Walls.[16] It should come as little surprise that white inmates, particularly young and compliant whites, benefited from the greater medical care available at the Walls, and that black, Mexican, and disobedient white inmates suffered disproportionately from medical neglect on state farms.

Over the course of the 1930s, the Texas prison's medical system became increasingly sophisticated. A new hospital at the Walls was completed in 1935, to the high praise of the prison administrators who built it.[17] Moreover, in 1941 a hospital at the State Farm Industries Unit was "equipped as a modern institution," serving inmates at prison farms scattered south of Houston. Tubercular prisoners were brought to Wynne Farm, which in 1941 was updated to give "first-class attention" to these infirm prisoners and also modernized so "that no contact is had between these patients and the non-tubercular inmates."[18] The construction of new buildings and increasing medical segregation guided physicians toward a progressive narrative that touted the always-improving medical care available. This narrative was not without merit: indeed, many inmates probably received medical attention that would have been unavailable to them prior to incarceration. That many services may in fact have been out of reach to the population at large bespeaks the broader social maldistribution of health, in which medical resources disproportionately benefited wealthy whites while neglecting poor whites, blacks, and Mexicans.[19]

By modern standards, medical care in California was superior to that of Texas. Leo Stanley, San Quentin's chief surgeon from 1913 until 1951, gave a brief and self-aggrandizing history of San Quentin's medical system. The facilities he found when he arrived, fresh from medical school and with no surgical experience, were appalling. "The ventilation was abominable, the beds were crowded together, air space was extremely limited." Equally disturbing were the social conditions, where hygienic segregation was as underdeveloped, to his taste, as racial segregation. "Whites, Negroes, and Indians commingled here indiscriminately," and the "surroundings were extremely sordid." Stanley oversaw the building of a new hospital with more air, more light, and more segregation.[20]

Along with his four paid assistants and inmate clerks and nurses, Stanley developed a well-ordered medical system. For regular treatments or ailments that arose over the course of a given day, prisoners gathered in morning and afternoon pill lines, and doctors were generally available for emergencies.[21] Most beneficial to the male prison population was the fact that after many years of progressive lobbying for a separate women's institution, women prisoners were removed from San Quentin and brought to the new facility in Tehachapi in 1934.[22] When the women left, the Women's Building at San Quentin, which Stanley had eyed greedily for years, became the men's new hospital. By 1942 medicine at San Quentin was more sophisticated than at most other prisons in the United States—noted prison reformer Austin MacCormick, who would soon tour the Texas system, placed it among "the best . . . in all the state institutions of the country."[23] This, as in most histories of medicine behind bars, was an unabashedly progressive narrative that hid as much as it told. While dangers to health in Texas prisons tended to come from inattention and general neglect—the lack of medical modernity— in California, medical danger could come from medical modernity itself. Inmates under Stanley's care were subject to putatively voluntary steriliza- tions and a battery of strange procedures, ranging from sleep experiments to implanting testicle materials from recently executed prisoners—and goats— into other men. Prisoners had access to modern physicians, but those physi- cians also had access to them as experimental subjects. Stanley was generous with this access, and he saw prison as providing unparalleled opportunities for research.[24]

As prisons assumed moral care and fiscal responsibility for inmates, the states, like slave owners of a previous era, sought to ensure a healthy and able-bodied population. Progressive ideals informed medical practice and bespoke the increasing power of an expert-driven state to regulate social hygiene. This had implications at both institutional and societal levels. Insti- tutionally, medical care could guarantee inmates' health; prisoners welcomed this, and it helped the institutions run smoothly. But medicine could also be used as disciplinary control and withheld as punishment. Unwell prisoners might be left untreated or simply forgotten. Nevertheless, inmates who fell ill on Texas prison farms later in the decade were more likely to be sent to the hospital at the Walls, rather than to suffer while still working on a prison farm. The goal, however, rarely stated outright but clear enough from many Texas annual reports' financial statements, was that the ill might become well enough to return to work. In California, somewhat more modern goals were referred to: believing that health was related to social hygiene more broadly, officials like Leo Stanley thought that the eradication of illness would lessen crime overall, and that physicians might offer a cure to crime itself.[25]

By the middle of the Depression decade, then, as the ill were congre- gated for treatment, most deaths at the Walls were due to illnesses rather than fights or gunshots. After its new hospital was completed and as inmates from much of the scattered prison system were sent there, death at the Walls, or at the nearby Wynne tubercular unit, came slowly. It crept up in coughs and wheezes, from meningitis and malignant lumps explained too late and infections treated ineffectively or too slowly. As a result of the more efficient transfer of ill inmates to the Walls across the decade, most of the dying done on other farms and in other units came from heat stroke and overwork—from accidents and "accidents," from sudden heart attacks, from stabbings or beatings by inmates, or from being shot by guards. Death became somewhat less frequent on the farms. But it could come suddenly, literally as a lightning strike, a falling tree, or an old grievance and a knife in the side. It could come mysteriously, as "accidental asphyxia," the cause of which is lost in the records. Prisoners on farms could still expect delay before being recognized as sufficiently ill to deserve transfer to the Walls, and in that time could suffer greatly: when G. B. Butler, ill with jaundice, was transferred on August 11, 1939, from Clemens Farm, to the New Unit Hospital, the transfer came too late. He died there three days later.[26] That same year, the expanded Walls Unit hospital neared capacity. Prison officials diagnosed this "condition" as "caused by more transfers from the farms to Huntsville Hospital for treatment."[27] Despite this, officials found reason for self-congratulation. In 1940, Dr. Butler proudly reported that "the Medical Departments of the recently visited prisons in Arkansas, Mississippi, and Louisiana are, as a whole, obsolete and inadequate compared to the Medical Department of our Texas Prison System."[28] This was a well-chosen and self-serving choice of comparisons.

Mortality rates in Texas and California prisons fluctuated during the 1930s. (See Table 7.3) Despite this, mortality rates in Texas generally declined, even as the prison population grew in total numbers. This probably reflected the centralization of the medical system at the Walls and at the Imperial Farm. In the same years California's mortality rate was broadly stable, and generally lower than Texas's. The decline was consistent, however, with national trends in the 1930s and across the twentieth century. The national mortality rates saw bumps in the second half of the decade, though they remained lower in 1940 than they were in 1930, and they would drop lower still in 1950.[29]

While this might be good news for those entering institutions later in the decade, prison inmates still tended to die earlier than their peers on the outside. Mortality rates in California and Texas penitentiaries were significantly higher than rates for the general populations of their respective states and of the nation overall. This was true despite the fact that the prisons consisted overwhelmingly of young men, who, given their youth, would presumably not die in large numbers. In Texas, twelve of the forty-two prisoners who died in 1940 (excluding those executed) were between sixteen and twenty-five years old, and they comprised some 29 percent of the dead for that year. Given that prison officials recorded 2,415 prisoners in this age group in 1940, a conservative estimate of the mortality rate for Texas prisoners aged sixteen to twenty-five comes to five deaths per thousand.[30] In the same year, the death rate for Texans of all races aged fifteen to twenty-four was 2.7 per thousand. In other words, the mortality rate for Texas prisoners was nearly twice that of the general population of the same age. The white Texan mortality rate for this age group in 1940 was 2.3 per thousand, and for "all other races" was 4.7 per thousand. Texas inmate mortality rates were thus higher than even the already disproportionately high rates for black and Mexican Texans.[31] If racism can be defined as "the state-sanctioned and/or extra-legal production and exploitation of group-differentiated vulnerabilities to premature death," serving a prison sentence compounded and expanded racism's biological dangers.[32]

Yet even behind bars, or especially behind bars, racism differentiated and allocated life chances. Data is unavailable from California, but evidence from Texas confirms what we might have already suspected—black prisoners died at higher rates than Mexican or white prisoners. Numbers differed by year, given the vagaries of escape attempts on different farms or the predilections of individual guards and inmates. But the clear trend was that black prisoners died at rates that could nearly double those for white or Mexican inmates (see table 7.1 below).[33] Only in 1931 and 1936 did whites die at higher rates (excluding executions) than African Americans.[34]

Black inmates suffered more violence and death than did white or Mexican prisoners; the same was true for inmates in maximum security facilities, where violence and death were concentrated, not controlled. Across the period 1929–1942, mortality rates at California's Folsom were almost 14 percent higher than at San Quentin, with Folsom's mortality rate averaging 10.1 and San Quentin's averaging 8.7 per thousand. When legal executions are removed, the mortality rate at Folsom in these years was 21 percent higher than at San Quentin. Folsom's noncapital mortality rate averaged nine per thousand prisoners; it was 7.1 per thousand prisoners at San Quentin. Lethal violence was also far higher at Folsom, with seven of eight system-wide deaths from stabbings or "nonaccidental skull fractures" taking place at Folsom, and one stabbing at San Quentin in 1933–1934. Moreover, suicide rates were also higher at Folsom. Though Folsom's population was smaller than San Quentin's, twice as many inmates killed themselves there, with .20 per thousand suicides at San Quentin and .72 per thousand at Folsom in 1933, and .35 per thousand

TABLE 7.1

Texas Prison Mortality Rates per Thousand Prisoners by Race (excluding execution)

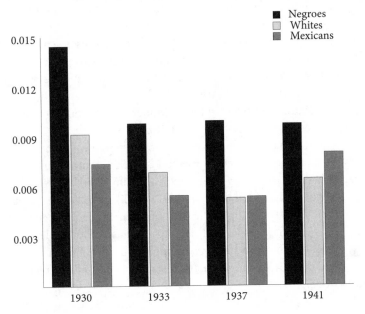

at San Quentin and 1.38 per thousand at Folsom in 1934. Together, these suicide rates dwarfed national averages, doubling the 1933 national rates and tripling them in 1934.[35]

The same was broadly true in the Lone Star State. There was of course no good place to be a Texas prisoner, but Eastham, the farm for recidivists, was especially rough. August 16, 1938, was a particularly bad day at Eastham State Farm,and can serve as an illustration. Two people were shot and two others drowned, presumably as they attempted to escape across the Trinity River. Two more people were shot dead the next day, and five days later another was stabbed to death. A month later, on September 28 and September 30, two more were worked to death, the causes of death listed not as overwork in the sun but as thermic fever.[36]

Prison medical records consistently differentiated between kinds of death. Officials were curious about the distinction between death from coronary thrombosis, cardiac failure, and aortic insufficiency, the better to administer the lives of the imprisoned—so that they could work in prison and return, ideally, as productive rather than enervated citizens.[37] But the more salient

A Dark Cloud Would Go Over | 197

distinction for prison authorities was between violent and nonviolent death, between death at the hands of another, and death from "natural causes."

Yet the difference between violent death and dying from natural causes is a political difference, and, as noted earlier, this is a key point. Though prison officials recorded sunstroke as a disease, an alternative argument is that sunstroke, or the more medicalized "thermic fever" *was* a violent death, differing only from legal execution in that those who died from it were not, in fact, sentenced to die. They were worked to death in the Texas sun, driven by the lash and the guards' hopes of having a bumper crop of cotton or sugar cane to help finance the running of the prison itself.

The Lone Star State is better known for oppressive heat than for its chilly winters, but anyone subjected to the sudden temperature drop of a "blue norther," when the jet stream blasts arctic air from Canada across the Great Plains without even a foothill to slow it, is unlikely to forget. Sleeping in drafty buildings and working in the cold and rain and without access to dry clothes would make it colder still. Perhaps because of forced labor in cold and wet fields, pneumonia was more common in Texas than it was in California. Pneumonia killed 10 percent of Texas prisoners and 4 percent of California prisoners.

Tuberculosis proved to be the second most likely cause of death for Texas prisoners between 1930 and 1941. Indeed, TB was second only to legal execution itself. While nearly one-fifth (18 percent) of inmates who died in Texas prisons in these years were put to death in the electric chair, 15 percent of the dead succumbed to tuberculosis in one form or another. Yet death from TB proved to be no more of a "natural" cause of death than capital punishment or thermic fever. Just as district attorneys pushed for capital sentencing based on the sex and race of the accused and the victim, tubercular morbidity and mortality were deeply implicated in the southern political economy. Diet and living conditions were key indicators of death or survival for people infected with TB. The specific demography of those who died in prison of tuberculosis is unavailable, but the conditions of overwork and the crowded and dilapidated housing characteristic of black life in the Jim Crow South meant that African Americans were dramatically overrepresented among its sufferers, and these conditions were exacerbated behind bars. According to historian Samuel Kelton Roberts Jr., approximately one-quarter of Americans who died from TB in 1929 were black, and the numbers were higher three years later. Poor whites also suffered from TB, but the largest Texas cities showed a dramatic racial disparity in the disease. In Houston and Dallas, pulmonary tuberculosis mortality rates for nonwhites in 1935 were roughly twice the white rates.[38]

Tuberculosis was even more lethal in California than it was in Texas, probably due to overcrowding at the Big House–style prisons of San Quentin and Folsom. Moreover, California's reliance on the Folsom quarry and the San Quentin jute mill meant that floating fibers and dust particles could facilitate tuberculosis infection or exacerbate its effects. As in the racial ghetto of Chinatown across the bay, tuberculosis remained a serious problem in San Quentin even as it diminished for more affluent populations across the country.[39]

Tuberculosis rates in California prisons were alarmingly high. Indeed, TB mortality rates were far above national averages. Even though California prisons held mostly white inmates, their TB mortality rates were much closer to rates for nonwhite populations on the outside. Taking 1933 and 1934 as a sample (these are the only years when both San Quentin and Folsom kept detailed medical records of deaths), TB death rates in California prisons were 2.4 and 2.33 per thousand. National averages for all races in the same years were some five times lower than California prison rates, with .568 and .534 deaths from TB per thousand. Nonimprisoned white rates were even lower, with .493 and .46 deaths per thousand. Rates for nonwhites in the outside world were in fact much closer to imprisoned death rates for TB. In marked contrast to white rates, death rates for "all other races" were 2.499 per thousand in 1933 and 2.421 per thousand in 1934.[40] The significance can be put in two simple ways. The first is that white prisoners died at rates *as if* they were nonwhite—they lost the health privileges of whiteness. The second is that nonwhites outside of prison died of tuberculosis at rates *as if* they were convicted criminals—that is, their deaths indicated a precarious lack of biological citizenship. (See table 7.2.)[41]

At the Wynne tubercular farm, the Huntsville Walls Unit, and elsewhere, inmates played key roles in caring for the sick and the dying. Inmate nurses were sometimes even rewarded with time deducted from their sentences and awards of meritorious conduct, particularly if they treated inmates with communicable diseases, such as spinal meningitis, or helped in the hospital during flu outbreaks.[42] The concern inmate nurses showed was remarkable, because it was perhaps more common for inmates to fight than to offer comfort.

Indeed, as we have seen, prisons sustained a world of nearly universal antagonism that made mutual support hard to achieve and harder still to maintain. Largely because of the dominating hierarchies they supported, overtly violent pain and death were all too common. Violence threatened from every direction—from guards, from other prisoners, and by prisoners

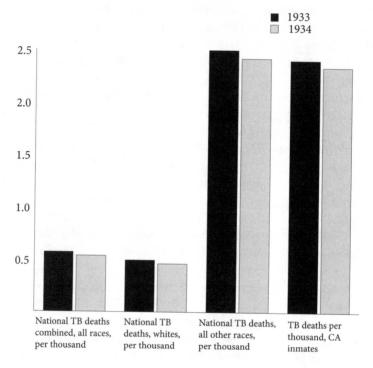

TABLE 7.2

Combined TB Mortality Rates in California Prisons,
and Nationally, by Race, 1933–1934

■ 1933
□ 1934

against their own bodies. Five percent of those who died in each state were killed by other inmates. Between 1930 and 1941, 11 percent of Texas prisoners killed died of gunshot wounds, while 2 percent of inmates killed in California were shot by guards.[43]

Violence could manifest itself and escalate with great speed, particularly if a prisoner disrespected a guard or disobeyed an order.[44] A black prisoner named Hugh Adams was born in Missouri, but he died at San Quentin. On the afternoon of December 28, 1931, Adams lit a cigarette in a no-smoking area. A guard named McVey commanded him to stop, but he looked at McVey and continued walking and smoking—a clear performance of disrespect. McVey pulled him out of the crowd and Adams began walking with him, but then (according to testimony) took off at a run and tried to blend in with a group of "other colored fellows."[45] Guards whistled for him to stop, and when he did not, they opened fire. Adams ducked under balconies and into alleys between buildings, and tried to climb gates. Before he was fatally shot, ricocheting bullets wounded seven other prisoners.

Officials testified that the 28-year-old Adams had been a troublemaker—he was accused of having had a knife a few days earlier and had reportedly run from guards then. It was possible that on this occasion he was trying to hide a knife or other contraband before being searched. Yet it seems clear enough that on this day, Adams was still well within the walls of the institution, and though he ran despite an order to stand still, there was no risk (to guards) or hope (from Adams's perspective) of escape. Disrespect and disobeying orders was never tolerable from prisoners, regardless of their race. Yet disrespect from a black prisoner was surely considered even more insubordinate, and to be dealt with harshly. In any event, when the smoke cleared and the investigation ended, all guards were exonerated from any wrongdoing. Adams was buried in San Quentin's graveyard, Potters' Field.

An inmate running from guards might expect trouble, but violence was impossible to predict. In the midst of a workday in late 1929, an inmate and a guard fought in the new section of the jute mill.[46] The guard hit the inmate with his club and began dragging him out, presumably to see the captain of the guard. Tension mounted as prisoners began to protest. "[T]he cons," in one guard's words, "had begun to boil up." C. F. Cobb watched the events unfold from an elevated, mesh-covered gun position suspended from the jute mill's ceiling. Cobb and a guard on the floor, likely George W. Lynch, had little luck getting the inmates back to work. Cobb "threw a shell in the gun and let the hammer down on safety," preparing to shoot if the situation escalated.

But just as the threat of an uprising quickly mounted, so too did it subside. Most inmates returned to work at their spinners and carders, but a few still hung around. Cobb kept an eye on them from his perch in the cage. "I sat down and was leaning over watching. . . . I bent over and started to straighten up again and the gun went off. That is all I know."[47] George Lynch, a guard standing below the cage, looked up and saw Cobb, "looking at the gun in a sort of a daze."[48] None of the men still milling around where the fight took place were hit, though, and Cobb must have breathed a sigh of relief. It was short lived.

Arthur C. Snead worked in the old section of the jute mill, two or three hundred feet away from the scuffle. Given the size and general din of the mill, Snead was probably unaware that anything out of the ordinary had even taken place. But that mattered little to the 24-year-old Virginian. What mattered was that Cobb forgot to put the safety back on his weapon, or take his finger off the trigger. What mattered to Snead was the trajectory of a bullet in a crowded space, and the bad luck of being where it struck.

Suicide

In his 1940 memoirs, San Quentin doctor Leo Stanley described the myriad ways he had seen prisoners take their lives,

> some having jumped from a height, some having hanged themselves in their cells, others having taken poison, and still others having soaked their clothes in oil and applied a match. One demented prisoner, snatching a razor from the barber's hand, slashed his throat from ear to ear and expired at my feet before anything could be done.[49]

For Stanley, the macabre list was an effective narrative device: it heightened his moral authority as a man in the trenches with the experience to be believed. He and others tried to save suicidal prisoners, from medical concern as well as to protect institutional reputations. He had no control over death, but he might control mortality.[50] Stanley also knew that others had long been fascinated by suicide, for academic as well as sensationalist reasons, and he played on both forms of interest in equal measures.[51] In the 1930s, suicide rates rose across the United States to a high in 1933 of 17.4 suicides per one hundred thousand Americans, a statistic that did not specify differences by race, class, sex, or age.[52] Larger and larger numbers of men, especially, blamed themselves rather than systemic forces for their families' poverty. If despair and self-loathing were one component of increased suicide in the Depression, concerns about social alienation remained consistent from earlier periods. Depression-era prisons, as with more recent ones, were sites of deliberate alienation. As Donald Cressey noted, keeping prisoners from identifying with each other was an important control strategy.[53] If killing, for some prisoners or guards, became a twisted form of alienated empowerment, suicide, for others, became an escape.

There is more than a grain of historical truth to the idea that death, and even self-mutilation, could become an escape from the tortures of prison life. Prison doctors like Texas's W. B. Veazy expressed surprise about "the apparent disregard the average inmate has for his health," but Veazy misunderstood the social devaluing of prisoners' bodies, a process to which prisoners were hardly immune.[54] How else are the many injuries that prisoners did to themselves intelligible, as they cut Achilles tendons and severed fingers and hands? Prison doctors treated twenty self-inflicted arm fractures in 1940 alone.[55] Prisoners injured themselves to avoid work in the fields—which infuriated farm managers—but also to control their own bodies, even through pain and destruction. The line between state-sanctioned punishment and self-destruction blurred.

Multiple tragedies drove people to hopelessness in the 1930s, and though sociological typologies can help make sense of the suicides that occurred, each had its own reasons. Whatever they were, prison made them worse. Yet one constant was the turmoil of missing family and loved ones, of the demise of the social ties beyond the walls. For the 33-year-old Analeto Nartates, it was the difficulty he faced in being deported to the Philippines. Unlike many Filipinos, after the nine years he had already spent at the Walled City, he actually looked forward to deportation.[56] Driven mad by the wait—and surely by his years at San Quentin—he attacked his cellmate. The ensuing fight was broken up by guards' warning shots. After Nartates was hospitalized, one doctor reported that he "was quite worried that he had not been deported, so he decided he would end his life."[57] He screamed incessantly and was under near-constant sedation: "On Saturday night he tried to commit suicide. He put his finger in a light socket and he put his head in the toilet bowl. On Sunday he refused to eat breakfast, saying that he wanted to die."[58] He attacked a hospital attendant and was put in a straightjacket because "he was using everything in there to injure himself and anyone who came in." After eight days in the hospital, at three in the morning on January 12, he died. Somehow, a coroners' jury determined that Nartates died from "natural causes," one of thirty-five such deaths at San Quentin in 1940. According to official records, Nartates' death was wholly unrelated to his desire to die. Nartates never returned to the Philippines. He, too, was buried in the San Quentin cemetery.

Les Shuttleworth was in a similar state of despair, though he did not attack anyone. The Department of Labor had a "hold" on him for deportation, but he did not mention any desire to return to his native Canada. The 25-year-old arrived at San Quentin in June 1932 on five counts of robbery and another "one to twenty" to be served consecutively. Shuttleworth had a good record, and was about to be promoted out of the jute mill. But Captain Brakefield reported that Shuttleworth had been morose. "He came up to see me several days ago from the mill. He was very much worried. In fact, he cried a little, but never asked for another job." But the job was not the problem: "[H]e left the impression that he didn't get any more mail from his people." A few days later, witnesses saw him climb through the restraining bars on the fourth tier. Charles Bennett explained, he "was creeping through the bars. He held onto the edge of the thing and he was trembling, and he gave himself a push and dived." Henry Nichols, Shuttleworth's former cellmate, reflected that he might have seen it coming, since Shuttleworth was so terrified about his sentence. Then, one morning, "he told me he wasn't going to worry about it any more. I thought afterwards that he might have figured on it then, thought about taking his own life."[59]

If suicide bespoke despair for some, for others it was a kind of escape. In a world where death and life mingled so intimately, being shot by a guard could have been a kind of release. It is impossible to know the motivations of the dead, but common sense in prison folklore holds that if a prisoner is tired of living, an escape attempt will guarantee death. Country musician Johnny Cash's song "The Wall" describes a prison inmate who tried to escape knowing that no one had survived an attempt before: "The newspapers called it a jailbreak plan, / But I know it was suicide." In *Passed On*, her literary history of black dying, Karla F. C. Holloway reflected on her son's death while attempting to escape from prison, and she places his life in the long history of African American life—and death—in escapes from historical or contemporary forms of unfreedom.[60]

Though Cecil Davis did not slash his wrist or tie a noose from a bedsheet, he did commit suicide.[61] The 33-year-old Davis was serving a two-year sentence on Texas's Retrieve Farm, then dedicated to white men over 25 years old of intermediate security risk and rehabilitative potential. Slightly more than a week after his arrival, Davis tried his first escape. At around 9:30 in the morning, while working with the Hoe Squad #9 near the Retrieve Club House, he looked directly at Captain Brown, in position on horseback behind the squad, and told him, "Captain, I am going, you can kill me if you want to." Davis dashed into the cane patch, and the nearest guards tried to shoot him but missed. Captain Brown, on horseback, overtook Davis after about three hundred yards. He talked to Davis for twenty minutes and convinced him to return. On the way back, Davis reportedly told Brown, "You might as well kill me, I'm not going back. . . . I'm not going to do this time." Reflecting on the day to investigators, Brown tried to explain just how difficult the trip back to the building was: "You don't realize how hard it was getting him back to the building and him talking that way to me."

On his return, a visiting physician examined Davis. Dr. Blair concluded, "There isn't anything wrong with him. It seems to me like he just wanted to run off." The doctor prescribed a favorite cure: Davis simply "needed to be put back to work." Davis was allowed to watch the picture show that night, and promised Captain Brown that he wouldn't try to escape again. Brown warned him, "You had better not run anymore because somebody might kill you. I gave you your life today." On the Retrieve Farm, Davis's life was not his own. For Captain Brown, riding hard after an escaping prisoner and convincing him to return was difficult work. It would have been easier to kill him.

Davis ran the following day. Brown shot him dead.

In her report on the investigation, prison board member Charlotte Teagle determined that the killing of Cecil Davis was very much justified. As a liberal member of the board, she commended Captain Brown "for his patience and good judgment in getting the prisoner back to the building under such trying conditions" the day before he killed him. She concluded that Davis was "in a very depressed state of mind" or was perhaps "mentally unbalanced" but that, in either case, "he placed himself in [a] position to be killed."

While the evidence of the report clearly indicated that Davis would rather die than spend two years at Retrieve, inmates' testimony begged questions. Most gave pointedly vague responses to Mrs. Teagle's questions. After receiving numerous answers of "No" or "No Ma'am," she asked, "You men don't do much talking. Why?" Eddie Canonico responded, "I came to do my time and give no trouble," though trouble to whom is ambiguous. C. B. Bland's answer was more than simply unresponsive: "I had rather not make any statement, but at the same time I am not casting any reflections on Captain Miller [the Retrieve Farm manager] personally, but for my own safety, since I am trying to secure my release, and for other reasons, I had rather not testify." The reasons for not testifying are unclear. Yet these were lost to the historical record when the dark cloud came over, and died with Davis on that hot July day.

Suicide, like self-mutilation, disgraced the prison. It belied the system's self-depictions of kindness and social correction. It also demonstrated the limits on what the state could in fact to do control (if not correct) its wards' minds or bodies. It showed a grim creativity, too, as prisoners used the means of their punishment to control their self-destruction. The cane knives Texas prisoners used at labor were repurposed for self-destruction.[62] Twenty-three-year-old Mack L. Johnson strangled himself with six feet of twine stolen from San Quentin's jute mill.[63] Just a year later another San Quentin inmate tried to jump to his death—using the physical space and architecture of the Big House to craft his own demise. Warden Clinton Duffy complained of yet *another* article in the newspaper about it. Surely moved by the public shaming as well as by his own liberalism, Duffy asked the Prison Board, "In view of the fact that several such unfortunate incidents have occurred, do you not think it would be feasible to build a wire screen on the second tier of cells to prevent inmates from jumping over the rail?" No action was taken; the estimated twenty-seven thousand dollars was more daunting than another death.[64] Yet it was also significant that Duffy's solution was a technocratic and architectural one, rather than one that addressed the causes of suicidal despair. Such was the nature of liberal reform.

When prisoners killed themselves in these ways, they used the space of the prison against themselves and against the prison itself. They revealed the limits of the state as a caregiving entity. They also demonstrated the highly limited range of options at their disposal for resisting the terms of their punishment, in this situation of radically constrained agency and being. When prisoners' lives were so thoroughly controlled, they could at least exert control over the destruction of their own bodies. When prisoners severed their own heel strings or cut off fingers and hands, they could avoid field labor until they healed. Yet tactics of shaming officials, if tactics they were, could only work if prison officials were concerned for the appearance of providing care. In Texas, Lee Simmons did not care at all.

The Shadow of the Cloud

The dangers of the prison were no secret, but the actual conditions and the distance from loved ones meant that prisoners' families might never know what happened to their kin.

Rosie Wilson, of Beckville, Texas, received a telegram on June 8, 1937, about her son, Johnnie. To say that the message is succinct is to put it mildly:

> Rosie Wilson, Colored,
>   Beckville, Texas.
>   Johnnie Wilson died last night eastham state farm weldon Texas advise
> by Western union immediately whether you want remains your expense.
>   H E Moore, Chief Bureau of record and
>   Identification Texas Prison System. 952am.[65]

Mrs. Wilson responded the same day that she would retrieve the body immediately. She was fortunate to have the money to bring her son home, and Johnnie, on some level, was fortunate that his mother wanted to bring him home at all, regardless of the crime he had committed. Yet when Otis Harris, the man she sent to retrieve her son's body, arrived at the prison, the terse clarity of H. E. Moore's telegram was lost behind the murkier truths of punishment. The body was missing. Mr. Harris

> saw one Mr. Wade, but could not get any satisfactory information as to where the body was, first saying that the body was here at Huntsville, in a death cell and after learning that Mr. Harris, was prepared to remove the body then he Mr. Harris, was advised that the body was at the Ferguson,

farm about sixty miles distant, and also advised him that if he went there he would very likely be denied admittance.

Wade advised Harris that most likely, "the body had alreay [sic] been intered [sic], and that she would have to pay $50.00 for embalming the body and that they had no facilities there for embalming the same." W. P. Barber, justice of the peace of Precinct Two of Panola County, expressed perhaps justifiable skepticism about why Rosie Wilson was having trouble receiving her son's body. "Now Govenor [sic], it appears that there is something very irregular about this affair, and it also appears that for some reason the officials did not want the body removed at all. Therefore by request of the citizens of this city, I am Respectfully asking that you have this matter investigated and advise me as to the cause and manner of his death." There is no indication in the files that Governor Allred responded at all. Nor do available medical records clarify matters. The 1937 annual report lists eight people who died at Eastham in this year, one each from stab wounds and pneumonia, and six from gunshots.[66] But it does not specify death by month, or how Wilson may have died. All that was clear was that a dark cloud passed over.

This sort of invisibility over the conditions of death was not solely caused by inefficiency or confusion, as may have been the case with Johnnie Wilson's death. Prison officials, then as now, were reluctant if not outright defiant about having anyone investigate the conditions of a prisoner's death. When Jimmy Arnold died on a Texas prison farm in 1930, general manager Lee Simmons listed the death as unfortunate, but free of foul play or negligence. J. A. Collier wrote to Lee Simmons and wanted to look into Arnold's death. Simmons was unequivocal: "You ask that you be permitted to make a private investigation of this matter, and I state to you frankly that I will not permit you, or anyone else to make private investigations of incidents that happen on state farms."[67] A decade later, C. V. Compton requested that the officials furnish statistics pertaining to prison violence. He was denied. "We are treated as though the prison officials are the arbitrary possessors of something that belongs to them individually," rather than servants accountable to the public. Good men, Compton said, Christians and taxpayers, "are virtually barred from interviewing inmates or even visiting this branch of our government unless we get permission from the Chairman of the Prison Board or the Manager of the Prison System, thus rendering it nearly impossible for us to learn of the atrocities that are daily taking place behind the gray walls."[68] Members of the prison board might, on rare occasions, mount an investigation, as was the case with Cecil Davis, but they were to be internal, not public, affairs. When outside investigators asked questions of the prison administration, they met a silence that would make a convict blush. The convict code had nothing on the fraternity of prison officials.

Bringing Home the Body

In her literary and historical analysis of death and dying for African Americans, Karla F. C. Holloway notes the ways that many black families have emphasized the coming together that death, all too common an experience for black families and one that often occurs all too early, can mean. Blacks who had left for the North frequently—when they could afford it—returned to the South for a relative's funeral. "We went home for a funeral. No questions. Nobody worried about what it cost or what we were doing with jobs or whatever. When somebody died—and I don't care how you were related—if you were family you went back home where you were supposed to be. With your family."[69] Yet in the Depression, this desire for a family reunited around death was thwarted by the hard fact of poverty and the inability to travel—either home, to mourn a family member gone wrong but now returned, or, in the case of the prison, to bring the body home.

After a prisoner died in Texas, from whatever causes, his or her family would receive word from prison officials. This word may have been the quick notice of an unexpected death, when the speed of decay and expense of embalming demanded a speedy, if unsympathetic, telegram. Yet many could not afford to claim their family member's remains and were less fortunate than Johnnie Wilson in that regard. Emma Tinney had no money to bring her son's body home and asked the governor's help. He refused.[70] One of Elmer Pruitt's parents responded to a warden's letter: "It is my desire to claim the body of my hopeless son, but I am unable, financially, to bear the expense."[71]

Bennie Randall's parents were in similar financial straits, and they turned to God because the state would do little. "To the Warden at Huntsville, sir in reply to your notice though it pains me to my heart to tell you, I cannot claim the body of my son, I am not able to bring the body here so you will be doing a great favor by giving him a Christian burial there. . . . I thank you in God's name, tell him I hope he has made his peace with God." Whether he made his peace or not, Randall was buried at the Huntsville cemetery, known to inmates as Peckerwood Hill.[72]

After her son was executed at San Quentin, Everett Gilbert Parman's mother wrote a letter to Clinton Duffy. Like her son in his final days, she, too, took solace in religion. She first asked that Duffy send her son's books, "especially his Bible with his name in it." The quotation below does not correct language in the original letter.

> I wish also to thank you from the bottom of my heart for the last visit with my son. Which was a pleasant one with his end only 3 days away. also Guard Harris for his many little courtsies shown me. I am happy my Son met his fate brave—as only the ones that knew him realy could under stand. how unjustly he died. Thank God his debt to society is paid to bad Some have to be used for examples. Justic is counted in $s. Wholesale murders always escape. it seems.[73]

While thanking Duffy and Harris for their personal kindness, she seethed at the structural injustices of her son's execution, and the economic inequality of state killing. We cannot know exactly to whom she referred as a wholesale murderer, but we can surmise that he was not poor.

Indigent prisoners, and of these there was a not inconsiderable number, might hope for a burial suit to be provided by the prison, as well as a coffin. In Texas, the suit was sewn by women prisoners at Goree, who made all of the prisoners' clothes. The coffins, too, were almost certainly made in the prison carpentry shop. In Texas in 1939, "Special Death Expenses" amounted to $794.81 of the prison's budget.[74] Chaplain C. E. Garret, who tended to the spiritual well-being of white Protestants in the "upper sector" of the prison system, oversaw some twenty-nine burial services in 1940 alone.[75] By the first days of World War II, the prison seemed to have found a bit of money to help return the bodies of the deceased. A hopeful matter indeed, as that sum more than exceeded the thirteen dollars spent on new grave markers and other funeral expenses for Peckerwood Hill.[76] Little was done to tend the graves of San Quentin's dead; only inmate volunteers would tend to the unmarked graves at Potter's Field, itself reportedly near a similarly neglected Miwok burial site.[77]

Surely among a prisoners' greatest fears was being lost to friends and family, of being dead to them, and alone. This was, of course, part of the frightful nature of incarceration and the alienation it produced in the name of social correction, but that spoke, in truth, to vengeful racialized exclusion. For those who were physically rather than symbolically dying, through capital sentence, a hacking cough, or a strange growth, the distance would be greater still. Prisoners surely hoped that in death, they might be returned home. In California, some desperately ill prisoners were permitted to rejoin

San Quentin's Potter's Field. Image 1925.004.006: "California State Prison Potter's Field, San Quentin, California" (ND), Folder 4, Leo L. Stanley Collection, San Quentin Photographs, Anne T. Kent Room, Marin County Public Library.

their families in their final days: this was a humane gesture, to be sure—though one should note that the practice also cut medical costs and massaged mortality rates downward, in administrators' favor.[78] Musician Merle Haggard expressed a common sentiment when he sang of the prisoner who longed to be buried far from the prison, and "beneath the green, green grass of home."[79] Sorry was the prisoner who was buried at Huntsville or in the makeshift cemetery on the prison farm, where headstones listed just an inmate number, sometimes marked with an "X" for execution.[80] Sad was the memory of the inmate whose family was so poor or so angry that they could not or would not bring the inmate home. Later, Peckerwood Hill would be called the Joe Byrd Memorial Cemetery, in honor of the official executioner at the Walls.

Prison chaplains oversaw inmates' burial on Peckerwood Hill. It was a vital part of their job. One hopes that the matter-of-fact tone in annual reports belied a deeper sentiment in this chaplain's ministrations: "In cases

TABLE 7.3
Mortality Rates in California and Texas Prisons, per thousand inmates

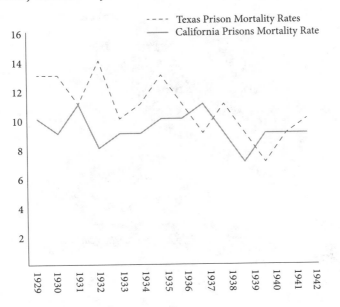

- - - - Texas Prison Mortality Rates
——— California Prisons Mortality Rate

TABLE 7.4
Causes of Death, California Prisons, 1933–34

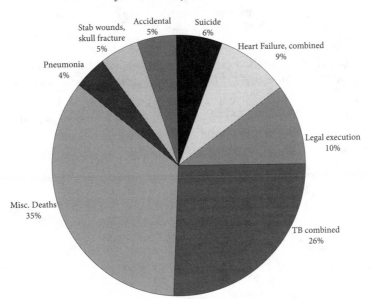

Stab wounds, skull fracture 5%

Accidental 5%

Suicide 6%

Heart Failure, combined 9%

Pneumonia 4%

Legal execution 10%

Misc. Deaths 35%

TB combined 26%

TABLE 7.5
Total Mortality in Texas Prison System, 1929–1941

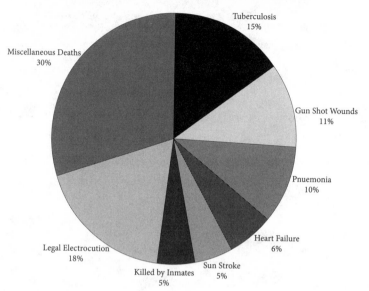

where the electrocuted men were not claimed by their relatives, I have conducted their funeral services; I have conducted funeral services for the men who died in the hospital and were buried in the prison cemetery. The funerals of the men from the Wynne Farm have been held at the cemetery of that farm, as that unit has no chapel nor any suitable place for services."[81]

One can imagine the short ceremony at Peckerwood Hill or at San Quentin's Potter's Field. The chaplain would say a few words, perhaps as the prisoners drafted to dig the grave listened on—glad, surely, that they were not being put in the ground and hoping that unlike this man, who would never leave the prison, their families would have the inclination and the means to bring them home.

212 | *A Dark Cloud Would Go Over*

Going Home

Say someday, someday, someday baby, I'll be home.
Someday you'll see me around. . . .
When I get lucky, I'll be home some day.

—Arthur "Ligtnin'" Sherrod, "Should A Been on the River in 1910"[1]

Doing time was hard, and getting out was hard, too. If prisoners hoped for an early release, they had a lot of work to do—bags to weave or cotton to pick, certainly, but also powerful friends to make, petitions to write, bureaucracies to navigate, and favors to ask. Through the 1930s, parole boards would gain increasing power over inmates' lives. Their ability to fix a sentence or set a release date incorporated what had once been judicial sentencing power into their administrative positions. Inmates and their families needed to learn what worked, and what did not, to help get them home.

Historian David Rothman argued that decisions about parole—who could leave the prison, when, and under what circumstances—were, at their core, "arbitrary and capricious."[2] His conclusion about the capriciousness of parole and release was a necessary correction to parole board officers' oft-stated but rarely validated belief that parole would gauge individual prisoners' redemption and eligibility for return to the outside world. Parole was less scientific than board members' ideological proclamations claimed, but it was also more complex than Rothman suggested. One might productively argue that capriciousness itself was a chief political effect of imprisonment—that the Kafkaesque unpredictability of the way punishment worked was perhaps unintended, yet central to relationships between the so-called criminal classes and the modern state.

But there was more than this. Local and extralocal patronage systems, political economic needs, institutional control, and tension between ideologies of vengeful punishment and performances of individual reform—all played a role. Leaving the prison, as much as entering it, showed different aspects of each state's penal modernity and its reimposition of hierarchies. From an inmate's petition for an early release to his or her time on parole and beyond, formal and informal mechanisms effectively deepened modes of difference and power. Despite increasing the bureaucratic formalism of penal modernity—more developed in California than in Texas—leaving the prison, and the question of whether one served a full sentence or received clemency, demonstrated how inmates navigated a gray zone between bureaucratic formalism and the long traditions of sovereign discretion and its selective dispensation of "mercy" through early release. Inmates faced benefits and dangers in each. An application might win an individual prisoner's parole, but it often did so by solidifying social hierarchies of race, nation, and gender. If an inmate played into the prescribed roles and validated the established social order, he or she just might leave a bit early.[3]

Though they shared a great deal, there were differences between the states. Release procedures differed by region, a fact that Rothman left unexplored. Officials in California, an aesthetically modern and liberal penal state, tended to favor an extensive parole program. Along with many progressive penologists of the day, they were convinced that parole was a necessary component of incarceration and release. Parole board members believed that all inmates should be released on parole for at least a short period, to supervise their transition to life and wage labor outside. California inmates were automatically considered for parole at the end of their minimum term.[4] Nevertheless, a fundamental component for determining eligibility for parole was the guarantee of outside work and a signed labor contract, still understood as the foundation of proper manly citizenship. In California, release decisions bespoke a bureaucratic capitalist modernity, an unsteady balance between the needs of running overcrowded institutions and the desire to control a surplus labor population in an economic crisis.

In contrast, the assumption in Texas was that prisoners should serve their full sentences, unless significant extenuating circumstances surrounding the crime were discovered.[5] Most Texas prisoners served their full terms. However, if they could demonstrate community support for their release, they might get out early. Yet "community support" did not mean just any set of advocates; it meant the support of elite white patrons. In Texas, personal connections and visible patronage went further in securing release than mere evidence of a job.

Put another way, release decisions in Texas tended to be local affairs, driven by inmates' location in the racial and class patronage networks of the communities where they were convicted, their acknowledgment of a subordinate place in those networks, and deference to the men above them. This symbolic deference could include literal financial debt. California release decisions were more formally bureaucratic and were explicitly indexed to outside wage employment rather than debt, though they, too, were structured by informal racial and gender anxieties. Over the 1930s, each state's institutions refined its procedures and guidelines for an inmate's release, as part of the process of developing state bureaucracies. Despite increasing legal formalism, garish threads of sovereign discretion still wound through the gray bureaucratic machinery, differentiating inmates by race, class, nation, and sex and determining the chances of their lives. Parole boards were increasingly professional and bureaucratic in the New Deal era, yet inmates who could perform to their liking might win the state's mercy. It came at a cost.

Administrative Histories

Parole was formally adopted in California in 1893, also the year when capital punishment was centralized.[6] In 1905, a committee appointed by the California legislature recommended expanded parole as a means of alleviating prison overcrowding. In 1910, California's first parole bureaucracy came into being, with a parole officer, an assistant parole officer, and a clerical worker stationed in San Francisco. Unable to make any visits beyond that city, the agency had little actual supervisory capacity. It reviewed monthly reports and processed paperwork after parolees had been convicted of another crime. Agents might contact the missing parolees' families, but this was the limit of their abilities.[7] In 1915, an Advisory Pardon Board was formed to help the governor decide on those prisoners who deserved full pardons, rather than just release on parole.

In 1931, the California legislature established the Board of Prison Terms and Paroles (BPTP), which assumed some of the duties of the State Board of Prison Directors. The board's aim was, first, to provide "protection to society" and, second, to accomplish "the reduction of the prison population and, through the Parole Officer, the adjustment of outgoing men to the responsibilities of normal life."[8] The BPTP would set both the final date of an inmate's term and the date when he or she could leave the institution and serve the remainder of the sentence on parole. "Because a parole will not be granted to a prisoner who has a continuous bad conduct record while in prison," the board wrote, "a powerful incentive is provided for good conduct. Thus parole acts as an aid in maintaining discipline within the prison."[9]

While the promise of parole was an effective means of inducing good behavior within prisons, it also had considerable financial appeal—particularly in the cash-strapped Depression. Supervising parolees was cheap, and, moreover, they might support families that might otherwise need public assistance.[10] There is little evidence that board members made individual parole decisions with costs or overcrowding in mind, but financial considerations had their place. Some twenty-five hundred prisoners were on parole in the 1933 fiscal year. After calculating the costs, the board proclaimed that having these people on parole saved the state more than $430,000. They made the same case at the end of the decade. Supporting a prisoner at San Quentin cost $210 per year, and one at Folsom, $213. Supervising a parolee cost just forty dollars.[11]

Wage labor remained the *sine qua non* of California's parole system, and a signed labor contract was a precondition for release. The requirement was based on the belief that wage labor was foundational to California's social order. In the difficult job market, inmates who could not find work would continue to languish, and the prison would absorb these surplus workers.[12] Reports lamented the lack of opportunities, "through no cause of those on parole . . . but unfortunately by a general period of depression . . . causing wholesale unemployment, affecting not only men on parole, but the general public as well."[13] Because the board continued to require signed labor contracts, the numbers of parolees released remained relatively static across the decade. Total numbers climbed early in the decade (from 2,176 in 1930 to 3,185 in 1932). Parolees gradually decreased to just 1830 in 1938. Numbers grew slowly in 1939, and then sharply as the economy improved and the war effort began in earnest. By 1942, 4,026 California prisoners were on parole, primarily at work in defense industries.[14]

Texas's history of executive clemency linked with and diverged from California's. Texas prisoners' forms of clemency went under many names: conditional pardons, full pardons, furloughs, reprieves, and emergency paroles, the last of which temporarily suspended an inmate's sentence so that he or she might leave the prison to testify in a trial or sit for another charge. On some occasions, governors extended temporary reprieves or furloughs and offered conditional pardons (essentially the same thing as parole). In 1893, the two people on the Board of Pardon Advisors made recommendations to the governor on clemency cases. In 1905, Texas's first parole law gave power to the Board of Prison Commissioners and the Board of Pardon Advisors to make rules and regulations for the pardon or parole of "meritorious prisoners." First-time offenders who had served two years or more than a quarter of their sentences were eligible, provided that they had not committed egregious crimes. In 1911, the legislature passed a law permitting the existence of a parole agent or supervisor, yet no system of supervision existed. Two years later an indeterminate sentencing law passed, which gave the governor the sole power to grant clemency or conditional pardons. The Board of Prison Commissioners still established the regulations under which a prisoner could be pardoned, but those rules had to be approved by the governor.[15] In 1929 the legislature abolished the two-member Board of Pardon Advisors and established a three-person Board of Pardons and Paroles. Board members served six-year terms and were appointed by governors subject to state senatorial approval. The governor selected one member to be the chairman, and the board chose the supervisor of paroles. The members of the board served in an advisory capacity only; governors could grant clemency with or without the board's recommendation.

Because clemency authority resided in the governor's office, each administration had its own personal characteristics. Ross Sterling, governor from 1931 to 1933, permitted early releases only through parole and furlough, and did not grant pardons. Miriam Ferguson, in office from 1933 to 1935, in contrast, mostly granted full or conditional pardons, with fewer paroles or furloughs. Governor Allred (1935–1939) had long protested against undue leniency in granting pardons, and accused Ferguson of corruption, much as Governor Moody had promised to clean up the corrupt "pardon orgy" under James Ferguson's administration.[16] In 1936 Allred supported a constitutional amendment that reduced the governor's role in pardon and parole procedures. Beginning in 1937, the newly organized Board of Pardons and Paroles had three members: one appointed by the governor, another appointed by the chief justice of the Texas Supreme Court, and the last by the presiding judge of the Texas Court of Criminal Appeals.

The 1936 law required board recommendation for gubernatorial pardons, reprieves, and commutations, but only the governor could revoke pardons. Governors could grant one thirty-day capital reprieve without recommendations. Taken as a whole, these were significant limitations on the governor's power. Nevertheless, when Allred became governor, he would grant conditional pardons, but now on the advice of the board: He issued some 650 conditional pardons and 50 paroles in 1937, and released another 175 through reprieves and furloughs. By World War II, the board released between two thousand and thirty-five hundred prisoners annually under conditional pardon.

Texas inmates were paroled or given conditional pardons in numbers that tracked fairly consistently with intakes across the decade. That is, the average daily prison population climbed from 4,868 in 1929 to 5,550 in 1931, and clemency decisions also climbed from 425 to 1,538 in 1932. The average population dipped slightly and then stabilized from 1932 to 1934, but then climbed sharply until 1939 (from 5,359 to 6,992). Clemency decisions followed a similar trajectory. They were generally stable from 1932 to 1934 (1,538 clemencies in 1932 and 1,550 in 1934) and then climbed to 1,942 paroles in 1940, climbing higher still in 1942, with greater numbers released as the economy improved and released prisoners could serve in the military or war industries.[17] Because Texas, unlike California, had no firm employment criteria for release, its board could act with a freer hand. Across the decade, proportions of inmates leaving Texas prisons through conditional pardons increased considerably.

Process and Procedures

Inmates began thinking about a pardon or parole from the moment they were sentenced. They and their families wrote letters almost immediately to anyone who might have a hand in securing an early release. They were right to try to contact the governor, for governors traditionally maintained pardon power. Yet increasing bureaucratization meant that greater numbers of people became involved in the parole and pardoning process, with the creation of mounting and overlapping departments.

In California, clemency procedures were relatively formal and required work from both inmates and officials. Inmates had to notify the district attorney and a local newspaper where they were convicted of their intent to apply for parole. Illiterate and non-English-speaking inmates were blatantly disadvantaged here. Governors and board members would contact sheriffs, district attorneys, and trial judges to furnish reports about the crime.[18] Judges and district attorneys were required to give reasons for their recommendations, and these were weighted heavily in clemency decisions.[19] Investigations were intended "to present a concise narrative of each prisoner and his crime," including his "life history and the particular circumstances of his crime." Board members also consulted the warden, resident physician, captain of the yard, and psychiatrist. With this information in hand, board members would evaluate the inmate's case. Thirty days before the board was scheduled to consider offering a parole or fixing an indeterminate sentence, it would send letters to the judge of the superior court where the applicant was tried and to the district attorney and sheriff of the county where he or she was sentenced. The press was also notified of considered and final actions on fixing terms.[20]

As elsewhere in the country, appointment to parole boards reflected connections rather than expertise in penological practice. That these were highly political appointments did not mean that the people appointed were bad spirited or wholly incompetent, though reformers lamented their lack of expertise. Board members were, as historian Vivian M. L. Miller found in Florida, generally "respectable" and well-intentioned people whose sensibilities were shaped by their class position and racial identities. They tended to be white members of the professional classes, including entrepreneurs, businesspeople, merchants, clergy, physicians, and insurance brokers, frequently with legal or law enforcement backgrounds and civic club connections.[21]

Charles L. Neumiller was the first chairman of California's Board of Prison Terms and Paroles. Born in Stockton in 1873, Neumiller attended Hastings College of the Law and worked for the Stockton district attorney before becoming a prominent business lawyer with impeccable Republican Party connections. He was a California delegate to the 1912 Republican National Convention, served as chair of the California Republican Party, and played a significant role in the Progressive Republican movement. The two other founding members of the board were Joseph H. Stephens, a Sacramento Rotarian, and Frank C. Sykes, who would serve in the San Francisco Public Schools War Production Training Program during World War II. Frederick L. Esola, a U.S. marshall, joined the board at the end of the decade.[22]

California board members' responsibilities were significant. The board determined the length of time an inmate would spend in locked prison, and set the date when the prisoner would leave. The decisions they made, especially in accordance with indeterminate sentencing laws, meant that their administrative and disciplinary determinations incorporated what had once been judicial sentencing power. Their proceedings followed the model of a trial—an inmate could speak on his or her own behalf, and so forth—but decisions were final, and there was neither relevant oversight nor capacity for review. Thus the parole board could revoke a parole or expand a prisoner's sentence to the maximum for any number of reasons.[23] Until the board determined a release date, prisoners were "deemed to be serving the maximum of the sentence provided for by law."[24]

Inmates commonly had their parole dates knocked back for disciplinary infractions. Unsurprisingly, board members found inmates who broke prison rules to be poor candidates.[25] Parole and the indeterminate sentence were intended to punish better, not less. But in fact they might have also punished more—sentences actually lengthened under indeterminate sentencing regimes. One parole board member blamed overcrowding on longer terms set under new parole regulations. The state, he said, was "holding men for longer terms within walls before parole or discharge than ever before in the history of California."[26] George Weaver had four of his nine months of parole rescinded for having a half-gallon of prison-made alcohol in his cell, and Hollis Booker was punished for "refusing to clean his machine in the jute mill after repeated warnings." Booker lost a year of parole.[27] Conversely, obedient inmates could have more parole granted to them, which meant getting out sooner. Estes Ray Brown gained an additional thirty days' parole upon the recommendation of the warden, "for meritorious conduct and industry." So too was Laura H. Ford granted an additional thirty days of parole, again, "for meritorious conduct and industry."[28] Meritorious conduct proved a flexible concept used to reward a range of compliant behaviors. Some of these went well beyond internal discipline, and even bled into labor repression outside of the prison. Ernest Ramsay, a union member imprisoned on questionable murder charges during a labor dispute, was promised an early parole by an Industrial Association officer, if he was willing to identify labor leader Harry Bridges as a Communist, and thus aid in the Australian radical's deportation. He would not.[29]

California prisoners appeared before Neumiller, Stephens, and Sykes to make their case while board members asked questions and perused the inmate's file. Prisoners were encouraged to make claims about their cases, and thus to be involved in the disciplinary process. This was, as Natalie Zemon Davis and scholars since have argued, an opportunity for inmates to craft alternative and plausible narratives for their lives and crimes. "The inmates," wrote board members, "are actuated by the knowledge that a full expression of the motives and causes which have contributed to their present state" would be considered.[30] As with inmates' and their families' letters to boards, this provided an opportunity for prisoners to tell their side of the story. Board officers felt that the testimony was useful for gaining deep insight into the inmate's case. Indeed, they marveled that inmates were a "surprisingly good source of information" as to their crime, history, and circumstances.[31] From these stories, "[T]he board is . . . given an opportunity to get an insight into the character and social viewpoint of the inmate under conditions which could not be duplicated in court."[32] Many of the men told compelling stories. "It is not uncommon for the board to hear a story so intimate and personal in nature that it could not or would not have been told in a court room. When information thus secured can be substantiated as true it can and very properly does effect [sic] the findings of the Board."[33] After giving testimony and answering a few questions, the inmate returned to the tumult and tedium of prison life, as board members made and recorded their decision.[34]

For California inmates, testimony was fraught with danger and potential. Plausible, verifiable, and, moreover, pleasing stories would help secure a parole or fix a shorter sentence. If an inmate had a surly attitude, if his or her record showed evidence of bad behavior (fighting or showing impudence to guards were common reasons), or if the inmate told an unappealing story, his or her sentence could be extended. Some inmates, board members recounted, "told stories that were obviously false. Many men of this type also revealed unwholesome social viewpoints and mental attitudes which give the Board an insight into their probable future behavior."[35] Inmates who told unpleasing stories were then classed as a "type," which then impacted their future chances for release. For some, this surely led to what recent critics have called the "innocent prisoners' dilemma": knowing that maintaining innocence to a parole board (and therefore not demonstrating remorse) will lead to a longer time in prison.[36]

For all their responsibilities to society and the prisoner, boards worked with surprising speed. California's parole board met 137 times in 1935–1936 and considered 4,614 parole or sentencing-determining cases. There is no indication of how long these meetings lasted, but simple division shows that around thirty-four cases were considered at each meeting. If the board met for an eight-hour day, then each inmate's case was considered for around fifteen minutes—this would have included time spent reading case histories, speaking with inmates to get their testimonies, hearing from prison officials, deliberating the case, and reaching a decision.[37] One study found that even when parole boards were provided with inmates' records days before their meetings, they rarely consulted them prior to making a decision. As one investigator noted in 1936, "Everything depended on the impression the prisoner made upon the board in response to their questions," and too often, questions had little to do with a prisoner's future prospects.[38]

Yet perhaps, on a relative scale, California's board was conscientious. Around the country, state parole boards spent just minutes on any case— at times just two or three minutes reading the file, meeting the inmate, and deciding his or her fate. At times, decisions were based on whether or not they liked the "look" of the inmate: some inmates were paroled literally because, in one board member's words, "This is a nice looking boy" or because "[t]hat man has a good face." And in another, "He is kind of a slob, but I think he is all right."[39] Many parole boards made snap evaluations that essentially retried the original case and charge rather than interpreted how rehabilitated an individual might be. Yet even the fifteen minutes that the California board spent seems inadequate, regardless of the material its members had before them.[40]

It is of course hard to know just how those meetings went, and how inmates' performances affected their chances of parole, though we can surmise that what board members read as affability and obedience—good speech, a respectful mien, clothes worn to the board's standards, hats doffed rather than worn at an angle—were rewarded. Board minutes list the results of those interviews, not the conversations themselves, thorough or cursory as they may have been. More revealing are the letters that remain, from court officers or jurors, or an inmate's family and community. In each case, and often they conflicted, pardon and parole records revealed tensions within communities, and the various networks and social hierarchies that animated life in Depression-era Texas and California. Clemency cases reveal a great deal about the nature of these societies—what was forgivable and what was not. As always, the specific class and race identities of offenders and victims were crucial, as was the quality of their connections to patronage networks.

The capriciousness that previous scholarship demonstrated did not mean that board decisions lacked their own logic. That logic just had less to do with the strict merits of an individual case, or at least those that could be determined in a few minutes, than it did with the way clemency applications meshed with dominant power relationships and understandings of behavior. And board members' understandings were always shaped, first, by how docile prisoners had been behind bars and then, secondarily, by dominant conceptions of respectability, patronage, race, sex, and class.

If an inmate had a good record, other elements would influence board members' discretionary powers. For men, having to support a family that might need public assistance without them was an important consideration. Being white increased the likelihood of parole, as did letters from influential people and court officers. Being black was an impediment. So was having served a previous sentence.[41]

While being nonwhite was detrimental to receiving parole nationwide, in some border states, such as California and Arizona, being ethnically Mexican proved to be a benefit to parole decisions. Far from this being a sign of relative social inclusion, ethnic Mexicans were paroled at high rates in California so that they could be expelled from the country. In the context of the Depression, whites fearing competition with impoverished and nonwhite migrants sought mass deportations of foreign nationals, especially Mexicans. Estimates vary as to the number of Mexicans driven from the United

States in the decade, but perhaps one million, with many American citizens among them, were expelled.[42] The California parole board, along with the Board of Pardons and Paroles in Texas, looked favorably on granting early release from prison to foreign nationals, provided they were willing to leave the country.[43] In early release they saw a cost-effective way to rid the prison and nation of undesirable foreign and racial elements.

In 1935 the California parole board requested and received fifteen thousand dollars from the legislature for a Deportation and Undesirable Alien Transfer Fund to help expel these prisoners. Doubly guilty—of foreignness and criminal conviction—"undesirable aliens" were to be doubly punished, first with a prison term and then with expulsion. The board deemed these individuals "not fit subjects to be returned to society in this country." Foreign nationals convicted of crimes, the board opined, should be "made to leave the country, thereby assuring the people of this State that these offenders will not be in a position to commit further criminal acts here." Lest anyone fear that deportees were getting off easy, the board ensured that they would only be paroled after serving a substantial portion of their sentences: exile was a supplement to punishment, not a replacement for it.[44] With funds appropriated by the legislature, both ends could be met. "The value of such a fund," they wrote, "cannot be over estimated."[45] The board encouraged "voluntary" deportation, too, with the promise of a shorter sentence and an offer to pay inmates' way from the deportation fund. Inmates commonly refused, but 133 inmates, nearly 14 percent of those paroled in 1938–1939, were deported to other countries.[46]

Mexican inmates tended to be more amenable to deportation in exchange for an early release than other so-called undesirable aliens. Historian F. Arturo Rosas found that Mexican prisoners preferred deportation to time in American prisons, a decision that reflected calculations of proximity and travel.[47] Despite the increasing vigilance of the border patrol and widespread expulsion drives in California, the U.S.-Mexico border remained porous, and Mexican inmates paroled for deportation could return with relative ease, even if doing so risked a return to prison.[48]

Chinese and Filipino prisoners were more reluctant to leave, despite the promise of early release. This was not because they found prison life any easier than Mexican prisoners but because legal proscriptions and the vast distances of the Pacific made the return trip harder. Within a month of the Tydings-McDuffie Act's passage, the California parole board informed the Immigration and Naturalization Service that it had 185 Filipino inmates they wanted to deport. In 1938–1939, ninety-six chose deportation, with the inability to ever return, over incarceration.[49] The rest "refused to make application," according to the frustrated board's report.[50] Even American citizens were encouraged to take an early parole if they left the nation. Fred Wong was encouraged to "return" to China, but he refused. "In view of this fact [of Wong's citizenship], the Parole Department can do nothing further on the case."[51]

Johnnie Sotelo was received at San Quentin in October of 1936, sentenced to two six-year sentences to run concurrently for drug crimes. When he served half his sentence, he would be eligible either for parole or for deportation to the Philippines. But just thirteen months after arriving at San Quentin, he requested that he be paroled in California instead. As many prisoners did across the country, he made his appeal on the foundation of the patriarchal family. Sotelo had a wife and small children and needed to stay in California "so that he might care for his family, as they are dependent on him." Were he forced to go to the Philippines, he did "not know whether he will be able to care for them or whether he will be able to send for them." The board took no action at the time, but they understood Sotelo's implication that his family might become a public charge if he, as the male breadwinner, could not care for them.[52] Sotelo, like many, chose prison over exile, and remained at San Quentin. Sotelo did his longer time and was ultimately released to the California streets to see his family again.

If racial and national identities were important in California release decisions, gender was crucial, too. Sotelo was wise to say that he needed to take care of his family—this was a big part of successful parole applications. Gender considerations weighed heavily in clemency decisions for both men and women. Women in both California and Texas might have their sentences cut short if they became pregnant immediately before conviction, and officials noted that no child should be born in a prison. But without official support, sentimental appeals could just as easily fall on deaf ears or be circumvented by protests. Women faced a harder time mounting these gendered appeals than men because, as convicted criminals, they were already understood as fallen women.[53]

Oklahoma-born Pauline Tibbits was arrested with her husband and another man for second-degree burglary in California's Stanislaus County in September 1939. She received a 1–15-year indeterminate sentence, later fixed at six years. When she applied for clemency, she wrote that she was not guilty of the offense for which she was convicted. Without substantial public and official support, this was a perennially risky strategy because it failed to show requisite contrition. She also claimed that if she were guilty, she had served enough time for the offense. Yet more pressing was the cost that her conviction placed on her children, born of a previous marriage. "My children need me. Their father is dead and they have no one but me to give them the care they need. My sister, in whose charge they are now, is not able to care for them either financially or otherwise."

While her claim as a mother who needed to look after her children may have played to the board's paternalist sentiment, those feelings were circumvented by Stanislaus County district attorney Leslie A. Cleary. Prosecuting attorneys like Cleary developed strategies to contain such appeals. "I do not regard her statements relative to her children," Cleary wrote, "as being any excuse for a pardon or commutation of sentence. A woman of this type would scarcely be a valuable influence on the children and if the sister is not able to care for them it is undoubtedly the duty of the state to take over the children and give them the best opportunity that is possible." Cleary's words against Tibbits's clemency may have also been freighted with a racial/behavioral subtext—she was an Okie, after all. Cleary continued: "Naturally the members of this Board realize that if pardons or commutations are to be granted on the basis of the sorrow or injury that the commission brings to another member of the criminal's family it would mean that very few who are criminals would ever remain in prison." Sentiment could only go so far, and no court officers supported her claims. Maligned as a bad mother, she lost her appeal, and her family's disruption, a collateral consequence of her incarceration, as recent critics have put it, was unacknowledged.[54]

If gendered appeals won neither Pauline Tibbits nor her children pity and thus failed to win her clemency, pardon board members and court officers found enough gendered pathos in Donald Vredenburg's story to commute his sentence. The 21-year-old Vredenburg pled guilty in January 1935 to first-degree robbery with a firearm. Vredenburg and accomplice Betty O'Neil had stolen a car at gunpoint and robbed two service stations en route to Eureka. Yet as his pardon board file reads, Vredenburg was as much a victim as the man whose car he stole or the owners of the gas stations he helped rob. They were all, so trial officers believed, subject to the will and manipulations of the femme fatale Betty O'Neil. "I believe this is one of those cases in which the woman was at fault," wrote the trial judge. Advisory pardon board members were convinced that Vredenburg, whose legs were partially paralyzed, was infatuated with O'Neil, and she duped him into committing the crimes to impress her. His gullibility and lack of dangerousness was further evidenced by the fact that he was arrested while coming out of a Eureka movie theater, while O'Neil was arrested in bed with the man she had come to Eureka to see. Vredenburg's youth, his disability, and his association with this "bad" woman convinced pardon board members that his sentence should be commuted to time served. District attorney Earl Warren thought that Vredenburg was a "pitiful figure because of his physical handicaps," and that "a hardened and dominating woman had taken advantage . . . of his physical and mental conditions." Warren would have pushed for probation in the trial, but was unable because Vredenburg used a gun in the crime. Even the man whose car he stole came to testify on his behalf. Vredenburg's sentence was commuted to time served in May 1936. Yet Warren was "strongly of the opinion that no such clemency should be shown to the girl in this particular case."[55]

In California, then, bureaucratic formalism played an important part in clemency decisions at the same time that board members used gut judgments in extending or refusing pity. The machinery of justice turned, and inmates were processed according to their prison records and behaviors, but discretion played a major part of the parole and release process. The decisions that parole boards made departed from formal legal structures—there was hardly time to fully assess individual prisoners' likelihood of social redemption or to foretell their future life. Instead, executive clemency, and the discretion it entailed, affirmed the hegemonies of race, sex, class, and nation.

Conditional Pardons in Texas

Not everyone in Texas understood the bureaucratic minutiae of how to apply for clemency, and even if they did, relatively few would have the connections that would grease the wheels to make it happen. Lines of communication, supplication, patronage, and control may have been easier to recognize in overtly hierarchical societies and more hidden in modern bureaucracies, but there was some of each in Texas. Governors' records are thick with letters from prisoners' families, imploring that their husbands or sons be released to help their families survive. Evie Silicaker wrote to Governor Allred on behalf of her husband, Buster, serving five years on the Harlem Farm. Secretary George Clarke informed her of the new process, which had become more confusing after Allred's reform to limit corruption in granting pardons.

> [I]f your husband has served one third of his sentence with a clear record and is eligible for clemency, I want to suggest that you have letters of recommendation from his trial officials and as many members of the jury as possible, as well as from reputable citizens who can testify as to his worthiness, sent to the Board of Pardons and Paroles, Austin, Texas. The Governor can grant no clemency to your husband until it has been recommended by that Board.[56]

Texas clemency applications were relatively informal. They did not need to be made in writing and then publicized in newspapers, as was the case in California and many other states. Texas Board of Pardons and Paroles chairman J. B. Keith gave two reasons for this informality. The pragmatic reason was that the legislature appropriated no money for such a process. The second reason was more benevolent, and one need not be overly cynical to suspect it followed from the first. A large proportion of the prison population was illiterate, and worse still, Keith opined, "without friends to assist them in preparing applications," hence "the adoption of this broad democratic rule of the Board."[57] Yet literacy, and the privilege it bespoke, and friends, who could testify to an applicant's worth, counted for a great deal. Unlike in California, prisoners would not make statements on their behalf—distances from Texas's scattered prison farms to the BPP office in Austin were too great. But the board would hear prisoners' families or advocates, and family and community appeals did play their parts, both for and against clemency. Keith noted that he was frequently called upon to speak with inmates' wives, mothers, daughters, and sons. "We do not, and we will not, refuse to hear them; but in our final discussions we are not guided by emotion. Stubborn facts and scientific principles finally determine the recommendations made by us."[58]

For all of this, one report found that the Board of Pardons and Paroles largely considered the offense, previous record, and warden or farm manager reports rather than "scientific" understandings of an inmate's rehabilitation. "Much emphasis has been placed on the question of whether the prisoner has served a term commensurate with his offense," though commensurability was based on board members' racially based perceptions of seriousness. "If no extenuating circumstances connected with the offense are presented," the report found, "the presumption has been that parole should be refused."[59]

When Governor Allred's secretary, George Clarke, recommended that Evie Silicaker gather signatures from jury members and reputable citizens to testify to her husband's worthiness, he gave good advice. He might have also added that she should stress the dire straits she and her family faced, and her family's need for a breadwinner and a strong man to lead it. Such assertions of the rightness of patriarchal control appealed to parole boards, fulfilling hegemonic understandings of proper families, which, in turn, were connected to proper and established social hierarchies. Such hierarchies were deeply established in Texas culture, and black, white, and Mexican inmates alike would do well to find a powerful planter or, increasingly, a businessman to advocate on their behalf.

As in California, inmates' "meritorious conduct" might shave months off time in prison. Helping guards maintain order was a key way for that conduct to be recognized; this was another benefit of being a building tender. African American inmate J. B. Brown was granted executive clemency for his outstanding work in the Dallas County jail, where he watched the insane prisoners. The sheriff could not afford a deputy, so he used the 6'2", 225-pound Brown. The Sheriff said Brown had "probably been the best trusty in the jail for the past 27 months," and he received a general parole for his service.[60] When Eastham prisoner Homer Parker saved a guard's life during an attempted prison break, he was promised the rare prize of a full pardon. He did not have long to enjoy it, though, as he was badly injured in the melee and would quite likely die. Nevertheless, "General Manager Simmons states that should he die full clemency should be granted, and if he gets well he is entitled to such recognition." Parker had served all but a few months of his sentence and "risked his own life to give aid to the guards . . . who were overpowered during the break." Parker won a full pardon and restoration of citizenship.[61]

Marshall R. Smith was a 26-year-old shoemaker, convicted in 1925 of murder in Clifton, Texas, and sentenced to from five to fifty years.[62] While he was behind bars, Smith distinguished himself a "splendid prisoner" who had won the "friendship of all the officers in the prison system." If the promise of clemency was a key to internal prison control and ensuring inmates' self-discipline, Smith was a great success. He served as a trustee, and was a contributing member of the Inmate Welfare League. Men like Smith offered proof that rehabilitation was possible and that the promise of parole worked. On the basis of that merit, and because his wife was ailing, he won a temporary furlough in 1930.[63] But there was tremendous public uproar when news got out that he was being considered for a pardon or an extension of his furlough. Smith had not killed a poor white man, like himself, which white juries would commonly have seen as worthy of punishment, or a black man, which might be wrong but perhaps understandable in certain circumstances, assuming that the black man was not closely associated with a powerful white family. Instead, Smith had killed Dr. Owen Carpenter, a respected professional and member of the Clifton community. Countless people signed petitions and sent individual letters to the BPP demanding that Smith not be released, repeatedly referring to the "cold-blooded" killing of one of the most prominent men of his town. Members of the Lions Club, trying jurors, and the presiding judge all protested against his release. Smith was caught between the institutional pressures to maintain parole to reward good behavior and keep inmate populations down, on the one hand, and, on the other, the external political pressure for revenge that came when a poor man killed a wealthy one.

The many signatures against Smith's release doubtless impacted the Board of Pardons and Paroles' calculations and clearly indicated where the most vocal elements of community sentiment lay. Many of the letters to Governor Sterling in 1930 and 1931 directly appealed to his own patronage system, with writers reminding Sterling of their support in his campaign and suggesting that he would do well to help them now.[64] But board members would have been forced to consider, to a small extent, the manner in which signatures were gathered. Some, it seems, were not wholehearted expressions of protest. In a letter to the Board of Pardons and Paroles, G. M. Sealy withdrew his name from the petition he signed. He regretted doing it, saying he had put down his name "on the spur of the moment and unthoughtedly [sic]." Moreover, he attested, "Many others did the same." Sealy's recantation took greater time and effort than signing the petition against Smith's clemency, and surely bespoke some consideration on his part. He was the only one who openly withdrew his name.[65]

Smith did have supporters, though. His wife solicited help from her employer, a Dallas dress manufacturer, who testified that she was "on the verge of a nervous breakdown" from working to support her two young sons. She needed her husband's help. Physician Chas. Sorrells treated Mrs. Smith's ailments and said that she "needed someone to take care of her and her children." These advocates confessed that they knew nothing about Smith's case and would defer to the board on those matters, but Mrs. Smith and her children badly needed their breadwinner at home, which, they trusted, the board could surely appreciate.[66]

Another writer gave strident support to Smith. Identifying only as "a good friend" of Mr. Smith, this writer challenged the narrative of the cold-blooded murder of one of Clifton's best citizens. This writer told the board that Dr. Owen Carpenter was hardly as upstanding as he was commonly portrayed. Most petitioners referred to Dr. Carpenter as a fine citizen, but this writer impugned Carpenter as not just a womanizer but also "one of the biggest gamblers in the state." He would "insult every women [if] he had half a chance." Moreover, Carpenter had "insulted Mrs smith [sic] once." In this writer's telling, Marshall Smith was the honorable man, who had merely done what he needed to do to protect the safety of his home. The writer also informed the board that "Mr smith warned Dr. Owen Carpenter not to go to his house. if he did he would kill him. if you had been Mr Smith you would tried [sic] to protect your home and family. as smith was trying to do."[67] Carpenter had money and influential friends, while Smith, this writer said, had neither. He was "a poor man and didn't have much." Yet, "there are a number of people here that can tell you the same as I that Mr Smith was trying to protect his family and home from harm. Now his poor little children and wife have to suffer."[68] Countless people signed their names in support of Smith's long-time punishment, perhaps compelled to do so while community members looked on. Yet despite offering strident support for Smith, this writer was reluctant to sign his or her name.

In the end, Smith's supporters won the day. Despite the letters against his release, the governor was impressed by prison officials who said they had never known such a good prisoner and who testified that "his influence with the other convicts" had been "of great help to the prison officers." Smith received a general parole in July 1931, and once he had made his way out of the prison, he garnered additional patrons to testify to his worthiness. Over the next year and a half, Smith would accumulate enough support to bolster his claims for a full pardon, which he received in 1933. His ailing wife and destitute children, oft mentioned in the statements supporting his release, would have him home.[69]

Black prisoners across the South understood the good and ill affects of white patronage, and few would hold their breath waiting for the pardon it might bring. "Well you might get a pardon," sang J. B. Smith, "if you don't drop dead."[70] Texas prisoners mythologized a white planter named Tom Moore, who entered the realm of black musical tradition in the 1930s.

> I was down in the penitentiary doing natural life,
> I heard about Tom Moore and I gave him a wire.
> He wrote back and told me, "I will set you free,
> But nigger I want to tell you, you got to slave for me."[71]

Moore would secure conditional pardons for black prisoners and drive them hard on his plantation. He would supply them with women, liquor, good food and lodging, and money to gamble. The oft-told story was that they could do whatever they wanted, as long as they stayed on his property. If they picked enough cotton, he would tell them, "If you keep yourself out of the graveyard, I'll keep you out of the penitentiary." The Moore family may have been an extreme example, but the obligation to work for the person who helped secure a conditional pardon was common within the spectrum of coercive labor relations across Texas and the South—not just during the convict lease period, but well into the twentieth century.

Vaxter Haskins, a 21-year-old black housekeeper, killed his neighbor, John Davis, in May 1935, in Collin County, north of Dallas. The facts of Vaxter Haskins's case are difficult to parse from existing records, but it appears that the conflict emerged from the relationship among Haskins, Davis, and Davis's wife. Black men who killed other black men typically received relatively short sentences, for southern judges and juries commonly ruled these as mere "Negro affrays." Haskins was sentenced to ten years on the Ramsey Farm.[72] Because of the low value placed on black or Mexican men's and women's bodies, the wrong of an injury against them was seen as relatively minor, regardless of the offender. Frederico Terrasas was convicted of raping a woman of "low type" and was paroled for deportation in a relatively short period. Had he raped a woman whiter or of higher status than himself, he might have been lynched, been executed, or at least served a longer time.[73]

Though Governor Allred instituted the Board of Pardons and Paroles in 1935 to modernize Texas politics and dismantle undue patronage and corruption, the oldest elements of southern rule held fast. The strategies that Haskins's advocates used, the leverage they applied, and their successes in influencing sentencing and parole practices reveal much about how a black man could get off a southern prison farm.[74] While Haskins labored at Ramsey, the white family he worked for lobbied on his behalf. Four months after his conviction, W. H. L. Wells wrote a letter to the parole board's Judge T. C. Andrews, requesting Haskins's immediate clemency. Wells identified himself as a "Confederate soldier ninety five years of age," told Andrews that Haskins worked on his farm, and testified to Haskins's "good character." Wells suggested that Haskins killed Johnnie Davis in self-defense, and that Davis was a Negro "of bad standing."[75] Davis's death was not, Wells believed, a great loss. The Confederate veteran's son, W. D. Wells, also wrote to the board testifying to Haskins's trustworthiness. He said Haskins was raised in East Texas by "good Southern darkey parents" and that he was "more like the old slave darkeys quite different from some of the negroes in Collin Co including the one he was forced to kill." The slave parallel felt appropriate to him—indeed, he wrote, the Wells family had planted a cotton crop just for Haskins to work.[76]

When John Davis's mother, Effie Drake, learned of clemency applications being made on Haskins's behalf, she also wrote to the Board of Pardons and Paroles. She asked that the board "not grant [Haskins] any relief whatever, as he murdered my son, in cold blood, murdered him to get his wife." She contended that Haskins had received a fair trial and ought to serve his term, and that "by all means he should not be shown clemency at such an early date as this as he has served barely six month, etc."[77] Though her letter was filed, it had little impact on the board's decision.

Many letters from the Wells clan followed. In early letters, they said that the seven months Haskins had served was "ample punishment." More pressing to the Wells family than due punishment, however, was that they wanted Haskins to work off the debt he owed them. "We have been out a great deal of expense," probably for the cotton crop they planted.[78] Mrs. W. D. Wells wrote to Andrews again in April 1936, requesting six months' furlough, reiterating the debt he owed, as well as Haskins's desire to settle the debt. "We need the negro badly and as we have spent quite a lot of money on him, he is anxious to repay us. We know he is deserving, otherwise we would not want him." They were especially eager for his release, since this was the summer work season. "[W]e need him worse now than any time . . . as we have no help." Mrs. Wells had visited him at Ramsey Farm, where she said he was "well-regarded by the officials," was appointed a trustee, and was making double time.[79]

On September 15, Andrews regretfully explained that Haskins's clemency had been denied. Andrews personally supported it, but the two other members of the board did not. None of the trial officers explicitly opposed Haskins's clemency, though one member said he thought the evidence was clear and that Haskins actually "got off light." Andrews recommended that they take up Haskins's case again, after he had served one-third of his sentence—the minimum term allowable. Andrews, whose growing affection for the Wells family came through in the letters, closed his missive by sending his regards to the elder Wells, the Confederate veteran.

Despite Andrews's kind words, Mrs. Wells responded with great disappointment. She tried to offer new evidence mitigating "our negro's" guilt. Davis had been crazy with unfounded jealousy, she said, and "determined to get revenge on somebody." More pointedly, she maligned the credibility of the white tenant farmers whose testimony was used to convict Haskins. "The white folks, Mr. Ham and son, who testified so bitterly against Vaxter are just ignorant tenants and prejudiced against us." She was incredulous, and drove the point: "Do you think that class should be recognized more than a man like Mr. Wells, who is 96 yrs old and has lived in the county sixty yrs[?]" Clearly, she thought poor white farmers' words deserved less recognition than her own family's distinguished lineage.[80] It seems the board agreed. After serving the minimum allowable term, Haskins was released on a conditional pardon.[81]

It is impossible to say with certainty what sort of relationship Haskins returned to with the Wells family when he was granted a conditional pardon in October 1937. Certainly all the elements of debt peonage were there. As historian Pete Daniel put it, "The seeds of peonage grew well in social and economic soil so fecund with oppression."[82] Along with the family's desire to help "good deserving darkeys" came the indebtedness that had bound black workers to powerful whites for generations. Nor is it clear what his relationship was within the black community, or with Effie Drake, whose son he killed. Haskins's release was founded on hundreds of years of white paternalist control undergirded by violence, but it also sat squarely in the contemporary cotton economy and the modern state. Yet time did move on—Texas was not frozen in the nostalgic past. Black prisoners across the South would be paroled to white employers in urban areas, too.[83]

Walking out the Gate

California inmates had to satisfy the parole board that they would lead law-abiding lives and find an employer who would contract to hire them for an early release. This was an important difference from Texas. Texas prisoners needed to demonstrate their location in supportive patronage networks. In California, the networks that parolees had to join were based on wage labor contracts. Given the faith that wage labor was foundational to the social order, employers were considered to be "the parolee's sponsor," who "must aid him in abiding the conditions of release." Employers, then, would serve as state agents and were obligated to "notify the board of any violation of the terms of parole."[84] If inmates had neither a job contract nor outside advocates, they would fester behind bars until their full sentence expired.

Finding an outside job was no small task, when even people without criminal records struggled to get work. Each year, hundreds of California inmates were unable to take paroles because they lacked verifiable employment. In 1936, more than 550 prisoners languished inside even though they could be released. Prison officials noted with considerable understatement that "the problem is serious in its effects on the morale of these inmates."[85] Many waited years, unable to be released for want of outside work. Dozens of parole-eligible California inmates died waiting for job contracts: fourteen in 1937, eleven in 1938, five in 1939, eleven more in 1940. An astounding thirty-seven died awaiting parole in 1941.[86]

Texas prisoner John Leslie Brown's day finally came on February 17, 1939. Waiting and working on Texas's Retrieve Farm, Brown probably knew that the parole board was meeting in Austin to consider his conditional pardon.

One can imagine his anticipation, waiting for a guard or trustee to deliver the mail and hand him the form-letter postcard. If it was good news, Brown would leave; if not, there was more cotton to be picked. On this day, Brown was fortunate.[87]

Before he could walk out of the gates, he would meet with the farm manager, a last chance to be advised and threatened about living right. Brown would have been reminded that even though he was not swinging a hoe on Retrieve Farm, he was still under state control. He would have been given an important form, entitled "Parolee General Rules and Conditions." The general rules listed prohibitions and regulations that Brown needed to follow precisely, rules circumscribing his rights until his sentence finally expired. Brown must immediately report to his parole supervisor, a member of Texas's all-volunteer County Parole Board. He must always be reachable by his supervisor. He must report his monthly income and expenditures; he must "absolutely abstain" from the use of all drugs and intoxicating liquors; he must seek written permission before leaving the county; and he must consent to other significant controls over his life, travel, and labor.

If Brown's role in the exit interview ritual was to listen patiently and attentively, the farm manager's lines were also scripted—especially after Texas's 1936 parole reforms. Wardens and farm managers were instructed to read the "Explanation of General Rules and Conditions," a form that was attached to the "Parolee General Rules and Conditions" but that was to be removed before the parolee was given the latter. Releasing officials must orally stress many of the same rules so that they would be "deeply impressed on the parolee's mind."[88]

The parolee "must be made to realize that his supervisor has control over *all* of his actions, even having the final say as to the parolee's employment and residence." Moreover, a "[s]upervisor has the power and authority to make requests or conditions *over and beyond* those which are set out for him in these rules and proclamations." Parolees would be informed, in no uncertain terms, that the supervisor's power was total, and wholly discretionary. Reformers would have good reason for concern about this kind of control. This was a good definition of modern sovereignty—if not precisely the power to kill, it was very much power over life and its possibilities.

Rules of evidence did not apply to the supervisory relationship, or to the way supervisors could send inmates back to prison. The example of drug use was stark: "The belief that a parolee has used drugs since he received his clemency or that he is contemplating the use of drugs will be sufficient grounds for revocation of his clemency." And even though parolees had to sign statements that they would abstain from all alcohol, the "Explanation of General Rules and Condtions" mentioned some discretionary ability here. The state office, it read, did not have "strenuous objections . . . to a parolee drinking a small amount of beer or light wine . . . with his meals" but cautioned that one drink often led to two, and so on. Parolees might be granted the privilege to drink a bit—an extension of discretion and mercy—but would be warned that they were more likely to have their parole revoked if they began down the slippery slope.[89]

This discretion and contradiction—parolees being made to sign a statement of total abstention from alcohol alongside the understanding that they might do so and that the supervisor might agree to permit it—entrenched the supervisor's discretionary rule over the parolee. This discretion reflected an ambiguity built into modern parole practice, from an inmate's petition for an early release to his or her time on parole and beyond, in which formal and informal mechanisms attempted to secure control and deepen hierarchy, even as inmates tried to navigate those systems and make them their own.

Conditions were different in California, but the restriction of civil liberties would have been familiar enough. The parole officers were told to be firm but friendly. After the parolee signed his papers, officers would give "much encouragement, hope and aid for betterment to the deserving, while keeping all prisoners on parole under surveillance and liable to be summarily retaken and returned to confinement for any violation of parole rules."[90] Moreover, wrote Ed H. Whyte, the state parole officer,

A concerted effort is made to create a bond of understanding and a spirit of friendliness to the subject released on parole, offering him council and every possible aid in his endeavor to maintain the success of his parole and to reclaim himself as a useful, honest, and beneficial citizen. He is treated by the Parole Officer's department solely as an individual and not as a class or a group; pains are being taken by that department to study his personality and individual makeup together with those characteristics so often peculiar to himself, so that he can thereby be handled accordingly.[91]

When prisoners were lucky enough to meet the procedural prerequisites for clemency, life on the outside could be harsh. There is no telling the number of prisoners who, on release, could not find or keep adequate employment. The stigma of being an ex-con was hard to shake, and impacted his or her ability to find work or get state relief. Singer Merle Haggard said that an ex-con was a "branded man, out in the cold," and others shared the feeling.[92] John Platt Emerson complained that on several occasions he had been "refused aid by the State Relief Administration and other alphabetical projects, they say on account of my having been in San Quentin."[93]

Inmates knew how hard it was to get work on the outside—many had been unemployed prior to their arrest, after all. But it would be harder still with a prison record. Ex–San Quentin inmate Charles Herbert confessed that "it's very difficult to obtain employment. It seems that no one is interested in giving a fellow with a [criminal] past a job. Believe me, it's most humiliating to have these personnel men swear at me." Even in the flush war years, ex-cons, he said, could be "barred from all this defense work going on. I don't believe it's quite fair."[94] Yet the board refused to change the employment requirement for parole, convinced that work was the answer to rejoining the outside world. They preferred overcrowding and compromised internal discipline to contravening the fundamental premise that wage labor was necessary to prevent a parolee's backsliding into crime.

Even when they had work, parolees might lose their jobs, or be exploited by the bosses whose signatures were the only thing standing between themselves and a return to prison. Parole officers noted parolees' vulnerability. A 1939 attorney general's report warned of the "considerable danger of the exploitation of parolees by unscrupulous employers when they are forced to accept any sort of job offer in order to be paroled."[95] Moreover, a state parole officer found that many parole violations were "caused by disagreement with employers as to wages and working conditions."[96] As Jonathon Simon has noted, the danger of abuse was inherent "in the powerful combination of the state's power to punish with private networks of social control in an industrial society."[97]

It is unclear whether Vaxter Haskins went into peonage with the Wells family or how many California parolees were subject to radical exploitation, but this and worse happened to others. Journalist Don Reid believed that some Texas parole supervisors were little more than "employers seeking cheap labor," and archival evidence supports his claim.[98] It may seem incredible, but Maggie Jackson requested that her daughter, Sallie Mae, be sent back to the Goree Farm to finish her sentence. Her daughter, who had been released to a private family, was "being treated like a dog" and worked for no pay. Sallie Mae sent a letter to her mother, which she forwarded to the governor, asking to be returned to the prison. The Connally family moved her from Orange, Texas, to Alexandria, Louisiana, against her will. When Mrs. Connally learned that Sallie Mae had written to her mother about the move, she got mad and told me that if I foole with her that she would open every let-ter that was mail to me and read it. I told her she was perfect welcome to do so. and then she told me that all negroes art to be slaves and Whup every 6 month in the year. I told her that I had all ways thought that what she wonted but that would never be again she would do that to me if she wasent afraid but I am her change be cause she must remember she gt one of the best out of prison. there is women in prison would have done whip her all over her house to long to talk and would has done gone back to the pen. . . . please don't worry about me be cause some day if life lastest we will all see each other now be good and remember me in your prays and I will do the same by you

> *From Sallie*
> *2236 Hill Ave*
> *Alexandria*
> *write the letter to the Gov.*[99]

Even for those not subject to peonage, there were final indignities in leaving the prison. Albert Sample recalled his final departure, which included a strip search as part of its ritual humiliation. His few possessions included the journals he had taken to keeping.

> My turn came, I put my clothes, shoes, and other personals on the counter. I completed the "Open your mouth, spread your cheeks" part as the young guard watched. He raked my shoes and clothes to one side, indicating it was okay to start putting them back on. I was almost finished buttoning my shirt and cramming my cigarettes and Zippo back in my pockets when he began to leaf through my composition tablets stacked on the counter.
> "What're these?" he asked.
> "Jus some books I've been keepin notes in."
> "How long you been here?"
> "A long time, Boss, seventeen years altogether."
> He pitched them into the barrel with the rest of the things they'd confis-cated. Five years of writing tossed into the trash.
> "You ought not have no trouble rememberin."[100]

Nevertheless, and regardless of what waited for them on parole or in freedom, leaving the prison was an exalted moment, and they had certainly known worse than this. Friends would congratulate the inmate, who might ask, as a work song did, "What you want me to tell your mama . . . when I go home?" The answer, from the remaining prisoner, "Tell her you left me rollin', buddy, but I ain't got long."[101]

San Quentin's Discharge Room. Image 1925.005.010, Folder 5, Leo L. Stanley Collection, San Quentin Photographs, Anne T. Kent Room, Marin County Public Library.

When his time came, he might help pass messages along, too, to loved ones left far behind.

San Quentin's prisoners would prepare by spending a few minutes in the institution's relatively well-appointed discharge room. It was narrow but long, with a carpeted floor, a plush chair, a cushioned bench to sit on when trying on the shoes and trousers they would wear on the outside. A few clerks were available to help fit the hats stacked on shelves along one wall, almost like an outside shop. Perhaps there was some pomade available, and one of the short ties that were the style of the day. A photo of Franklin Roosevelt watched as they prepared to leave the institution.[102] If they were going on parole, they would need to go directly to their parole supervisor and their employer and walk a fine line—or at least appear to—until their sentences were up and they were out of formal surveillance. But in any case, David Lamson gave a sense of leaving the institution.

> Then one afternoon of pouring rain the lieutenant appeared at the cell door. . . . We went out across the yard to the clothing room, bent to the storm. A new outfit was waiting for me; they were expecting me. But the garments carried no number. The linen was white. The suit was brown. The clothes were my own, the ones I had worn into the prison thirteen months earlier. They had been laundered and cleaned and put away, against the outside chance that I might be going back again. And the outside chance had won.
>
> Going across the Garden Beautiful to the little iron door that led Out-side, I looked up at the Row. I knew that behind each door a man stood, watching me. The rain and the screens on the door hid them from me. They would be waving to me, waving good-bye. I waved back to them, furtively after the prison habit, and a little shamefacedly because I was fortunate.[103]

He was fortunate because he was on his way out. Moreover, he was white, was literate, and had a bit of money, a supportive family and friends, and even a decent suit. In its combination of parole and its meager efforts at social welfare, the state would look after people who did not. White men like Lamson would come to expect the new-found and hard-fought entitlements from the government, while nonwhite men, and all women, would fight for recognition as subjects who deserved the same. They would walk out of San Quentin, ten state-issued dollars in their state-issued pockets to get them started—maybe as much as twenty, if the Board of Prison Directors thought they had performed some meritorious service. They would climb onto the cheapest bus headed to their place of conviction, or someplace else that cost less than ten dollars to reach.[104] If they left Texas's Walls Unit, they would walk past its tall, red brick walls, and under the town's leafy trees, toward the bus station—no ride on Bud Russell's One Way Wagon this time. They would probably walk past white-suited trustees, who might take a short break from their responsibilities to watch them go. The New Deal government was firmly in place and rumors of war in Europe grew stronger, even if the economy was not yet on firm ground. They would carry the lessons, scars, and nightmares of hard time with them, the aura and stigma of being an ex-con, and anxiety about a return. Many would find themselves on the wrong side of the law again—the requirements of parole too trying or the legitimate economy too exclusive to permit otherwise. But for now, at least, they were on their own.

Epilogue

San Quentin prison, like the rest of the Golden State and the rest of the nation, went on high alert on December 7, 1941. Unlike previous emergencies, when desperate prisoners tied sheets together to escape from a window or burrowed under the thick walls, this threat came from outside rather than within. Authorities were concerned that dimmed nighttime floodlights could hide escaping prisoners, but they were even more afraid that the lights would guide Japanese bombers attacking the Bay Area. Instead of fighting with each other, international war gave prisoners and authorities a common enemy. They could all agree that the Germans and the Japanese were the greater threat to the inconsistent promise of American life, to which prisoners held fast even from behind bars. Japanese Americans, marked by race and executive order as "enemy aliens," were forced into wartime Concentration Camps—carceral structures that contained this newfound threat to national security. As enemy aliens, they provided a figurative opposite to the patriotic inmates held in state prisons.

Prisoners were quick to realize the new ideological terrain created by the war, and were sincere when they declared that though they might be criminals, they were still Americans. San Quentin prisoner H. Buderus von Carlshausen asked, "Remember Pearl Harbor? We have remembered! We the half million who have lost the right to call ourselves citizens, but—thank God!—not the right to call ourselves Americans!"[1] The enthusiasm meshed with improved conditions. California's massively overcrowded institutions grew quieter as prisoners ensnared by the Depression were paroled or finished their sentences, and as numbers of the newly received dwindled. Good jobs in war industries and the demand for soldiers across the armed forces drained the pool of potential inmates. Prisons emptied as industrial machinery hummed and wallets filled with defense dollars. Armaments factories and military service—consent-based disciplinary institutions likewise stratified by race and gender—took over the role that prisons had played in the 1930s, but generally conferred prestige rather than insult, and directed violence abroad rather than within.

Not only were there fewer state prisoners during the Second World War, but labor assignments diversified. Work proved to be a key source of prisoners' identification as patriotic Americans. Indeed, highly masculine social realist imagery abounded in California's inmate publications, in which prisoners canning food for the war effort portrayed themselves as driving a stake in the heart of Nazism. Furthermore, prisoners in San Quentin took on new industrial roles for the war effort. They stamped cafeteria trays and did laundry for the navy; they wove antisubmarine nets to be strung below the surface of the San Francisco Bay. Prisoners worked for wages in harvest camps, picking food to feed the nation and be sent to the front lines. They also fought forest fires, protecting material resources for the nation and the war effort. They wove cargo nets and made landing boats, and even donated cigarettes to "the boys" on the front lines. More striking still, San Quentin and Folsom inmates donated gallons and gallons of their blood to the war effort, which led to jokes that some of their wildness might give soldiers extra courage on the battlefield.[2] Other inmates, serving long sentences or life terms, wanted to sign on to desperate missions on "suicide squads," where their deaths would restore the patriotic honor they had forgone in life. Still others volunteered for medical experimentation supervised by the U.S. Navy's Department of Scientific Research.[3] But the luckiest were the parolees, now able to fight: on March 13, 1942, the *San Quentin News* reported that the parole board agreed that any man leaving prison who enlisted in the armed forces would receive a full discharge and be reclassified from 4-F to 1-A.[4] Fighting a war became their means toward full reincorporation into the nation.

And though black prisoners continued to receive the worst treatment in California prisons, some used the contradictions between fighting a war against fascism abroad while living under Jim Crow to better their conditions at home. There was a "Double V" movement behind prison walls, too. In late 1943 W. Mills wrote to members of the Alco Investigating Committee demanding an end to racial segregation at Folsom. "In times such as these," wrote Mills, "with America fighting for survival in this world struggle, it is an insult and disgrace to the Atlantic Charter, Bill of Rights and American Constitution to continue to humiliate us Negroes with all kinds of Jim Crow rules." He continued, "My people since 1619 have worked, fought, bled, suffered and some died to build and protect this country. What more has any other race did? What more can we do?" Despite the long tenure of African Americans in the United States, and the sacrifice and contributions they made to the nation, he and other black inmates continued to be treated "as though we are not human."[5]

When prisoners described themselves as patriots rather than as criminals, and when they placed themselves in a national narrative of inclusion beyond the confines of common criminality, they attempted to redefine the terms of punishment. "Love-of-country," von Carlshausen wrote, "is an emotion rooted too deep for 'the law' to destroy, even in hardened criminals."[6] Prisoners' expressions of nationalism were an effort to destigmatize themselves, to change the terms of the discourse by which they were outcast. In this way, war allowed prisoners to rearticulate the meaning of incarceration and criminality in opposition to the more distant racial and national otherness of Japanese and German enemies. It was an astute decision, and it sat well with government officials. It was no mere coincidence that prisoners' patriotism developed rapidly in a context in which the United States Department of Justice asked that prison officials record and register all "alien" inmates of the institution, in accordance with the Alien Registration Act of 1940.[7]

Despite the many changes the war brought to Texas and California prisons, each would continue to travel the paths of its respective penal modernity. Wartime prison populations fell in Texas, as they did in California. But by every account, conditions in Texas prisons changed for the worse. Perhaps this occurred because the prison's agricultural production had expanded so greatly during the Depression that the prison system itself, like the economy of the previous decade, had reached a crisis of overproduction. There were too few inmates to make the farms run, too few inmates to be contained efficiently, too few laborers—either waged or in shackles—for the prison to operate as smoothly as it once had.[8]

As we have seen, Investigator Austin MacCormick blamed the guards and the buildings. The most competent guards joined the military, and a great many others were lured away by bigger paychecks in defense work. This left at best questionable personnel in charge of the wards of the state; MacCormick thought many were heavy drinkers, and if they were not drunk, most were still "inexperienced or incompetent" and quick to brutalize inmates.[9] The prison tanks remained a sore spot, too, and MacCormick believed that cellblocks, like those in California, would eliminate the prevalence of violence. The ugly history of postwar Texas showed that he was wrong.

Despite MacCormick's error, he was not totally off the mark. One difference between the California and Texas experience was the very nature of their penal modernities, and their relative configurations of architecture and violence. San Quentin's thick walls continued to control inmates' movements, despite a decreased guard corps. In Texas's scattered penal farms, only armed guards and BTs stood between prisoners and escape. Wartime guards seemed to perceive a new equation in the balance of power. If there were fewer guards to control prisoners, they had to mete out more violence, and building tenders continued to offer their services. Investigators believed the BTs rose to the occasion and dominated the remaining prisoners, which resulted in escape attempts, gross violence and assault, and self-mutilation.

Texas prison officials had long been in the habit of reporting the best of circumstances, and continued to do so during the war, despite widespread and expanding brutality. Nineteen forty-three was a particularly profitable year, they boasted, with good crops and sales to the army. The prison did relatively little building due to wartime material shortages, but nevertheless finished a manager's residence at Blue Ridge and Ramsey, a guard's dormitory at Harlem, and a blacksmith shop and warehouse at Wynne. They also connected power lines for the Darrington, Eastham, Clemens, Retrieve, and Ferguson farms so that they could have commercially generated electrical power.[10] Yet two years later, members of the classification committee admitted to some difficulties they faced during the war. The classification committee was understaffed, but they still assiduously divided prisoners into black, white, and Mexican units. However, they would not devote the resources necessary to "classify" all incoming inmates, even with the decreased wartime intake. "It is again noted that the present staff is unable to write summaries on all cases, and that no attempt is made to make written reports or summaries on Latin-American and Negro cases." White prisoners might be differentiated between potentially rehabilitated citizens and the dangerous and forever excluded incorrigibles. As before, black and Mexican prisoners were denied whatever gains classification might confer—and thus violent and nonviolent, and young and old prisoners remained undifferentiated.[11] As earlier, all black and, to a lesser extent, Mexican prisoners, regardless of crime, were treated as the very worst of those among them. Blackness and Mexicanness were effectively, and punitively, equated with irredeemable criminality. And though prison officials enjoyed the relatively smaller numbers of inmates during the war years, they nevertheless looked to the end of the war with a sense of foreboding. They knew full well that the numbers of inmates would rise along with postwar demobilization, as soldiers accustomed to violence returned home.

After the Second World War, California and Texas prisons continued along their respective paths of reformist and revanchist modernity. With the significant financial resources and the dreams that characterized postwar California's middle-class planners as much as its poor migrants, California's prison officials met the postwar challenge with energy and self-proclaimed expertise. The California Department of Corrections would apply new modes of progressive penological theory more fully than any other state in the nation. Under the guidance of pioneer penologist Richard McGee, its officials wedded psychotherapeutic practices with indeterminate sentencing, intensive surveillance with vocational training. Therapeutic correction, based on psychology and ascendant notions of "bibliotherapy" (in which prison libraries would serve as "hospitals of the mind"), took center stage in new reform ideologies.[12] California's therapeutic ideal found its best expression in the Chino Institution for Men, opened in 1942 to much self-congratulation.[13] Chino superintendent Kenyon J. Scudder believed that "prisoners were people," not convicts, and should be treated accordingly.[14] They undertook an intensive expansion of the prison system itself, adding new facilities to ease overcrowding and improve the differentiation of inmates by classification. There were just two prisons in California at the beginning of the 1930s, and four when the war ended. Californians continued their experiments with progressive penology, developing library and educational systems and expanding outside forest camps in an effort to instill a kind of citizenship-in-training that joined military-style mobilization with ideologies of redemptive labor at public works.[15] Inmates branded as homosexual were stridently, if always incompletely, policed. California's prisons became increasingly black and Latino in the postwar years, populated by the new streams of domestic and international migrants to California's federally funded defense plants, but also to agroindustrial farms, and, later, service industries.

Texas's postwar prison system would continue on much the same path as it had traveled before: running tough, low-cost institutions, stressing hard agricultural labor, racial dominance, and unstinting brutalization for anything other than subservience. Nevertheless, Texas prison officials, too, would receive their share of plaudits. O. B. Ellis headed the Texas system after the war and implemented a handful of overdue changes, while staying true to the dictum of hard work and total discipline. Even the *American Journal of Corrections* proclaimed that under Ellis, "Texas's prison system [has moved] from near the bottom of the ladder to near the top."[16] California might lead the nation in penal reforms, but George Beto, Ellis's replacement, who, according to inmate legend, ruled Texas prisons "with a Bible in one hand, and a bat in the other," kept costs at rock bottom and extended its model of control penology.[17] His low-cost prisons were the envy of governors' budget committees around the nation. When riots shook other institutions, Texas prisoners were quiet. Their quiescence was the fruit of domination rather than consent, the application of violence rather than its diminution. "We had total control, absolute literal control," a former guard recalled.[18]

Yet politics inside and outside the institutions forced change. In California, radical inmate critics like George Jackson took advantage of San Quentin's library for self-education, and voiced increasingly strident challenges to the prison as an agent of racist colonialism, in which ghetto residents and the Vietcong were similar victims of imperialism. Jackson understood that revolutionary challenges hardly demonstrated the contrition parole boards wanted to see before setting a release date, but he also understood that progressive reforms, like the indeterminate sentence, allowed for tight administrative control without review. Jackson came to equate this cornerstone feature of progressive penology with the rule of fascism, and argued that in prison, the liberal velvet glove came off to reveal the truth of America's iron fist. When Jackson was shot down by guards in 1970—and before the showcase trial of which he would be a part—the prisoners in New York's Attica rebelled. This prompted yet another crackdown by revanchist politicians.[19]

In Texas, prisoners' rights activists and jailhouse attorneys challenged the constitutionality of the system, and particularly its reliance on building tenders and unbridled violence. Self-educated inmate writers like Fred Cruz, David Ruíz, and Lawrence Pope filed federal suits against the state for violation of their constitutional rights. With the aid of civil rights attorneys, they effectively put the state on trial. In the landmark case *Ruíz v. Estelle*, Judge William Wayne Justice ruled that the Texas Department of Corrections was in violation of the Constitution, and put the system under federal oversight. "No human being, regardless of how disfavored by society, shall be subjected to cruel and unusual punishment or be deprived of the due process of the law. . . . Regrettably, state officials have not upheld their responsibilities to enforce these principles." The BT system was to be abolished, and numerous reforms would be taken in order to meet "evolving standards of decency." Yet this initiative was short-lived. Prison officials fought court-imposed changes at every step.[20]

The lynchpin years came in the 1970s, and California's and Texas's penal paths slowly began to converge. The prisoners' rights movement corresponded with worldwide social protests, prompting a crisis in international capitalism and, along with fiscal restructuring around currency markets, accelerating the change that geographer David Harvey called the transition from a Fordist-Keynesian mode of production to one of flexible accumulation. Subsequent processes of capital mobility accelerated deindustrialization in the United States, as industry sought more profitable locations of production in order to pay lower wages and to be less limited by the strictures placed on capital by nation-states, characterized in the United States as the "New Deal Order."[21] But even as welfare state provisions and national regulations on markets waned, repressive state oversight, especially in military and policing functions, grew increasingly comprehensive. Tactics of social control centered most stringently on urban America, and, more specifically, on nonwhites—African American, Latino, and Asian American youth—and police forces drew on military counterinsurgency techniques to control poor communities. Moreover, increasing disciplinary technologies of record keeping and the control of space were imported from the prison into everyday police tactics.[22] New Right critiques of liberal penology grew and took root alongside the growing "southern strategy," paring off disaffected and economically precarious whites from the Democratic Party. Capitalizing on the fear of urban and black civil unrest, criminologists provided fodder for the idea that "nothing works" to diminish criminality and that long-term incapacitation of criminals—akin to the control models Texas developed so effectively—was the only solution. Fed by expansive (and expensive) wars on crime and, later, on drugs, prison populations skyrocketed. Much as the convict lease helped crush the political gains earned by African Americans through Civil War and Reconstruction, late modern crime control and mass incarceration offered a putatively color-blind means of dismantling the victories hard won in the civil rights movement, known to many as the "Second Reconstruction." It is hardly a coincidence that the decline in black suffrage due to felony convictions followed barely a generation after the 1965 Voting Rights Act.[23]

As the hard shift from an industrial to a postindustrial economy began, prison populations increased dramatically, filling with black and brown young men. California's institutions had moved from penal progressivism to fully embracing the therapeutic ideals of bibliotherapy and psychological treatment to the most recent era, characterized by an increasingly punitive criminology favoring near-total confinement.[24] Fearful of prisoners' supposed hypermasculinity, some hardliners called for the removal of weightlifting and other exercise equipment, eliminating one of the "successes" of midcentury penology. Texas's vengeful penality, which had to respond to prisoners' rights reforms but rebounded, harder still, expanded similarly, to rejoin California. Texas embarked on the largest prison-building program known to the democratic world. California's voters are driven to the polls by hard-line fear of black criminals and brown immigrants—a perennial southern and Anglo borderland strategy; but so too do Texas prisons now favor arch-modern architectural controls, which may have reached near-total expression in California's Pelican Bay supermax prison, where "administrative segregation" ("ad-seg") cells eliminate nearly all human contact. In 1871, *Ruffin v. Commonwealth* ruled that prisoners were legally dead, but prisoners' legal status as *civiliter mortus* was overturned as a result of prisoners' rights legislation, with rulings determining that "[t]here is no Iron Curtain drawn between the Constitution and the prisons of this country."[25] Nevertheless, with contemporary penal innovation of total confinement, many are effectively buried alive. Barry Gibbs lost nineteen years of his life to the criminal justice system. "They took my identification, they took everything from me," he explained. "I lost my son, I lost my family, I lost my friends. . . . I lost my dignity, and I lost my honor." It took an unrelenting fight for him to regain them. Relating the history of that injustice is one step forward.[26]

Punishment must be understood beyond its commonsense definition as a consequence of criminal acts. Just as Edwin Owen historicized the notion of crime from a San Quentin cell in 1933, so too are modes of punishment historically specific expressions of social power and conflict. Prisons are active sites of cultural formation where the state—that strange complex of institutions, discourses, practices, and forces, set in motion by people and shaping them in turn—tries to reproduce its version of good order. The state, as an institution, a bureaucracy, an entity, and an idea, is made in the process.

Members of the multiracial and transnational working classes were forcibly gathered in Depression-era prisons. In Texas and California in particular, inmates ranged from around the country and around the world, but more than any other feature, they shared the common ground of being poor. In the midst of radical economic crisis and widespread critiques of capitalism as a social and economic system, prisons might have become locations of working-class politicization. But this was rarely the case. The Popular Front became a vibrant working-class movement outside the walls, but prisons, as powerful pedagogical institutions of state control, delineated between racial groups and undermined the potential of cross-racial working-class identification. The mordant processes of incarceration affected inmates' identities: they were quickly and thoroughly divided into groups. Obedient whites were offered kinds of social citizenship and retraining (or were told they were offered this redemption), while Native American, Asian American, Mexican, and, to a greater extent than the others, African American prisoners were fully subordinated. Texas's institutions were a segregationist planner's dream, places where complete racial and spatial differentiation, impossible on the outside, could actually be attempted. California's prisons came closer to replicating its urban centers, where segregation was less formal, but de facto Jim Crow was real enough. White prisoners in each state claimed the prerogatives that their skin privilege entailed, to be sure, and as a result of this and more, conflicts permeated the institution: conflicts of an alienated working class divided against itself, and conflicts between prisoners of all sorts and their keepers.

The meanings and privileges of gender, and especially masculinity, were reified and transformed as prisoners were sorted and sorted themselves. At times, prisoners' understandings meshed with those of keepers: some conceptions of manhood were shared across the bars. At others, male prisoners and keepers held opposing definitions of manhood, suitable to their needs, positions, and visions. The meaning of being a man—with its connections to power, work, self-control, and providing for family, its place in sex roles, and its connection to violence—was a field in which all prisoners participated. Prisoners were forced into a world in which masculinity was ever more intimately linked to dominating control. This took different forms in each state, with con bosses in California and building tenders in Texas, but the connections between hegemonic masculinity and control, which suppressed both alternative masculinities and all femininities was more deeply carved. As states, especially California, medicalized, pathologized, and penalized homosexuality, the number of ways of being a "normal" man decreased, as did the possibilities of caring relationships behind bars.

No less than the individual bodies, behaviors, and identities that prisons strove to create (but also destroyed), these state institutions also tried to enforce the ideological and territorial borders of the nation. They differentiated between those who might be redeemed as citizens—white, obediently industrious, and heterosexual—and those who needed still more punishment: everyone else, though with some gradations of suffering and reward. African Americans especially, and those prisoners reproduced as racial (rather than ethnic) others in American prisons, would remain behind prison walls or, upon release, would be returned to scratch out a living in barrios, ghettos, impoverished rural towns, or factories in the fields. Housing covenants no less than harsh policing would enforce racial segregation. They also determined who would be expelled from the nation. When prison officials reported Filipino, Chinese, or Mexican "aliens," among others, to the Immigration and Naturalization Service for deportation, they drew indelible lines of national otherness.

In every case, punishment was a symptom and a front of political economic transformation. Prisons brought together forces of racial dominance, protection of class relations, and regulation of violence under the roof of the state, which would try to master them all. The underside, and thus the foundation, of the modern American state was thereby forged, attempting new modes of social control but never shying away from the oldest forms of violence. A full and expanding spectrum of domination and redemption were expressed in Texas and California prisons—of forced labor, ambivalent pleasures, training and therapy, of bone-grinding pain and death. The racial, sexual, and national contours of the nation were made, and contested, in institutions that formed the final sanction available to the state. In this way, the state helped save the capitalist economy, structured by racial and gender dominance, from the crises that capitalism itself had created.

As I write the final words to this book in 2010, conditions are eerily similar to those of the 1930s. A global financial crisis, dubbed "the Great Recession," has wrought havoc on the world's economy. Banks and nations threaten to crash. Dark clouds of oil drift through the depths of the Gulf of Mexico, much as towering dust clouds once darkened midwestern skies. It is as yet unclear how state or federal governments will respond to these economic, environmental, and human catastrophes, wrought, then as now, by periods of unregulated capitalism. The differences between the 1930s and today's prison systems are obvious. The scope of prisons today beggars belief and has far vaster human and societal consequences. Then, a racially structured rehabilitative ideal did exist, though it generally benefited whites only and rarely had the funding its advocates desired. Even that modest rehabilitative ideal was lost in the 1990s, when politicians called for harsher punishments and longer sentences. In the Depression, a prison system was overcrowded with seven thousand inmates, but many of today's operate with more than a hundred thousand. There is something of a social safety net in the twenty-first century, a legacy of the New Deal, though benefits are rarely adequate and run out too quickly. Yet the ranks of the unemployed are growing. In early 2010 the Bureau of Labor Statistics counted fifteen million people unable to find work, with 6.3 million Americans among the "long-term unemployed."[27] These numbers, of course, are muted by the prison system itself, which has already removed 2.3 million people from the count. At the same time, the corrections industry is a massive employer. It spends $212 billion per year and pays the wages of 2.4 million people, more than Wal-Mart and McDonald's combined.[28]

In 2008, there were 173,670 inmates in California's ninety-odd state prisons. If county jail inmates are included, some 255,808 Californians were behind bars. In Texas, the total imprisoned population (including prisons and jails) was 239,040. Of these, 172,506 were in state prisons—a rate of 639 per 100,000.[29] Nationally, more than one in one hundred adults in America are locked behind bars, with dramatic racial disparities. One in nine black men aged 20–29 is incarcerated. One in sixty white men aged 20–24 is behind bars, and one in twenty-four Hispanic men is in jail or prison. When probation and parole are factored in, the numbers are starker still: one in thirty-one adults, more than 7.3 million people, is under some form of criminal justice control.[30]

It is too soon to tell how the opposing pressures of a growing budget crisis and mounting unemployment will come together in twenty-first-century prisons, but the budgets are greatly overextended. California spent $8.8 billion on penal systems in 2007. Texas, with slightly more inmates than California, spent $3.3 billion.[31] In the face of a $20 billion deficit in 2010—some analysts call California a failed state—Governor Schwarzenegger proposed releasing large numbers of nonviolent, nonserious prisoners, at a proposed savings of $1.1 billion. His proposal met with a cool reception from legislators in both parties, none of whom wanted to appear "soft" on crime.[32] Nevertheless, there is some indication that tight budgets will force states to cut prison spending. One way to do so would be to release low-level offenders, as Schwarzenegger proposed. Another would involve cutting costly rehabilitative programs without replacing them. A third, highly likely possibility is expanding prison labor as a profit-making (or cost-minimizing) venture. The Prison Industries Enhancement Act was passed in 1979 and effectively unmade the 1929 Hawes-Cooper Act, bringing the Fordist-Keynesian period of prison labor to a close. The resurgent exploitation of prisoners' labor was limited by relatively cheap opportunities available in overseas export processing zones, but this, too, may change.

Questions of cost rather than morality have been the driving force of today's (still meager) efforts at reform and alternatives to incarceration. According to a report from the Pew Center for the States, "the breathtaking rise in correctional costs is triggering alarm in statehouses around the nation. . . . [B]y broadening the mix of sanctions in their correctional tool box, they can save money and still make lawbreakers pay."[33] Even with the centrist Obama presidency, the political and practical distance between federal government and state prison regimes is vast. State prisons, now as in the 1930s, are broadly insulated from federal policy. Without vibrant local political support, even federal judicial oversight (as in Texas in the 1990s) can be largely ignored.[34]

But political support might grow. It remains to be seen whether or not the "hope" that the Obama campaign captured in 2008 will move away from bipartisan centrism and will call for substantive change. After all, for the past twenty years, bipartisanship around crime has meant collusion in building and filling more prisons with more people of color. If popular movements might learn some lessons from the long civil rights movement, as it took shape within prison walls and without, and if the democratic globalization movement—perhaps an analogue to the Popular Front—can reach across prison walls as much as it has looked across national borders, the future will remain open. At least the future need not be one so dominated by mass incarceration. It may be one where the promise of democratic belonging and broader well-being is understood as undermined by inequitable political economies and rigid border control, rather than by racialized criminal scapegoats or by migrant economic refugees fleeing worse lives elsewhere. If no movement emerges, or if it fails to confront forces of restrictionist nativism, liberal reformism, or revanchism, mass incarceration will remain our legacy.

Notes

ABBREVIATIONS IN NOTES

BPTP   Board of Prison Terms and Paroles
CAH   Center for American History
CAHR   California History Room
CASL   California State Library
CSA   California State Archives
TSLAC   Texas State Library and Archives Commission
MCCO   Marin County Coroner's Office
MCFPL   Marin County Free Public Library
PIRA   Prison Industries Reorganization Administration

INTRODUCTION

1. Edwin Owen, "History of Crime," *The Bulletin*, January 10, 1933.

2. David M. Kennedy, *Freedom fom Fear: The American People in Depression and War, 1929–1945* (New York: Oxford University Press, 1999), 59, 87, 77.

3. Scoop Lankford, in Studs Terkel, ed., *Hard Times: An Oral History of the Great Depression* (New York: Washington Square Press, 1970), 407. Lankford's suggestion resonates with Giorgio Agamben's work on biologically and politically expendable subjects, a matter explored in greater detail throughout *Doing Time*. Agamben, *Homo Sacer: Sovereign Power and Bare Life*, trans. Daniel Heller-Roazen (Stanford, CA: Stanford University Press, 1998).

4. Quoted in Steven Mintz and Susan Kellog, *Domestic Revolutions: A Social History of American Family Life* (New York: Free Press, 1988), 138; and in Michael S. Kimmel, *Manhood in America: A Cultural History*, 2d ed. (New York: Oxford University Press, 2006), 132.

5. See United States Department of Commerce/United States Bureau of the Census, *Prisoners in State and Federal Prisons and Reformatories* (Washington, DC: United States Government Printing Office). Examination of reports from 1929 through 1937 shows the uniformly high rank among Texas and California prison populations, for both inmates received and total populations.

6. Frank L. Rector, *Health and Medical Service in American Prisons and Reformatories* (New York: National Society of Penal Information, 1929), 21.

7. Quoted in David J. Rothman, *Conscience and Convenience: The Asylum and Its Alternatives in Progressive America*, rev. ed. (New York: Aldine de Gruyter, 2002 [1980]), 196.

8. United States Department of Commerce/Bureau of the Census, *Prisoners in State and Federal Prisons and Reformatories, 1937: Statistics of Prisoners Received and Discharged during the Year for State and Federal Penal Institutions* (Washington, DC: United States Government Printing Office, 1939), 15.   U.S. Bureau of the Census, *Prisoners in State and Federal Prisons and Reformatories from 1926 through 1946* (Washington, DC: U.S. Government Printing Office, 1926–1946).

9. Elliot J. Gorn, *Dillinger's Wild Ride: The Year That Made America's Public Enemy Number One* (New York: Oxford University Press, 2009); Claire Bond Potter, *War on Crime: Bandits, G-Men, and the Politics of Mass Culture* (New Brunswick, NJ: Rutgers University Press, 1998); Jonathan Munby, *Public Enemies, Public Heroes: Screening the Gangster Film from "Little Caesar" to "Touch of Evil"* (Chicago: University of Chicago Press, 1999); Sean McCann, *Gumshoe America: Hard-Boiled Crime Fiction and the Rise and Fall of New Deal Liberalism* (Durham, NC: Duke University Press, 2000); Rebecca N. Hill, *Men, Mobs, and Law: Anti-Lynching and Labor Defense in U.S. Radical History* (Durham, NC: Duke University Press, 2008).

10. David J. Rothman, *The Discovery of the Asylum: Social Order and Disorder in the New Republic* (Boston: Little, Brown, 1971); and Rothman, *Conscience and Convenience*; David Garland's penal trilogy: *Punishment and Welfare: A History of Penal Strategies* (Hants, England: Gower, 1985), *Punishment and Modern Society: A Study in Social Theory* (Chicago: University of Chicago Press, 1990), *The Culture of Control: Crime and Social Order in Contemporary Society* (Chicago: University of Chicago Press, 2001); Alex Lichtenstein, *Twice the Work of Free Labor: The Political Economy of Convict Labor in the New South* (New York: Verso, 1996); Rebecca M. McLennan, *The Crisis of Imprisonment: Protest, Politics, and the Making of the American Penal State, 1776–1941* (Cambridge: Cambridge University Press, 2008). And, famously, Michel Foucault, *Discipline and Punish: The Birth of the Prison*, trans. Alan Sheridan (New York: Vintage, 1979). Mary Bosworth voiced a similar critique in *Explaining U.S. Imprisonment* (Thousand Oaks, CA: Sage, 2010), 4–5.

11. For poignant demonstration from recent Texas prisons, Robert Perkinson, *Texas Tough: The Birth of America's Prison Empire* (New York: Metropolitan Books, 2010), 23–30.

12. E. P. Thompson, *The Making of the English Working Class* (New York: Vintage, 1966), 12.

13. Michael Ingatieff cautions that the state cannot bear the full load of responsibility for moral sanctions behind crime and punishment, and his argument might be extended to the maintenance of racial difference. He argues that "it is a serious over-estimation of the role of the state to assume that its sanctioning powers were the exclusive source of the social division between criminal and respectable." I agree, and *Doing Time* thus assesses the roles that white prisoners played in maintaining racial hierarchies, and the roles that citizens played in justifying punishment. However, like labor historian Brian Kelly, I argue that we are remiss to exonerate the state and capital from their roles in maintaining social divisions. Just as Kelly argues that scholars must "bring the employers back in" to explain racial divisions among Alabama coal miners in the early twentieth century, I examine how states officially reproduced gendered racial hierarchies, and rendered it system supportive. Michael Ingatieff, "State, Civil Society, and Total Institution: A Critique of Recent Social Histories of Punishment," in David Sugarman, ed., *Legality, Ideology, and the State* (London: Academic Press, 1983), 183–211; Brian Kelly, *Race, Class, and Power in Alabama Coalfields, 1908–21* (Urbana: University of Illinois Press, 2001). On Antonio Gramsci, Stuart Hall, "Gramsci's Relevance for the Study of Race and Ethnicity," in David Morley

and Kuan-Hsing Chen, eds., *Stuart Hall: Critical Dialogues in Cultural Studies* (London: Routledge, 1996).

14. On the pedagogical intent of penal institutions, see Michael Meranze, *Laboratories of Virtue: Punishment, Revolution, and Authority in Philadelphia, 1760–1835* (Chapel Hill: University of North Carolina Press, 1996); Peter Linebaugh, *The London Hanged: Crime and Civil Society in the Eighteenth Century* (New York: Cambridge University Press, 1992); Douglas Hay, et al., *Albion's Fatal Tree: Crime and Society in Eighteenth-Century England* (London: Allen Lane, 1975); Michel Foucault, *Discipline and Punish*; Robert Olwell, *Masters, Slaves, and Subjects: The Culture of Power in the South Carolina Low Country, 1740–1790* (Ithaca, NY: Cornell University Press, 1998); Louis P. Masur, *Rites of Execution: Capital Punishment and the Transformation of American Culture, 1776–1865* (New York: Oxford University Press, 1989).

15. Garland, *Punishment and Modern Society*, 252.

16. Biennial reports for California prisons showed laborers vastly outweighing any other occupational category of prisoners. Numbers of laborers received at the prison grew from 343 in 1931 to 607 in 1937. See biennial reports of the State Board of Prison Directors of the State of California, archived at the California State Library, Government Publications Room. In Texas, laborers received increased from 595 in 1932 to 796 in 1938. See Annual reports of the Texas Prison Board, 1929–1945, archived at the Texas State Library.

17. Gorn, *Dillinger's Wild Ride*, 22.

18. United States Department of Commerce/Bureau of the Census, *Prisoners in State and Federal Prisons and Reformatories, 1937*, 13. On gambling and illegal economies, see Linda Espana-Maram, *Creating Masculinity in Los Angeles's Little Manila: Working-Class Filipinos and Popular Culture, 1920–1950* (New York: Columbia University Press, 2006), 51–72; Davarian L. Baldwin, *Chicago's New Negroes: Modernity, the Great Migration, and Black Urban Life* (Chapel Hill: University of North Carolina Press, 2007); Shane White, Stephen Garton, Stephen Robertson, Graham White, *Playing the Numbers: Gambling in Harlem between the Wars* (Cambridge, MA: Harvard University Press, 2010).

19. Christopher L. Tomlins, *The State and the Unions: Labor Relations, Law, and the Organized Labor Movement in America, 1880–1960* (Cambridge: Cambridge University Press, 1985). On cross-racial working-class cultures, George J. Sánchez. "Working at the Crossroads: American Studies for the Twenty-first Century; Presidential Address to the American Studies Association, November 9, 2001," *American Quarterly* 54, no. 1 (March 2002); Luiz Alvarez, *The Power of the Zoot: Youth Culture and Resistance during World War II* (Berkeley: University of California Press, 2008); George Lipsitz, *Rainbow at Midnight: Labor and Culture in the 1940s* (Urbana: University of Illinois Press, 1994); Clora Bryant, et al., *Central Avenue Sounds: Jazz in Los Angeles* (Berkeley: University of California Press, 1998); Daniel Widener, "'Perhaps the Japanese Are to Be Thanked?' Asia, Asian Americans, and the Construction of Black California," *Positions* 11, no. 1 (2003), 135–181; Lizabeth Cohen, *Making a New Deal: Industrial Workers in Chicago, 1919–1939* (Cambridge: Cambridge University Press, 1990); Michael Denning, *The Cultural Front: The Laboring of American Culture in the Twentieth Century* (New York: Verso, 1997).

20. My understanding of "class" is influenced by Ira Katznelson's theorization of levels of class formation. Katznelson offers four "levels" of class: the first is the macro-economic "objective" level of capitalist economic development: in this case, of the economic crises faced across Texas and California (and their peripheries) in the 1930s. The second level is

of specific socioeconomic relations, including such features as the specific conditions of labor relations, be they for a migrant worker, a sharecropper, a cook, or, here, someone in the San Quentin jute mill or on a Texas prison farm. In Katznelson's assessment, participants' understandings of those conditions (approval or disapproval, etc.), matter little in defining class at these levels. The third level is of "groups, sharing dispositions," akin to E. P. Thompson's understanding of the way people do (or do not) define themselves and their actions in class ways. It also includes the meanings people make to understand and act on their world. Katznelson's fourth level of class formation is of overtly political action—traditionally understood as trade unionism. Ira Katznelson, "Levels of Class Formation," in Patrick Joyce, ed., *Class* (Oxford: Oxford University Press, 1995), 142–49. Neither race nor gender nor nation have explicit place in Katznelson's levels, however, which I argue are necessary for understanding how prisoners were alienated from each other, as well as from nonprisoners.

21. Georg Rusche and Otto Kircheimer, *Punishment and Social Structure* (New Brunswick, NJ: Transaction Publishers, 2003), originally published 1939. In barest terms, Rusche and Kirchheimer argued that prisons controlled labor supplies by containing unproductive workers in a time of labor surplus, and that punishment has less to do with actual acts defined as criminal than with political-economic necessities and social fears. Despite economic reductionism that ignored politics of race and gender or the effects of culture, their understanding that incarceration subjects surplus members of the working class to state control remains astute. *Doing Time* follows in Rusche and Kirchheimer's tradition, with critiques. I do not assert a mechanistic connection between labor markets and imprisonment rates and find other elements such as race, ethnicity, and nationality to be salient features of penal practice. For recent critiques, see Loïc Wacquant, "Deadly Symbiosis: When Ghetto and Prison Meet and Mesh," *Punishment and Society* 3, no. 1 (1998): 121, note 3; Garland, *Punishment and Modern Society*, 83–110.

22. On prisons as vanguard sites, George Jackson, *Soledad Brother: The Prison Letters of George Jackson* (Chicago: Hill, 1994 [1970]), and *Blood in My Eye* (Baltimore, MD: Black Classic Press, 1990 [1972]); Angela Y. Davis, *Angela Davis: An Autobiography* (New York: International Publishers, 1989 [1974]); raúlrsalinas, *raúlrsalinas and the Jail Machine: My Weapon Is My Pen* (Austin: CMAS, University of Texas Press, 2006); Eric Cummins, *The Rise and Fall of California's Radical Prison Movement* (Stanford, CA: Stanford University Press, 1994); Dylan Rodríguez, *Forced Passages: Imprisoned Radical Intellectuals and the U.S. Prison Regime* (Minneapolis: University of Minnesota Press, 2005); Alan Eladio Gómez, "'Nuestras Vidas Corren Casi Paralelas': Chicanos, *Independentistas*, and the Prison Rebellions in Leavenworth, 1969–1972," *Latino Studies* 6 (2008): 64–96. On the long civil rights movement, Nikhil Pal Singh, *Black Is a Country: Race and the Unfinished Struggle for Democracy* (Cambridge, MA: Harvard University Press, 2005), 6. On prisoners' rights within the long civil rights movement, Robert T. Chase, "Civil Rights on the Cell Block: Race, Reform, and Violence in Texas Prisons and the Nation" (Ph.D. dissertation, University of Maryland at College Park, 2009).

23. Ranajit Guha, "The Prose of Counterinsurgency," in Ranajit Guha and Gayatri Chakravorty Spivak, eds., *Selected Subaltern Studies* (New York: Oxford University Press, 1988).

24. On cross-racial working-class cultures, Sánchez, "Working at the Crossroads"; Alvarez, *The Power of the Zoot*; Lipsitz, *Rainbow at Midnight*; Bryant et al., *Central Avenue Sounds*; Cohen, *Making a New Deal*.

25. My thoughts on racial formation draw most explicitly on Michael Omi and Howard Winant, *Racial Formations in the United States: From the 1960s to the 1990s*, 2d ed. (New York: Routledge, 1994), but also on Ian F. Haney-López, *White by Law: The Legal Construction of Race* (New York: New York University Press, 1996). On gender identities as a process, see especially Judith Halberstam, *Female Masculinities* (Durham, NC: Duke University Press, 1998), 25. My thought also parallels Margot Canaday's conceptualization of state regulation of homosexuality. "The state," Canaday writes, "did not merely implicate but also *constituted* homosexuality in the construction of a stratified citizenry." *The Straight State: Sexuality and Citizenship in Twentieth-Century America* (Princeton, NJ: Princeton University Press, 2009), 4. Loïc Wacquant productively places incarceration among successive "peculiar institutions" of racial, spatial, and labor control, whose foundational matrix was slavery. His analysis would have been strengthened with attention to westward expansion, and the displacement and domination of Mexicans and Native Americans, as an equally important foundational matrix. See Wacquant, "Deadly Symbiosis"; and Perkinson, *Texas Tough*, 52–55.

26. See Hal Draper, *Karl Marx's Theory of Revolution*. Vol. 2, *The Politics of Social Classes* (New York: Monthly Review Press, 1978), 453–78; also, David F. Greenberg, ed., *Crime and Capitalism: Readings in Marxist Criminology*, expanded and updated ed. (Philadelphia: Temple University Press, 1993).

27. Jean-Christophe Agnew, "Capitalism, Culture, and Catastrophe," in James W. Cook, Lawrence B. Glickman, and Michael O'Malley, eds., *The Cultural Turn in U.S. History: Past, Present, and Future* (Chicago: University of Chicago Press, 2008), 383–413.

28. On December 31, 1938, there were 140 women prisoners in Texas, out of a total of 6,989. 1938 Texas Prison Board Annual Report, 139. There were 144 women on hand in California prisons on June 30, 1933, of a total of 8,886. 1933–1934 Biennial Report, 17, 152.

29. The literature on women in prison is growing, belatedly but rapidly. Richard Morales, "A History of the California Institution for Women, 1927–1960: A Woman's Regime (Ph.D. dissertation, University of California at Riverside, 1980); Nicole Hahn Rafter, *Partial Justice: Women in State Prisons, 1800–1935* (Boston: Northeastern University Press, 1985); Estelle B. Freedman, *Their Sisters' Keepers: Women's Prison Reform in America, 1830–1930* (Ann Arbor: University of Michigan Press, 1981); Anne M. Butler, *Gendered Justice in the American West: Women Prisoners in Men's Penitentiaries* (Urbana: University of Illinois Press, 1997); Shelly Bookspan, *A Germ of Goodness: The California Prison System, 1851–1944* (Lincoln: University of Nebraska Press, 1991), 69–92; Mary Ellen Curtin, *Black Prisoners and Their World: Alabama, 1865–1900* (Charlottesville: University Press of Virginia, 2000), 113–29; Lucia Zedner, "Wayward Sisters: The Prison for Women," in Norval Morris and David J. Rothman, eds., *The Oxford History of the Prison: The Practice of Punishment in Western Society* (New York: Oxford University Press, 1998), 295–342; Kali N. Gross, *Colored Amazons: Crime, Violence, and Black Women in the City of Brotherly Love, 1880–1910* (Durham, NC: Duke University Press, 2006); Cheryl D. Hicks, "'Bright and Good Looking Colored Girl': Black Women's Sexuality and 'Harmful Intimacy' in Early-Twentieth-Century New York," *Journal of the History of Sexuality* 18, no. 3 (2009); Mary Bosworth, *Explaining U.S. Imprisonment* (Thousand Oaks, CA: Sage, 2010). On late-twentieth- and early-twenty-first-century women in prison, Human Rights Watch/Women's Rights Project, *All Too Familiar: Sexual Abuse of Women in U.S. State Prisons* (New York: Human Rights Watch, 1996); Beth E. Richie, *Compelled to Crime: The Gender*

Entrapment of Battered Black Women (New York: Routledge, 1996); Christina Rathbone, *A World Apart: Women, Prison, and Life behind Bars* (New York: Random House, 2005); Rickie Solinger, Paula C. Johnson, Martha L. Raimon, Tina Reynolds, Ruby C. Tapia, eds., *Interrupted Life: Experiences of Incarcerated Women in the United States* (Berkeley: University of California Press, 2010).

30. Canaday, *Straight State*, 5.

31. I understand gender not as fixed to specific bodies or biology, but as a historically shifting set of power relations informed by understandings of sexual difference. In the prison context; see especially Dana Britton, *At Work in the Iron Cage: The Prison as Gendered Organization* (New York: New York University Press, 2003); Don Sabo, Terry S. Kupers, and Willie London, eds., *Prison Masculinities* (Philadelphia: Temple University Press, 2001); Regina Kunzel, *Criminal Intimacy: Prison and the Uneven History of Modern American Sexuality* (Chicago: University of Chicago Press, 2008). More broadly, Judith Butler, *Gender Trouble: Feminism and the Subversion of Identity* (New York: Routledge, 1999); E. Anthony Rotundo, *American Manhood: Transformations in Masculinity from the Revolution to the Modern Era* (New York: Basic Books, 1993); George Chauncey, *Gay New York: Gender, Urban Culture, and the Making of the Gay Male World, 1890–1940* (New York: Basic Books 1994); Gail Bederman, *Manliness and Civilization: A Cultural History of Gender and Race in the United States, 1880–1917* (Chicago: University of Chicago Press, 1995); R. W. Connell, *Masculinities* (Berkeley: University of California Press, 1995); Judith Halberstam, *Female Masculinities* (Durham, NC: Duke University Press, 1998); Michael S. Kimmel, *Manhood in America: A Cultural History*, 2d ed. (New York: Oxford University Press, 2006).

32. On penal modernism as a singular (if complex) historical formation, Garland, *Culture of Control*, 27–73. Perkinson rightly criticizes historiographical focus on the Northeast, "the birthplace of rehabilitative penology," and argues instead for a much heavier emphasis on Texas and "the South, the fountainhead of subjugationist discipline." *Texas Tough*, 8. It is a necessary critique, but the contrast risks what some call the myth of southern exceptionalism, which may make what transpired for rehabilitation elsewhere seem better than it was. See Matthew D. Lassiter and Joseph Crespino, eds., *The Myth of Southern Exceptionalism* (New York: Oxford University Press, 2010), and especially Heather Ann Thompson's "Blinded by a 'Barbaric' South: Prison Horrors, Inmate Abuse, and the Ironic History of American Penal Reform," 74–95.

33. For the 1910 investigation, see the Texas legislature, *Report of the Penitentiary Investigating Committee, including All Exhibits and Testimony Taken by the Committee*, 1910, archived at the University of Texas's Center for American History, Austin, Texas. See also Robert Reps Perkinson, "The Birth of the Texas Prison Empire, 1865–1915" (Ph.D. dissertation, Yale University, 2001); Paul M. Lucko, "The Governor and the Bat: Prison Reform during the Oscar B. Colquitt Administration, 1911–1915," *Southwestern Historical Quarterly* 106, no. 3 (June 2003); Lucko, "A Missed Opportunity: Texas Prison Reform during the Dan Moody Administration, 1927–1931," *Southwestern Historical Quarterly* 96 (July 1991); Lucko, "Counteracting Reform: Lee Simmons and the Texas Prison System, 1930–1935," *East Texas Historical Journal* 30 (Fall 1992); and Lucko, *Handbook of Texas Online*, s.v. "Texas Committee on Prisons and Prison Labor," http://www.tsha.utexas.edu/handbook/online/articles/TT/mdtva.html (accessed August 19, 2005). Broadly, Robert Perkinson, *Texas Tough*.

34. Ruth Wilson Gilmore, *Golden Gulag: Prisons, Surplus, Crisis, and Opposition in Globalizing California* (Berkeley: University of California Press, 2007).

35. The best histories of the Elmira regime are Alexander W. Pisciotta, *Benevolent Repression: Social Control and the American Reformatory-Prison Movement* (New York: New York University Press, 1994); and McLennan, *The Crisis of Imprisonment.*

36. Gresham M. Sykes, *The Society of Captives: A Study of a Maximum Security Prison* (Princeton, NJ: Princeton University Press, 1972 [1958]); also, Charles Bright, *The Powers That Punish: Prison and Politics in the Era of the "Big House," 1920–1955* (Ann Arbor: University of Michigan Press, 1996), 107–91.

37. Jorge A. González, "Cultural Fronts: Towards a Dialogical Understanding of Contemporary Cultures," in James Lull, ed., *Culture in the Communication Age* (London: Routledge, 2001), 107–31, esp., 113, 111. Emphasis in original.

38. Rogers M. Smith, *Civic Ideals: Conflicting Visions of Citizenship in U.S. History* (New Haven, CT: Yale University Press, 1997), 6.

39. Cesare Lombroso, *Criminal Man,* trans. and introduced by Mary Gibson and Nicole Hahn Rafter (Durham, NC: Duke University Press, 2006).

40. Frantz Fanon, *The Wretched of the Earth* (New York: Grove, 2005 [1961]). For more recent and parallel analyses, see John Comaroff and Joan Comaroff, eds., *Law and Disorder in the Postcolony* (Chicago: University of Chicago Press, 2006).

41. Linebaugh, *The London Hanged.*

42. Nell Irvin Painter, "Soul Murder and Slavery: Toward a Fully-Loaded Cost Accounting," in Linda K. Kerber, ed., *U.S. History as Women's History* (Chapel Hill: University of North Carolina Press, 1995), 125–46.

43. Peter Way, *Common Labour: Workers and the Digging of North American Canals, 1780–1860* (Cambridge: Cambridge University Press, 1993).

44. Consider Shelly Bookspan, *A Germ of Goodness: The California State Prison System, 1851–1944* (Lincoln: University of Nebraska Press, 1991). This is changing, however. For recent dissertations on Texas prisons, Paul M. Lucko, "Prison Farms, Walls, and Society: Punishment and Politics in Texas, 1848–1910" (Ph.D. dissertation, University of Texas at Austin, 1999); Robert Reps Perkinson, "The Birth of the Texas Prison Empire, 1865–1915" (Ph.D. dissertation, Yale University, 2001). An early venture in the political economy of prisons was Barbara Jeanne Yaley's "Habits of Industry: Labor and Penal Policy in California, 1849–1940" (Ph.D. dissertation, University of California at Santa Cruz, 1980). More recently, McLennan's *Crisis of Imprisonment* brought class struggle over inmate labor to the fore across a broad swath of American history. For a rare look into postwar, pre–prison-industrial-complex California, see Theodore Hamm, *Rebel and a Cause: Caryl Chessman and the Politics of the Death Penalty in Postwar California, 1948–1974* (Berkeley: University of California Press, 2001); Volker Janssen, "Convict Labor, Civic Welfare: Rehabilitation in California's Prisons, 1941–1971" (Ph.D. dissertation, University of California at San Diego, 2005); and Janssen, "When the 'Jungle' Met the Forest: Public Work, Civil Defense, and Prison Camps in Postwar California," *Journal of American History* 96, no. 3 (2009): 702–26. For Texas, see Norwood Henry Andrews III, "Sunbelt Justice: Politics, the Professions, and the History of Sentencing and Corrections in Texas since 1968" (Ph.D. dissertation, University of Texas at Austin, 2007); Robert T. Chase, "Race, Reform, and the Rehabilitative Prison in New York and Texas, 1945–1990" (Ph.D. dissertation, University of Maryland, 2009); and Perkinson, *Texas Tough.*

45. Thanks to Mark Edele for reminding me of this.

46. Cindy Hahamovitch, *The Fruits of Their Labor: Atlantic Coast Farmworkers and the Making of Migrant Poverty* (Chapel Hill: University of North Carolina Press, 1997). See also Stephen Skowronek, *Building a New American State: The Expansion of National Administrative Capacities, 1877–1920* (New York: Cambridge University Press, 1982); Theda Skocpol, "Political Response to Capitalist Crisis: Neo-Marxist Theories of the State and the Case of the New Deal," in Melvin Dubofsky, ed., *The New Deal: Conflicting Interpretations and Shifting Perspectives* (New York: Garland, 1992), 25–107.

47. Theda Skocpol, *Protecting Soldiers and Mothers: The Political Origins of Social Policy in the United States* (Cambridge, MA: Harvard University Press, 1992). Gwendolyn Mink, *The Wages of Motherhood: Inequality in the Welfare State, 1917–1942* (Ithaca, NY: Cornell University Press, 1995); Linda Gordon, *Pitied but Not Entitled: Single Mothers and the History of Welfare* (Cambridge, MA: Harvard University Press, 1998). For the British penal context, Garland, *Punishment and Welfare*.

48. On prison as a spatial and political fix to crisis, Gilmore, *Golden Gulag*.

49. McLennan, *The Crisis of Imprisonment*, 11. McLennan's usage of "postindustrial" refers to early-twentieth-century prison labor systems, rather than the character of U.S. political economy since the 1980s.

50. Warren I. Susman, *Culture as History: The Transformation of American Society in the Twentieth Century* (New York: Pantheon, 1973).

51. Bright, *The Powers That Punish*, 1.

52. Achielle Mbembe, "Necropolitics," trans. Libby Meintjes, *Public Culture* 15, no. 1 (2003). Also, consider prison activist and economic geographer Ruth Wilson Gilmore's definition of "racism" as "the state-sanctioned and/or extra-legal production and exploitation of group differentiated vulnerabilities to premature death." See her "Race and Globalization," in R. J. Johnson, Peter J. Taylor, Michael J. Watts, eds., *Geographies of Global Change: Remapping the World*, 2d ed. (Malden, MA: Blackwell, 2002), esp. 261.

CHAPTER 1

1. Robert Joyce Tasker, *Grimhaven* (New York: Knopf, 1928), 6–7.

2. Ibid., 12.

3. David Lamson, *We Who Are About to Die: Prison As Seen by a Condemned Man* (New York: Scribner's, 1935), 29–33.

4. *Thirty Minutes behind the Walls*, Program 140, November 27, 1940. Center for American History, University of Texas at Austin.

5. Harry W. Jamison testimony, January 4, 1944. Volume X: Witnesses Before the Governor's Committee on Investigation of San Quentin Prison, 1,935. California State Archives, Earl Warren Papers—Governor's Committee on Penal Affairs—1943–44. F3640:965.

6. *Thirty Minutes behind the Walls*, Program 150, February 5, 1941.

7. Andrew L. George, *The Texas Convict: The Thrilling and Terrible Experiences of a Texas Boy* (Austin, TX: Ben C. Jones, 1893), 139. Cited by Robert Reps Perkinson, "The Birth of the Texas Prison Empire, 1865–1915" (Ph.D. dissertation, Yale University, 2001), 437–38. On mortification and ritual degradation, Irving Goffman, *Asylums: Essays on the Social Situation of Mental Patients and Other Inmates* (New York: Penguin, 1961), esp. 30–40.

8. "Prison Sale," *Time*, June 17, 1940, online at http://www.time.com/time/magazine/article/0,9171,789910,00.html (accessed July 9, 2010).

9. J. B. Smith, "Bud Russell," *Ever Since I Been a Man Full-Grown* (Takoma Records, 1965).

10. Quoted in Bruce Jackson, *Wake Up Dead Man: Afro-American Worksongs from Texas Prisons* (Cambridge, MA: Harvard University Press, 1972), 8.

11. "Bud Russell Funeral Rites Planned Wednesday at Blum"; "Oldtime Lawmen Gather to Pay Final Tribute to Bud Russell," February 3, 1955. Newspaper articles accessed online at http://texashideout.tripod.com/russell.html (July 9, 2010).

12. Leo Leonidas Stanley, M.D., "Twenty Years at San Quentin," *The Centaur of Alpha Kappa Alpha* 39, no. 2 (January 1934), CASL California History Room, 389–99, 443–44, 443.

13. Leo L. Stanley, *Men at Their Worst* (New York: D. Appleton-Century, 1940), 2.

14. See Richard Terdiman's introduction to Pierre Bourdieu's "The Force of Law: Toward a Sociology of the Juridical Field," trans. Matthew Adamson, *Hastings Law Journal* 38, no. 5 (1987): 805–55. Also Michel Foucault, *Discipline and Punish: The Birth of the Prison*, trans. Alan Sheridan (New York: Vintage Books, 1979), which charted much of this terrain. But while Foucault offered powerful insight into subjection and carceral power, racial formation remained a blind spot. What Foucault misses, and which scholars such as Ian F. Haney-López and Melissa Nobles address, is the ways in which states adjudicate group and especially racial identities through techniques of mapping bodies (via citizenship law and court cases, or in the census). Haney-López, *White by Law: The Legal Construction of Race* (New York: New York University Press, 1996); Nobles, *Shades of Citizenship: Race and the Census in Modern Politics* (Stanford, CA: Stanford University Press, 2000).

15. Pierre Bourdieu and Loïc Wacquant, "Symbolic Violence," in Nancy Scheper-Hughes and Philippe Bourgois, eds., *Violence in War and Peace: An Anthology* (Malden, MA: Blackwell, 2004), 272–74, esp. 273.

16. John Comaroff, "Foreword," in Mindie Lazarus-Black and Susan F. Hirsch, eds., *Contested States: Law, Hegemony, and Resistance* (New York: Routledge, 1994). Also Walter Johnson, *Soul by Soul: Life inside the Antebellum Slave Market* (Cambridge, MA: Harvard University Press, 1999), 46.

17. W. E. B. DuBois, *Souls of Black Folk* (New York: Vintage Books, 1990 [1903]), 8–9. Gloria Anzaldua and other border theorists have articulated a similar "mestiza consciousness," and awareness of doubling. *Borderlands/La Frontera: The New Mestiza* (San Francisco: Aunt Lute, 1987).

18. Elliot J. Gorn, *Dillinger's Wild Ride: The Year That Made America's Public Enemy Number One* (New York: Oxford University Press, 2009), 122.

19. No. HS-24. Federal and State Prisoners by Jurisdiction and Sex: 1925 to 2001, U.S. Bureau of Justice Statistics, *Prisoners in State and Federal Institutions on December 31, annual, and Correctional Populations in the United States, annual,* http://www.ojp.usdoj.gov/bjs/prisons.htm.

20. Data from table 1.1 is drawn from U.S. Bureau of the Census. *Prisoners in State and Federal Prisons and Reformatories,* from 1926 through 1946 (Washington, DC: U. S. Government Printing Office, 1926–1946). Data in table 1.2 is from No. HS-24. Federal and State Prisoners by Jurisdiction and Sex: 1925 to 2001, U.S. Bureau of Justice Statistics, *Pris-*

oners in State and Federal Institutions on December 31, annual, and Correctional Populations in the United States, annual, http://www.ojp.usdoj.gov/bjs/prisons.htm. Data in table 1.3 comes from "California State Prison and Parole Population, 1918–1942," biennial report of the State Board of Prison Directors, 1940–1942, 19. This does not include populations on parole. Data in table 1.4 is calculated from annual reports.

21. Carey McWilliams, *Factories in the Field: The Story of Migratory Farm Labor in California* (Boston: Little, Brown, 1939); Ronald Takaki, *Strangers from a Different Shore: A History of Asian Americans* (New York: Penguin, 1989); Sucheng Chan, *Asian Americans: An Interpretive History* (New York: Twayne, 1991); Lisa Lowe, *Immigrant Acts: On Asian American Cultural Politics* (Durham, NC: Duke University Press, 1996); Quintard Taylor, *In Search of the Racial Frontier: African Americans in the American West, 1528–1990* (New York: Norton, 1998), Gunther Peck, *Reinventing Free Labor: Padrones and Immigrant Workers in the North American West, 1880–1930* (New York: Cambridge University Press, 2000); James N. Gregory, *American Exodus: The Dust Bowl Migration and Okie Culture in California* (New York: Oxford University Press, 1989); Dorothy B. Fujita-Rony, *American Workers, Colonial Power: Philippine Seattle and the Transpacific West, 1919–1941* (Berkeley: University of California Press, 2003).

22. On global capital and labor, David Harvey, *Spaces of Capital: Toward a Critical Geography* (London: Routledge, 2001); and Harvey, *The Condition of Postmodernity: An Inquiry in the Origins of Cultural Change* (London: Blackwell, 1990); in Texas, David Montejano, *Anglos and Mexicans in the Making of Texas, 1836–1986* (Austin: University of Texas Press, 1987); Neil Foley, *The White Scourge: Mexicans, Blacks, and Poor Whites in Texas Cotton Culture* (Berkeley: University of California Press, 1997); Emilio Zamora, *The World of the Mexican Worker in Texas* (College Station: Texas A&M University, 1995); Emma Pérez, *The Decolonial Imaginary: Writing Chicanas into History* (Bloomington: Indiana University Press, 1999). Among California immigration histories in this period and before, see Sucheng Chan, *Asian Americans*; Takaki, *Strangers from a Different Shore*; Alexander Saxton, *The Indispensable Enemy: Labor and the Anti-Chinese Movement in California* (Berkeley: University of California Press, 1971); George J. Sánchez, *Becoming Mexican American: Ethnicity, Culture, and Identity in Chicano Los Angeles, 1900–1945* (New York: Oxford Universty Press, 1993); David Gutiérrez, *Walls and Mirrors: Mexican Americans, Mexican Immigrants, and the Politics of Ethnicity* (Berkeley: University of California Press, 1995); Devra Weber, *Dark Sweat, White Gold: California Farm Workers, Cotton, and the New Deal* (Berkeley: University of California Press, 1994); Carey McWilliams, *Factories in the Fields: The Story of Migratory Farm Labor in California* (Boston: Little, Brown, 1939); Shirley Ann Wilson Moore, *To Place Our Deeds: The African American Community in Richmond, California* (Berkeley: University of California Press, 2000); Lawrence B. de Graaf, Kevin Mulroy, and Quintard Taylor, eds., *Seeking El Dorado: African Americans in California* (Los Angeles: Autry Museum of Western Heritage; Seattle: University of Washington Press, 2001); Marilynn S. Johnson, *The Second Gold Rush: Oakland and the East Bay in World War II* (Berkeley: University of California Press, 1993); Gregory, *American Exodus*.

23. Todd DePastino, *Citizen Hobo: How a Century of Homelessness Shaped America* (Chicago: University of Chicago Press, 2003), 76, 81–83.

24. Domingo Tomez, #24120, Folsom Inmate Case Files, California State Archives. I have not been able to locate files on Berg or Young. Like the vast majority of individual prisoners' records in California, they may have been destroyed.

25. Consider George Lipsitz, *Rainbow at Midnight: Labor and Culture in the 1940s* (Urbana: University of Illinois Press, 1994), and Lipsitz, *Dangerous Crossroads:Popular Music, Postmodernism, and the Poetics of Place* (New York: Verso, 1994); Matt Garcia, *A World of Its Own: Race, Labor, and Citrus in the Making of Greater Los Angeles, 1900–1970* (Chapel Hill: University of North Carolina Press, 2001), esp. chapter 6; George J. Sánchez, *Becoming Mexican American* and "Working at the Crossroads: American Studies for the Twenty-first Century; Presidential Address to the American Studies Association, November 9, 2001," *American Quarterly* 54, no. 1 (March 2002); David Reyes and Tom Waldman, *Land of a Thousand Dances: Chicano Rock 'n' Roll from Southern California* (Albuquerque: University of New Mexico Press, 1998); Clora Bryant et al., *Central Avenue Sounds: Jazz in Los Angeles* (Berkeley: University of California Press, 1998); Manuel Peña, *The Mexican American Orquesta: Music, Culture, and the Dialectic of Conflict* (Austin: University of Texas Press, 1999); Bill C. Malone, *Country Music, U.S.A.*, rev. ed (Austin: University of Texas Press, 1985); Luis Alvarez, *The Power of the Zoot: Youth Culture and Resistance during World War II* (Berkeley: University of California Press, 2008). For innovation among urban historians, Mark Wild, *Street Meeting: Multiethnic Neighborhoods in Early Twentieth-Century Los Angeles* (Berkeley: University of California Press, 2005); Allison Varzally, *Making a Non-White America: Californians Coloring Outside Ethnic Lines, 1925–1955* (Berkeley: University of California Press, 2008); Scott Kurashige, *The Shifting Grounds of Race: Black and Japanese Americans in the Making of Multiethnic Los Angeles* (Princeton, NJ: Princeton University Press, 2008); Nayan Shah, "Between 'Oriental Depravity' and 'Natural Degenerates': Spatial Borderlands and the Making of Ordinary Americans," in Mary L. Dudziak and Leti Volpp, eds., *Legal Borderlands: Law and the Construction of American Borders; Special Issue of American Quarterly* 57, no. 3 (2005): 703–25.

26. May 4, 5, 1929, Minutes, San Quentin Board of Prison Directors Minutes, 1929–30, 160–61. CSA, Department of Corrections Records, F3717:1004.

27. Data calculated from biennial reports. Also, Barbara Jeanne Yaley, "Habits of Industry: Labor and Penal Policy in California, 1849–1940" (Ph.D. dissertation, University of California at Santa Cruz, 1980), table III-6, p. 262.

28. Data calculated from biennial reports.

29. Data calculated from biennial reports.

30. Calculated from Texas Prison System annual report, 1929.

31. Calculated from annual reports.

32. Calculated dividing the number of prisoners reporting that occupation in 1938 by the prison population on December 31, 1938. See 1938 Annual Report.

33. Calculated by combining all prisoners received by occupation from 1930–1941 biennial reports.

34. Calculated from data in biennial reports. San Quentin information is based on data from 1930–1941, but lacks information from 1934. Folsom data lacks information for 1930 and 1932. Both are based on information for prisoners on hand, rather than prisoners received.

35. Data from Texas Prison System annual reports.

36. Biennial reports. Data is unavailable for 1930 and 1932, and was excluded from these calculations.

37. Compiled from biennial reports. Property crimes from Folsom are defined here as burglary, first degree; burglary, second degree; burglary, attempt; forgery and checks; receiving stolen property; robbery, first degree; robbery, second degree; robbery, attempt;

theft and fraud; theft (auto). Violent crimes from Folsom are defined as assaults; manslaughter; murder, first degree; murder, second degree; rape and attempted rape; weapons. Property crimes from San Quentin are defined as burglary, first degree; burglary, second degree; burglary, attempt to commit; robbery, first degree; robbery, second degree; robbery, attempt to commit. Violent crimes at San Quentin are defined as assaults; manslaughter; weapons; murder, first degree; murder, second degree; rape and attempted rape.

38. Data for Table 1.10 From annual reports (data unavailable from 1931 and 1932). These are prisoners on hand, rather than prisoners received. Property crimes here include theft of auto, by bailee, of hogs, horses, mules, fowls, from person, and miscellaneous theft; burglary, of private residence, of private residence at night, of railroad car. Rape includes term and life sentences. Data for Table 1.11 from annual reports.

39. United States Census, U.S. Census Bureau,http://www.census.gov/population/documentation/twps0056/tab19.pdf. Also, material drawn from biennial reports of the California State Board of Prison Directors. Populations taken on June 30 of each year.

40. United States Census, U.S. Census Bureau, http://www.census.gov/population/documentation/twps0056/tab58.pdf. Also, material drawn from annual reports of the Texas State Prison System.

41. Donald R. Walker, *Penology for Profit: A History of the Texas Prison System, 1867–1912* (College Station: Texas A&M University Press, 1988), 114.

42. Angela Y. Davis with Eduardo Mendieta, *Abolition Democracy: Beyond Empire, Prisons, and Torture* (New York: Seven Stories Press, 2005), 37–38; Joy James, "Introduction," in Joy James, ed., *The New Abolitionists: (Neo)Slave Narratives and Contemporary Prison Writings* (Albany: SUNY Press, 2005), xxvii–xxix; Amy Dru Stanley, "Beggars Can't Be Choosers: Compulsion and Contract in Postbellum America," *Journal of American History* 78 (March 1992): 1265–93; Teresa Zackodnik, "Fixing the Color Line: The Mulatto, Southern Courts, and Racial Identity," *American Quarterly* 53, no. 3 (September 2001): 420–51, esp. 424–25; Khalil Gibran Muhammad, *The Condemnation of Blackness: Race, Crime, and the Making of Modern Urban America* (Cambridge, MA: Harvard University Press, 2010); Bryan Wagner, *Disturbing the Peace: Black Culture and the Police Power after Slavery* (Cambridge, MA: Harvard University Press, 2009), 126–41, 153–58.

43. Radical criminologists have long made this claim. See, for example, Ian Taylor, Paul Walton, Jock Young, *The New Criminology: For a Social Theory of Deviance* (London: Routledge and Kegan Paul, 1973). See also Edward L. Ayers, *Vengeance and Justice: Crime and Punishment in the Nineteenth-Century American South* (New York: Oxford University Press, 1984); Zackodnik, "Fixing the Color Line"; Bourdieu, "The Force of Law."

44. Simon A. Cole, *Suspect Identities: A History of Fingerprinting and Criminal Identification* (Cambridge, MA: Harvard University Press, 2001). According to Cole, the mappings of criminals' bodies and identities were intended to track a behavioral history in text, and link a body to that file and the history it contained. Walter Johnson argues that the histories slave traders wrote of their slaves did more than just record questionable facts to facilitate a market transaction. "By detaching slaves from their history and replacing human singularity with fashioned salability, the traders were doing more than selling slaves: they were making them." Johnson, *Soul by Soul*, 129.

45. This is akin to Marx's understanding of how "living" labor is converted into the "dead" labor of capital itself. *Capital*, vol. I, trans. Ben Fowkes (New York: Penguin, 1992), chapters 6 and 7 and p. 342.

46. Cole, *Suspect Identities*, 149.

47. Most significant were the changing political economic context of depression and war, the change from a labor surplus to a labor shortage, the racialization and stigmatization of domestic ("Okie" and black southern) and international immigrants, complicated by the global colonial and core-periphery relationships between the United States and Mexico, the Philippines, China, Japan, and India, among others. All of this shifted, too, in the context of the Second World War. On bureaucratic versus folk definitions of race, Loïc J. D. Wacquant, "For an Analytic of Racial Domination," *Political Power and Social Theory* 11 (Greenwich, CT: JAI Press, 1997).

48. I learned of Ocie Hoosier's ancestry from Lele Celeste Simmons, Ocie Hoosier's granddaughter, to whom I am grateful. Personal communication, October 15, 2007, copy in author's possession. Also, Hoosier's listing in the Convict Record and Conduct Register, TSLAC.

49. See Department of Corrections Records, San Quentin Inmate Identification Cards. These are archived by inmate number. CSA.

50. Thanks to Lucy Barber, California state archivist, in this discussion of the significance of the red ink in writing "Negro." Specific segregation and maltreatment of inmates marked as "Negro" was consistent throughout the system, and was different from the way Mexican and different ethnoracially other prisoners were treated. This was much like the racial segregation in the mess hall, where, according to California prison investigators in 1943–1944, black prisoners were the only ones to be racially segregated from the rest—and this was true for living quarters as well. Mexican prisoners ate in the same general areas as "white" prisoners, though we might assume that there was some segregation here, too, given the prevailing standards of white supremacy across society.

51. Cesare Lombroso, "The Savage Origin of Tattooing," *Appleton's Popular Science Monthly* 48 (1896): 793–803, quotation 793. Cited by Cole, 58. The irony of a tattoo—an acquired physical mark—signaling inherent bodily criminality was apparently lost on Lombroso. Nevertheless, Lombroso read prisoners' tattoos in much the same way that antebellum slave buyers read scars—as evidence of "deformity" of character or inherent criminality. See Johnson, *Soul by Soul*, 145–46.

52. Joe Carcella, San Quentin #48267, gave Smock, #54341, a tattoo, and lost good time as punishment. San Quentin Minutes of the Board of Prison Terms and Paroles, October 11, 1933, 170. CSA, F3717:1072. Also Jane Caplan, ed., *Written on the Body: The Tattoo in European and American History* (Princeton, NJ: Princeton University Press, 2000).

53. None of these books had call numbers at the California State Archives when I undertook research. Archivists recommended that they be cited by their shelf location. For San Quentin Women: C5168; and for Black and Yellow #2 and #3: C5169.

54. Jas. Mori, 57735; Willie Williams, 57738; Herbert Chan, 57742; Iasian Ali, 58419. Black and Yellow #2 and #3: C5169.

55. Cordelia McWee, 52181; Alice Halverson, 52298; Cassie Turner, 45174; Josephine Lee, 45204; Maria Gonzalez, 45300; Rose Massucco, 52440; Lida Harden, 52762. SQ Women: C5168, CSA. On the 1924 Immigration Act, see Mae M. Ngai, "The Architecture of Race in American Immigration Law: A Reexamination of the Immigration Act of 1924," *Journal of American History* (June 1999), http://www.historycooperative.org/journals/jah/86.1//ngai.html (accessed November 22, 2003).

56. On the diffracted nature of whiteness and "Nordic" and "Mediterranean" types, Kennan Malik, *The Meaning of Race: Race, History, and Culture in Western Society* (New York: New York University Press, 1996), 125; Foley, *White Scourge;* Matthew Frye Jacobson, *Whiteness of a Different Color: European Immigrants and the Alchemy of Race* (Cambridge, MA: Harvard University Press, 1998).

57. Alwyn Barr, *Black Texans: A History of African Americans in Texas, 1528–1995* (Norman: University of Oklahoma Press, 1996), 141. Consider, too, the lengthy prison investigations and testimony of 1910 and 1913. *Report of the Penitentiary Investigating Committee, 1910;* Robert Perkinson, *Texas Tough: The Rise of America's Prison Empire* (New York: Metropolitan Books, 2010), 160, 171–72.

58. Perkinson, *Texas Tough,* 177–204; Robert T. Chase, "Civil Rights on the Cell Block: Race, Reform, and Violence in Texas Prisons and the Nation" (Ph.D. dissertation, University of Maryland at College Park, 2009).

59. *Official Program Souvenir of the 8th Annual Prison Rodeo,* 5, TSLAC, Box 1998/038-404, Folder "Rodeo Program 1939." The classification program is also described in the 1938 Annual Report.

60. *Official Program Souvenir of the 8th Annual Prison Rodeo,* 5, TSLAC, Box 1998/038-404, Folder "Rodeo Program 1939."

61. Montejano, *Anglos and Mexicans,* 159–78, esp. 160–63.

62. Francisco Serrano, #63610, TSLAC Escape records, 1851–1943, Volume 1998/038-270; Conduct register 1998/038-213, Convict record 1998/038-164. See also J. W. Dunlop testimony, December 7, 1943, Volume IV: Witnesses Before the Governor's Committee on Investigation of Folsom Prison, 734–57. CSA, Earl Warren Papers—Governor's Committee on Penal Affairs—1943–44. F3640:959.

63. Cubans would become "white" in U.S. immigration rhetoric in the context of Cold War anticommunism. Cheris Brewer Current, "Normalizing Cuban Refugees: Representations of Whiteness and Anti-Communism in the USA during the Cold War," *Ethnicities* 8, no. 1 (2008): 42–67.

64. Francisco Serrano, #63610, TSLAC Escape records, 1851–1943, Volume 1998/038-270; Conduct Register 1998/038-213, Convict Record 1998/038-164.

65. San Quentin Board of Prison Directors Minutes, 1933–34, CSA, Corrections Records, F3717:1007. See entry for May 25, 1935, 328. No records remain for Fong Suey Lung, #52931, or Jo Lee, #53645.

66. Stanley, "Twenty Years at San Quentin," 365 S7.

67. San Quentin Board of Prison Directors Minutes, 1939–40, CSA, Corrections Records, F3717:1010. See entry for July 10, 1940.

68. Chan, *Asian Americans,* 33–35; Saxton, *The Indispensable Enemy.*

69. On Texas "houseboys," see Chase, "Civil Rights on the Cell Block," esp. 156–60.

70. H. Buderus von Carlshausen, written under the name "Roark Tamerlane," "America—Add Stars to Our Stripes!" 20–21. Unpublished manuscript, California State Library, California History Room, 365 C284.

71. William J. Ryan Testimony, December 6, 1943, evening session. Volume III: Witnesses Before the Governor's Committee on Investigation of Folsom Prison, 631–70. CSA, Earl Warren Papers—Governor's Committee on Penal Affairs—1943–44. F3640:958. Consider also Kendrick Ian Grandison's discussion of black balconies in segregated churches and theaters in "Negotiated Space: The Black College Campus as

a Cultural Record of Postbellum America," *American Quarterly* 51, no. 3 (Sept. 1999): 529–79, esp. 575, n. 18.

72. William J. Ryan Testimony, Volume III: Witnesses Before the Governor's Committee on Investigation of Folsom Prison, 631–70, esp. 650–54. CSA, Earl Warren Papers—Governor's Committee on Penal Affairs—1943–44. F3640:958.

73. Consider C. H. Daseking's December 6, 1943, testimony, Volume III: Witnesses Before the Governor's Committee on Investigation of Folsom Prison, 584–625, esp. 600–602. CSA, Earl Warren Papers—Governor's Committee on Penal Affairs—1943–44. F3640:958.

74. Letter to from Blinsky to Clinton Duffy, in Joseph Blinsky file, SQ#60270.

75. J. B. Smith, "No More Good Time in the World for Me," *Ever Since I Been a Man Full-Grown* (Takoma Records, 1965).

CHAPTER 2

1. Ethan Van Blue, "Hard Time in the New Deal: Racial Formations and the Cultures of Punishment in Texas and California in the 1930s" (Ph.D. dissertation, University of Texas at Austin, 2004), chapter 2; Rebecca M. McLennan, *The Crisis of Imprisonment: Protest, Politics, and the Making of the American Penal State, 1776–1940* (Cambridge: Cambridge University Press, 2008); Glen A. Gildemeister, *Prison Labor and Convict Competition with Free Workers in Industrializing America, 1840–1890* (New York: Garland, 1987).

2. Alex Lichtenstein, *Twice the Work of Free Labor: The Political Economy of Convict Labor in the New South* (London: Verso, 1996); Stanley B. Greenberg, *Race and State in Capitalist Development* (New Haven, CT: Yale University Press, 1980); McLennan, *Crisis of Imprisonment*, 87–136.

3. California Taxpayers' Association, Inc., "Report on Prison Labor in California," Los Angeles, CA, 1930, 18. Archived at the Bancroft Library, F862.8.C228.

4. California Taxpayers' Association, Inc., "Report on Prison Labor in California," 19.

5. Ibid., 28.

6. Editor, "A Word of Acknowledgement," *The Bulletin*, January 1925, 3, 19. CASL Government Publications Room.

7. Roy F. Basler et al., eds., *The Collected Works of Abraham Lincoln*, vol. 2 (New Brunswick, NJ: Rutgers University Press, 1953), 364. In Gunther Peck, *Reinventing Free Labor: Padrones and Immigrant Workers in the North American West, 1880–1930* (Cambridge: Cambridge University Press, 2000), 9.

8. For New York, McLennan, *Crisis of Imprisonment*, 270; on the progressive penological vision, see David J. Rothman, *Conscience and Convenience: The Asylum and Its Alternatives in Progressive America*, rev. ed. (New York: Aldine de Gruyter, 2002 [1980]); for critiques of this system in New York's Elmira, Alexander W. Pisciotta, *Benevolent Repression: Social Control and the American Prison Reformatory Movement* (New York: New York University Press, 1994).

9. Clinton T. Duffy testimony, Volume X: Witnesses Before the Governor's Committee on Investigation of San Quentin Prison, 1886. CSA, Earl Warren Papers—Governor's Committee on Penal Affairs—1943–44. F3640:965.

10. This was a common tactic for early-twentieth-century prison officials. See Rebecca McLennan, "Citizens and Criminals: The Rise of the American Carceral State, 1890–1940" (Ph.D. dissertation, Columbia University, 1999).

11. Prison Industries Reorganization Administration, *The Prison Labor Problem in California*, 1937, tables 3, 4, pp. 16–17.

12. Tom Gaghan, "At Work in the Jute Mill," *The Bulletin*, May–June 1935, 22–24, CASL Government Publications Room.

13. "The San Quentin Jute Mill," *The Bulletin*, January 1933, 21. CASL Government Publications Room. Zubler's concern for prisoners' well-being was admirable, but we might ask who mandated punishment for not making task if not he, the superintendent of the jute mill. Further, the premise of his article was a classic in penological thinking: we acknowledge that conditions were bad in the past; because we acknowledge it, conditions must be much better today.

14. California Taxpayers' Association, Inc., "Report on Prison Labor in California."

15. Lowrie, *My Life in Prison*, 138, cited in Barbara Jeanne Yaley, "Habits of Industry: Labor and Penal Policy in California, 1849–1940" (Ph.D. dissertation, University of California at Santa Cruz, 1980), 277.

16. H. Buderus von Carlshausen, aka "Roark Tamerlane," "America!—add stars to our stripes," typescript, CASL California History Room, 365 C284, 26.

17. Leo Leonidas Stanley, M.D., "Twenty Years at San Quentin," *The Centaur of Alpha Kappa Alpha* 39, no. 2 (January 1934): 390. CASL California History Room.

18. See Dwight Meyers testimony (no convict number listed), Governor's Hearings/ Transcript of Hearings vs. State Board of Prison Directors, vol. 3. CSA, Dept. of Penology Records, F3450: vols. 1–4, 6 (vol. 5 missing), 1,323–31.

19. Leo L. Stanley, "Tuberculosis in San Quentin," read before the California Medical Association, 67th Annual Session, Pasadena, May 9–12, 1938. Reprinted in *California and Western Medicine* 49, no. 6 (December 1938) and 50, no. 1 (January 1939), Bancroft Library, F863.66 S72.

20. San Quentin Minutes of the Board of Prison Terms and Paroles, November 25–26, 1935, meeting, 485. CSA, F3717:1073. Gray's San Quentin number was 56141.

21. San Quentin Minutes of the Board of Prison Terms and Paroles, December 1935 meeting, 496. CSA, F3717:1073. Contreras's San Quentin number was 56463.

22. Brown was listed as San Quentin #54389, but is archived in the Folsom Inmate Case Files as Folsom #21990.

23. Homer Breakfield testimony, Frank Kelley Inquisition, No. 2020, held San Quentin, August 7, 1934, 2. Marin County Coroners' Office.

24. "The San Quentin Jute Mill," *The Bulletin*, January 1933, 21. CASL Government Publications Room.

25. San Quentin Board of Prison Directors Minutes, 1938–39, 218, November 9, 1939. F3717:1009, CSA.

26. "Special Crime Study Commission" Report, 1939. Cited in Yaley, "Habits of Industry," 281. The tenor of this quotation is very different from the story written in *The Bulletin* about the jute mill, in which the inmate author praises the jute mill's capacity for making responsible men and citizens deserving of parole. While the members of the commission probably wanted to modernize the productive capacity of San Quentin Industries, while also benefiting inmates in classic liberal reformer style, Hal Eble, the imprisoned author, was put in the position of *defending* the jute mill as a positive good in his and other prisoners' lives. He was forced to do so to enable the claim that he was a good man and a deserving citizen. This was among the contradictions of prisoner-authored writings:

while they had perhaps the best reasons and, among prisoners, were most able to publicly criticize their conditions of labor, they also needed to defend the conditions of labor created by prison authorities in order to make a claim on productive citizenship and proper manhood.

27. Edwin Owen, "Craftsmanship in Desks and Men," *The Bulletin*, October 1932, 14.

28. See Gail Bederman, *Manliness and Civilization: A Cultural History of Gender and Race in the United States, 1880–1917* (Chicago: University of Chicago Press, 1995).

29. Robert Joyce Tasker, *Grimhaven* (New York: Knopf, 1928), 53–54. After he was transferred to a different job, he later referred to the moulding machine he walked by as "her." He also called the machine his "passing love," his "old flame," and referred to their new relationship as one between "fickle lovers." 83.

30. Hal Eble, "DUDS and SUDS: San Quentin Installs Modern Laundry," *The Bulletin*, November 1932, 8, 23. "Helen of Troy Had a Word for It" (no author), *The Bulletin*, November/December 1935, 21. Also, Regina Kunzel, *Criminal Intimacy: Prison and the Uneven History of Modern American Sexuality* (Chicago: University of Chicago Press, 2008), 85.

31. W. H. West, Volume III: Witnesses Before the Governor's Committee on Investigation of Folsom Prison, 681. CSA, Earl Warren Papers—Governor's Committee on Penal Affairs—1943–44. F3640:958

32. Donald Clemmer, *The Prison Community* (New York: Holt, Rinehart, and Winston, 1958 [1940]), 277.

33. Clemmer identified the "con ethic" as more of a guiding philosophy than a hard and fast set of rules. Prisoners commonly invoked the con ethic, but almost as common as these invocations were stories of prisoners turning each other in to officials, in order to even personal scores and to secure better assignments for themselves. Clemmer, *The Prison Community*.

34. Clemmer, *The Prison Community*, 163. Capitalization in original.

35. John C. Hurst, San Quentin #63585, Folsom Inmate Case files.

36. Edward D. Clark, Volume II: Witnesses Before the Governor's Committee on Investigation of Folsom Prison, 292–303. CSA, Earl Warren Papers—Governor's Committee on Penal Affairs—1943–44. F3640:957.

37. Clemmer, *The Prison Community*, 77–78. The knitting mill, however, was intended for younger, white inmates, and maintained a few Negro porters. Thus black prisoners in more privileged locations were still frequently racially subordinated.

38. Clemmer, *The Prison Community*, 77.

39. James H. Freeman, Folsom 23820, Folsom Inmate Case Files, CSA.

40. Clifton Longan, Folsom 21270, Folsom Inmate Case Files, CSA.

41. W. Mills, Folsom #21935, November 30, 1943, letter to Julian Alco, Earl Warren Papers—Administrative Files—Corrections—Governor's Prison Committee—Correspondence (Folder 5), 1943–44.

42. Theodore Hamm, *Rebel and a Cause: Caryl Chessman and the Politics of the Death Penalty in Postwar California, 1948–1974* (Berkeley: University of California Press, 2001), 95–106.

43. Wesley Robert Wells, *My Name Is Wesley Robert Wells*, foreword by Buddy Green (San Francisco: State Defense Committee for Wesley Robert Wells, 1951), 6.

44. Ibid.

45. Ibid., 13.

46. On World War II hate strikes and racially segmented labor markets, George Lipsitz, *Rainbow at Midnight: Labor and Culture in the 1940s* (Urbana: University of Illinois Press, 1994); Judy Yung, *Unbound Feet: A Social History of Chinese Women in San Francisco* (Berkeley: University of California Press, 1995); Marilynn S. Johnson, *The Second Gold Rush: Oakland and the East Bay in World War II* (Berkeley: University of California Press, 1993); Kevin Starr, *Embattled Dreams: California in War and Peace, 1940–1950* (New York: Oxford University Press, 2002). Also, Chester Himes, *If He Hollers Let Him Go* (New York: Thunder's Mouth Press, 2002).

47. Wells, *My Name Is Wesley Robert Wells*, 14.

48. Ibid., 6. A prisoner named Wells was apparently going to be transferred to San Quentin during the 1943 Folsom investigation. But the prison chaplain, Reverend McKerrigher, and psychiatrist, Dr. Schmidt, testified that he and others transferred would "raise hell" at San Quentin, because they were so mean. Wells, whom they constantly referred to as a "colored fellow," was refusing to work. A prisoner named Parker also refused to do the work that he was assigned to, and both had sworn to be uncooperative. One of the investigators asked if they could put the Folsom transfers "up on the shelf." He said they could, but that they could still raise hell there, that they would start booing in the mess hall, and then the rest of the prisoners would join in. "[I]f three or four of those men get in the mess hall and start booing there will be trouble." See Dr. David G. Schmidt testimony, Psychiatrist at San Quentin, Volume VI: Witnesses Before the Governor's Committee on Investigation of San Quentin Prison, 1,175–99, esp. 1,191. CSA, Earl Warren Papers—Governor's Committee on Penal Affairs—1943–44. F3640:961.

49. Folsom Inmate Case Files, R. W. White, #23921. CSA, F3745:575.

50. Albert Ellsworth Jackson Jr., SQ #50939, Folsom #21611, Folsom Inmate Case Files, CSA.

51. Ibid.

52. Chernin, "Convict Road Work in California" (Ph.D. dissertation, University of California at Los Angeles, 1938), 84.

53. Prison Industries Reorganization Administration, *The Prison Labor Problem in California*, 1937, iii.

54. Alex Lichtenstein, "The Private and the Public in Penal History: A Commentary on Zimring and Tonry," in David Garland, ed., *Mass Imprisonment: Social Causes and Consequences* (London: Sage, 2001), 171–78.

55. On Colorado road camps, see Elinor Myers McGinn, *At Hard Labor: Inmate Labor at the Colorado State Penitentiary, 1871–1940* (New York: Peter Lang, 1993); Chernin, "Convict Road Work in California," 8–11.

56. Chernin, "Convict Road Work in California," 15–19.

57. "Sixth Biennial Report of the Division of Highways to the Director of Public Works," in *Appendix to Journals of Senate and Assembly*, 48th Session, 1929, vol. 4, p. 51. CASL Government Publications Room.

58. Chernin, "Convict Road Work in California," 26, 32, 40–41.

59. Chernin, "Convict Road Work in California," 40; Lloyd L. Voigt, *History of California State Correctional Administration from 1930 to 1948* (San Francisco, 1949), 43–48.

60. David Montejano, *Anglos and Mexicans in the Making of Texas, 1836–1986* (Austin: University of Texas Press, 1987); Carey McWilliams, *Factories in the Field: The Story of*

Migratory Farm Labor in California (Boston: Little, Brown, 1939); Kitty Calavita, *Inside the State: The Bracero Program, Immigration, and the I.N.S.* (New York: Routledge, 1992); Devra Weber, *Dark Sweat, White Gold: California Farm Workers, Cotton, and the New Deal* (Berkeley: University of California Press, 1994).

61. Chernin, "Convict Road Work in California," 48.

62. On the "necessity" of unfree labor in a location of labor scarcity, see Stanley B. Greenberg, *Race and State in Capitalist Development: Comparative Perspectives* (New Haven, CT: Yale University Press, 1980); Alex Lichtenstein, *Twice the Work of Free Labor: The Political Economy of Convict Labor in the New South* (New York: Verso, 1996); Peck, *Reinventing Free Labor*; Howard Lamar and Leonard Thompson, eds., *The Frontier in History: North America and Southern Africa Compared* (New Haven, CT: Yale University Press, 1981), introduction; also Chernin, "Convict Road Work in California," 8.

63. Chernin, "Convict Road Work in California," 52.

64. California Highway Commission biennial report, 1926, 144. Cited by Yaley, "Habits of Industry," 293–95.

65. Mr. Milliken, California Highway Commission, fifth biennial report, 1926, appendix J, 144, quoted in Chernin, "Convict Road Work in California," 66–67.

66. California Division of Highways, second biennial report, 1920, 111–13, quoted in Chernin, "Convict Road Work in California," 100–101; Volker Janssen, "When the 'Jungle' Met the Forest: Public Work, Civil Defense, and Prison Camps in Postwar California," *Journal of American History* 96, no. 3 (2009): 702–26, esp. 706.

67. Biennial report of the State Board of Prison Directors of the State of California, 1933–34, 8. CASL Government Publications Room.

68. Chernin, "Convict Road Work in California," 106.

69. Chernin, "Convict Road Work in California," 108.

70. "How to Qualify for Road Camps," *The Bulletin*, January 1925, 11. CASL Government Publications Room.

71. The quotation is Chernin, "Convict Road Work in California," 114.

72. Chernin, "Convict Road Work in California," table II, p. 122.

73. Chernin, "Convict Road Work in California," 83.

74. Chernin, "Convict Road Work in California," 90–96.

75. Chernin, "Convict Road Work in California," 101.

76. Chernin, "Convict Road Work in California," 84.

77. Prison Industries Reorganization Administration, *The Prison Labor Problem in California*, 1937, 29.

78. San Quentin Minutes of the Board of Prison Terms and Paroles, March 6–8, 1940, 339–40. CSA, F3717:1077. "Sixth Biennial Report of the Division of Highways to the Director of Public Works," in *Appendix to Journals of Senate and Assembly*, 48th Session, 1929, vol. 4, p. 53. CASL Government Publications Room.

79. "Sixth Biennial Report of the Division of Highways to the Director of Public Works," in *Appendix to Journals of Senate and Assembly*, 48th Session, 1929, vol. 4, p. 55. CASL Government Publications Room.

80. Mr. Milliken, Superintendent of Prison Camps, in California Highway Commission, fifth biennial report, 1926, appendix J, 144, quoted in Chernin, "Convict Road Work in California," 66–67.

81. "Seventh Biennial Report of the Division of Highways to the Director of Public Works," in *Appendix to Journals of Senate and Assembly*, 49th Session, 1931, vol. 3, p. 68. CASL Government Publications Room.

82. San Quentin Minutes of the Board of Prison Terms and Paroles, November 6, 1935, BPTP minutes, 463. CSA, F3717:1073. Harrison's SQ number was 48563, and Salgot's was 50901.

83. "Sixth Biennial Report of the Division of Highways to the Director of Public Works," in *Appendix to Journals of Senate and Assembly*, 48th Session, 1929, vol. 4, p. 53. CASL Government Publications Room.

84. Chernin, "Convict Road Work in California," 143.

85. Escapes from Chino Forest and Work Camps, CSA, Earl Warren Papers—Administrative Files—Corrections—Governor's Prison Committee—California Institution for Men at Chino—1941–44, F3640:989. Prisoners interviewed here were from Chino, from forest camps, and from the Mira Loma work camp. Also, Janssen, "When the 'Jungle' Met the City," esp. 713, 722.

86. November 9, 1934, Minutes, San Quentin Minutes of the Board of Prison Terms and Paroles, 34–35, CSA, F3717:1073.

87. Chernin, "Convict Road Work in California," 144.

88. R. D. Burdick, "Oroville to Keddie," *The Bulletin*, June 1933, 5. CASL Government Publications Room.

CHAPTER 3

1. "Adress [sic] of Lee Simmons, General Manager of the Texas Prison System, to Inmates of Huntsville Prison on Tuesday, April 15, 1930, at 12:30 P.M." TSLAC, Governor Moody Records, Box 1984/024-45.

2. Ibid.

3. For an excellent treatment of the evolution of the Texas prison business model in the postwar period, Robert T. Chase, "Civil Rights on the Cell Block: Race, Reform, and Violence in Texas Prisons and the Nation, 1945–1990" (Ph.D. dissertation, University of Maryland at College Park, 2009), chapters 3 and 4. On the theory and practice of control penology as practiced in Illinois' Stateville Penitentiary, see James B. Jacobs, *Stateville: The Penitentiary in Mass Society* (Chicago: University of Chicago Press, 1977); and for the personal relationships between Stateville's Warden Regan and Texas's Beto in the postwar period, Chase, "Civil Rights on the Cellblock," chapter 3.

4. 1930 Annual Report, 2-B, 3-B.

5. 1933 Annual Report, 14.

6. 1939 Annual Report, 19.

7. 1940 Annual Report, 22.

8. 1939 Annual Report, 15–16.

9. Prison Industries Reorganization Administration, *The Prison Labor Problem in Texas: A Survey by the Prison Industries Reorganization Administration*, 32–33. TSLAC, aT365 p938 OS.

10. Don Hudson, "The Texas Department of Criminal Justice's Central Unit Main Building and Its Historical Significance: A Brief Study; The Evolution of Texas Penology" (Texas Historical Commission, Texas Department of Criminal Justice, 2001), 6–7.

11. Hudson, "The Texas Department of Criminal Justice's Central Unit Main Building," 13.

12. Annual report of the Texas Prison Board, 1938, archived at the Texas State Library, 19.

13. Convict Record and Conduct Register on Joel L. Denley, #84690. TSLAC, Convict Record Book Domain 83261-85270, archived as 1998/038-23, and Conduct Register domain 79301-84740, archived as 1998/038-167.

14. On the 1880s origins of racial differentiation in Texas prisons and labor, Robert Reps Perkinson, "The Birth of the Texas Prison Empire, 1865–1915" (Ph.D. dissertation, Yale University, 2001); Ethan Blue, "A Parody on the Law: Organized Labor, the Convict Lease, and Immigration in the Making of the Texas State Capitol," *Journal of Social History* 43, no. 4 (2010); 1021–44.

15. Farm Manager's Report, TSLAC, Box 1984/024-45. The word "negroes" is in lower case in the original.

16. PIRA, *The Prison Labor Problem in Texas*, 9.

17. 1935, 1936 annual reports.

18. 1934 Annual Report, 42-A.

19. 1934 Annual Report, 32—this number also included "other leather goods."

20. 1934 Annual Report, 13–14.

21. 1929 Annual Report, B-2, B-3.

22. Ohio Inspection Bureau, "Report on the Ohio State Penitentiary Fire, Columbus, Ohio, April 21, 1930," available online at http://www.nfpa.org/assets/files//PDF/Research/Ohio_State_Penitentiary.pdf (accessed July 31, 2010). For a description of the Ohio fire, Chester Himes, *Yesterday Will Make You Cry* (New York: Norton, 1998 [1953]), 94–108. J. W. Dewesse, State Fire Marshal Report, May 10, 1930. Moody Records, Box 1984/24-45, TSLAC.

23. PIRA, *The Prison Labor Problem in Texas*, 9.

24. PIRA, *The Prison Labor Problem in Texas*, 10–11.

25. *Thirty Minutes behind the Walls*, Program 93, December 27, 1939.

26. Martha Ann Turner, "Within the Walls: Texas Prison Folklore," in Francis Edward Abernethy, ed., *T for Texas: A State Full of Folklore* (Dallas: E-Heart Press, 1982), 196–209, esp. 202.

27. *Thirty Minutes*, Program 23, August 24, 1938. Foucauldians will be interested to know that McAdams himself worked at the inner-sole table. See also 1938 Annual Report, 21, 59–60; PIRA, *The Prison Labor Problem in Texas*, 10–11.

28. Hudson, "Central Unit Main Building and Its Historical Significance," 7.

29. *Thirty Minutes*, Program 17, July 13, 1938.

30. *Official Souvenir Program of the 8th Annual Prison Rodeo, 1938*, 55. TSLAC, Box 1998/038-404, Folder "Rodeo Program 1939." Note that this folder is mislabeled.

31. PIRA, *The Prison Labor Problem in Texas*, 11.

32. *Thirty Minutes*, Program 17, July 13, 1938.

33. Quoted by Charlotte A. Teagle, *History of the Welfare Activities of the Texas Prison Board, 1927–1940*, 110. TSLAC, Texas Department of Corrections Records, Box 1998/038-127.

34. Teagle, *History of the Welfare Activities of the Texas Prison Board*, 124.

35. Chase, "Civil Rights on the Cell Block," 135.

36. Chase, "Civil Rights on the Cell Block," esp. 134–35.

37. J. B. Smith, "No More Good Time in the World for Me," *Ever Since I Been a Man Full-Grown* (Takoma Records, 1965).

38. Paul M. Lucko, "The Governor and the Bat: Prison Reform during the Oscar B. Colquitt Administration, 1911–1915," *Southwestern Historical Quarterly* 106, no. 3 (January 2003): 396–417, esp. 405.

39. 1934 Annual Report, 65; Map of Ramsey State Farm, 1934, Stevenson box 4-14/148, Folder: Texas Prison System, TSLAC.

40. 1934 Annual Report, 42, 44, 45.

41. Farm Manager's Report, TSLAC, Box 1984/024-45.

42. Chase, "Civil Rights on the Cell Block," esp. 129. On Dog Sergeants and high riders, J. B. Smith, "The Danger Line," *Ever Since I Have Been A Man Full-Grown* (Takoma Records, 1965).

43. 1938 Annual Report, 17.

44. Chase, "Civil Rights on the Cell Block," 128–29.

45. R. J. Flanagan, General Manager, Correspondence to H. W. Sayle, October 15, 1927, Recapitulation of Flour and Meal issued, October 15, 1927, Box 1984/024-45, TSLAC; also, Chase, "Civil Rights on the Cell Block," esp. 156–60.

46. Lee Simmons, *Assignment Huntsville: Memoirs of a Texas Prison Official* (Austin: University of Texas Press, 1957), 83–84.

47. 1937 Annual Report, 10.

48. January 2, 1939, meeting, Documents of the Texas Prison Board, Minutes and Meeting Files, June 1927–December 1941, Box 1998/038-8, Folder July 1938–May 1939, TSLAC.

49. Bruce Jackson, *Wake Up Dead Man: Afro-American Worksongs from Texas Prisons* (Cambridge, MA: Harvard University Press, 1972), 1.

50. The first quotation is from Jerry Quate, oral history conducted by Robert T. Chase, March 12, 2007, housed at the Institute for Oral History, Baylor University. Both are in Chase, "Civil Rights on the Cell Block,"135–37.

51. Quoted in Jackson, *Wake Up Dead Man*, 35.

52. Turner, "Within the Walls," 201.

53. PIRA, *The Prison Labor Problem in Texas*, 11–12. Donald Clemmer confirmed a similar trend in his more aesthetically modern prison. Inmates working in the quarry were able to loaf approximately 5 to 10 percent of the time, while workers in the "important shops" were idle between 50 and 60 percent of the time. *The Prison Community* (New York: Holt, Rinehart, and Winston, 1958 [1940]), 275. Thus prisoners in the socially degraded jobs worked longer and harder hours than their peers in more privileged positions.

54. Quoted in C.V. Compton, *Flood Lights behind the Gray Walls: An Expose of Activities* (Dallas: C.V. Compton, 1942), 33.

55. Michael Eubanks oral history, conducted by Robert T. Chase, quoted in Chase, "Civil Rights on the Cell Block," 140.

56. Whipping Orders Executed in April 1930, TSLAC, Box 1984/024-45. On inter-prisoner violence, see chapter 4. For other whipping orders, see Moody Papers, TSLAC, Oversize Box 124.

57. C. C. Johns, *Thirty Minutes*, Program 19, July 27, 1938.

58. A. L. McDonald, *Thirty Minutes*, Program 54, March 24, 1939.

59. See, for example, Lawrence W. Levine, *Black Culture and Black Consciousness: Afro-American Folk Thought from Slavery to Freedom* (New York: Oxford University Press, 1978); Peter H. Wood, *Black Majority: Negroes in Colonial South Carolina from 1670 through the Stono Rebellion* (New York: Norton, 1974); Frederick Douglass, *Narrative of the Life of Frederick Douglass, An American Slave, Written by Himself* (New York: Signet Books, 1968), 31–32. Also, Alan Lomax Collection Compact Disc *Don'tcha Hear Poor Mother Calling: Historical Recordings from Parchman Farm, 1947–48; Prison Songs, Volume Two* (Rounder Records, 1997).

60. Albert Race Sample, *Racehoss: Big Emma's Boy* (Austin, TX: Eakin Press, 1984), 172–73.

61. Quoted in David M. Oshinsky, *"Worse Than Slavery": Parchman Farm and the Ordeal of Jim Crow Justice* (New York: Free Press, 1996), 147.

62. Jackson, *Wake Up Dead Man*, 111–18; Oshinsky, *"Worse Than Slavery,"* 146.

63. Jackson, *Wake Up Dead Man*, 26.

64. Quoted in Oshinsky, *"Worse Than Slavery,"* 145.

65. "Hammer Ring," on *Prison Worksongs* (Arhoolie Records, 1959), recorded at Angola Penitentiary.

66. Johnny Butler and Gang, "Early in the Mornin,'" on *Prison Worksongs*.

67. See versions A–G in Jackson, *Wake Up Dead Man*, 194–200.

68. Jackson, *Wake Up Dead Man*, 18.

69. Jackson, *Wake Up Dead Man*, 151.

70. Oshinsky, *"Worse Than Slavery,"* 217–22; Cecil Brown, *Stagolee Shot Billy* (Cambridge, MA: Harvard University Press, 2003).

71. Jackson, *Wake Up Dead Man*, 184–92.

72. Bama, interview with Alan Lomax, "What Makes a Work Song Leader," *Prison Songs: Historical Recordings from Parchman Farm, 1947–1948; Volume One, Murderous Home*, from the Alan Lomax Collection (Rounder Records, 1997), track 12.

73. Bob Wills's "Twenty-One Years" was among the most frequently recorded songs of the 1930s and was commonly on jukeboxes and the radio. This song lamented the singer's distance from home and his loneliness in prison, and, like many black prisoners' work songs, rhetorically inverts the positions of the singer and the governor, who could pardon him. See Jean A. Boyd, *"We're the Light Crust Doughboys from Burrus Mill": An Oral History* (Austin: University of Texas Press, 2003), 32. For lyrics, see Dorothy Horstman, *Sing Your Heart Out, Country Boy* (New York: 1976), 303, cited online at http://www.bobdylanroots.com/21.html. Also, Américo Paredes, *With His Pistol in His Hand* (Austin: University of Texas Press, 1958).

74. Merle Haggard, "Huntsville," *Prison* (EMI, 2001).

75. Turner, "Within the Walls: Texas Prison Folklore," esp. 203.

76. Governor Allred Proclamation 17635, 23 July, 1937. TSLAC, Allred Box 1985/024-96, Folder: Texas Prison System, General Correspondence and Proclamations July 1937.

77. Haggard, "I'm a Lonesome Fugitive," *Prison*.

78. Prisoners who severed their Achilles tendons were called "heel stringers" in a 2001 joint Texas Historic Commission/ Department of Criminal Justice publication. Cited in Hudson, "Central Unit Main Building and Its Historical Significance," 15.

79. *Thirty Minutes*, Program 13, June 15, 1938.

80. In similar fashion, Walter Johnson describes how slaves could control some tiny degree of their own destinies by threatening suicide if they were sold or moved away from

families. Many prisoners also transformed their own bodies by severing fingers in order to be less easily sold. Johnson, *Soul by Soul: Life inside the Antebellum Slave Market* (Cambridge, MA: Harvard University Press, 1999), 33–34.

81. James C. Scott, *Domination and the Arts of Resistance: Hidden Transcripts* (New Haven, CT: Yale University Press, 1990); Walter Johnson, "On Agency," *Journal of Social History* 37, no. 1 (Fall 2003): 113–24.

82. R. Craig Copeland, "The Evolution of the Texas Department of Corrections" (M.A. thesis, Sam Houston State University, 1980), 56.

83. Letter to Gov. Coke Stevenson from Anthony Sayers, #94054, Retrieve State Farm, TSLAC, Stevenson Box 414/136, Folder "Prison System 1943" 12/04/1943.

84. Oshinsky describes white prisoners' rebelliousness at forced agricultural labor and at the performances of subservience at Parchman Farm, suggesting that white prisoners protested more frequently and more violently than black prisoners. I interpret the reason for this different rebelliousness as white male prisoners' prideful rejection of forcible feminization and racialization inherent to rituals of subservience. A group of religious advocates for prisoners opined that when white men were forced to "doff their caps" to visitors, and forced to be "humble and servile at all times," they would be equally forced to rebel or to kill themselves. No matter what a white prisoner's status might have been before incarceration, "he comes out just a cotton chopper or a cotton picker"—certainly a racialized identification. And whites in the 1930s increasingly rejected association with labor in cotton fields as part of their racial and working identities. See Oshinsky, "*Worse Than Slavery*," 165. Jim Crow life forced black southerners to "perform" subservience as a survival strategy, even if it was just a matter of "wearing a mask," as poet Paul Laurence Dunbar put it. Black oppositional practices took other forms.

CHAPTER 4

1. Albert Race Sample, *Racehoss: Big Emma's Boy* (New York: Ballantine Books, 1984), 163.

2. Ibid., 166–67.

3. Ibid., 170.

4. In this chapter I bring Pierre Bourdieu's notion of symbolic capital into a modified, dynamic, structural-functionalist model of incarceration, which, while somewhat out of favor today, still offers considerable insight. Unlike midcentury structural-functionalists, I concentrate on racial-gender formations and acknowledge how "structures" change. See Bourdieu, *Outline of a Theory of Practice*, trans. Richard Nice (New York: Cambridge University Press, 1977), esp. 171–97. Also, Donald Clemmer, *The Prison Community* (New York: Holt, Rinehart and Winston, 1958 [1940]); Gresham M. Sykes, *The Society of Captives: A Study of a Maximum Security Prison* (Princeton, NJ: Princeton University Press, 1972 [1958]); Erving Goffman, *Asylums: Essays on the Social Situation of Mental Patients and Other Inmates* (New York: Penguin, 1961). For a critique of the convict code literature, Regina Kunzel, *Criminal Intimacy: Prison and the Uneven History of Modern American Sexuality* (Chicago: University of Chicago Press, 2008), 168, drawing on Lee Carroll, "Race, Ethnicity, and the Social Order of the Prison," in Robert Johnson and Hans Toch, eds., *The Pains of Imprisonment* (Beverly Hills, CA: Sage Publications, 1982).

5. David Graeber, *Toward an Anthropological Theory of Value: The False Coin of Our Own Dreams* (New York: Palgrave, 2001), 86.

6. Kunzel, *Criminal Intimacy*.

7. On masculinities as relational, contested, and historically and regionally contextual, R. W. Connell, *Masculinities* (Berkeley: University of California Press, 1995); R. W. Connell and James W. Messerschmidt, "Hegemonic Masculinity: Rethinking the Concept," *Gender and Society* 15, no. 6 (2005): 829–59; Judith Halberstam, *Female Masculinity* (Durham, NC: Duke University Press, 1998); and the pieces in Don Sabo, Terry A. Krupers, and Willie London, eds., *Prison Masculinities* (Philadelphia: Temple University Press, 2001).

8. R. Craig Copeland, "The Evolution of the Texas Department of Corrections" (M.A. thesis, Sam Houston State University, 1980), 43.

9. Steve J. Martin and Sheldon Ekland-Olson, *Texas Prisons: The Walls Came Tumbling Down* (Austin: Texas Monthly Press, 1987), 17.

10. PIRA, *The Prison Labor Problem in Texas: A Survey by the Prison Industries Reorganization Administration*, 4. TSLAC, aT365 p938 OS.

11. See chapter 7.

12. Quoted in Bruce Jackson, *Wake Up Dead Man: Afro-American Worksongs from Texas Prisons* (Cambridge, MA: Harvard University Press, 1972), 9.

13. State Legislature, *Special Committee on Penitentiary, Report* (Austin, 1871), TSLA, cited in Robert T. Chase, "Civil Rights on the Cell Block: Race, Reform, and Violence in Texas Prisons and the Nation, 1945–1990" (Ph.D. dissertation, University of Maryland at College Park, 2009), 49.

14. David M. Oshinsky, *"Worse Than Slavery": Parchman Farm and the Ordeal of Jim Crow Justice* (New York: Free Press, 1996), 140–50.

15. In January 1943 five inmates overpowered and killed the BT on Harlem Farm. January 25, 1943, letter from Mr. and Mrs. A. C. Smith to Governor Coke Stevenson. Stevenson Box 4-14/136, Folder Texas Prison System 1943, TSLAC.

16. Chase, "Civil Rights on the Cellblock," 204; Ben M. Crouch and James W. Marquart, *An Appeal to Justice: Litigated Reform of Texas Prisons* (Austin: University of Texas Press, 1989), 89.

17. Chase, "Civil Rights on the Cellblock," 220. In the postwar period, according to Chase's fine study, BTs would absorb the control of commodity markets that California con bosses held in the 1930s, rendering BTs' control of other prisoners even more expansive.

18. C. V. Compton, *Flood Lights behind the Gray Walls: An Exposé of Activities* (Dallas: C.V. Compton, 1942), 26.

19. Sample, *Racehoss*, 164–65.

20. Quoted in Compton, *Flood Lights*, 29.

21. Dorothy Thompson #86388, described in "The Curious Sentence of Convict #86388," Texas Prison Museum, http://www.txprisonmuseum.org/article.html (accessed July 22, 2010).

22. Susan Brownmiller, *Against Our Will: Men, Women, and Rape* (New York: Simon & Schuster, 1975). For a recent discussion of Brownmiller, Kunzel, *Criminal Intimacy*, esp. 171–74.

23. Wilbert Rideau and Billy Sinclair, "Prison: The Sexual Jungle," in *Male Rape*, ed. Anthony Scacco (New York: AMS Press, 1982), 4. Quoted in Kunzel, *Criminal Intimacy*, 173.

24. Sample, *Racehoss*, 162, 213–14. On southern male homosexuality more broadly, John Howard, *Men Like That: A Southern Queer History* (Chicago: University of Chicago Press, 2001).

25. Copeland cites "Stone, 16, 1974," but the reference is not in his bibliography. It was probably from an interview that Copeland conducted. Copeland, "The Evolution of the Texas Department of Corrections," 63.

26. Kunzel, *Criminal Intimacy*, 153.

27. Sample, *Racehoss*, 157.

28. March 1 and April 12, 1937, Texas Prison Board Meeting Minutes, TSLAC, Box 1998/038-8, Folder: Minutes September 1936–July 1937. Documents of the Texas Prison Board, Minutes and Meeting Files, June 1927–December 1941.

29. March 7, 1938, meeting, Texas Prison Board Meeting Minutes, TSLAC, Box 1998/038-8, Folder: Minutes January–May 1938: Documents of the Texas Prison Board, Minutes and Meeting Files, June 1927–December 1941.

30. "Dallas Civic Figure C.V. Compton Dies," Dallas *Times Herald*, June 13, 1960, n.p. Biographical Vertical Files, Center for American History, Austin. See also Compton's January 28, 1943, communication and report to Governor Coke Stevenson. Coke Stevenson Papers, Folder: Prison System 1943, Box 4-14/136, TSLAC.

31. Compton, *Flood Lights*, 8, 10–11.

32. Annual report, 1941, 7.

33. *Dallas Morning News*, February 14, 1941, quoted in Compton, *Flood Lights*, 12–13.

34. Annual report, 1941, 7.

35. Compton, *Flood Lights*, 19–20, 34.

36. Compton, *Flood Lights*, 16–17. Chase, "Civil Rights on the Cell Block," 76.

37. See Copeland, "The Evolution of the Texas Department of Corrections," 57. One sheriff explained the technique he was taught: the officer handcuffed a suspect and stood on the handcuff chain, "pinning the man's hands to the floor and cutting off blood flow to his hands until they began to turn blue. The officer then reached down and straightened the man's fingers. This was intensely painful, and any marks on the prisoner's wrists could be dismissed as having been caused by his struggles to escape the handcuffs." Thad Sutton, *The Texas Sheriff: Lord of the County Line* (Norman: University of Oklahoma Press, 2000), 111.

38. April 2, 1940, meeting; November 24, 1940, Special Meeting. Texas Prison Board Meeting Minutes, TSLAC, Box 1998/038-8, Folder: Minutes January–September 1940. Documents of the Texas Prison Board, Minutes and Meeting Files, June 1927–December 1941. On Mississippi's trustee-shooters, Oshinsky, "*Worse Than Slavery*," esp. 140–50.

39. Cynthia Linzy oral history with Carl Luther McAdams, October 26, 1987, Texas Prison History Museum, quoted in Chase, "Civil Rights on the Cell Block," 177.

40. Austin MacCormick, Report on Texas Prisons, 1947, Jester Papers, TSLAC, Box 4-14/113, quoted in Chase, "Civil Rights on the Cell Block," 71.

41. MacCormick, Report, quoted in Chase, "Civil Rights on the Cell Block," 68.

42. See Chase, "Civil Rights on the Cellblock."

43. Lee Watts Inquest No. 2079, July 22, 1940, MCCO.

44. Edward L. Ayers, *Vengeance and Justice: Crime and Punishment in the Nineteenth-Century American South* (New York: Oxford University Press, 1984), esp. 13–18, 247–76.

45. Raymond Boyd Inquest No. 1985, January 16, 1933, MCCO. The first quotation is from Brakefield, the second from assistant resident physician Herbert M. Every.

46. Wesley Robert Wells, *My Name Is Wesley Robert Wells*, foreword by Buddy Green (San Francisco: State Defense Committee for Wesley Robert Wells, 1951), 7.

47. "San Quentin Felon Stabbing Victim: Georgian Shoved, Uses Knife on Fellow Prisoner," San Francisco *Examiner*, January 12, 1938. Clippings File, Box: San Quentin, Folder: San Quentin Prison—History, 1930s. Anne T. Kent California Room, Marin County Free Public Library.

48. Shane White, "The Clearing House Blues, or 'Numbers' in Harlem," presented at the University of Western Australia, August 25, 2010.

49. William J. Ryan Testimony, Volume III: Witnesses Before the Governor's Committee on Investigation of Folsom Prison, 645. CSA, Earl Warren Papers—Governor's Committee on Penal Affairs—1943–44. F3640:958. On items prisoners gambled with, also see Clemmer, *The Prison Community*, 240.

50. Clemmer, *The Prison Community*, 239.

51. Clemmer, *The Prison Community*, 240.

52. Robert Joyce Tasker, *Grimhaven* (New York: Knopf, 1928), 59. The tobacco-sugar exchange rate is on page 57.

53. H. Buderus von Carlshausen, aka "Roark Tamerlane," "America!—add stars to our stripes," 18. Manuscript archived at CASL California History Room, 365 C284.

54. Quoted by Investigator Alco, Volume III: Witnesses Before the Governor's Committee on Investigation of Folsom Prison, 633. CSA, Earl Warren Papers—Governor's Committee on Penal Affairs—1943–44. F3640:958.

55. Capt. Joseph H. Fletcher, Volume VI: Witnesses Before the Governor's Committee on Investigation of San Quentin Prison, 1356–57. CSA, Earl Warren Papers—Governor's Committee on Penal Affairs—1943–44. F3640:961.

56. Ibid., 1,358.

57. C. H. Daseking testimony, Volume III: Witnesses Before the Governor's Committee on Investigation of Folsom Prison, CSA, Earl Warren Papers—Governor's Committee on Penal Affairs—1943–44. F3640:958. The reference to "jute balls" is on 598, and the reference to river water instead of milk is from 607. The American River ran next to the Folsom prison.

58. Hal Eble, "Ye Olde San Quentin Printe Shoppe," *The Bulletin*, January 10, 1933, 19–20. CASL Government Publications Room.

59. W. H. West, Volume III: Witnesses Before the Governor's Committee on Investigation of Folsom Prison, 670–85, esp. 679. CSA, Earl Warren Papers—Governor's Committee on Penal Affairs—1943–44. F3640:958.

60. C. H. Daseking, Volume III: Witnesses Before the Governor's Committee on Investigation of Folsom Prison, 586. CSA, Earl Warren Papers—Governor's Committee on Penal Affairs—1943–44. F3640:958.

61. Goffman, *Asylums*, 180.

62. Sykes, *Society of Captives*, esp. 40–62; David B. Kalinich, *The Inmate Economy* (Lexintgon, MA: Heath, 1980), 15–21, 75–76.

63. W. H. West, Volume III: Witnesses Before the Governor's Committee on Investigation of Folsom Prison, 670–85, esp. 684. CSA, Earl Warren Papers—Governor's Committee on Penal Affairs—1943–44. F3640:958.

64. "Convict Escapes from Farm, Is Captured in San Francisco," Sacramento *Bee* 27, 1943, p. 1 col. 7, p. 20 col. 4.

65. Albert H. Mundt, Volume V: Witnesses Before the Governor's Committee on Investigation of Folsom Prison, 935–65. CSA, Earl Warren Papers—Governor's Committee on Penal Affairs—1943–44. F3640:960. Both quotations are from 946. On Lloyd Sampsell as the education department con boss, see Osborne testimony, 3, CSA Earl Warren Papers—Administrative Files—Corrections—Governor's Prison Committee—Confidential Witness (Folder 11), 1942–44. F3640:982.

66. Mundt testimony, Volume V: Witnesses Before the Governor's Committee on Investigation of Folsom Prison, 935–65, esp. 947. CSA, Earl Warren Papers—Governor's Committee on Penal Affairs—1943–44. F3640:960.

67. Osborne testimony, 3.

68. Los Angeles *Times*, March 7, 1923. In Folsom Inmate Case Files, Burroughs McGraw, 22230. F3745:519.

69. October 6, 1941, letter from W. B. Albertson, Superintendent of Camp 33F, Keene, CA, to Albert H. Mundt, Assistant Secretary, Board of Prison Terms and Paroles. Archived in Folsom Inmate Case Files, Burroughs McGraw, 22230. F3745:519.

70. W. H. Baxter letter to Clinton T. Duffy, October 27, 1942. Archived in Folsom Inmate Case Files, Burroughs McGraw, 22230. F3745, 519.

71. Lyle Egan, Volume IV: Witnesses Before the Governor's Committee on Investigation of Folsom Prison, 811. CSA, Earl Warren Papers—Governor's Committee on Penal Affairs—1943–44. F3640:959.

72. Jack B. Olympius, Volume III: Witnesses Before the Governor's Committee on Investigation of Folsom Prison, CSA, Earl Warren Papers—Governor's Committee on Penal Affairs—1943–44. F3640:958. On meals and playing cards, see 697. On the hat as a gift to McGraw, Fred G. Schoon, Volume V: Witnesses Before the Governor's Committee on Investigation of Folsom Prison, 921–29. CSA, Earl Warren Papers—Governor's Committee on Penal Affairs—1943–44. F3640:960.

73. McGraw to Plummer, March 2, 1943, from San Quentin. In Folsom Inmate Case Files, Burroughs McGraw, 22230. F3745:519.

74. Daniel Forsythe, Volume III: Witnesses Before the Governor's Committee on Investigation of Folsom Prison, 706–16. CSA, Earl Warren Papers—Governor's Committee on Penal Affairs—1943–44. F3640:958. Forsythe was double-crossed by McGraw because in 1936, Forsythe had rigged a bet to eat eighteen candy bars in the L.A. County jail. McGraw had bet four hundred dollars that Forsythe would do it, and Forsythe threw the bet. So, McGraw sold him out to Plummer when he had some evidence that Forsythe was involved in some trickery in the prison. McGraw had a long memory; this was part of his effectiveness as a "politician."

75. Egan, Volume IV: Witnesses Before the Governor's Committee on Investigation of Folsom Prison, 818. CSA, Earl Warren Papers—Governor's Committee on Penal Affairs—1943–44. F3640:959.

76. Quoted by Alco, Volume III: Witnesses Before the Governor's Committee on Investigation of Folsom Prison, 633. CSA, Earl Warren Papers—Governor's Committee on Penal Affairs—1943–44. F3640:958.

77. Egan testimony, 813.

78. Egan testimony, 815–16.

79. Egan testimony, 815–16.

80. Martin Eng, Volume II: Witnesses Before the Governor's Committee on Investigation of Folsom Prison, 307–11. The quotations are from 308, 309. CSA, Earl Warren Papers—Governor's Committee on Penal Affairs—43–44. F3640:957.

81. Tasker, *Grimhaven*, 124.

82. San Francisco *Chronicle*, March 21, 1939, p. 1 col. 3.

83. Von Carlshausen, aka "Roark Tamerlane," "America!—add stars to our stripes," 9. Underlining in original.

84. "San Quentin Food Strike Fails, 4000 Foodless," February 2, 1939, Clipping Files, Box: San Quentin Prison, Folder: San Quentin Prison—History, 1930s. Kent Room, MCFPL.

85. "San Quentin's Food O.K., Says Prison Board," February 5, 1939, Clipping Files, Folder: San Quentin Prison—History, 1930s, Box: San Quentin Prison, Kent Room, MCFPL.

86. "Quentin Strike Virtually Over," February 3, 1939, Clipping Files, Folder: San Quentin Prison—History, 1930s, Box: San Quentin Prison, Kent Room, MCFPL. On Johnson and "the Modesto Boys," see the Marine Fireman's Union history, at http://www.mfoww.org/history.htm (accessed December 1, 2005); Bruce Nelson, *Workers on the Waterfront: Seamen, Longshoremen, and Unionism in the 1930s* (Urbana: University of Illinois Press, 1990), 171–72; California State Federation of Labor circular, October 10, 1935, Labor Archives and Research Center, San Francisco State University: California State Federation of Labor, Minutes of Meetings of Executive Council, etc., 1930–1938.

87. "New Quentin Strike Looms," February 6, 1939, Clipping Files, Folder: San Quentin Prison—History, 1930s, Box: San Quentin Prison, Kent Room, MCFPL.

88. Von Carlshausen, "America!—add stars to our stripes," 10.

89. Ibid.

90. Ibid., 11. Italicized sections were emphasized in the original in red; underlining in the original.

91. Governor's Hearings/Transcript of Hearings vs State Board of Prison Directors, vol. 1, 300–301. CSA, Dept of Penology Records, F3450: vols. 1–4, 6.

92. Most of the following narrative draws from Mr. Murphy, one of the representatives of the state against the prison board. Governor's Hearings/Transcript of Hearings vs State Board of Prison Directors, vol. 1, pp. 61–64. CSA, Dept of Penology Records, F3450: vols. 1–4, 6.

93. "42 Grilled in San Quentin's Food Strike," March 22, 1939, Clipping Files, Folder: San Quentin Prison—History, 1930s, Box: San Quentin Prison, Kent Room, MCFPL.

94. A list of twenty-nine food-strike prisoners and their "official" punishments is in the April 22, 1939, San Quentin Board of Prison Directors Minutes, 1939–40, CSA, Department of Corrections Records, F3717:1010, 1–15. Among the strikers, I have only been able to locate case files for Joseph Blinksy, Alfred Ferreira Jardine, and Phil Rosen. Demographic data is thus unavailable, but ten of the twenty-nine listed here worked in the jute mill. Their struggle may well have been associated with their position on or near the bottom of the productive and labor economy. Alfred Ferreira Jardine, 55370, was also among the strikers, but was not listed among those punished here. Jardine, arrested for burglary in 1924, was listed as racially Portuguese, was born and raised in California, and described himself as a laborer with no real trade. New York–born Phil Rosen, 60171, was listed as

"Jewish" for his "color" in official records, was a laborer, and had been arrested for two counts of first-degree robbery. Joseph Blinsky, listed as white and born in West Virginia, was arrested for grand theft and worked in the jute mill. No occupation was listed in his files.

95. See von Carlshausen. In his description of the Spot, which matched von Carlshausen's precisely, Murphy suggested that the idea for the Spot as a disciplinary technique was developed by Lewis. Governor's Hearings/Transcript of Hearings vs State Board of Prison Directors, vol. 1, p. 63. CSA, Dept of Penology Records, F3450: vols. 1–4, 6.

96. Bell, Governor's Hearings/Transcript of Hearings vs State Board of Prison Directors, vol. 1, pp. 179–80. CSA, Dept of Penology Records, F3450: vols. 1–4, 6.

97. Ibid., 61–65.

98. Bell testimony, Governor's Hearings/Transcript of Hearings vs State Board of Prison Directors, vol. 1, p. 189. CSA, Dept of Penology Records, F3450: vols. 1–4, 6.

99. Bell testimony, Governor's Hearings/Transcript of Hearings vs State Board of Prison Directors, vol. 1, pp. 186–87. CSA, Dept of Penology Records, F3450: vols. 1–4, 6.

100. Governor's Hearings/Transcript of Hearings vs State Board of Prison Directors, vol. 1, p. 419. CSA, Dept of Penology Records, F3450: vols. 1–4, 6.

101. Governor's Hearings/Transcript of Hearings vs State Board of Prison Directors, vol. 1, p. 420. CSA, Dept of Penology Records, F3450: vols 1–4, 6.

102. Clemmer argued that guards received a psychic wage from dominating their wards. "[B]y dominance over a helpless group, prison workers are able to tickle their egos and obtain some satisfaction through the power of authority. . . . [P]rison guards who, all through their lives, have been in a subordinate position, loudly command a cowed, helpless inmate to perform such and such an act." *The Prison Community*, 185.

103. *The Prison Community*, 185.

104. Governor's Hearings/Transcript of Hearings vs State Board of Prison Directors, vol. 1, p. 66. CSA, Dept of Penology Records, F3450: vols. 1–4, 6 (vol. 5 missing).

105. Bell testimony, Governor's Hearings/Transcript of Hearings vs State Board of Prison Directors, vol. 1, p. 190. CSA, Dept of Penology Records, F3450: vols. 1–4, 6 (vol. 5 missing). This closely parallels a black Texas prisoner's description of guard violence:

> One time Captain Powell was whipping a boy with that bat and he kept a hollerin', "Oh lordy, oh lordy!" And then finally he bust him again and he say "Oh lordy, Captain!" And the Captain said, "I thought you'd get around to me directly." 'Cause he wanted him to know that Jesus wasn't whippin' him, it was *him* whippin' him. And Jesus couldn't help him neither.

In Bruce Jackson, ed., *Wake Up Dead Man: Afro-American Worksongs from Texas Prisons* (Cambridge, MA: Harvard University Press, 1972), 9. Italics in original.

106. Governor's Hearings/Transcript of Hearings vs State Board of Prison Directors, vol. 1, pp. 48–49. CSA, Dept of Penology Records, F3450: vols. 1–4, 6 (vol. 5 missing).

107. Ibid., p. 50.

108. San Quentin Board of Prison Directors Minutes. The Spot was abolished in the June 29, 1940, Minutes, 451; and the discussion of dismantling the Dungeon took place in the August 10, 1940, Minutes, 482. F3717:1009, CSA.

109. Von Carlshausen, "America!—add stars to our stripes," 11–12. Spelling and punctuation in original.

110. Leo L. Stanley, *Men at Their Worst* (New York: D. Appleton-Century, 1940), 201.

111. Ethan Blue, "The Strange Career of Leo Stanley: Remaking Manhood and Medicine at San Quentin Penitentiary," *Pacific Historical Review* 78, no. 2 (2009): 210–41.

112. Nan Alamilla Boyd, *Wide Open Town: A History of Queer San Francisco to 1965* (Berkeley: University of California Press, 2003), 9, 28, 43–44, 86–87; George Chauncey, *Gay New York: Gender, Urban Culture, and the Making of the Gay Male World, 1890–1940* (New York: Basic Books, 1994), 65–97; Kunzel, *Criminal Intimacy*, 45–76.

113. Kunzel, *Criminal Intimacy*, 80.

114. My thoughts are indebted to Halberstam, *Female Masculinity*.

115. Elise Chernier, "Segregating Sexualities: The Prison 'Sex Problem' in Twentieth-Century Canada and the United States," in Carolyn Strange and Alison Bashford, eds., *Isolation: Places and Practices of Exclusion* (London: Routledge, 2003), 71–85, esp.74.

116. Malcolm Braly, *False Starts: A Memoir of San Quentin and Other Prisons* (Boston: Little, Brown, 1976), 159, quoted in Kunzel, *Criminal Intimacy*, 73.

117. J. W. Dunlop, Volume IV: Witnesses Before the Governor's Committee on Investigation of Folsom Prison, 734–57, esp. 751–52. CSA, Earl Warren Papers—Governor's Committee on Penal Affairs—1943–44. F3640:959.

118. W. H. West, Volume III: Witnesses Before the Governor's Committee on Investigation of Folsom Prison, 670–85, esp. 674. CSA, Earl Warren Papers—Governor's Committee on Penal Affairs—1943–44. F3640:958.

119. J. W. Dunlop, Volume IV: Witnesses Before the Governor's Committee on Investigation of Folsom Prison, 734–57, esp. 752–52. CSA, Earl Warren Papers—Governor's Committee on Penal Affairs—1943–44. F3640:959.

120. Verso of photo 1925.013.010, Folder 13, Leo L. Stanley Collection, San Quentin Photographs, Kent Room, MCFPL.

121. Johnny to Billy, 1954, Folder 48-A, and Eddie to "Darling," June 2, 1950, Folder 48-B, in San Quentin, Prison Collection, Kinsey Institute. Quoted in Kunzel, *Criminal Intimacy*, 186–87.

122. James W. Robinson, Volume II: Witnesses Before the Governor's Committee on Investigation of Folsom Prison, 345–53, esp. 350. CSA, Earl Warren Papers—Governor's Committee on Penal Affairs—1943–44. F3640:957. Also, Chauncey, *Gay New York*, 59.

123. Kunzel, *Criminal Intimacy*, 187–88.

124. Kunzel, *Criminal Intimacy*, 64–65.

125. Ryan testimony, Volume II: Witnesses Before the Governor's Committee on Investigation of Folsom Prison, 399–436, esp. 428. CSA, Earl Warren Papers—Governor's Committee on Penal Affairs—1943–44. F3640:957.

126. W. E. Kamp, Volume II: Witnesses Before the Governor's Committee on Investigation of Folsom Prison, 270–92. CSA, Earl Warren Papers—Governor's Committee on Penal Affairs—1943–44. F3640:957.

127. Ryan testimony, Volume II: Witnesses Before the Governor's Committee on Investigation of Folsom Prison, 399–436, esp. 425. CSA, Earl Warren Papers—Governor's Committee on Penal Affairs—1943–44. F3640:957.

128. Folsom Inmate Case Files, CSA, R. W. White, San Quentin #57479, Folsom #23921.

129. Ryan testimony, Volume II: Witnesses Before the Governor's Committee on Investigation of Folsom Prison, 428. CSA, Earl Warren Papers—Governor's Committee on Penal Affairs—1943–44. F3640:957.

130. Regina G. Kunzel, "Situating Sex: Prison Sexual Culture in the Mid-Twentieth-Century United States," *GLQ* 8, no. 3 (2002): 253–70, esp. 262.

131. See George Chauncey, *Gay New York*; Allan Bérubé, *Coming Out under Fire: The History of Gay Men and Women in World War Two* (New York: Plume, 1991); Kunzel, "Situating Sex"; Kunzel, *Criminal Intimacy*; Estelle B. Freedman, "The Prison Lesbian: Race, Class, and the Construction of the Aggressive Female Homosexual, 1915–1965," *Feminist Studies* 22, no. 2 (Summer 1996): n.p., online at http://infotrac.galegroup.com/itweb/viva_uva?db=ITOF (accessed June 19, 2004); Estelle B. Freedman, "'Uncontrolled Desires': The Response to the Sexual Psychopath, 1920–1960," in Kathy Peiss and Christina Simmons, eds., *Passion and Power: Sexuality in History* (Philadelphia: Temple University Press, 1989), 199–225; Chernier, "Segregating Sexualities."

132. Quoted in Robert Perkinson, *Texas Tough: The Rise of America's Prison Empire* (New York: Metropolitan Books, 2010), 219.

133. Quoted in Michael D. Brown, "History of Folsom Prison, 1878–1978" (Represa, CA: Folsom Graphic Arts, 1978).

134. K. L. Buchanan, Volume III: Witnesses Before the Governor's Committee on Investigation of Folsom Prison, 492–518, esp. 514. CSA, Earl Warren Papers—Governor's Committee on Penal Affairs—1943–44. F3640:958.

135. Ibid., 515.

136. Ryan, Volume II: Witnesses Before the Governor's Committee on Investigation of Folsom Prison, 427. CSA, Earl Warren Papers—Governor's Committee on Penal Affairs—1943–44. F3640:957.

137. Letter from Mundt to the Governor. CSA, Earl Warren Papers—Administrative Files—Corrections—Governor's Prison Committee—Folsom State Prison (Folder 15) 1942–43, F3640:986.

138. Ibid.

139. W. T. Kamp, Volume II: Witnesses Before the Governor's Committee on Investigation of Folsom Prison, 275. CSA, Earl Warren Papers—Governor's Committee on Penal Affairs—1943–44. F3640:957.

140. J. J. Solberg, Volume II: Witnesses Before the Governor's Committee on Investigation of Folsom Prison, 386–91. CSA, Earl Warren Papers—Governor's Committee on Penal Affairs—1943–44. F3640:957.

141. Plummer testimony, Volume V: Witnesses Before the Governor's Committee on Investigation of Folsom Prison, 1023–40, esp 1038–39. CSA, Earl Warren Papers—Governor's Committee on Penal Affairs—1943–44. F3640:960

142. Though Plummer was hardly an avowedly reformist warden, hard-line keepers have commonly accused progressive prison officials of homosexuality. New York prison reformer Thomas Mott Osborne was accused of homosexuality in 1915, an accusation that effectively discredited his policies and ruined his career. So, too, Miriam van Waters, superintendent of Massachusetts Reformatory for Women at Framingham, was accused of being a lesbian. See Rebecca M. McLennan, *The Crisis of Imprisonment: Protest, Politics, and the Making of the American Penal State, 1776–1940* (Cambridge, MA: Cambridge University Press, 2008), 411–12; Kunzel, *Criminal Intimacy*, 144.

143. Letter from Mundt to the Governor. CSA, Earl Warren Papers—Administrative Files—Corrections—Governor's Prison Committee—Folsom State Prison (Folder 15) 1942–43, F3640:986.

144. Clinton T. Duffy and Al Hirschberg, *Sex and Crime* (Garden City, NY: Doubleday, 1965), 29. Quoted in Kunzel, *Criminal Intimacy*, 80.

145. On the development of therapeutic and expert treatment (and reaction against it) see Theodore Hamm, *Rebel and a Cause: Caryl Chessman and the Politics of the Death Penalty in Postwar California, 1948–1974* (Berkeley: University of California Press, 2001); Kunzel, *Criminal Intimacy*, esp. chapters 3 and 4.

CHAPTER 5

1. *Thirty Minutes*, Program 1, March 23, 1938. Transcripts available from the University of Texas's Center for American History, Austin, Texas.

2. On complaints about brutality in Texas prisons, see Governor Sterling papers, Box 301-467, Folder "Texas State Prison System, Complaints, Feb 12, 1931–Sept 15, 1932," Texas State Library and Archives Commission. For complaints a decade later, see Governor Stevenson papers, Box 4-14/164, Folder "Texas Prison Board 1942," and Box 4-14/136, Folder "Prison System Referral."

3. The confluence of broadcast capital and state interests in *Thirty Minutes* was striking. Robert McChesney argues that American broadcast capital successfully wrested control of the airwaves from state regulation in 1927 and 1934 on the premise that for-profit broadcasters would sponsor "public-interest" programming on the state's behalf. Governmental regulation of the airwaves was, broadcasters argued, tantamount to totalitarian control of sources of information. *Thirty Minutes behind the Walls* was a perfect example of for-profit broadcasting on the state's behalf. WBAP "contributed" airtime and network channels to "the public good" while securing their own place and importance in the governmentally regulated public sphere. See Robert McChesney, *Telecommunications, Mass Media, and Democracy: The Battle for Control of U.S. Broadcasting, 1928–1935* (New York: Oxford University Press, 1993); Jason Loviglio, "*Vox Pop*: Network Radio and the Voice of the People," in Michelle Hilmes and Jason Loviglio, eds., *The Radio Reader: Essays in the Cultural History of Radio* (New York: Routledge, 2002), 94; also, Susan Smulyan, *Selling Radio: The Commercialization of American Broadcasting, 1920–1934* (Washington, DC: Smithsonian Institution Press, 1994).

4. Charlotte A. Teagle, *History of Welfare Activities of the Texas Prison Board, 1927–1940*, TSLAC, Department of Corrections Records, Box 1998/038-124, 171; *Thirty Minutes*, Program 156, March 19, 1941; Skip Hollandsworth, "O Sister, Where Art Thou?" *Texas Monthly*, May 2003.

5. Warren I. Susman, *Culture as History: The Transformation of American Society in the Twentieth Century* (New York: Pantheon, 1984 [1973]). The disciplinary effects of mass media and athletics in prisons has largely escaped historians' and media studies scholars' attention, despite recent debates over cable television and weightlifting equipment behind bars. However, see Blake McKelvey, *American Prisons: A History of Good Intentions* (Montclair, NJ: Patterson Smith, 1977), 137, 261–62, 294. On the causes and consequences of the demise of contract inmate labor in the Northeast, see Rebecca M. McLennan's *The Crisis of Imprisonment: Protest, Politics, and the Making of the American Penal State, 1776–1941* (New York: Cambridge University Press, 2008), and McLennan, "Punishment's 'Square Deal': Prisoners and Their Keepers in 1920s New York," *Journal of Urban History* 29, no. 5 (July 2003): 597–619.

6. Most criminal justice and lynching scholars focus on visual spectacles, witnessed in person. *Thirty Minutes* demands analysis in the era of mass communication and the realm of sound rather than sight. With the financial and technological aid of radio broad-

casting capitalists, prison radio offered an expansive economy of power to display the condemned, broadcast into homes rather than a public square or in public labor. As such, it was an aural innovation in creating what Michelle Brown recently identified as "penal spectatorship," subjects partially constituted through relationships with carceral media. Michelle Brown, *The Culture of Punishment: Prison, Society, and Spectacle* (New York: New York University Press, 2008). Michael Meranze, *Laboratories of Virtue: Punishment, Revolution, and Authority in Philadelphia, 1760–1835* (Chapel Hill: University of North Carolina Press, 1996); Peter Linebaugh, *The London Hanged: Crime and Civil Society in the Eighteenth Century* (New York: Cambridge University Press, 1992); Douglas Hay, et al., *Albion's Fatal Tree: Crime and Society in Eighteenth-Century England* (London: Pantheon, 1975); Michel Foucault, *Discipline and Punish: The Birth of the Prison*, trans. Alan Sheridan (New York: Vintage Books, 1979); Robert Olwell, *Masters, Slaves, and Subjects: The Culture of Power in the South Carolina Low Country, 1740–1790* (Ithaca, NY: Cornell University Press, 1998); Louis P. Masur, *Rites of Execution: Capital Punishment and the Transformation of American Culture, 1776–1865* (New York: Oxford University Press, 1989); David Garland, *Punishment and Modern Society: A Study in Social Theory* (Chicago: University of Chicago Press, 1990); Peter Stallybrass and Allon White, *The Politics and Poetics of Transgression* (Ithaca, NY: Cornell University Press, 1986).

7. Indeed, *Thirty Minutes* must be seen as a twentieth-century version of slave celebrations, in which inmates, like slaves before them, were made to appear satisfied with their incarceration despite omnipresent violence. See Frederick Douglass, *Narrative of the Life of Frederick Douglass* (New Haven, CT: Yale University Press, 2001), 55–56; Saidiya V. Hartman, *Scenes of Subjection: Terror, Slavery, and Self-Making in Nineteenth-Century America* (New York: Oxford University Press, 1997).

8. David M. Oshinsky, *"Worse Than Slavery": Parchman Farm and the Ordeal of Jim Crow Justice* (New York: Free Press, 1996).

9. Barbara Dianne Savage describes the denial of black speakers' voice on radio broadcasts as a central feature in the politics of representation, and also as a goal of black political movements around radio broadcasting. A speaking role on the radio would indicate parity in "the symbolically equalizing formality of political discourse," a role that was systematically repressed. Savage, *Broadcasting Freedom: Radio, War, and the Politics of Race, 1938–1948* (Chapel Hill: University of North Carolina Press, 1999), 198, 200.

10. George Lipsitz, *Rainbow at Midnight: Labor and Culture in the 1940s* (Urbana: University of Illinois Press, 1994).

11. Jorge A. González, "Cultural Fronts: Towards a Dialogical Understanding of Contemporary Cultures," in James Lull, ed., *Culture in the Communication Age* (London: Routledge, 2001, 106–31. While Susman argued that American culture in the 1930s was that of a thoroughly hegemonic middle class, analysis of *Thirty Minutes behind the Walls* substantiates Michael Denning's findings of greater cultural conflict in *The Cultural Front: The Laboring of American Culture in the Twentieth Century* (New York: Verso, 1997). But unlike either Susman or Denning, I argue that the popular cultures of punishment in the 1930s should be understood as fields of social conflict: contested, appropriated, and made use of in multiple directions by different people, at different times.

12. Speech, understood as the ability to participate in social forms and protests recognizable to the state, was denied to racialized prisoners. Music, however, is a far less stable medium for communication, and its protests and alternative imaginations remained silent

to state officials, narratives, and transcriptions and thus to received understandings of historical source material. Indeed, the *Thirty Minutes* transcripts are full of prison officials' and white inmates' spoken words, but are devoid of black or Mexican men's, or women prisoners', speech. Officials recognized nonwhite and women prisoners' musical appeal when they played music to ensure listenership, but there remained, I contend, aspects of musical performance that superseded disciplinary intentions. Michael Warner suggested a difference between creating a "public," which might develop direct links with a state, and a "counterpublic," which requires similar processes of creation and sustenance. Counterpublic discourses can generate their own communities, he suggests, but these have an ambivalent relationship to and effect on governments. "Publics more overtly oriented in their self-understandings to the poetic-expressive dimensions of language—including artistic publics and many counterpublics—lack the power to transpose themselves to the level of the generality of the state." It is frequently the inability of the communities formed by counterpublic discourse to effect social change at the level of law or the state (for whatever reason) that leads critics to see counterpublics as nonpolitical. Michael Warner, "Publics and Counterpublics," *Public Culture* 14, no. 1 (2002), 49–90, esp. 83–84.

13. This makes sense: today's mass incarceration of poor people of color for drug offenses is certainly reminiscent of the postbellum South's criminalization of petty theft and vagrancy, and, as in the lease period, private industries have made bids to resume control of today's bloated prisons. In addition, Progressive and New Deal limits on private profit from convict labor were compromised by the 1979 Prison Industries Enhancement Act, and private companies can hire prisoners once more. On the convict lease, see Edward L. Ayers, *Vengeance and Justice: Crime and Punishment in the Nineteenth-Century American South* (New York: Oxford University Press, 1984);, Alex Lichtenstein, *Twice the Work of Free Labor: The Political Economy of Convict Labor in the New South* (New York: Verso, 1996); Matthew Mancini, *One Dies, Get Another: Convict Leasing in the American South, 1866–1928* (Columbia: University of South Carolina Press, 1996); Karin A. Shapiro, *A New South Rebellion: The Battle against Convict Labor in the Tennessee Coalfields, 1871–1896* (Chapel Hill: University of North Carolina Press, 1998); Mary Ellen Curtin, *Black Prisoners and Their World, Alabama, 1865–1900* (Charlottesville: University of Virginia Press, 2000). On lynch violence, W. Fitzhugh Brundage, *Lynching in the New South: Georgia and Virginia, 1880–1930* (Urbana: University of Illinois Press, 1993); Grace Elizabeth Hale, *Making Whiteness: The Culture of Segregation in the South, 1890–1940* (New York: Pantheon, 1998); William D. Carrigan, *The Making of a Lynching Culture: Violence and Vigilantism in Central Texas, 1836–1916* (Urbana: University of Illinois Press, 2004); James W. Marquart, Sheldon Ekland-Olson, and Jonathan R. Sorensen, *The Rope, the Chair, and the Needle: Capital Punishment in Texas, 1923–1990* (Austin: University of Texas Press, 1994); David Garland, "Penal Excess and Surplus Meaning: Public Torture Lynchings in Twentieth-Century America," *Law and Society Review* 39, no. 4 (2005); Charles J. Ogletree Jr. and Austin Sarat, eds., *From Lynch Mobs to the Killing State: Race and the Death Penalty in America* (New York: New York University Press, 2006).

14. This description draws from *The Echo*, January 1943, TSLAC, microfilm Reel 1 (June 1933–December 1948), p. 3 col. 5, p. 5 col. 2; and *Thirty Minutes*, Program 102, February 28, 1940.

15. Robert Elliot Burns, *I Am a Fugitive from a Chain Gang* (Warner Bros. Pictures, 1932). *Thirty Minutes behind the Walls* also strove to counteract sensationalist and romantic

representations of banditry, crime, and punishment. On bandits' and bank robbers' mystique in the Depression, as well as the federal government's attempts to quash their allure, see Claire Bond Potter, *War on Crime: Bandits, G-Men, and the Politics of Mass Culture* (New Brunswick, NJ: Rutgers University Press, 1998).

16. Savage, *Broadcasting Freedom*, 6.

17. *Thirty Minutes*, Program 1, March 23, 1938. The italics are mine.

18. Clinton T. Duffy Testimony, Volume VI: Witnesses Before the Governor's Committee on Investigation of San Quentin Prison, 1285. CSA, Earl Warren Papers—Governor's Committee on Penal Affairs—1943–44, F3640:961. Susan Douglas also argues that intellectuals debated whether radio should be used for "entertainment" or for "education." The highbrow/educational advocates, frequently social elites, advocated for the radio's potential to educate and lift up "the masses," while the more crass advertising executives celebrated the lowbrow potential of entertainment as a way to sell ever more consumer goods to that same "mass" audience. Prison radio planners sought to use both together: lowbrow entertainment to "hook" the masses they wanted to instruct with the educational/disciplinary features of the shows. Susan J. Douglas, *Listening In: Radio and the American Imagination* (Minneapolis: University of Minnesota Press, 2004 [1999]), 88. See also Jackson Lears, *Fables of Abundance: A Cultural History of Advertising in America* (New York: BasicBooks, 1994).

19. *The Echo*, March 1938, 8.

20. "Prison Radiocasts," *The Echo*, March 1939, 4.

21. *Thirty Minutes*, Program 52, March 15, 1939. O'Daniel placed faith in God and in humane punishment to redeem errant Texans, but his actual practices of legislating for better prison conditions did not always meet the rhetoric espoused here.

22. *Thirty Minutes*, Program 16, July 6, 1938.

23. *The Echo*, March 1941, p. 9 col. 3.

24. *Thirty Minutes*, Program 15, June 29, 1938.

25. *Thirty Minutes*, Program 3, April 6, 1938.

26. *Thirty Minutes*, Program 19, July 27, 1938.

27. On white supremacy and prison reform in Texas, see Paul M. Lucko, "Prison Farms, Walls, and Society: Punishment and Politics in Texas, 1848–1910" (Ph.D. dissertation, University of Texas at Austin, 1999); Robert Reps Perkinson, "The Birth of the Texas Prison Empire, 1865–1915" (Ph.D. dissertation, Yale University, 2001).

28. *Thirty Minutes*, Program 25, September 7, 1938. New buildings became something of a fetish in the prison reform narrative, signifying institutional progress. Throughout the Texas Prison System's annual reports in the 1930s, new buildings were framed as the saviors of an archaic system.

29. *Thirty Minutes*, Program 20, August 3, 1938.

30. *Thirty Minutes*, Program 13, June 15, 1938. Prison doctors kept erratic records on inmate self-mutilation, but they treated twenty self-inflicted arm fractures in 1940. Annual report of the Texas Prison Board, 1940, 188.

31. *Thirty Minutes*, Program 106, March 27, 1940.

32. Within transcripts, race was referenced by recourse to malapropism and dialectal transcription for racially other voices. On racial denigration and textual representation, see Tommy L. Lott, *The Invention of Race: Black Cultures and the Politics of Representation* (Malden, MA: Wiley-Blackwell, 1999), 84–110; Gavin Jones, *Strange Talk: The Politics of Dialect Literature in Gilded Age America* (Berkeley: University of California Press, 1999).

33. Consider Angela Y. Davis, *Women, Race, and Class* (New York: Random House, 1981; Jacqueline Jones, *Labor of Love, Labor of Sorrow: Black Women, Work, and the Family from Slavery to the Present* (New York: Vintage, 1995 [1985]); Tera W. Hunter, *To' Joy My Freedom: Southern Black Women's Lives and Labors after the Civil War* (Cambridge, MA: Harvard University Press, 1997); Amy Dru Stanley, *From Bondage to Contract: Wage Labor, Marriage, and the Market in the Age of Slave Emancipation* (New York: Cambridge University Press, 1998).

34. *Thirty Minutes*, Program 139, November 20, 1940. For another "youngster" interview, see Program 15, June 29, 1938. On the gendered nature of punishment and the fears of disordered (i.e., nonpatriarchal) homes as a primary cause of crime, see Christine Stansell, *City of Women: Sex and Class in New York, 1789–1860* (New York: Knopf, 1986); David J. Rothman, *The Discovery of the Asylum: Social Order and Disorder in the New Republic* (Boston: Little, Brown, 1971).

35. *Thirty Minutes*, Program 139, November 20, 1940.

36. Linda Gordon, *Pitied but Not Entitled: Single Mothers and the History of Welfare* (Cambridge, MA: Harvard University Press, 1998); Devra Weber, *Dark Sweat, White Gold: California Farm Workers, Cotton, and the New Deal* (Berkeley: University of California Press, 1994); Christopher L. Tomlins, *The State and the Unions: Labor Relations, Law, and the Organized Labor Movement in America, 1880–1960* (Cambridge: Cambridge University Press, 1985).

37. *Thirty Minutes*, Program 6, April 27, 1938.

38. Gayatri Spivak, "Can the Subaltern Speak," in Cary Nelson and Lawrence Grossberg, eds., *Marxism and the Interpretation of Culture* (Urbana: University of Illinois Press, 1988), 271–313.

39. *Thirty Minutes*, Program 24, August 31, 1938. Italics added.

40. See LeRoi Jones/Amiri Baraka, *Blues People: Negro Music in White America* (New York: Morrow Quill, 1963). On infrapolitics, see Robin D. G. Kelley, *Race Rebels: Culture, Politics, and the Black Working Class* (New York: Free Press, 1996), 8–9. On black working-class vernacular religious culture, Evelyn Brooks Higginbotham, "Rethinking Vernacular Culture: Black Religion and Race Records in the 1920s and 1930s," in Wahneema Lubiano, ed., *The House That Race Built* (New York: Pantheon, 1997), 157–77.

41. *Thirty Minutes*, Program 85, November 1, 1939.

42. On radio comedy in the 1930s, see Douglas, *Listening In*, 100–123. James C. Scott, *Domination and the Arts of Resistance: Hidden Transcripts* (New Haven, CT: Yale University Press, 1990); Kelley, *Race Rebels*. On blackface minstrelsy, see Eric Lott, *Love and Theft: Blackface Minstrelsy and the American Working Class* (New York: Oxford University Press, 1993).

43. On finding subaltern agency within the interstices of the historical record, see Emma Pérez, *The Decolonial Imaginary: Writing Chicanas into History* (Bloomington: Indiana University Press, 1999). On contests over the publics and counterpublics generated by popular culture, see Warner, "Publics and Counterpublics."

44. On dignity as a category of analysis, see Luis Alvarez, *The Power of the Zoot: Youth Culture and Resistance during World War II* (Berkeley: University of California Press, 2008).

45. Angela Y. Davis, *Blues Legacies and Black Feminism: Gertrude "Ma" Rainey, Bessie Smith, and Billie Holiday* (New York: Pantheon, 1998), caption to photo facing page 141.

46. Skip Hollandsworth, "Blue Notes," *Texas Monthly*, May 2003. Online at texas-monthly.com (accessed September 27, 2006).

47. Skip Hollandsworth, "O Sister, Where Art Thou?" *Texas Monthly*, May 2003. Online at texasmonthly.com (accessed June 21, 2003). Lele Celeste Simmons, Ocie Hoosier's granddaughter, fondly recalled her grandfather's harmonica playing when she was a child. Personal correspondence, October 15, 2007, in author's possession.

48. Scott Yanow, *Trumpet Kings: The Players Who Shaped the Sound of Jazz Trumpet* (San Francisco: Backbeat Books, 2001), 304–6.

49. It is a strange irony that the Lomaxes' recording interests were almost precisely the inverse of prison officials' and WBAP transcribers'. The WBAP transcripts documented only speaking roles on the show, and these were overwhelmingly white prisoners and officials solidifying prison pedagogy. Yet the Lomaxes sought out almost exclusively black prisoners' music, and even then, "unpopular" work songs, spirituals, and field hollers rather than marketable and radio-ready music. While black and Mexican voices were marginalized on the program, white and Mexican prison musicians' songs escaped the Lomaxes' attention on this recording trip. See the May 14, 1939, Lomax Fieldnotes from Goree State Farm, 1939 Southern Recording Trip Fieldnotes, Section 12: Huntsville, Texas, and vicinity; May 11–14, accessed from the Library of Congress Online, September 26, 2006.

50. Lomax recorded a "Convict Quartet" singing "Ride On, King Jesus," on May 12, 1939, and it was performed by the "Negro Four" on *Thirty Minutes*, Program 57, April 19, 1939. The quartet consisted of William Brown, Terrell Conley, Eugene Blacker, and Alvin Brown. The Negro Choir played "Great Day" on *Thirty Minutes* on September 21, 1938, Program 27; it was recorded by a quartet by Lomax May 11, 1939.

51. Hollandsworth, "Blue Notes," *Texas Monthly*, May 2003. Online at texasmonthly.com (accessed September 27, 2006).

52. Hollandsworth, "Blue Notes."

53. May 14, 1939, Lomax Fieldnotes from Goree State Farm, 1939 Southern Recording Trip Fieldnotes, Section 12: Huntsville, Texas, and vicinity; May 11–14, Accessed from the Library of Congress Online September 26, 2006.

54. Ibid.

55. Ibid.

56. Hollandsworth, "O Sister, Where Art Thou?"

57. To hear Ace Johnson's "Rabbit in the Garden," consult the Lomax recording *Black Texicans* from Rounder Records. It is transcribed as "Rabbit" in the Lomax 1939 Fieldnotes, though no recording is available from the Library of Congress website. My thoughts on "Rabbit in the Garden" are deeply indebted to conversations with Scott Saul and Charles Fairchild, and I thank them both.

58. Lawrence W. Levine, *Black Culture and Black Consciousness: Afro-American Folk Thought from Slavery to Freedom* (New York: Oxford University Press, 1978), 371.

59. "Old Rattler" was one such mythical dog (among many real ones) in Texas prisons. Consider the April 16, 1939, work song, "Ole Rattler," sung by Tommy Woods and other prisoners, recorded at Clemens State Farm, in which prisoners sing about the dog tracking down an escaped prisoner. Lomax 1939 Southern Recording Trip Fieldnotes Section 4: West Columbia and Clemens State Farm, Brazoria County, Texas; April 15–17. The version of "Ole Rattler" by Moses "Clear Rock" Platt and James "Iron Head" Baker, on *Big Brazos:*

Texas Prison Recordings, 1933 and 1934 (Rounder Records), has a barking sound similar to Johnson's dog in "Rabbit." See also Bruce Jackson, *Wake Up Dead Man: Afro-American Worksongs from Texas Prisons* (Cambridge, MA: Harvard University Press, 1972).

60. Lipsitz, *Rainbow at Midnight*, 312.

61. Edward L. Ayers, *Promise of the New South: Life after Reconstruction* (New York: Oxford University Press, 1992), esp. 377; see also Bill C. Malone, *Country Music, USA* (Austin: University of Texas Press, 1985), 4–6.

62. Lott, *Love and Theft.*

63. Lipsitz, *Rainbow at Midnight*, 303–33, esp. 309–13. Also, González, "Cultural Fronts." Furthermore, as in Michael Warner's retheorization of public spheres, I argue that the text-based public messages of *Thirty Minutes* were aligned to the state-oriented messages of discipline, while the affective and embodied community generated by musical segments accessed a potential counterpublic. Michael Warner, "Publics and Counterpublics," esp. 83–84, 86–89.

64. This is an exceptionally difficult argument to prove, given the disciplinary parameters of historical research. The rules of evidence (and there is a great deal of cultural work that goes into validating what is and is not historical fact) dictate that I focus research on the culturally sanctioned facts of words transcribed in the historical record: in this case, these were the interviews, which proved to be heavily laden with ideological baggage legitimizing the state and capital's politics (though not free from contradiction). In the extant transcripts, only the names of songs were recorded, rather than the songs themselves, and arguments about music's subversive potential and the interplay between identities and allegiances must remain tentative among material that is skewed toward the state's representations. So too must assessment of audience response be tentative.

65. *Thirty Minutes*, Program 152, February 19, 1941. Indeed, that Hattie Ellis, the "blues singing negress," took requests and sang Judy Garland's "Over the Rainbow" (on Program 108, April 10, 1940) speaks well to cultural fluidity in music behind bars. It also challenges the historiographical notion that prisons were repositories of undiluted folkloric culture, as investigated by various folklorists in the middle decades of the twentieth century. Understanding of the ways in which popular culture crossed prison walls similarly complicates the hermetic totality of "total institutions." See John A. Lomax and Alan Lomax, *Negro Folk Songs as Sung by Lead Belly* (New York: Macmillan, 1936); Jackson, *Wake Up Dead Man*; Erving Goffman, *Asylums: Essays on the Social Situation of Mental Patients and Other Inmates* (London: Penguin, 1961). On the western swing version of "Under the Double Eagle," see Lipsitz, *Rainbow at Midnight*, 322.

66. *Thirty Minutes*, Program 84, October 25, 1939.

67. *Thirty Minutes*, Program 66, June 21, 1939.

68. *Thirty Minutes*, Program 63, May 31, 1939.

69. Lott, *Love and Theft.*

70. Osie [sic] Hoosier, Convict Number 83277, Conduct Register and Convict Records, TSLAC.

71. Malone, *Country Music, USA*, 9.

72. On racial transgression as well as the further delineation of racial difference via sexuality in urban vice districts, see Kevin J. Mumford, *Interzones: Black/White Sex Districts in Chicago and New York in the Early Twentieth Century* (New York: Columbia University Press, 1997).

73. *The Echo*, January 1940, 8.

74. *Thirty Minutes*, Program 15, June 29, 1938. The conflation of racialization and "happiness" was striking. Consider the following, from Program 5, April 20, 1938: "And here are those four grinning Darkies who make up the prison's Negro Quartette. . . . Let's listen to them sing 'Precious Lord!'" Indeed, this racialization and the trope of the grin/smile even extended to the seemingly secure white social position of the vice-president of the prison board: "Next, we are pleased to introduce to you another old time Texan . . . *a genial, robust Irishman whose characteristics include a flashing smile and all the ready wit and wisdom of his race* . . . Col. W. R. Dulaney, of Houston, Texas" (Program 5, April 20, 1938, emphasis added). It is interesting that as an Irishman, he'd be introduced with a reference to his "smile," akin to the "grinning" of black participants on the show, in racialized characteristics like those of Amos 'n' Andy and other minstrel show acts. Interestingly, while this invocation of the Irish as a separate race falls outside Matthew Frye Jacobson's overarching periodization in the consolidation of ethnic whiteness-as-Caucasian, it also suggests a division among elite whites, in addition to the racialized poor whites that Neil Foley explores. Perhaps this was an effort by a social subordinate to ridicule and racially mark his "superior." See Jacobson, *Whiteness of a Different Color: European Immigration and the Alchemy of Race* (Cambridge, MA: Harvard University Press, 1998), esp. 39–138; Neil Foley, *The White Scourge: Mexicans, Blacks, and Poor Whites in Texas Cotton Culture* (Berkeley: University of California Press, 1997).

75. Personal communication with Lele Celeste Simmons, Ocie Hoosier's granddaughter. October 15, 2007, copy in author's possession.

76. Manuel Peña, *The Mexican American Orquesta: Music, Culture, and the Dialectic of Conflict* (Austin: University of Texas Press, 1999), 132. Importantly, rumba itself emerged from the blending of African and Hispanic musical styles in Cuba and the Caribbean.

77. *Thirty Minutes*, Program 64, June 7, 1939; Program 71, July 26, 1939; Program 116, June 5, 1940; see also Peña, *Mexican American Orquesta*, esp. 132.

78. In this, it seems more than a coincidence when Peña explains that urban, middle-class, swing-influenced orquesta music was called *jitóne* (derived from "hightone"), and opposed to rural, working-class ranchero music. Peña, *Mexican American Orquesta*, 2, 122–23. Such a distinction articulated racialized, as well as class components within Mexican American music.

79. Charlotte A. Teagle, *History of Welfare Activities of the Texas Prison Board, 1927–1940*, TSLAC, Department of Corrections Records, Box 1998/038-124, 171. On audience surveillance, see Douglas, *Listening In*, 124–60, esp. 158–59.

80. *Thirty Minutes*, Program 151, February 12, 1941.

81. Loviglio, "*Vox Pop*," 90, 91.

82. See the May 14, 1939, John and Ruby Lomax fieldnotes from Goree State Farm. "1939 Southern Recording Trip Fieldnotes, Section 12: Huntsville, Texas, and vicinity; May 11–14." Accessed from the Library of Congress Online, September 26, 2006.

83. *Thirty Minutes*, Program 103, March 6, 1940; Program 85, November 1, 1939; Program 107, April 3, 1940; Program 74, August 16, 1939.

84. *Thirty Minutes*, Program 81, October 11, 1939.

85. *Thirty Minutes*, Program 58, April 11, 1939.

86. *Thirty Minutes*, Program 95, January 10, 1940.

87. "250,000 Radio Listeners Write," *The Echo*, March 1942, 2.

88. "Broadcast Staff Receives Variety of Fan Letters," *The Echo*, March 1940, 1, 2.

89. "Fan Mail Sets New Record as Local Staff Is Swamped," *The Echo*, March 1940, 1, 12.

90. *Thirty Minutes*, Program 142, December 11, 1940. Emphasis in original.

91. James N. Gregory, *American Exodus: The Dust Bowl Migration and Okie Culture in California* (New York: Oxford University Press, 1989), esp. 150.

92. *Thirty Minutes*, Program 153, February 26, 1941.

93. Hartman, *Scenes of Subjection*, 46.

94. From the file of L. C. Newman, #277, quoted in Marquart et al., *The Rope, the Chair, and the Needle*, 35–36.

95. Hollandsworth, "O Sister, Where Art Thou?"

96. "Broadcast Staff Receives Variety of Fan Letters," *The Echo*, March 1940, 1, 2.

97. *Thirty Minutes*, Program 49, February 22, 1939.

CHAPTER 6

1. *The Echo*, August 1935, p. 10 cols. 1, 2, 3, TSLAC microfilm Reel 1 (June 1933– December 1948).

2. Elliot Gorn, *The Manly Art: Bare-Knuckle Prizefighting in America* (Ithaca. NY: Cornell University Press, 1986), 138, in Michael S. Kimmel, *Manhood in America: A Cultural History*, 2d ed. (New York: Oxford University Press, 2006), 94.

3. "Fans Celebrate Close of Baseball Season," *The Bulletin*, October 1923, 17, 18.

4. "All San Quentin Thrills as Field Meet Nears," *The Bulletin*, July/August 1935, 28. CASL Government Publications Room.

5. "Court Smith Is New San Quentin Warden," *The Bulletin*, March/April 1936, 22, CASL Government Publications Room.

6. Pierre Bourdieu, "Programme for a Sociology of Sport," *In Other Words: Essays Towards a Reflexive Sociology* (Stanford, CA: Stanford University Press, 1990), 156–67; Roland Barthes, "The Tour de France as Epic," in *The Eiffel Tower and Other Mythologies*, trans. Richard Howard (New York: Hill and Wang, 1979), 79–90; John Bale, *Landscapes of Modern Sport* (New York: St. Martin's Press, 1994).

7. Alexander W. Pisciotta suggests that officials at Elmira first opened a gymnasium in 1890, thus seizing inmates' bodies as locations of athletic training earlier than McKelvey claims, and that baseball, basketball, track and field and football developed at Elmira in the late 1880s. Unlike McKelvey, Pisciotta is ambiguous as to whether or not these were innovations made by prisoners or by officials. Nevertheless, Pisciotta positions athletics as a new form of social control rather than as an element of hegemonic contest. Pisciotta, *Benevolent Repression: Social Control and the American Reformatory-Prison Movement* (New York: New York University Press, 1994), 24–25.

8. Blake McKelvey, *American Prisons: A History of Good Intentions* (Montclair, NJ: Patterson Smith, 1977), 137.

9. McKelvey, *American Prisons*, 261–62.

10. Rebecca McLennan's "Punishment's 'Square Deal': Prisoners and Their Keepers in 1920s New York," *Journal of Urban History* 29, no. 5 (July 2003): 597–619, also describes the innovation of structured leisure in prison regimes. Focusing on the varied sources of the new penal approaches, McLennan stresses that structured leisure in prison developed from prisoners' protests, labor union activity, and political movements, rather than simply from the prison officialdom.

11. Kimmel, *Manhood in America*, 80–95.

12. "So-Long, Dominoes, Hello Baseball!" *The Bulletin*, February 1933, 22. CASL Government Publications Room.

13. Hal Eble, *The Bulletin*, July 10, 1933.

14. Lee Simmons, *Assignment Huntsville: Memoirs of a Texas Prison Official* (Austin: University of Texas Press, 1957), 85, 86.

15. See McKelvey, *American Prisons*, 294; and Norbert Elias and Eric Dunning, *Quest for Excitement: Sport and Leisure in the Civilizing Process* (Oxford, England: Basil Blackwell, 1986), especially Elias's "Introduction," 19–62, and their jointly written "The Quest for Excitement in Leisure," 63–90. Rather than seeing violence as an essential component of the human condition increasingly contained by state institutions and practices of "civility," as Elias and Dunning suggest, I understand prison violence as *produced* and exacerbated by incarceration, which is then sublimated through self-discipline and sport.

16. Alison M. Wrynn, "The Recreation and Leisure Pursuits of Japanese Americans in WWII Internment Camps," in George Eisen and David K. Wiggins, eds., *Ethnicity and Sport in North American History and Culture* (Westport, CT: Greenwood Press, 1994), 117–31. George Eisen demonstrated that Nazis were active supporters of recreation, play, and leisure programs in Theresienstadt, the Jewish ghetto, because, Nazis reasoned, such programs "might have a calming effect on the agitated population." Eisen, *Children and Play in the Holocaust: Games among the Shadows* (Amherst: University of Massachusetts Press, 1988), 44; cited by Wrynn, 118.

17. *1938 Little Olympics Program*, "Baseball . . . ," pasted in the *Little Olympics Scrapbook, 1933–1941*. Not paginated. Archived in the San Francisco Olympic Club's records.

18. Yet as Judith Butler suggests, "Exceeding is not escaping, and the subject exceeds precisely that to which it is bound." Butler, *The Psychic Life of Power: Theories in Subjection* (Stanford, CA: Stanford University Press, 1997), 17–18.

19. For a Gramscian model of sport brilliantly applied to early-twentieth-century immigrant "assimilation" projects, see S. W. Pope, "Introduction," in S. W. Pope, ed., *The New American Sport History: Recent Approaches and Perspectives* (Urbana: University of Illinois Press, 1997).

20. Hugh Fullerton, quoted in Pope, *Patriotic Games: Sporting Tradition in the American Imagination, 1876–1926* (New York: Oxford University Press, 1997), 73.

21. James L. Johnston, *Prison Life Is Different* (Boston: Houghton Mifflin, 1937), 303.

22. *1938 Little Olympics Program*, "Baseball."

23. See "Baseball Program for San Quentin All-Stars v. Southern Pacific Rail Road Club," online at http://cprr.org/Museum/Ephemera/Baseball_SPRR_San_Quentin.html; also, *1938 Little Olympics Program*, "1937–38 Entertainment Reviews," not paginated. Pasted in the *Little Olympics Scrapbook, 1933–1941*, archived in the San Francisco Olympic Club's records. On sports and corporate paternalism, see Toby Moore, "Dismantling the South's Cotton Mill Village System," in Philip Scranton, ed., *The Second Wave: Southern Industrialization, from the 1940s to the 1970s* (Athens: University of Georgia Press, 2001), 114–45. On organized labor's use of sport in community formation, see Lizabeth Cohen, *Making a New Deal: Industrial Workers in Chicago, 1919–1939* (Cambridge: Cambridge University Press, 1990), 323–60.

24. Photograph of Chinese team, 1915. San Quentin Photo Album, Kent Room, MCFPL, accessed online July 26, 2010.

25. "Baseball Program for SQ All-Stars v. Southern Pacific Rail Road Club," Sunday, July 24, 1932, accessed online at http://cprr.org/Museum/Ephemera/Baseball_SPRR_San_Quentin.html.

26. Johnston, *Prison Life Is Different*, 305.

27. See the Olympic Club's homepage at http://www.olyclub.com/visitors/vis_home.asp. Thanks to Bill Callan, the Olympic Club's official historian, for allowing me access to their records. Regrettably, however, they would not permit reproduction of the photographs here.

28. Kenneth Lamott, *Chronicles of San Quentin: The Biography of a Prison* (New York: David McKay, 1961), 205. Olympic Club members seem to have been motivated by the upswell of urban, elite social reform movements in the Progressive Era striving to minimize urban tension and increase "Americanization" through a physical training and play movement. See Mark Dyreson, *Making the American Team: Sport, Culture, and the Olympic Experience* (Urbana: University of Illinois Press, 1998), esp. 20–22, 187–93.

29. Johnston, *Prison Life Is Different*, 306.

30. *Wall City News*, August 7, 1941, 1, CASL Government Publications Room, P875.W3. Texas Rodeo planners would have disagreed.

31. *Wall City News*, August 16, 1930, 4, CASL Government Publications Room, P875.W3.

32. Image A.1925.001.032, folio [17], 1930 San Quentin Field Meet Album, Leo Stanley Collection, Anne T. Kent Room, Marin County Library.

33. Numerous descriptions of the Little Olympics below draw from photographs collected in *The Little Olympics Scrapbook, 1933–1941*, compiled by Jack C. Patrick, and housed in the Olympic Club Records, Lakeside Club, San Francisco, CA. The scrapbook is not paginated.

34. Luis Alvarez, *The Power of the Zoot: Youth Culture and Resistance during World War II* (Berkeley: University of California Press, 2008).

35. *Wall City News*, Aug. 16, 1930, p. 4, CASL Government Publications Room, P875.W3.

36. "All San Quentin Thrills as Field Meet Nears," *The Bulletin*, July/August 1935, 28.

37. Lamott, *Chronicles of San Quentin*, 205.

38. From photographs collected in *The Little Olympics Scrapbook, 1933–1941*, Not paginated.

39. Jack C. Patrick, *The Little Olympics Scrapbook, 1933–1941*, Not paginated.

40. Lamott, *Chronicles of San Quentin*, 204–5.

41. Allen Gutman, *The Erotic in Sport* (New York: Columbia University Press, 1996).

42. "The Greatest Show on Earth!" *The Represa News*, July 5, 1935, p. 2 col. 3. CASL Government Publications Room, P800 R5.

43. The rodeo offers an opportunity to investigate processes of what Michelle Brown calls penal spectatorship and mass culture—replete with its many ambivalences—in the early decades of its formation. Brown, *The Culture of Punishment: Prison, Society, and Spectacle* (New York: New York University Press, 2008).

44. *Thirty Minutes*, Program 81, October 4, 1939.

45. *Thirty Minutes*, Program 80, September 27, 1939.

46. *Official Program Souvenir of the 8th Annual Prison Rodeo*, 5, TSLAC, Box 1998/038-404, Folder "Rodeo Program 1939."

47. Eric Hobsbawm and Terrence Ranger, eds., *The Invention of Tradition* (New York: Cambridge University Press, 1992); Richard R. Flores, *Remembering the Alamo: Memory, Modernity, and the Master Symbol* (Austin: University of Texas Press, 2002). On the political significance of the cowboy image in the Depression, see James N. Gregory, *American Exodus: The Dust Bowl Migration and Okie Culture in California* (New York: Oxford University Press, 1989), 222–38; Bill Malone, *Country Music, U.S.A.*, 2d ed. (Austin: University of Texas Press, 2002), 137–75.

48. Simmons, *Assignment Huntsville*, 111.

49. *Official Program Souvenir of the 12th Annual Prison Rodeo*, TSLAC, Box 1998/038-404, Folder "Rodeo Program 1942" (no pagination in program).

50. *Official Program Souvenir of the 8th Annual Prison Rodeo*, 13. TSLAC, Box 1998/038-404, Folder "Rodeo Program 1939."

51. Ibid., 11.

52. Mary Waurine Hunter, "No Holds Barred: Best Possible Morale Builder is Bone-Cracking Prison Rodeo," *Texas Parade*, November 1941, 16–17, 25. Archived at CAH.

53. *Thirty Minutes*, Program 79, September 20, 1939.

54. *Thirty Minutes*, Program 22, August 17, 1938. Bold in original.

55. *Thirty Minutes*, Program 20, August 3, 1938.

56. Elizabeth Atwood Lawrence, *Rodeo: An Anthropologist Looks at the Wild and the Tame* (Knoxville: University of Tennessee Press, 1982), 208–10.

57. Dick Hebdige, *Subculture: The Meaning of Style* (New York: Routledge, 1997 [1979]). In the context of a judged and regimented rodeo event, *style* mattered for scoring and for prestige. Bodily *style* (agility, timing, improvisation, rather than the clothes that Hebdige emphasizes), however, was not intrinsically subversive, since it was the element by which prison athletes were ranked, judged, and applauded by prisoners, fans, and administrators alike.

58. Hunter, "No Holds Barred." "Best Possible Morale Builder is Bone-Cracking Prison Rodeo," *Texas Parade* 6, no. 6 (November 1941): 16–17, 25. Archived at CAH

59. Gena Caponi-Tabery, "Jump for Joy: Jump Blues, Dance, and Basketball in 1930s African America," in John Bloom and Michael Nevin Willard, eds., *Sports Matters: Race, Recreation, and Culture* (New York: New York University Press, 2002), 39–74, esp. 57–58. Caponi-Tabery borrows a term from composer Olly Wilson, which he called a "soul focal moment." According to Caponi-Tabery, a soul focal moment

> is not gratuitous showmanship—its artistry is functional and accomplishes what the moment requires, but with a degree and twist of virtuosity that is unnecessary and unexpected. The audience gasps in surprise, exclaims with pleasure, bursts into applause, and audience and player are united in appreciation for the endless inventiveness of human expression. The soul focal moment is showy, to be sure, but this is not a one-person show, for the soul focal moment elevates a community, and its master is the ultimate team player.

60. Alan M. Kline, *Baseball on the Border: A Tale of Two Laredos* (Princeton, NJ: Princeton University Press, 1997), xiv.

61. B. Jacoby and H. McGillacutty, "A Look Back at a Texas Tradition," in *Clock Wise*, November 1986, 9–11. TSLAC, Box 1998/038-404: Clippings, Brochures, Programs for the Rodeo, Folder 1, "Clippings about the Rodeo, 1931–1986."

62. *Thirty Minutes*, Program 132, October 2, 1940.

63. The perversity of a Juneteenth celebration behind prison walls bears note. Here was a celebration of the emancipation of African Americans from slavery within an explicitly racist location of forced labor and unfreedom. Juneteenth and other celebrations had a great deal in common with holiday revelry on plantations of the antebellum South.

64. *The Echo*, October 1935, p. 10, col. 4, TSLAC microfilm Reel 1 (June 1933– December 1948). Rob Ruck also notes that many black baseball fans dressed very well, to see and be seen, at Negro League games. *Sandlot Seasons: Sport in Black Pittsburg* (Urbana: University of Illinois Press, 1987).

65. *Thirty Minutes*, Program 64, June 7, 1939.

66. *The Echo*, July–August 1939, p. 8 col. 1, TSLAC microfilm Reel 1 (June 1933– December 1948).

67. Juneteenth was too important to be canceled because of weather. Perhaps this was so because of its singularity, as opposed to the more common occurrence of white baseball games.

68. *The Echo*, June 1940, p. 1 col. 5, p. 7 col. 4, TSLAC microfilm Reel 1 (June 1933– December 1948).

69. "Huntsville, TX." The Handbook of Texas Online. http://www.tsha.utexas.edu/handbook/online/articles/view/HH/heh3.html (accessed December 12, 2002).

70. David Waldstreicher, *In the Midst of Perpetual Fetes: The Making of American Nationalism* (Chapel Hill: University of North Carolina Press, 1997), 350.

71. Dyreson, *Making the American Team*, 38.

72. Clara Phillips, "Greek Games in San Quentin," *The Bulletin*, February 1933, 9, CASL Government Publications Room.

73. Ibid.

74. Dyreson, *Making the American Team,* 110.

75. Phillips, "Greek Games in San Quentin."

76. See the January 7, 1944, testimony of Elvira Clift, Tehachapi Sewing Room Warder, Volume XI: Witnesses Before the Governor's Committee on Investigation of the California Institution for Women at Tehachapi, CSA, Earl Warren Papers—Governor's Committee on Penal Affairs—1943–44. F3640:966.

77. *Official Souvenir Program for the Eleventh Annual Prison Rodeo*, 1941, 44. TSLAC, Box 1998/038-404, Folder "Prison Rodeo Program, 1941."

78. Tehachapi's athletics program was modest. Like the Goree Farm, they had occasional dances, but inmates also told officials that they wanted a tennis court and a baseball diamond. Volume XI: Witnesses Before the Governor's Committee on Investigation of the California Institution for Women at Tehachapi, CSA, Earl Warren Papers—Governor's Committee on Penal Affairs—1943–44. F3640:966.

79. *Thirty Minutes*, Program 21, August 10, 1938.

80. See *The Echo*, August 1935, p. 1 col. 2, p. 2 col. 1, for a description of the Fourth of July dance.

81. The prison used a binary opposition between public and private spheres to distinguish the gendered performances of sport versus dance, but there are clearly highly erotic components of masculine sports, too. Guttman, *The Erotic in Sports*; Elias, "Introduction" in Elias and Eric Dunning, *The Quest for Excitement.*

82. *Thirty Minutes*, Program 21, August 10, 1938.

83. Tera W. Hunter, *To 'Joy My Freedom: Southern Black Women's Lives and Labors after the Civil War* (Cambridge, MA: Harvard University Press, 1997), 168–86; Nigel Thrift, "The Still Point: Resistance, Expressive Embodiment, and Dance," in Steve Pile and Michael Keith, eds., *Geographies of Resistance* (London: Routledge, 1997), 124–51, esp. 147.

84. *The Echo*, August 1935, p. 1 col. 2, p. 2 col. 1, TSLAC microfilm Reel 1 (June 1933–December 1948).

85. *Thirty Minutes*, Program 21, August 10, 1938.

86. Hattie Ellis, Lavena Austin, Mozelle Stewart, Ella Mae Fitzpatrick, Gene Raymond, Jimmie Lee Hart, and Doris McMurray, "Cap'n Don't 'Low No Truckin'-Round in Here," and the Lomax field notes, May 11–14, 1939, State Penitentiary and Goree Farm. John and Ruby Lomax 1939 Southern Recording Tour, available online at http://memory.loc.gov/ammem/lohtml/lohome.html. Both accessed March 31, 2009.

87. *Thirty Minutes*, Program 21, August 10, 1938.

88. Ibid.

89. Estelle B. Freedman notes that fears of interracial lesbian sex prompted the racial segregation of women prisoners in New York's Bedford Hills prison. While the institution had previously been racially integrated, in accordance with the warden's principles on racial equality, a 1915 legislative investigation found this to be a serious problem. But more than racial antagonism, of which Freedman found little evidence, legislators' main concern was that black and white women were having sex with each other. Freedman, *Their Sisters' Keepers: Women's Prison Reform in America, 1830–1930* (Ann Arbor: University of Michigan Press, 1984), 139–40.

90. See Cheryl D. Hicks, "'Bright and Good Looking Colored Girl': Black Women's Sexuality and 'Harmful Intimacy' in Early-Twentieth-Century New York," *Journal of the History of Sexuality* 18, no. 3 (2009): 418–56; Regina G. Kunzel, "Situating Sex: Prison Sexual Culture in the Mid-Twentieth-Century United States," *GLQ* 8, no. 3 (2002): 293–70; Estelle B. Freedman, "The Prison Lesbian: Race, Class, and the Construction of the Aggressive Female Homosexual, 1915–1965," *Feminist Studies* 22, no. 2 (Summer 1996). Kunzel describes numerous mid-twentieth-century prison authors who wrote about interracial lesbian relationships in prisons, and in which white women actively sought out black sexual partners. Contemporary writers rationalized white women's desire for black partners by explaining that white women saw black women as masculine, and therefore as worthwhile sex partners. Estelle B. Freedman writes, "In this interpretation, white women were not really lesbians, for they were attracted to men, for whom Black women temporarily substituted." Cited in Kunzel, 262. It is likely that Goree matron M. V. Heath was familiar with this literature, and the cultural forms it expressed, and thus even more firmly justified racial segregation for women in this sexualized atmosphere. Little is said by any of these authors, however, about the black women's feelings and desires in the matter. See also Judith Halberstam, *Female Masculinity* (Durham, NC: Duke University Press, 1998).

CHAPTER 7

1. Augustus "Track Horse" Haggerty, "Mama, Mama," *Big Brazos: Texas Prison Recordings, 1933 and 1934*; "San Quentin Slanguage," *Western Folklore* 17, no. 2 (1955): 135–36; Jimpson and singers, "The Murderer's Home," *Prison Songs*, Vol. 1: *Murderous Home—Historical Recordings from Parchman Farm, 1947–48* (Rounder Records, 1997).

2. This is particularly true of capital punishment literature. Charles J. Ogletree Jr. and Austin Sarat's *From the Lynch Mob to the Killing State* does well to stress the connection between nineteenth-century extralegal lynch violence and twenty-first-century legal execution, yet analyzes capital punishment as if it exists in isolation from other carceral forms. Decoupling lynching, ordinary punishment, and the death penalty has allowed many scholars to neglect a broader critique of prisons. Execution is but one element within the necropolitical regime of American incarceration and its role in modern and late modern state formation. Death penalty scholars would do well to reckon with the many forms of social, civil, and biological death behind bars. Charles Ogletree Jr. and Austin Sarat, "Introduction," *From the Lynch Mob to the Killing State: Race and the Death Penalty in America* (New York: New York University Press, 2006), 14. Angela Y. Davis and Eduardo Mendieta, *Abolition Democracy: Beyond Empire, Prisons, and Torture* (New York: Seven Stories Press, 2005), esp. 95–97. For an important critique within death penalty literature, Timothy V. Kaufman-Osborn, "A Critique of Contemporary Death Penalty Abolitionism," *Punishment and Society* 8, no. 3 (2006): 365–83. On prison abolition, Angela Y. Davis, *Are Prisons Obsolete?* (New York: Seven Stories Press, 2003); Joy James, "Introduction," in Joy James, ed., *The New Abolitionists: (Neo)Slave Narratives and Contemporary Prison Writings* (Albany: State University of New York Press, 2005); Dylan Rodríguez, *Forced Passages: Imprisoned Radical Intellectuals and the U.S. Prison Regime* (Minneapolis: University of Minnesota Press, 2006), esp.185–222.

3. My thoughts are indebted to geographer Ruth Wilson Gilmore's definition of "racism" as "the state-sanctioned and/or extra-legal production and exploitation of group differentiated vulnerabilities to premature death." See her "Race and Globalization," in R. J. Johnson, Peter J. Taylor, Michael J. Watts, eds., *Geographies of Global Change: Remapping the World*, 2d ed. (Malden, MA: Blackwell, 2002), esp. 261.

4. 8 September 1930 Meeting of the Texas Prison Board. Texas State Library and Archives Commission, Documents of the Texas Prison Board, Minutes and Meeting Files, June 1927–December 1941, Box 1998/038-8, Folder: Minutes, August–November 1930; also, Annual report of the Texas Prison Board, 1930, "Mortality Statistics," 7-D.

5. Ethan Blue, "'A Dark Cloud Will Go Over': Pain, Death, and Silence in Texas Prisons in the 1930s," *Humanities Research* 14, no. 2 (2007): 5–24; Giorgio Agamben, *Homo Sacer: Sovereign Power and Bare Life*, trans. Daniel Heller-Roazen (Stanford, CA: Stanford University Press, 1996).

6. William D. Carrigan, *The Making of a Lynching Culture: Violence and Vigilantism in Central Texas, 1836–1916* (Urbana: University of Illinois Press, 2004); David Garland, "Penal Excess and Surplus Meaning: Public Torture Lynchings in Twentieth-Century America," *Law and Society Review* 39, no. 4 (2005); Grace Elizabeth Hale, *Making Whiteness: The Culture of Segregation in the South, 1890–1940* (New York: Vintage Books, 1998); James W. Marquart, Sheldon Ekland-Olson, and Jonathan R. Sorensen, *The Rope, the Chair, and the Needle: Capital Punishment in Texas, 1923–1990* (Austin: University of Texas Press, 1994); W. Fitzhugh Brundage, *Lynching in the New South: Georgia and Virginia, 1880–1930* (Urbana: University of Illinois Press, 1993).

7. Numbers are drawn from James W. Marquart, Sheldon Ekland-Olson, and Jonathan R. Sorenson, *The Rope, the Chair, and the Needle: Capital Punishment in Texas, 1923–1990* (Austin: University of Texas Press, 1994), appendix B; Sheila O'Hare, Irene Berry, and Jesse Silva, *Legal Executions in California: A Comprehensive Registry, 1851–2005* (Jeffer-

son, NC: MacFarland, 2006). See also Bureau of Justice Statistics, "Number of Persons Executed in the United States, 1930–2005," available online at http://www.ojp.usdoj.gov/bjs/glance/tables/exetab.htm (accessed April 17, 2006).

8. Leo L. Stanley, *Men at Their Worst* (New York: D. Appleton-Century, 1940), 310.

9. Theodore Hamm, *Rebel and a Cause: Caryl Chessman and the Politics of the Death Penalty in Postwar California, 1948–1974* (Berkeley: University of California Press, 2001), 22.

10. C. W. Potter, "A History of Influenza," *Journal of Applied Microbiology* 91 (2001): 572–79.

11. Claudio Lomnitz, *Death and the Idea of Mexico* (New York: Zone Books, 2005), 16.

12. Quoted in Bruce Jackson, ed., *Wake Up Dead Man: Afro-American Worksongs from Texas Prisons* (Cambridge, MA: Harvard University Press, 1972), 3.

13. Lankford, in Studs Terkel, ed., *Hard Times: An Oral History of the Great Depression* (New York: Washington Square Press, 1970), 407.

14. On medicine in prison as metaphor and practice, David J. Rothman, *Conscience and Convenience: The Asylum and Its Alternatives in Progressive America* (New York: Aldine de Gruyter, 2002 [1980]), 56; Ethan Blue, "The Strange Career of Leo Stanley: Remaking Manhood and Medicine at San Quentin State Penitentiary, 1913–1951," *Pacific Historical Review* 78, no. 2 (2009); Joe Sim, *Medical Power in Prisons: The Prison Medical Service in England, 1774–1989* (Buckingham, England: Open University Press, 1990); Douglas C. McDonald, "Medical Care in Prisons," in Michael Tonry and Joan Petersilia, eds., *Crime and Justice. Vol. 26, Prisons* (Chicago: University of Chicago Press, 1999), 427–78.

15. See *Report of the Penitentiary Investigating Committee, 1910*; and *Report of the Penitentiary Investigating Committee, 1913*, CAH, University of Texas.

16. Paul Lucko, "Prison Farms, Walls, and Society: Punishment and Politics in Texas, 1848–1910" (Ph.D. dissertation, University of Texas at Austin, 1999); Robert Reps Perkinson, "The Birth of the Texas Prison Empire, 1865–1915" (Ph.D. dissertation, Yale University, 2001); Matthew J. Mancini, *One Dies, Get Another: Convict Leasing in the American South, 1866–1928* (Columbia: University of South Carolina Press, 1996).

17. Annual report, 1935, 108.

18. Annual report, 1941, 7–8.

19. Edward H. Beardsley, *A History of Neglect: Health Care for Blacks and Mill Workers in the Twentieth-Century South* (Knoxville: University of Tennessee Press, 1987); Samuel Kelton Roberts Jr., *Infectious Fear: Politics, Disease, and the Health Effects of Segregation* (Chapel Hill: University of North Carolina Press, 2009).

20. Leo L. Stanley, "Tuberculosis in San Quentin," read before the California Medical Association, 67th Annual Session, Pasadena, May 9–12, 1938. Reprinted in *California and Western Medicine* 49, no. 6 (December 1938) and 50, no. 1 (January 1939): 10, 11. Bancroft Library, University of California at Berkeley.

21. Leo Leonidas Stanley, M.D., "Twenty Years at San Quentin," *The Centaur of Alpha Kappa Kappa* 39 no. 2 (January 1934). California State Library, California History Room.

22. See Shelly Bookspan, *A Germ of Goodness: The California State Prison System, 1851–1944* (Lincoln: University of Nebraska Press, 1991), 69–93; Richard Morales, "History of the California Institution for Women, 1927–1960: A Women's Regime" (Ph.D. dissertation, University of California at Riverside, 1980); Anne M. Butler, *Gendered Justice in the American West: Women Prisoners in Men's Penitentiaries* (Urbana: University of Illinois

Press, 1997); Estelle B. Freedman, *Their Sisters' Keepers: Women's Prison Reform in America, 1830–1930* (Ann Arbor: University of Michigan Press, 1981); Nicole Hahn Rafter, *Partial Justice: Women in State Prisons, 1800–1935* (Boston: Northeastern University Press, 1985).

23. Austin H. MacCormick, ed., *Handbook of American Prisons and Reformatories*, 5th ed. Vol. 2, *Pacific Coast States, 1942* (Lebanon, PA: The Osbourne Association, 1942), xxiv.

24. L. L. Stanley, "An Analysis of One Thousand Testicular Substance Implantations," *Endocrinology* 6 (1922): 787–94, esp. 789. Ethan Blue, "'A Dark Cloud Will Go Over'" and "The Strange Career of Leo Stanley."

25. Blue, "The Strange Career of Leo Stanley."

26. 4 September 1939 Minutes of the Texas Prison Board, Box 1998/038-8, Documents of the Texas Prison Board, Minutes and Meeting Files, June 1927–December 1941, Folder July–November 1939, TSLAC.

27. Annual report, 1939, 118.

28. 1 July 1940 Minutes of the Texas Prison Board, Box 1998/038-8, Documents of the Texas Prison Board, Minutes and Meeting Files, June 1927–December 1941, Folder January–September 1940, TSLAC.

29. Herbert S. Klein, *A Population History of the United States* (Cambridge: Cambridge University Press, 2004), graph A.4, 259. See appendix: Mortality Rates in California Texas and Prisons, per thousand inmates.

30. I suggest that this is conservative because many of the youngest white prisoners were concentrated at the Walls, which probably diminished the mortality rates there.

31. Forrest E. Linder and Robert D. Grove, for the Federal Security Agency, United States Public Health Service, National Office of Vital Statistics, *Vital Statistics Rates in the United States, 1900–1940* (Washington, DC: United States Government Printing Office, 1947), 159. Prisoner mortality rates and age categorizations from Statistical Record Ledgers, 1998/038-241, Texas State Archives.

32. Gilmore, "Race and Globalization," 261.

33. Calculated from *Texas Statistical Registers*, TSLAC, 1998/038-240; 1998/038-241; 1998/038-242.

34. The numbers are small in a given year—though not to families of the dead—and must be treated with caution. The relatively small number of Mexicans in the prison and among the dead also poses a statistical problem of sorts, since a handful of deaths—from an escape attempt, for example—in a certain year radically transforms mortality rates.

35. Calculated from biennial reports and from Forrest E. Linder and Robert D. Grove, *Vital Statistics Rates in the United States, 1900–1940* (Washington, DC: United States Government Printing Office, 1947), table 17: "Specific Death Rates for Selected Causes, by Race: Death Registration States of 1900 for 1900–1940," 305.

36. Annual report, 1938, 192–93.

37. The development of pathology signaled a more invasive state, to better regulate life. Sharon Patricia Holland, *Raising the Dead: Readings of Death and (Black) Subjectivity* (Durham, NC: Duke University Press, 2000), 30.

38. Roberts, *Infectious Fear*, 33, fig. 1–10, 36.

39. Nayan Shah, *Contagious Divides: Epidemics and Race in San Francisco's Chinatown* (Berkeley: University of California Press, 2001); Roberts, *Infectious Fear*, 39–40.

40. Calculated from biennial reports and from Forrest E. Linder and Robert D. Grove, *Vital Statistics Rates in the United States, 1900–1940* (Washington, DC: United States

Government Printing Office, 1947), table 17, "Specific Death Rates for Selected Causes, by Race: Death Registration States of 1900 for 1900–1940," 305. Note that Mexicans are counted among nonwhites in these two years of the *Vital Statistics Rates*.

41. Calculated from physicians' reports included in biennial reports, and from *Vital Statistics Rates*, table 17: "Specific Death Rates for Selected Causes, by Race: Death Registration States of 1900 for 1900–1940," 299.

42. See, for example, the 5 May 1941 prison board meeting, which ruled that six prisoners would be given ninety days' credit on their sentences for treating a prisoner with spinal meningitis. Documents of the Texas Prison Board, Minutes and Meeting Files, June 1927–December 1941, Box 1998/038-8, Folder November 1940–May 1941, TSLAC.

43. It seems that the spatial distribution of prisoners in the field and plantation system of Texas prisons produced more lethal violence than did the Big House model, where the violence was that of spatial control and architecture rather than weaponry. This is some validation of Foucault's point about spatial control and the diminution of recognizable physical violence.

44. The following description comes from Hugh Adams Inquest, No. 1967, December 29, 1931, MCCO. Also, San Quentin Board Prison Director's Minutes, CSA, Department of Corrections Records, F3717:1006.

45. Connolly testimony, Adams Inquest, 3.

46. The following description is from Arthur C. Snead Inquest, No. 1874, September 26, 1929, MCCO.

47. C. F. Cobb testimony, Snead Inquest, No. 1874, MCCO.

48. George W. Lynch testimony, Snead Inquest, No. 1874, MCCO.

49. Leo L. Stanley, *Men at Their Worst* (New York: D. Appleton-Century, 1940), 390.

50. Michel Foucault, *Society Must Be Defended: Lectures at the Collège de France, 1975–1976* (New York: Picador, 2003), 248.

51. Emile Durkheim's 1897 study identified suicide with modernity, wherein diminished social cohesion enables the taking of one's own life. The "freest" people—those without traditional social ties—he believed, were the most likely to kill themselves. Sigmund Freud in 1917 argued that suicide was, in fact, aggression, the hatred against an oppressor turned inward. See Émile Durkheim, *Suicide*, trans. John A. Spaulding and George Simpson (London: Routledge Classics, 2002 [1897]). Also, Alvin Poussaint and Amy Alexander, "Suicide in Black and White: Theories and Statistics," in Lewis R. Gordon and Jane Anna Gordon, eds., *The Blackwell Companion to African-American Studies* (Malden, MA: Blackwell, 2006), 265–78, esp. 269.

52. Poussaint and Alexander, "Suicide in Black and White," 270.

53. Donald R. Cressey, "Foreword" to the 1958 reissue of Donald Clemmer, *The Prison Community* (New York: Holt, Rinehart, and Winston, 1958 [1940]), ix.

54. Annual report, 1936, 161. See also Abigail Groves, "Blood on the Walls: Self-Mutilation in Prison," *Australian and New Zealand Journal of Criminology* 37, no. 1 (2004): 49–64.

55. For data on fractured arms in Texas, annual report, 1940, 188.

56. The description of Nartates' death is drawn from Board of Prison Director's Minutes, February 10, 1940, 297–98, CSA, Department of Corrections Records, F3717:1009; Aneleto Nartates Inquest, No. 2074, January 19, 1940, MCCO; San Quentin Prison Cemetery List, CSA.

57. Reynolds testimony, Nartates Inquest, No. 2074, 8.

58. Reynolds testimony, Nartates Inquest.

59. Les (aka Wes) Shuttleworth, Inquest No. 1994, May 15, 1933, MCCO.

60. Karla F. C. Holloway, *Passed On: African American Mourning Stories—A Memorial* (Durham, NC: Duke University Press, 2002). Recent research has linked confrontation with criminal justice to suicide. In "Suicide in Black and White," Poussaint and Alexander cite a 1970 New Orleans study showing that nearly 50 percent of black men who committed suicide had a history of conflict with local authorities, notably the police, while only 10 percent of whites who committed suicide had similar confrontations. Further, in 1989, Lindsay Hayes found that suicide was the leading cause of death in American jails, while an earlier study found that the suicide rate in detention facilities was roughly nine times higher than it was in the general population. This led Poussaint and Alexander to conclude that "the possibility of suicide or suicidal behavior increases after individuals come into contact with the criminal justice system." See "Suicide in Black and White," 275. On suicide in prison, see Alison Leibling, "Prisoner Suicide and Prison Coping," in Tonry and Petersilia, eds., *Crime and Justice*. Vol. 26, *Prisons*, 283–359.

61. The description of Davis's escape/suicide is drawn from the "Investigation by Mrs. C. A. Teagle on July 29, 1940, at Retrieve State Farm of the Death of Inmate Cecil Davis, No. 94887," and Teagle's 2 August 1940 report to the prison board, O'Daniel Records, Box 2001/138–110, Folder Texas Prison Board Joint Meeting with Texas A&M Board of Directors, TSLAC.

62. Robert T. Chase, "Civil Rights on the Cell Block: Race, Reform, and Violence in Texas Prisons and the Nation, 1945–1990" (Ph.D. dissertation, University of Maryland at College Park, 2009), 59.

63. "Quentin Convict Hangs Self," *San Francisco Examiner*, February 7, 1939, n.p., Marin County Free Public Library, Anne T. Kent California Room, Clippings File: Box: San Quentin, Folder: San Quentin Prison—History, 1930s.

64. December 30, 1940, meeting. Board of Prison Directors, January 16, 17 Minutes, 1941, 135. CSA, F3717:1011.

65. The communication between H. E. Moore and Rosie Wilson and the letter from W. P. Barber to Governor Allred are in TSLAC, Allred Box 1985/024-96, Folder: Texas Prison System, General Correspondence and Proclamations, June 1937. Following paragraphs draw upon these sources.

66. Annual report of the Texas Prison Board, 1937, 180.

67. August 27, 1930, letter from Simmons to J. A. Collier, Moody Box 43, Folder: Proclamations for Various Convicts, August 15–November 14, 1930, TSLAC.

68. C. V. Compton, *Flood Lights behind Gray Walls: An Exposé of Activities; The Flaming Truth Revealed by Officials and Inmates of the Texas Penitentiary System* (1942), 6, 4. CAH, Austin, Texas.

69. Holloway, *Passed On*, 29.

70. Mrs. Emma Tinney to Moody, Folder Texas Prison System, October 7–20, 1930, Governor Moody Records 1984/24, Box 45, TSLAC.

71. Quoted in Marquart, Ekland-Olson, and Sorensen, *The Rope, the Chair, and the Needle*, 30.

72. Marquart, Ekland-Olson, and Sorensen, *The Rope, the Chair, and the Needle*, 30.

73. See Everett Gilbert Parman, #62480, San Quentin Execution Files Box 3, F3918:126.

74. The 1939 Annual Report listed "Special Death Expenses" among the costs in the General Administrative section. Burial outfits came to $220.81, coffins cost $379 that year, and $195 was allocated for "inquests," though the actual investigations over killing were unnamed. Annual report of the Texas Prison Board, 1939, 49.

75. Annual report, 1940, 175–77.

76. See "Non-current Appropriations to Date," annual report, 1941, 20, which listed A-735 "Returning Bodies of Deceased Convicts to Indigent Relatives for Burial": $487.52, and B-622 "Returning Bodies of Deceased Convicts to Indigent Relatives for Burial": $600.00. On grave markers, see "Special Death Expenses," in the 1941 Annual Report, 29.

77. George Nevin, "Ten Years Later, Caretaker Back at Prison Cemetery," March 1, 1975. Folder: San Quentin Prison—History, 1900–1929, Box, San Quentin Prison, Clippings files, MCFPL.

78. See "Chief Surgeon's Report," tenth annual report of the Board of Prison Terms and Paroles, July 1, 1940–June 30, 1941, 28. CASL Government Publications Room.

79. Merle Haggard, "Green, Green Grass of Home," *Prison* (EMI, 2001).

80. Robert Perkinson, *Texas Tough: The Rise of America's Prison Empire* (New York: Metropolitan Books, 2010), 17.

81. Annual report, 1930, 2-G.

CHAPTER 8

1. "Should a Been on the River in 1910," in Bruce Jackson, ed., *Wake Up Dead Man: Afro-American Worksongs from Texas Prisons* (Cambridge, MA: Harvard University Press, 1972), 75.

2. David J. Rothman, *Conscience and Convenience: The Asylum and Its Alternatives in Progressive America*, rev. ed. (New York: Aldine de Gruyter, 2002 [1980]), 173.

3. Among histories of parole and pardon, Sheldon L. Messinger, "Strategies of Control" (Ph.D. dissertation, University of California at Los Angeles, 1969); Sheldon L. Messinger, John E. Berecochea, David Rauma, and Richard A. Berk, "The Foundations of Parole in California," *Law & Society Review* 19, no. 1 (1985): 69–106; Natalie Zemon Davis, *Fiction in the Archives: Pardon Tales and Their Tellers in Sixteenth-Century France* (Stanford, CA: Stanford University Press, 1987); Jonathon Simon, *Poor Discipline: Parole and the Social Control of the Underclass, 1890–1990* (Chicago: University of Chicago Press, 1993); Carolyn Strange, ed., *Qualities of Mercy: Justice, Punishment, and Discretion* (Vancouver: University of British Columbia Press, 1996); Martha A. Myers, *Race, Labor, and Punishment in the New South* (Columbus: Ohio State University Press, 1998); Vivien M. L. Miller, *Crime, Sexual Violence, and Clemency: Florida's Pardon Board and Penal System in the Progressive Era* (Gainesville: University Press of Florida, 2000); Stephen Garton, "Managing Mercy: African Americans, Parole, and Paternalism in the Georgia Prison System, 1919–1945," *Journal of Social History* 36, no. 3 (2003): 675–99. On sovereignty, Giorgio Agamben, *Homo Sacer: Sovereign Power and Bare Life*, trans. Daniel Heller-Roazen (Stanford, CA: Stanford University Press, 1996). Studies of parole can reveal the macro-politics of political economics and state formations, which speak to the timing of incarceration and release practices (as in Myers and Simon); the micro-level theatrics of a parole board meeting, with performances of contrition structured by board members' gender, class, and race

expectations (as in Davis, Garton, and Miller); and the meso-level politics of institutional control (as in Simon and Messinger). For a fine study on the stigmatization of recent ex-prisoners and difficulty in finding employment, Devah Pager, *Marked: Race, Crime, and Finding Work in an Era of Mass Incarceraion* (Chicago: University of Chicago Press, 2007).

4. *The Attorney General's Survey of Release Procedures,* vol. 4,(Washington, DC: United States Government Printing Office, 1939), 141.

5. Prison Industries Reorganization Administration, "The Prison Labor Problem in Texas," 1937, 68–69, quoted in *The Attorney General's Survey of Release Procedures,* vol. 1 (Washington, DC: United States Government Printing Office, 1939), 1,071, n. 28.

6. Parole decisions demonstrate forms of what Foucault termed "biopolitical control," and the processes he left unaddressed in modern liberal state power, which Mbembe calls "necropolitics." That parole and capital punishment were solidified and centralized in California in the same year bespeaks the interweaving of these twined powers of state-hood—executing with the one hand and releasing surveilled and self-controlling living subjects with the other. Parole and death are not commonly understood as joined control mechanisms, but should be.

7. Simon, *Poor Discipline,* 46, 47, 48 n. 10, 53.

8. California BPTP, 1932–1933, 2. Quoted in Messinger, "Strategies of Control," 61.

9. California BPTP, 1932–1933, 11. Quoted in Messinger, "Strategies of Control," 61.

10. Simon, *Poor Discipline,* 49

11. Second annual report BPTP, July 1, 1932–June 30, 1933, 16; Ninth annual report of the BPTP, July 1, 1939–June 30, 1940, 12.

12. This suggests greater applicability of Marxist criminologists Georg Rusche and Otto Kircheimer's thesis (that capitalist prisons become repositories of surplus workers in economic crises) to California prisons than to southern prisons. Stephen Garton's and Martha A. Myers's studies of Georgia critiqued Rusche and Kircheimer's position, noting that while incarceration increased in depressions, so too did parole. See Rusche and Kircheimer, *Punishment and Social Structure* (New Brunswick, NJ: Transaction, 2003 [1939]); Garton, "Managing Mercy," and Myers, *Race, Labor, and Punishment.* Also Richard A. Berk, Sheldon L. Messinger, David Rauma, and John E. Berecochea, "Prisons as Self-Regulating Systems: A Comparison of Historical Patterns in California for Male and Female Offenders," *Law and Society Review* 17, no. 4 (1983): 547–86.

13. *State Board of Prison Directors, 1930,* 98, in Simon, *Poor Discipline,* 60.

14. These numbers are gathered from the chart "California State Prison and Parole Population, 1918–1942," Biennial report of the State Board of Prison Directors, 1940–1942, 19; and from California BPTP annual reports, 1932–1942.

15. This synthesis is drawn broadly from Paul M. Lucko, "Board of Pardons and Paroles," *Handbook of Texas Online,* s.v. "Board of Pardons and Paroles," http://www.tsha.utexas.edu/handbook/online/articles/BB/mdbjq.html (accessed December 20, 2006); Parole Division, "History of Parole in Texas," http://www.tdcj.state.tx.us/parole/parole-history.htm (accessed July 31, 2008).

16. Robert Perkinson, *Texas Tough: The Rise of America's Prison Empire* (New York: Metropolitan Books, 2010), 203.

17. Numbers are gathered from annual reports and combine furloughs, reprieves, paroles, and full and conditional pardons. When not given in annual reports, average daily populations were calculated from the populations on the last day of each month.

18. California Penal Code 1929, 705, in Lloyd L. Voigt, *History of the California State Correctional Administration from 1930 to 1948* (San Francisco, 1949), 62.

19. California Statutes 1929, chap. 300, p. 605, in Lloyd L. Voigt, *History of the California State Correctional Administration from 1930 to 1948* (San Francisco, 1949), 62–63.

20. First report of the BPTP, 1931–1932, 26–28.

21. Rothman, *Conscience and Convenience*, 162–63; Miller, *Crime, Sexual Violence, and Clemency*, 53–84.

22. First Report of the BPTP, 1931–1932, 23–24; "Neumiller and Beardslee Firm History," online at http://neumiller.com/history.html (accessed August 6, 2008); also, "The Political Graveyard: Index to Politicians," http://politicalgraveyard.com/bio/nemanich-neveu.html (accessed August 6, 2008); "San Francisco Public Schools: War Production Training Program," ca. 1942, at http://www.books-about-california.com/Pages/War_Production_Training.html (accessed August 6, 2008); also http://www.usmarshals.gov/district/ca-c/general/history.htm (accessed August 11, 2008).

23. Simon, *Poor Discipline*, 123.

24. *Attorney General's Survey of Release Procedures,* vol. 1 (Washington, DC: United States Government Printing Office, 1939), 175.

25. *The Attorney General's Survey of Release Procedures,* vol. 4 (Washington, DC: United States Government Printing Office, 1939), 470–72, 486.

26. Rothman, *Conscience and Convenience*, 193–97, esp. 196.

27. June 11–12, 1935, Minutes, 283–84, and June 25, 26, 1935, Minutes, 304. San Quentin Minutes of the BPTP, F3717:1073. CSA.

28. October 1, 2, 1935, Minutes, 403. San Quentin Minutes of the BPTP, F3717:1073. CSA.

29. See the transcript of "The Shipboard Murder Case," esp. Ramsay testimony, 31–32, housed at the Bancroft Library. Online at http://www.archive.org/stream/laborradical-ismoosteirich/laborradicalismoosteirich_djvu.txt (accessed January 5, 2009).

30. Second annual report BPTP, July 1, 1932–June 30, 1933, 3.

31. Fourth annual report BPTP, July 1, 1934–June 30, 1935, 21.

32. Fourth annual report BPTP, July 1, 1934–June 30, 1935, 21.

33. Fourth annual report BPTP, July 1, 1934–June 30, 1935, 21.

34. *The Attorney General's Survey of Release Procedures,* vol. 1, 156.

35. Fourth annual report of the BPTP, July 1, 1934–June 30, 1935, 21.

36. Daniel S. Medwed, "The Innocent Prisoners' Dilemma: Consequences of Failing to Admit Guilt at Parole Hearings," University of Utah Legal Studies Paper No. 06-05; *Iowa Law Review* 93 (2008): 491–557.

37. Fifth annual report of the BPTP, July 1, 1935–June 30, 1936, 10.

38. *The Attorney General's Survey of Release Procedures,* vol. 4, 169–71.

39. Ibid., 169; also, Rothman, *Conscience and Convenience*, 170, 171.

40. Rothman, *Conscience and Convenience*, 164–73.

41. *The Attorney General's Survey of Release Procedures,* vol. 4, 486–88.

42. Francisco E. Balderrama and Raymond Rodríguez, *Decade of Betrayal: Mexican Repatriation in the 1930s* (Albuquerque: University of New Mexico Press, 1995), 121–22.

43. F. Arturo Rosales, *¡Pobre Raza! Violence, Justice, and Mobilization among México Lindo Immigrants, 1900–1936* (Austin: University of Texas Press, 1999), 170.

44. Fourth annual report BPTP, July 1, 1934–June 30, 1935, 13.

45. Ibid.

46. Eighth annual report BPTP, July 1, 1938–June 30, 1939, 27.

47. Rosales, ¡Pobre Raza! 170.

48. Consider Pete Sanchez #24240, CSA, Folsom Inmate Case Files, F3745:578.

49. Ninth annual report BPTP, July 1, 1939–June 30, 1940, 35. Inmates who chose to be paroled for deportation could get additional time off their sentences. Philip Switzer, Tom Valles, Robert Starkey, and Alex Miraluboff each received about a month's parole advance in order to join a Department of Immigration "deportation party" leaving San Francisco on August 19, 1939. In concrete terms, time off sentences would probably be a matter of months rather than years, but there is little doubt that the parole board would see an inmate's willingness to be deported as evidence of compliance, and this would benefit parole considerations and sentencing dates. See August 3, 4, 1939, Minutes, San Quentin Minute Books, BPTP, 1934–1937, CSA F3717:1076.

50. Consider Art Marron (56701), September 22–23, 1936, meeting, San Quentin Board of Prison Directors Minutes, 1934–37, CSA, Department of Corrections Records, F3717:1074, 308

51. Lew Quong (53965), Lim Lee (55544), Fred Wong (54039), Minutes 22–23, 1936, San Quentin Board of Prison Directors Minutes, 1934–37, CSA, Department of Corrections Records, F3717:1074, 306–7

52. Johnnie Sotelo (59440), November 3, 4 5, 1937, Minutes, San Quentin Minute Books, BPTP, 1934–1937, CSA F3717:1075, 205. This could be risky—Sotelo's family might be deported for this very reason.

53. Nicole Hahn Rafter, Partial Justice: Women, Prisons, and Social Control (Edison, NJ: Transaction Publishers, 1990).

54. APB Case 483-1940. Pauline Tibbits's convict number at Tehachapi was No. 483, and her husband, Paul Tibbets, was San Quentin No. 63971. On the effects of women's incarceration on families, Beth E. Richie, "The Social Impact of Mass Incarceration on Women," in Marc Mauer and Meda Chesney-Lind, eds., Invisible Punishment: The Collateral Consequences of Mass Imprisonment (New York: New Press, 2002), 136–49.

55. Advisory Pardon Board Reports, Case 118-1935, F3717:1214. CSA.

56. Clarke to Silicaker, January 20, 1938, Allred Box 1985/024-96, Folder Texas Prison System, General Correspondence and Proclamations, January 1938; on Buster Silicaker, see E. A. Seale to Silicaker, January 22, 1938.

57. Address of J. B. Keith, Chairman of the Board of Pardons and Paroles, to the State Parole Conference, April 12, 1940, 4. O'Daniel Box 2001/138-11, Folder: Parole Conference at Huntsville, April 12, 1940, TSLAC.

58. Ibid., 8.

59. PIRA, "The Prison Labor Problem in Texas," 1937, 68–69, quoted in The Attorney General's Survey of Release Procedures, vol. 1, 1071, n. 28.

60. Proclamation of the Governor of the State of Texas, no. 27648, 23 May 1935, Allred Box 1985/024-95, Folder 2: Texas Prison System: General Correspondence and Proclamations, May 1935.

61. Proclamation of the Governor of the State of Texas, No. 27635, 17 May 1935, Allred Box 1985/024-95, Folder 2: Texas Prison System: General Correspondence and Proclamations, May 1935.

62. Texas Secretary of State, Statutory Documents Section, Box 2007/046-9: Folder: Smith, Marshall R., 1930–1931, TSLAC.

63. Moody letter to Jake Tirey, March 12, 1930, Texas Secretary of State, Statutory Documents Section, Box 2007/046-9: Folder: Smith, Marshall R., 1930–1931; Governor's Proclamation #5700, Governor's Clemency Proclamations/Governor's Proclamations on Microfilm: Group I, 1917–1943: Vol. 12, Reel 1615, Governor Dan Moody, TSLAC.

64. For example, Hilton Howell letter to Gov. Sterling, January 29, 1931, Texas Secretary of State, Statutory Documents Section, Box 2007/046-9: Folder: Smith, Marshall R., 1930–1931 (two folders).

65. G. M. Sealy letter to Board of Pardons, February 25, 1930, Texas Secretary of State, Statutory Documents Section, Box 2007/046-9: Folder: Smith, Marshall R., 1930–1931 (two folders).

66. S. A. Mincer letter to Ross Sterling, June 15, 1931; Sorrells letter to Ross Sterling, June 16, 1931, Texas Secretary of State, Statutory Documents Section, Box 2007/046-9: Folder: Smith, Marshall R., 1930–1931, TSLAC.

67. Anonymous letter to Moody, January 24, 1929, Texas Secretary of State, Statutory Documents Section, Box 2007/046-9: Folder: Smith, Marshall R., 1930–1931 (two folders). Mixed punctuation in the original.

68. Ibid.

69. Governor Sterling Proclamation #21549, July 22, 1931; Governor Sterling Proclamation #23569, January 10, 1933. Governor's Clemency Proclamations/Governors' proclamations of full and conditional pardons on microfilm: Group II, 1913–1988: Vol. 329, Reel 1631, and Vol. 333, Reel 1632, Governor R. S. Sterling, TSLAC.

70. J. B. Smith, "No More Good Time in the World for Me," *Ever Since I Been a Man Full-Grown* (Takoma Records, 1965).

71. "Mr. Tom Moore," in Jackson, ed., *Wake Up Dead Man*, 60–61.

72. Garton, "Managing Mercy," 686.

73. Proclamation No. 27806, July 8, 1935, Allred Box 1985/024-95, Texas Prison System: General Correspondence and Proclamations, Folder June–July 1935. TSLAC.

74. Garton, "Managing Mercy," 682–85.

75. W. H. L. Wells letter to T. C. Andrews, August 30, 1935, Texas Secretary of State, Statutory Documents Section, Box 2007/046-7, Folder Vaxter Haskins, 1935–1937. TSLAC.

76. W. D. Wells to T. C. Andrews, May 2, 1937, Texas Secretary of State, Statutory Documents Section, Box 2007/046-7, Folder Vaxter Haskins, 1935–1937. TSLAC.

77. Effie Drake correspondence to Board of Pardons and Paroles, October 11, 1935, Texas Secretary of State, Statutory Documents Section, Box 2007/046-7, Folder Vaxter Haskins, 1935–1937. TSLAC.

78. Letter to T. C. Andrews, December 2, 1935, Texas Secretary of State, Statutory Documents Section, Box 2007/046-7, Folder Vaxter Haskins, 1935–1937. TSLAC.

79. Mrs. W. D. Wells to Andrews, April 13, 1936, Texas Secretary of State, Statutory Documents Section, Box 2007/046-7, Folder Vaxter Haskins, 1935–1937. TSLAC.

80. Mrs. W. D. Wells letter to T. C. Andrews, September 16, 1936, Texas Secretary of State, Statutory Documents Section, Box 2007/046-7, Folder Vaxter Haskins, 1935–1937. TSLAC.

81. The last record in the file is from Mrs. Annie Wells, who requested that all correspondence regarding Vaxter Haskins be sent to herself and John Wells, instead of Will Wells. She said that "the negro expressed a desire to live with us," and they almost certainly benefited from his labor when he was released. Why, how, or even if Haskins made this clear to Annie Wells can only be speculated upon. It is the only place where his voice is referred to in the

parole application. Annie Wells to T. C. Andrews, July 14, 1937, Texas Secretary of State, Statutory Documents Section, Box 2007/046-7, Folder Vaxter Haskins, 1935–1937. TSLAC.

82. Pete Daniel, *The Shadow of Slavery: Peonage in the South, 1901–1969* (Urbana: University of Illinois Press, 1990), 21.

83. Garton, "Managing Mercy," 688.

84. *The Attorney General's Survey of Release Procedures,* vol. 1, 159.

85. Fifth annual report of the BPTP, July 1, 1935–June 30, 1936, 14.

86. See the annual reports of the BPTP.

87. For Brown's postcard, see O'Daniel Box 2001/138-98: Board of Pardons and Paroles, 1939–1941, Folder: Board of Pardons and Paroles, Correspondence, 1939–41, TSLAC.

88. "Parolee General Rules and Conditions," and "Explanation of General Rules and Conditions," O'Daniel Box 2001/138-100, Folder: Voluntary County Parole Boards, 1939–1940.

89. Ibid. Emphasis in original.

90. First Report of the BPTP, 1931–1932, 30. CASL Government Publications Room.

91. Ibid., 41–42.

92. Merle Haggard, "Branded Man," *Prison* (EMI, 2001).

93. APB Case 16-1938, Advisory Pardon Board, F3717:1218, "1938, Book No. 1"

94. Charles Herbert to Leo Stanley, May 31 and May 9, 1942. Anne T. Kent California Room, Marin County Civic Center Library, Leo L. Stanley Collection, Box 3, Folder 3 Miscellaneous Correspondence.

95. Attorney General's Report, 1939, 186, quoted in Simon, *Poor Discipline,* 58.

96. State Board of Prison Directors, 1928, 86, quoted in Simon, *Poor Discipline,* 58.

97. Simon, *Poor Discipline,* 58.

98. Don Reid, with John Gurwell, *Have a Seat, Please* (Huntsville: Texas Review Press, 2001), 165.

99. Governor Moody Records 1984/24, Box 40, TSLAC, Folder: Proclamations for Various Convicts, Jan. 1–Feb. 6, 1930.

100. Albert Race Sample, *Racehoss: Big Emma's Boy* (New York: Ballantine Books, 1984), 322–23.

101. J. B. Smith, "Ever Since I Been a Man Full Grown," in Bruce Jackson, ed., *Wake Up Dead Man: Afro-American Worksongs from Texas Prisons* (Cambridge, MA: Harvard University Pres, 1972), 158.

102. See image 1925.005.010, entitled "Discharge room where prisoners are outfitted when being discharged," no date. Folder 5. Leo L. Stanley Collection, San Quentin Photographs, Anne T. Kent California History Room, Marin County Free Library, Marin County Civic Center, San Rafael, California.

103. David Lamson, *We Who Are About to Die: Prison As Seen by a Condemned Man* (New York: Scribner's, 1935),

104. *Attorney General's Survey of Release Procedures,* vol. 1, 175.

EPILOGUE

1. H. Buderus von Carlshausen, aka "Roark Tamerlane," "America!—add stars to our stripes," unpublished typescript, 3, 2. Emphasis in original. CASL California History Room, 365 C284.

2. On San Quentin, see ibid., 82. For Folsom, see Lyle Egan, Classification Clerk, "Calendar of Highlights in Folsom Prison History: Chronologically Arranged," CSA, Earl Warren Papers—Administrative Files—Corrections—Governor's Prison Committee—Folsom State Prison, Folder 15, 1942–43, F3640:986. Approximately three hundred inmates wanted to donate blood on April 20, 1944, to the poorly named Cutter Laboratory. They would be paid four dollars per pint. April 21, 1944, State Board of Prison Directors Minutes, San Quentin, Folsom, and Chino, 1944, 9. CSA, Department of Corrections Records, F3717:1040.

3. On experimentation with flu vaccines, see San Quentin, Folsom, and Chino Minutes Summary Books, 1943–1945, January 23, 1943, CSA, F3717:1039. Also, Allen M. Hornblum, *Acres of Skin: Human Experiments at Holmesburg Prison: A True Story of Abuse and Exploitation in the Name of Medical Science* (New York: Routledge, 1998); Ethan Blue, "The Strange Career of Leo Stanley: Remaking Manhood and Medicine at San Quentin State Penitentiary, 1913–1951," *Pacific Historical Review* 78, no. 2 (2009): 236–37.

4. Cited in von Carlshausen, 33.

5. November 30, 1943, letter from W. Mills (No. 21935) to Alco. CSA, Earl Warren Papers—Administrative Files—Corrections—Governor's Prison Committee—Correspondence (Folder 5), 1943–44.

6. Von Carlshausen, 81.

7. San Quentin Board of Prison Directors Minutes, 1940–42, September 14, 1940, 8. CSA, Department of Corrections Records, F3717:1011.

8. The differing conditions that Texas and California prisoners faced in the new economic circumstances of the war also complicate the idea that conditions behind bars improve during periods of labor demand and deteriorate in times of labor surplus. This seemed to be true for California's industrial regime, but was not the case in Texas, which continued to rely on hard agricultural labor and had a disproportionately black and Mexican inmate population.

9. See Robert T. Chase, "Civil Rights on the Cell Block: Race, Reform, and Violence in Texas Prisons and the Nation, 1945–1990" (Ph.D. dissertation, University of Maryland at College Park, 2009), with quotations from the MacCormick Report, esp. 63–64.

10. Annual report of the Texas Prison Board, 1943, 9, 12–13.

11. Annual report of the Texas Prison Board, 1945, 71.

12. The quotation is from San Quentin librarian Herman Spector, cited in Eric Cummins, *The Rise and Fall of California's Radical Prison Movement* (Stanford, CA: Stanford University Press, 1994), 26, and Alan Eladio Gómez, "Resisting Living Death at Marion Federal Penitentiary, 1972," *Radical History Review* 96 (2006): 61.

13. On the correctional-therapeutic model, see Shelly Bookspan, *A Germ of Goodness: The California State Prison System, 1851–1944* (Lincoln: University of Nebraska Press, 1991), 93–118; Daniel Glasser, *Preparing Convicts for Law-Abiding Lives: The Pioneering Criminology of Richard A. McGee* (Albany: State University of New York Press, 1995); Cummins, *Rise and Fall of California's Radical Prison Movement*; Theodore Hamm, *Rebel and a Cause: Caryl Chessman and the Politics of the Death Penalty in Postwar California* (Berkeley: University of California Press, 2001); Volker Janssen, "Convict Labor, Civic Welfare: Rehabilitation in California's Prisons, 1941–1971" (Ph.D. dissertation, University of California at San Diego, 2005).

14. Kenyon J. Scudder, *Prisoners Are People* (Garden City, NY: Doubleday, 1952).

15. Volker Janssen, "When the 'Jungle' Met the Forest: Public Work, Civil Defense, and Prison Camps in Postwar California," *Journal of American History* 96, no. 3 (2009): 702–26.

16. Quoted in Robert Perkinson, *Texas Tough: The Rise of America's Prison Empire* (New York: Metropolitan Books, 2010), 230.

17. Perkinson, *Texas Tough*, 232. The "Bible and bat" phrase is from Chase, "Civil Rights on the Cellblock," 160–67.

18. Steve Martin, quoted in Perkinson, *Texas Tough*, 233.

19. Dylan Rodriguez, *Imprisoned Radical Intellectuals and the U.S. Prison Regime* (Minneapolis: University of Minnesota Press, 2005), 113–44; Rebecca N. Hill, *Men, Mobs and Law: Anti-Lynching and Labor Defense in U.S. Radical History* (Durham, NC: Duke University Press, 2008), Ch 6.

20. Perkinson, *Texas Tough*, 251–85, quotations from Justice on 278–79. Also, Chase, "Civil Rights on the Cellblock," chaps. 5–8; Steve J. Martin and Sheldon Ekland-Olson, *Texas Prisons: The Walls Came Tumbling Down* (Austin: Texas Monthly Press, 1987); Ben M. Crouch and James W. Marquart, *An Appeal to Justice: Litigated Reform of Texas Prisons* (Austin: University of Texas Press, 1989).

21. David Harvey, *The Condition of Postmodernity: An Enquiry into the Origins of Social Change* (Malden, MA: Blackwell, 1990).

22. See Christian Parenti, *Lockdown America: Police and Prisons in the Age of Crisis* (London: Verso, 1999); Angela Y. Davis, *The Angela Y. Davis Reader*, ed. Joy James (Malden, MA: Blackwell, 1998), 61–73; Davis, "Globalism and the Prison Industrial Complex: An interview with Angela Davis," interviewed by Avery F. Gordon, *Race & Class* 40, nos. 2–3 (1998–1999): 145–57; Ruth Wilson Gilmore, "Globalization and U.S. Prison Growth: From Military Keynesianism to Post-Keynesian Militarism," *Race & Class* 40, nos. 2–3 (1998–1999): 179–88.

23. Manning Marable, *Race, Reform, and Rebellion: The Second Reconstruction in Black America, 1945–1990*, rev. 2d ed. (Jackson: University Press of Mississippi, 1991); Alex Lichtenstein, "The Private and the Public in Penal History: A Commentary on Zimring and Tonry," in David Garland, ed., *Mass Imprisonment: Social Causes and Consequences* (London: Sage, 2001), 171–78. Among recent efforts to explain late-modern American hyperincarceration, Ruth Wilson Gilmore, *Golden Gulag: Prisons, Surplus, Crisis, and Opposition in Globalizing California* (Berkeley: University of California Press, 2007); David Garland, *The Culture of Control: Crime and Social Order in Contemporary Society* (Chicago: University of Chicago Press, 2001); Michael Tonry, *Malign Neglect: Race, Crime, and Punishment in America* (New York: Oxford University Press, 1995).

24. Garland, *Culture of Control*; Lorna A. Rhodes, *Total Confinement: Madness and Reason in the Maximum Security Prison* (Berkeley: University of California Press, 2004).

25. *Wolf v. McDonnell*, 481 US 539 (1974), quoted in Kimberly E. Gilmore, "States of Incarceration: Prisoners' Rights and U.S. Prison Expansion after World War II (Ph.D. dissertation, New York University, 2005), 6.

26. Barry Gibbs, "Exonerated," *The Moth: Stories Told*, July 5, 2010. Available online at http://www.themoth.org/.

27. Peter S. Goodman, "Despite Signs of Recovery, Chronic Joblessness Rises," *New York Times*, February 20, 2010. Accessed online July 22, 2010.

28. Perkinson, *Texas Tough*, 2.

29. Numbers are from The Sentencing Project, http://www.sentencingproject.org/map/map.cfm (accessed July 20, 2010); Gilmore, *Golden Gulag*, 7–8; California Department of Corrections and Rehabilitation, "California's Correctional Facilities," no date, online http://www.cdcr.ca.gov/Visitors/docs/CDCRmap_03-07.pdf (accessed October 4, 2007).

30. Pew Center on the States, "One in 100: Behind Bars in America 2008" (Washington, DC: Pew Charitable Trusts, 2008), 34; Pew Center on the States, "One in 31: The Long Reach of American Corrections" (Washington, DC: Pew Charitable Trusts, 2009), table A-1.

31. Pew Center on the States, "One in 100," 11, 14–16, 30.

32. Pew Center on the States, "One in 100," 13; Jerry Adler, "California: America's First Failed State?" *Newsweek*, January 26, 2010, http://www.newsweek.com/2010/01/25/california-america-s-first-failed-state.html (accessed July 22, 2010).

33. Pew Center on the States, "One in 100," 21.

34. Perkinson, *Texas Tough*, 327.

Index

Adamek, John, 142, 146
Adams, Hugh, 200–201
Advisory Pardon Board (California),
  215–217, 225
African American prisoners,
  death, 192, 196, 199–200, 208;
  demography in California, 36–37;
  demography in Texas, 37–38;
  discrimination against, 7, 38, 49–50,
    66–67, 80, 145–149, 242, 248–250;
  labor, 58–59, 64–67, 80, 84–86, 88–95;
  masculinities, 7, 49, 51, 55, 76, 89–90,
    93–94, 172–173, 182–183, 187;
  medical care, 193;
  migration, 24, 27–30;
  parole, 222, 230–233;
  protest, 66–67, 242;
  racialization, 170;
  subordination of, 7, 10;
  supposed incorrigibility, 6, 222, 244;
  worksongs, 91–95
agency, 14, 40, 96–98
Agricultural Adjustment Act, 12
Alco, Julian, 70
Alco Investigation (1943–1944), 66,
  101–102, 114–115, 128–132, 242
Ali, Iasian, 43
Alien Registration Act (1940), 243
alienation, 6, 118, 202
Allred, James V, 135, 139–140, 207, 217,
  226–227, 231
American Indian prisoners. *See* Native
  American prisoners
American Journal of Corrections, 245
Andrews, T. C., 231–232

Angola Farm, Louisiana, 80
architectural controls, 243–244, 302n43
Armstrong, Louis, 150
Arnold, Jimmy, 207
Ashurst-Sumners Act (1934), 17, 18, 54, 136
Asian American prisoners,
  demography in California, 36–37;
  deportation, 203, 223–224;
  labor, 48, 61;
  migration, 24, 27–30;
  racial-gender formations, 44, 48–49, 61,
    75, 224, 248–250;
  suicide, 203
Attica rebellion (1971), 246
"Auburn Plan," 49
Ayers, Edward L., 154

Barber, W. P., 207
Barrow, Clyde, 3, 95, 98, 139
baseball, 136, 138, 162, 164, 166–169, 174,
  180, 182, 184, 188
Baxter, W. H., 115
Bell, Mona, 178
Bennett, Charles, 203
Berg, Charles, 27
Bertillion, Alphonse, 39–41;
  Bertillionage, 21, 40
Beto, George, 245
biometrics, 3, 20–24, 39–41, 264n44
biopolitics, 19, 305n6
biopower, 190
Bird, J. H., 180
Black Power, 9
black prisoners. *See* African American
  prisoners

Chinese and Chinese American prisoners
    (*cont.*)
    deportation, 223–224;
    discrimination against, 50. *See also*
        Asian American prisoners
Chino Institution for Men, 26, 48–49, 245
citizenship,
    labor, 54–55, 214, 245;
    opposition to criminality, 9–11, 13, 137,
        248–250;
    sport, 164, 184
Civilian Conservation Corps, 17
Clarke, George, 226–227
class formation, 16–17, 255–256n20
Classification and Segregation Program, 46
Cleary, Leslie A., 225
Clemens State Farm, 80, 190, 195
Clemmer, Donald, 62, 64, 110–111, 269n33,
    274n53, 282n102
Cloud, Tom Iron, 159
Cobb, C. F., 201
Collier, J. A., 207
colonialism, 5, 9, 13–14, 40, 43, 246, 265n47
Compton, C. V., 106–108, 207
con boss system,
    bureaucratic authority, 112, 129, 133;
    charisma, 114;
    commodity exchange, 112–113;
    complex networks, 116, 280n74;
    covert markets, 112;
    formal tasks, 112–113;
    guard frustration, 115, 118;
    influencing prison administration, 114,
        116–117;
    investigations into, 101–102, 114–118,
        129–130, 132;
    masculinities within, 101, 113–114;
    state support, 112–118
con ethic, 62, 68, 101, 109–110, 208, 269n33
consumption, 17–19, 68, 73, 136, 166
Contreras, Alfredo, 58
convict code. *See* con ethic
convict lease system, 11–12, 14, 16–17, 45, 54,
    77, 80, 189–190, 192, 230
Copeland, R. Craig, 105

Cotton Pickers Glee Club, 176
covert economies, 109–112
Cressey, Donald, 202
crime, definition of, 1
criminal syndicalism, 42
criminalization, 5, 14, 24;
    racialization, 244;
    rearticulation in wartime, 241–243,
        287n13
Cruz, Fred, 246
Cultural Front (Denning), 8

dance, 185–187
Daniel, Pete, 233
Darrington State Farm, 106, 244
Davis, Angela Y., 149
Davis, Cecil, 204–205, 207
Davis, John, 231–232
Davis, Natalie Zemon, 220
"Dedicated to You" (Ellis), 151
"Deep Elm Blues" (Hoosier), 155
Denning, Michael, 8–9
death,
    conceptualizing, 189–191, 197–198;
    maximum security prisons, 196;
    poverty, 198;
    racism, 196, 198–201. *See also* mortality
debt peonage, 12, 233
Deep Secrets behind Gray Walls (Compton),
    106
Denley, Joel, 80
Department of Labor, 203
Department of Public Works, 59, 63
deportation, 2;
    economic crisis, 30, 203, 249;
    parole, 28, 30, 222–224, 231, 307n49
depression,
    border formation, 2, 28, 30, 222;
    crime during, 1–4, 8, 32–34, 153;
    criminalization, 5, 14, 24, 241–243, 248;
    low budgets, 53, 77–78, 192, 216;
    migration, 6, 27, 30;
    modernity, 12, 190, 192, 194;
    overcrowding, 3, 24, 50–51, 102, 250;
    patriarchal crisis, 145;

reform, individual (*cont.*)
  unimportance of, 12;
  white privilege, 6, 64, 67, 142. *See also*
    rehabilitation
reform, institutional,
  construction programs, 288n28;
  economic incentives, 251;
  execution, 137;
  failures, 19, 109, 205, 234, 246–247,
    252;
  industrialization, 79, 142, 268n26;
  internal administrative conflict, 13,
    132–134, 284n142;
  medicine, 194;
  parole, 219, 226, 234;
  prompted by prisoners, 101–102,
    106–109, 124, 128, 134;
  reform movements, 5, 11, 15, 45, 69–70,
    106–109, 122–124, 128–32, 205,
    244–245, 295n28;
  segregation, 11, 45–48, 102
rehabilitation, 10;
  classification, 45–46;
  evidence for parole, 227–228;
  labor ideologies, 55–56–61, 70, 79;
  mass culture, 135, 141, 158;
  sport, 164, 169;
  violence, 107
Reid, Don, 236
resistance, 50, 52;
  state resistance to reform, 17, 133;
  understandings of, 97–98, 108. *See also*
    agency; escape; food strike; labor,
    prisoners'; protest; sabotage
Retrieve State Farm, 79, 92, 97, 100,
  204–205, 233–234, 244
"Ride on, King Jesus," 150
Rimskij-Korsakov, Nikolai, 152
road camps (California). *See* honor camps
  Roberts, Samuel Kelton, Jr., 198
Rockefeller, Laura Spellman, 45
Roosevelt, Franklin, 139, 239
Rosas, F. Arturo, 223
Rothman, David, 213–214
Rousseau, V. J. "Lucky", 159–160
Ruffin v. Commonwealth (1871), 2, 248

Ruíz, David, 246
Ruíz v. Estelle, 246
Rusche, Georg, 8
Russell, Bud, 21–22, 239
Ryan, William J., 67, 127, 130

sabotage, 15, 58, 97–98
Salazar, Candelario, 146–147
Salgot, Roy, 74
Sample, Albert Race, 92, 104, 106, 237
Sampsell, Lloyd, 114–116, 129
San Quentin News, 242
San Quentin on the Air, 136, 139
San Quentin State Penitentiary,
  architecture and space, 12, 44, 48–52,
    124, 129, 132, 205, 342;
  bureaucratic organization, 12, 132;
  death, 202–204, 208–212;
  discharge ritual, 238–240;
  early history, 12;
  entry ritual, 20–23, 39, 42;
  labor, 48–64, 75–78, 96, 112–114,
    201–202, 242;
  library, 246;
  medicine, 76, 191, 193–200;
  multiracial institution, 5;
  parole from, 214–216, 218–226, 233,
    235–236, 242;
  population, 3, 24, 26, 28–34, 36–37;
  scandals, 16, 101, 118–124;
  sex in, 124–128, 132–134;
  sport, 164, 166–174, 183–185;
  wartime, 241–243;
  See also con boss system; honor camps
Sayers, Anthony, 97
Schmelling, Max, 163
Schwarzenegger, Arnold, 251
Scottsboro "boys," 3
Scudder, Kenyon J., 245
Sealy, G. M., 229
segregation, 6, 11–12, 45–50, 52, 64–67, 75,
  99, 127, 132, 182, 187, 193, 242, 248–249,
  265n50, 298n89
self-mutilation, 96–98, 108–109, 143,
  201–202, 205–206, 275–276n80
Serrano, Francisco, 47–48

Texas State Prison Board, 79, 84–85, 87, 102, 106–108, 135–136, 143, 181, 190, 205, 207
theft, 8, 14–15, 19, 34–35, 43, 58, 65–66, 74, 103, 113, 154–155
Third World, 9
Thirty Minutes behind the Walls, 135–162, 181, 186
Thompson, E. P., 5
Tibbits, Pauline, 224–225
Tinney, Emma, 208
Toldon, Simon, 182
Tomez, Domingo, 27–28
torture, 106–107, 121–124, 142, 278n37
Trade Department, 66
tuberculosis (TB), 193, 198–200, 211–212
Turner, Cassie, 43
"Twelfth Street Rag" (Bowman), 154
Tydings-McDuffie Act (1934), 223

"Under the Double Eagle" (Mexican Stringsters), 154
unemployment, 1

van Waters, Miriam, 132, 284n142
Veazy, W. B., 202
violence,
  among working class populations, 2, 13–15;
  criminological and historiographical understandings, 13–15, 189–190;
  efforts to limit, 106–109; 122–124, 207–208;
  guard violence, 121–124, 142;
  intraprisoner, 88–89;
  masculine honor, 109–110;
  persistence, 18, 137, 188;
  space, 302n43;
  state, 15, 199–201;
  sublimation in sport, 163, 166–167, 294n15;
symbolic violence, 23. *See also* self-mutilation, sexual violence, torture
Volstead Act. *See* Prohibition
von Carlshausen, H. Buderus, 111, 118–120, 124, 241, 243, 282n95. *See also* Tamerlane, Roark

Voting Rights Act (1965), 247
Vredenburg, Donald, 225–226

"The Wall" (Cash), 204
Waring, Fred, 150
Warner, James L., 141
Warner, Michael, 286–287n12
Warren, Earl, 129, 132, 226
Watts, Lee, 109–110
WBAP, 135–136, 138–140, 143, 149–150, 157, 159
We Who Are About to Die (Lamson), 20
Weaver, George, 220
Weeks, Happy, 154
welfare state, 16–17, 19, 136, 166, 191, 239, 247. *See also* New Deal
Wells, W. D., 231–232
Wells, W. H. L., 231–232, 236
Wells, Wesley Robert, 66–67, 110
West, W. H., 113, 117
"When the Gates Swing Open," 151
whipping, 15, 80, 86, 87, 88, 91, 138; efforts to abolish, 106–107. *See also* torture
White, Ed H., 235
White, Robert W. "Cannibal," 67
White prisoners,
  demography in California, 36–37;
  demography in Texas, 37–38;
  labor, California, 40, 58–59, 64–67, 75;
  labor, Texas, 79–80, 82–83, 95, 137, 145;
  masculinities, 6, 61, 172;
  migration, 24, 27–30;
  parole, 222, 227;
  perception of reformability, 6–7, 39;
    45–46, 58, 137, 142, 146, 153, 161, 180, 188, 244;
  privilege, 6–7, 10, 41, 52, 59, 66, 80, 83, 188, 199, 249;
  racial identity, 41–42, 44;
  racism of, 6, 9–10, 49–50, 52, 66–67, 110, 155, 248–249, 254n13;
  resistance, 95, 276n84
whiteness,
  differentiated, 44–47, 64–65, 75, 155–157, 199, 228, 232, 244, 292n74;
  gendered performance, 172;

whiteness (*cont.*)
  health benefits, 192–193, 196, 199–200;
  marked by criminality, recidivism, or
    recalcitrance, 39, 45, 64–65, 99, 139;
  as redeemability, 39, 41, 58–59, 99, 106,
    142, 146, 153, 161, 188;
  undermining class solidarity, 9–10
Williams, Jack, 177
Williams, Willie, 43
Wilson, Johnnie, 206–208
Wilson, Rosie, 206–207
Wilson, Teddy, 139
women activists, 11
women prisoners, 10;
  athletics, 183–187;
  clemency strategies, 224–225;
  labor, 143–144; 209;
  masculinities, 185–187, 298n89, 289n90;
  musicians, 143, 146, 150–152, 161;
  racial hierarchies, 42–44, 184–185;
  segregation, 187, 193–4. *See also*
    Tehachapi State Penintentiary; Goree
    State Farm
Women's Department, 183
Wong, Fred, 224
work songs, 21, 91–95;
  cooperation within, 92–94;
  masculinities, 93–94;
  negotiation with guards, 92;
  resistant, 94–95, 98;
  sexuality, 93;
  temporality, 92–93
working class,
  class formation, 16–17, 255–256n20;
  cross-racial solidarity, 138, 153–154,
    159–161, 255n19;
  death, 198;
  inmate demography, 7, 31–33;
  in the 1930s, 8;
  masculinities, 163–164, 180;
  social movements, 8–9;
  punishment exacerbating racial/gender
    conflicts within, 6–11, 157, 248–250;
  violence within, 2, 13–15
Wretched of the Earth (Fanon), 14
Wynne State Farm, 47, 81, 96, 193–194, 199,
  212, 244

Yanow, Scott, 150
"You Can't Stop Me from Dreaming"
  (Wilson), 139
Young, Charles, 27
Young, George, 141
Young, Jack, 110
Yuen, George, 48

Zoot Suit Riots, 170
Zubler, E. F., 57

About the Author

ETHAN BLUE is Assistant Professor of History at the University of Western Australia. His work has appeared in *Pacific Historical Review, Journal of Social History, Radical History Review, Humanities Research, Law, Culture, and the Humanities, Australasian Journal of American Studies,* and *Bad Subjects.*